CRITICAL METHODS IN POLITICAL AND CULTURAL ECONOMY

CRITICAL METHODS IN POLITICAL AND CULTURAL ECONOMY

Editor

Darby Linton

Socialy
PRESS
AN IMPRINT OF SCITUS ACADEMICS

Critical Methods in Political and Cultural Economy
Edited by **Darby Linton**

This Book is Printed on Acid-Free Paper.

ISBN: 978-1-68117-780-9
Library of Congress Control Number: 2017938804

Socialy Press
(An Imprint of Scitus Academics),
616, Corporate Way, Suite 2, 4766,
Valley Cottage, NY 10989

www.scitusacademics.com

Notice

Printed in United States of America.

PREFACE

Cultural political economy is a rising post-disciplinary approach that emphases the role of the cultural change to the analysis of the expression between the economic and the political and their embedding in broader sets of social relations. Explicit arguments in favor of 'cultural political economy' as such emerged in several contexts in the 1990s as part of and/or in reaction to the then existing cultural change. Given the range of cultural turns and the starting points from which they have been made as well as the widely different definitions of political economy, there is no consent among scholars on the nature of cultural political economy.

Critical Methods in Political and Cultural Economy seeks to forge a new collaborative path that builds a critical ethic and modes of inquiry within International Political Economy. Contributed chapters advance the cultural political economy and seek to articulate its promising research ethic. The text introduces cultural political economy as a distinctive approach in the social sciences, including policy studies. It combines critical semiotic analysis and critical political economy. It grounds its approach to both in the practical necessities of complexity reduction and the role of meaning-making and structuration in turning unstructured into structured complexity as a basis for 'going on' in the world. It explores both semiosis and structuration in terms of the evolutionary mechanisms of variation, selection, and retention and, in this context, also highlights the role of specific forms of agency and specific technologies.

The contributors explore how research on sense- and meaning-making can deepen critical studies in political economy, illuminating its role in critiquing the specific categories, contradictions and crisis-tendencies of capitalism. Scholars and students of heterodox, cultural, political and institutional economics will find this book a comprehensive guide.

TABLE OF CONTENTS

1

POLITICAL ECONOMY OF FISCAL UNIONS

Jan Fidrmuc

Department of Economics and Finance, Brunel University,Uxbridge, United Kingdom

ABSTRACT

Fiscal unions often use fiscal transfers to counter asymmetric shocks, but such transfers may be politically controversial. I present a model of a two-region fiscal union with region-specific shocks where the threat of secession imposes a limit on fiscal redistribution between regions. I show that both correlation of shocks across regions and their persistence over time are important for political support for integration. The gains from inter-regional risk sharing are potentially large when shocks are negatively correlated and temporary. In contrast, unions with negatively correlated permanent shocks are likely to be fragile.

Keywords: Fiscal federalism; Risk sharing; Disintegration; Median voter

1. INTRODUCTION

One of the most intriguing questions of economics concerns the conditions under which deeper integration is possible and the circumstances that make integration fail. And fail it does remarkably often: more than 100 new countries emerged in the course of the 20thcentury alone. Clearly, political and cultural motives such as a sense of separate identity and nationalism are of paramount importance as factors behind secessionist tendencies. Nevertheless, economic considerations also play an important role. Among them, the fact that unions tend to use fiscal policy to redistribute income across regions is often controversial. Such fiscal unions can feature inter-regional transfers that have been agreed upon, negotiated, and formalized explicitly, or that occur because of centralized automatic stabilizers such as progressive income tax, unemployment benefits, and the like. Disagreements about inter-regional fiscal redistribution can become an important driver of disintegration; fiscal transfers, and their perceived unfairness, played an important role in the break-up of Czechoslovakia and have significantly contributed to inter-regional tensions in Belgium, Spain, and the United Kingdom.

Nevertheless, fiscal transfers also have an important benefit in that they facilitate risk sharing. This aspect of integration has been highlighted by, among others, Beetsma and Jensen (2005), Gal and Monacelli (2008), and Farhi and Werning (2013). These studies emphasize the benefits – higher welfare due to consumption smoothing – that accrue to the participating countries when they enter into a mutual-insurance arrangement. As Farhi and Werning (2013) point out, these benefits are particularly large when fiscal policy is the only tool at the government's disposal (for example, when a country gives up independent monetary policy in order to participate in a currency union and thus loses the ability to use monetary policy to counter asymmetric shocks) and when financial markets are incomplete (because regions and individuals cannot use financial products to insure against shocks). Furthermore, the bigger and the more persistent are the shocks, the more attractive it is to form a fiscal union (Farhi and Werning, 2013).

The aforementioned contributions, while insightful, focus on the economic and welfare implications of fiscal unions. In this paper, instead, I consider the political economy of such arrangements. In a nutshell, a mutual-insurance arrangement that is optimal *ex ante* may be rejected by one of the parties *ex post*, once the shocks are realized. I formulate a model that is a dynamic version of the static model of Bolton and Roland (1997). It features a union composed of two countries with a centrally provided public good. As long as integration continues, fiscal policy reflects the union median voter's preferences which, in turn, depend on the aggregate effect of regional shocks.[1] The two regions thus constitute an implicit fiscal union: fiscal redistribution occurs through centralized fiscal policy rather than by means of explicit inter-regional transfers. The regions, however, have the option to secede and implement their own preferred fiscal policy if the utility gain from doing so outweighs the cost of secession. Because of the shocks, a union that was previously stable can break-up following a particular regional shock, whether positive or negative. The opposite is also true; a region that preferred independence initially can come to prefer integration in the wake of a particular shock.

The analysis suggests that two aspects of shocks are important: the symmetry (or correlation) of shocks across regions and their persistence over time. With respect to the former, holding everything else constant, positively correlated (symmetric) shocks are good for the stability of integration. This is because the shocks change both regions' preferred fiscal policies in a similar manner: either both prefer more extensive redistribution or both prefer to scale it down. In this, my results echo the main finding of the optimum currency area theory (Mundell, 1961 and McKinnon, 1963), which considers currency unions with common monetary rather than fiscal policy. The situation becomes more complicated when shocks are negatively correlated. In this case, fiscal-policy preferences diverge but the regions benefit from mutual insurance: under centralized fiscal policy, the region with a positive shock makes a net transfer to the region hit by a negative shock. This is where persistence of shocks proves crucial. With temporary shocks, the disutility from having suboptimal fiscal policy is short-lived and may be compensated by the benefits from risk sharing. When shocks are permanent, however, fiscal transfers become largely deterministic and unidirectional. The cost of having to put up with suboptimal fiscal policy, likewise, becomes long lasting. As a result, either region, or both, can prefer to secede in such a case so as to implement the region's preferred fiscal redistribution.

To illustrate the workings of the model, consider the disintegration of Czechoslovakia in 1993.[2] The model predicts that a previously stable union can unravel due to asymmetric and persistent shocks. In Czechoslovakia's case, the shock was precipitated by the economic reforms initiated in 1990–91. While the reform took place in both parts of Czechoslovakia, it affected Slovakia much more severely than the Czech Republic: per-capita GDP fell by 12 percent in the Czech Republic during 1991–92 and by 20 percent in Slovakia; Czech unemployment, similarly, remained low, 2.6 percent in 1992, while the Slovak figure was 11.8 percent (see Fidrmuc et al., 1999, and Fidrmuc, 2000). This asymmetric effect of the reform shock was largely due to the greater dependence of Slovakia on trade with the former Eastern Block: much of the Slovak industry was built during the communist period so that the economy was highly dependent on trade with other communist countries (see Fidrmuc et al., 1999, and the references therein). This trade essentially collapsed after the communist regime and central planning were abandoned. The reform thus constituted a negative and persistent shock, which affected Slovakia more severely and more persistently than the Czech Republic.[3] The greater cost of reform translated into greater support for redistribution in Slovakia than in the Czech Republic, which was reflected in the outcomes of the 1992 election (Fidrmuc, 2000).

The nature of the reform-induced shocks should have given an incentive to the Czech Republic to push for a break-up: it experienced a less-severe shock and it was also richer and therefore cross-subsidized Slovakia fiscally.[4] However, the Czech Republic was twice the size of Slovakia (10 million vs 5 million) so that it had much more sway over fiscal policy than Slovakia. It was, therefore, the poorer country that pushed for the break-up. As I argue below, the poor region may prefer secession if income inequality in the union is high enough and/or the negative shock is sufficiently severe: then, the poor region can choose to secede in order to impose higher taxes and redistribute more, even if this comes at a cost of losing the fiscal transfer from the rich region.

Therefore, the break-up of Czechoslovakia can be attributed, at least in part, to the asymmetric repercussions of the economic reforms, and to the size and persistence of the adverse shock experienced by Slovakia. Had the shocks been more symmetric, or had the asymmetric repercussions in Slovakia been of less persistent nature, Czechoslovakia might have well survived.[5]

There is already a rich body of literature analyzing the incentives that countries face to secede: Alesina and Spolaore, 1997, Alesina and Spolaore, 2003a and Alesina and Spolaore, 2003b, Alesina et al. (2000), Alesina and Perotti (1998), Bolton and Roland (1997), Goyal and Staal (2004), Le Breton and Weber (2003), Hindriks and Lockwood (2009), and Lülfesmann et al. (2015). However, much of this literature (with the exception of Alesina and Perotti, 1998, whose paper I discuss below) is static in nature: they consider the trade-off between heterogeneity of preferences and efficiency gains from integration (or efficiency loss from disintegration), without giving much thought to the factors that might drive preferences further apart or closer together as time passes. My analysis, in contrast, is concerned with offering insights on the reasons why unions that were originally stable subsequently break up.

Alesina and Perotti (1998) also consider fiscal integration between regions that are subject to idiosyncratic shocks. Their analytical framework, however, differs from mine in several important aspects. First, they consider shocks that are permanent and perfectly negatively correlated across regions. As such, their analysis does not allow inferences on the importance of either correlation or persistence of shocks. Second, they model shocks in a way that ensures that they do not affect income distribution and, correspondingly, they do not change the preferences over fiscal policy in the participating regions. Therefore, shocks in their model make the tax base stochastic but not the tax rate. Third, they assume that income distribution in each region is discontinuous: individuals belong to three discrete income classes. This means that the median voter in the union is always the same, regardless of the shocks. This, together with their assumption on the nature of shocks, implies that the tax rate under fiscal centralization becomes stochastic: specifically, it depends only on the shock to the region of the median voter. The tax base, in contrast, is constant under fiscal centralization because the region-specific shocks cancel each other out. Hence, their main conclusion is essentially the same as that of the static political economy literature discussed above: while fiscal integration offers some benefits in terms of risk sharing (the tax base that it constant over time), this comes at the cost of increased heterogeneity in policy preferences (tax rate that changes depending on the shocks' realization).

The paper is structured as follows: The next section introduces the model. Section 3 outlines the regions' incentives for secession and shows how stability of integration is determined by the nature of shocks. Section 4 concludes.

2. THE MODEL

I consider a union composed of two regions denoted by $k = a, b$. For simplicity, the regions are assumed to be of equal size (I discuss later the implications of assuming asymmetrically sized or multiple regions). The aggregate output of region k at time t consists of a deterministic and a stochastic term:

$$Y_{k,t} = \overline{Y}_k + E_{k,t} \tag{1}$$

where $\overline{Y}_k$ is the deterministic term and represents the region's potential output which I assume to be constant over time (adding a constant-trend growth rate would represent a trivial modification which I do not pursue for the sake of simplicity). $E_{k,t}$ is the stochastic component of region k's output in period t; this term can be either positive or negative. The stochastic component is intended to capture any factors that are idiosyncratic to the region and cause its output to fluctuate over time. As such, it can include business cycle fluctuations due to demand or supply shocks, weather- and climate-related shocks, natural disasters. discoveries of natural resources, and the like. I assume that the region-specific shocks are independent of each other but, as I discuss in more detail below, each shock can have spillover effect on the other region. Finally, the output of the union is given as the sum of the regional outputs.

The region's output can be expressed in per-capita terms:

$$y_{k,t} = \bar{y}_k + \varepsilon_{k,t} \tag{2}$$

where $\bar{y}_k$ is the average deterministic income and εk is the per-capita income shock. I assume that the region-specific shock follows an AR(1) process

$$\varepsilon_{k,t} = \rho_k \varepsilon_{k,t-1} + \eta_{k,t} \tag{3}$$

where $\eta k,t$ is white noise with a zero mean and variance σk^2. I assume that the persistence parameter, ρk, is between zero and one, $0 \leq \rho k \leq 1$: if shocks have persistent effect, they do not cause oscillation (assuming negative persistence parameter would be relatively trivial as it would merely reverse the signs of the effects discussed below; it is, nevertheless, difficult to imagine shocks that would take such form). The union's average output is then

$$y_t = \frac{\bar{y}_a + \bar{y}_b}{2} + \frac{\varepsilon_{a,t} + \varepsilon_{b,t}}{2} = \bar{y} + \varepsilon_t \tag{4}$$

where, for notational purposes, parameters lacking a subscript are those pertaining to the union as a whole.

Each individual similarly has a deterministic income every period: for individual i in region k , this is denoted as $\bar{v}_{ik}$. Individual incomes are assumed to take values between υ and V, where υ is a positive number that is high enough to ensure that no low-income individual experiences a negative income after an adverse shock.[6] I make certain specific assumptions about the distribution of individual incomes:

1. Income distribution is skewed so that the median income, $\bar{v}_{mk}$, is always smaller than or equal to the average income, $\bar{v}_{mk} \leq \bar{y}_k$ and $\bar{v}_m \leq \bar{y}$, where subscripts *mk* and *m* denote the median individuals in region *k* and in the union, respectively.

2. The distribution function, while skewed, is continuous.[7]

3. All individuals living in region *k* encounter the same shock, $\varepsilon k,t$ so that individual i 's actual income is $v_{ik,t} = \bar{v}_{ik} + \varepsilon_{k,t}$. While this assumption may be too restrictive, the results of my model would hold also when assuming that the individual shocks encountered by all individuals living in the same region are positively correlated or even less restrictively, that only the average and median incomes are subject to similar shocks.

4. The union median income, $um_{,}t$, is subject to the average shock, εt.

The fourth assumption may come across as counter-intuitive: the median individual must be either from region *a* or *b* and therefore is exposed to the shock affecting that region only. However, after the shocks are realized, the income distributions in the two regions shift relative to each other. Therefore, while the regional median voters are always the same individuals, the union's median individual is different every period (unless the two regional shocks exactly cancel out). The identity of the union median voter changes after every realization of the two regional shocks in such a way that the income of the new median voter differs from the income of the previous period's median voter by an amount that equals to the average shock. Therefore, assumption (4) follows from the assumption that the regional income distributions are continuous, and it constitutes a crucial difference between my model and that of Alesina and Perotti (1998), who assume that the union median voter always belongs to the same country (and her identity does not depend on the shocks).[8] In contrast, in my model, the union's fiscal policy depends on the average economic conditions in the union: it is the level of median income and not the nationality of the median-income individual that matters for fiscal redistribution.[9]

The following numerical example helps illustrate the rationale behind assumption (4): Region *a* has 150 citizens with income distribution such that the poorest individual has an income of 100, the next individual has 100.5, then 101, and so on in increments of 0.5 until the 49th individual whose income is 124. The 50th individual's income is 125, followed by 126, and so on in increments of 1 until the 150th individual whose income is 225. The income distribution in region *b* is identical with one exception: it has 149 citizens and the highest income is 224 (this ensures that the population of the union of these two regions is an odd number and the union median income can be clearly ascribed to a specific individual or individuals). The average income, at 154.2, exceeds the median income of 150. Each region has exactly one individual with an income of 150 and therefore the pivotal voter can originate from either *a* or *b*. Now consider the case where region *b* individuals are hit by a per-capita shock of 20 while incomes in region *a* remain unaffected. Correspondingly, the median income in *a* remains the same as before while the median income in *b* falls by 20. The union median income falls by 10–140 (with the average income in the union now being 144.2). Note that not only the median income but also the identity of the median voter changes. Before the shock, there were two individuals with an income of 150, one in each region. The one in *a* still has the same income, whereas her counterpart in *b* now has an income of 130, and neither of them is the union's median individual after the shock. As before, the new median voter can be either from *a* or *b* as both will have exactly one individual with an income of 140. Whether the new median voter is from *a* (and therefore experiences no shock) or from *b* (and has seen her income falling by 20) does not matter. What matters (as is explained in the discussion of how the tax rate is determined in the following two paragraphs) is the level of median income in the union and how it compares to the mean income.

Individuals derive utility from consumption of private and public goods with an increasing and concave utility function: $u'(.) > 0$ and $u''(.) < 0$. I assume that there is no lending or borrowing either by individuals or by the government. This assumption means that neither individuals nor the government can smooth the profile of consumption over time by accumulating or running down savings so that any consumption smoothing that occurs is the result of inter-regional risk sharing. The government has two instruments of fiscal policy at its disposal: a linear tax and a public good. Taxation is distortionary: levying a tax of t is associated with a cost of $\frac{t_t^2}{2}$. Since there is no saving or borrowing by the government, the budget is balanced every period. The public good is thus financed by the total amount of tax revenue collected less the cost of taxation:

$$g_t = \left(t_t - \frac{t_t^2}{2}\right) y_t. \tag{5}$$

Each individual receives the same amount of the public good. Private and public goods are assumed to be perfectly substitutable so that the utility function is linear in consumption. The consumption of individual *i* from region *k* then is:

$$c_{ik,t} = (1 - t_t) v_{ik,t} + \left(t_t - \frac{t_t^2}{2}\right) y_t. \tag{6}$$

The tax rate is determined by a union-wide vote. I assume voting takes place each period after the regional shocks have become known. Since voters' preferences are single-peaked and the individuals cannot save to smooth consumption intertemporarily, the tax rate will be chosen so as to maximize the median voter's consumption in period *t*:

$$t_t^*\left(y_t, v_{m,t}\right) = \frac{y_t - v_{m,t}}{y_t} \tag{7}$$

The tax rate thus depends on the skewness of income distribution: the greater the difference between the average and median incomes, the higher the tax rate.

The regions' preferences over fiscal policy may differ from the preferences of the union median voter. In particular, each region's optimal tax rate is the rate that maximizes consumption of that region's median-income voter:

$$t^{*}_{k,t}\left(y_{k,t}, v_{mk,t}\right) = \frac{y_{k,t} - v_{mk,t}}{y_{k,t}}. \tag{8}$$

Fiscal policy as chosen by the union median voter responds to region-specific shocks. In particular, the tax rate is counter-cyclical:

$$\frac{\partial t^{*}_{t}}{\partial \varepsilon_{k,t}} = -\frac{1}{2}\frac{y_t - v_{m,t}}{y_t^2} < 0$$

so that the tax rate rises during a recession and falls during a boom. This is because the shock alters the skewness of income distribution, as captured by the ratio $\frac{v_{m,t}}{y_t}$. On the other hand, the public good is pro-cyclical:

$$\frac{\partial g_t}{\partial \varepsilon_{k,t}} = \frac{1}{4}t_t^2 > 0.$$

Importantly, the union tax rate and public good provision change, as argued above, not because the preferences of the union's median voter change but because a different individual with a different income becomes pivotal in the union *after* the regional shocks have been realized.

The fact that fiscal policy responds to regional shocks stems from the preceding assumptions that the shocks are additive and the same shocks affect both the median and the average incomes. This implies that the poor are more vulnerable to shocks than the rich: since the shock is the same for everyone, it constitutes a greater share of the deterministic income of poor individuals. This can be rationalized by the fact that the ability to diversify risks tends to increase with income: the poor typically derive most or all of their earnings from labor while investment income can be an important component of earnings for the rich. The alternative assumption of multiplicative shocks, in contrast, would result in the shocks having no effect on fiscal policy: additive shocks alter the skewness of income distribution, $\frac{v_{m,t}}{y_t} = \frac{\overline{v}_{m,t} + \varepsilon_t}{\overline{y} + \varepsilon_t}$, whereas multiplicative shocks cancel out, $\frac{v_{m,t}}{y_t} = \frac{\overline{v}_{m,t}(1 + \varepsilon_t)}{\overline{y}(1 + \varepsilon_t)}$.[10]

The region's preferred tax rate thus depends on that region's income distribution and the realization of the region-specific shock. Unless the income distributions and shocks are identical in both regions, their preferred tax rates will be different from each other and both will, in turn, differ from the union tax rate. Therefore, without efficiency gains, economies of scale, or other benefits of integration, the two regions would always prefer independence and fiscal autonomy to fiscal integration.

3. SHOCKING ASPECTS OF FISCAL INTEGRATION

3.1. Integration vs secession

The tax rate in Eq. (7) maximizes the consumption of the union's median voter during each period. The tax rates preferred by the two regional median voters are generally different from the union tax rate as well as from each other: they would be the same only if the two regions had the same income distributions *and* faced exactly the same shocks. Integration thus carries the cost of compromising over fiscal policy. On the other hand, integration brings about two important benefits. First, it implies efficiency gains and economies of scale because of free trade, unrestricted flow of factors of production, and access to a larger market. Second, and this is particularly important in the context of my analysis, integration is associated with risk sharing. Note that risk sharing and inter-regional redistribution are not explicitly determined in the present model: the regions do not vote on or bargain about inter-regional transfers. Instead, risk sharing occurs automatically because tax collection and fiscal transfers are determined at the union-wide level: they reflect the union-wide income distribution and the average of the two regional shocks. Moreover, risk sharing is only a side effect of fiscal policy: its main objective is redistribution from rich to poor. The rich region may be making a net transfer to the poor one even if the former is hit by a negative shock, as long as it remains richer than the poor region – but the size of the net transfer is sensitive to the shock.

Each period, the regions decide whether to remain in the union or secede. This decision takes place before the region-specific shocks are realized. Therefore, the decision is based on the expectations of current period's shocks, which in turn depend on the past shocks and their persistence. I assume that the persistence of past shocks is common knowledge. The decision on fiscal policy, on the other hand, is made after the shocks have been revealed and therefore taxes and transfers reflect the actual realization of shocks in the current period. The union breaks up whenever at least one region votes for secession.

Secession comes at a cost $\lambda_{k,t} \leq 0$, which I assume to be independent of the regional shocks. This cost reflects the loss of efficiency due to disintegration as well as the cost of creating a new regional government, military, etc. The cost is likely to be substantial immediately after breaking up the union and may fall thereafter. Specifying a particular time profile for this cost is not material for the model's results, however, given that the decision on secession reflects the shocks and the cost of secession is independent of those. Finally, the cost need not be symmetric: one of the regions can find secession less costly, for example, because of considerations such as national pride, patriotism, or historical legacies.

Given majority voting, the decision to secede therefore depends on whether the region's median voter is better off under integration or under secession, taking into account the difference between the region's preferred fiscal policy and the union's fiscal policy (this difference in turn depends on the realizations of region-specific shocks) and the efficiency loss due to secession. We can formalize this as follows (to simplify the notation, I use subscript *k* when referring to the region's own variables while $-k$ denotes variables pertaining to the other region):

Definition 1.

Region k has an incentive to secede if the median voter expects greater consumption under secession than under integration, i.e. secession brings about a positive expected gain from secession

$$\Delta_{k,t} \equiv E_t\left[c_{mk,t}\left(\varepsilon_{k,t},\lambda_{k,t}\right)-c^{u}_{mk,t}\left(\varepsilon_{k,t},\varepsilon_{-k,t}\right)\right]>0 \tag{9}$$

Here, $c^{u}_{mk,t}(\varepsilon_{k,t}, \varepsilon_{-k,t})$ is the consumption of region *k*'s median voter in case of continued integration. Given that the shocks are autocorrelated, (9) can be rewritten as follows:

$$\Delta_{k,t} \equiv c_{mk,t}\left(\rho_k\varepsilon_{k,t-1},\lambda_{k,t}\right)-c^{u}_{mk,t}\left(\rho_k\varepsilon_{k,t-1},\rho_{-k}\varepsilon_{-k,t-1}\right)>0 \tag{10}$$

The outcome of the vote on secession therefore depends on the realization of previous period's shocks and their persistence.

As a digression, Eq. (9) is a necessary but not sufficient condition for secession. Whether secession occurs depends on the net present value of the gain from secession, $NPVS_{k,t} \equiv \sum_{s=0}^{\infty} \delta^{s} E_t \Delta_{k,t+s}$ (assuming secession is irreversible). The sufficient condition for secession then is $NPVS_{a,t} + NPVS_{b,t} > 0$, reflecting the fact that as long as at least one region prefers integration, it can offer concession to the other region to prevent it from seceding.[11] This, however, would introduce the possibility of strategic behavior, especially if $\lambda_{k,t}$ is not observable: either region could threaten to leave the union in order to elicit concessions from the other region. While interesting, such considerations are largely orthogonal to the question of the effect of shocks on integration. Therefore, I do not include them in this paper but they are discussed (briefly) in the final section.

To evaluate the expected gain from secession, note that under integration, the consumption of individual *i* in region *k* is:

$$c^{u}_{ik,t}\left(\varepsilon_{k,t},\varepsilon_{-k,t}\right) = v_{ik,t} + \frac{1}{2}\frac{y_t - v_{m,t}}{y_t}\left[\left(y_t - v_{ik,t}\right) + \left(v_{m,t} - v_{ik,t}\right)\right] \tag{11}$$

Correspondingly, the consumption of region *k*'s median voter under integration is

$$c^{u}_{mk,t}\left(\varepsilon_{k,t},\varepsilon_{-k,t}\right) = v_{mk,t} + \frac{1}{2}\frac{y_t - v_{m,t}}{y_t}\left[\left(y_t - v_{mk,t}\right) + \left(v_{m,t} - v_{mk,t}\right)\right]. \tag{12}$$

Finally, the consumption of region *k*'s median voter under secession is the following (note that it incorporates the cost of secession, $\lambda_{k,t}$):

$$c_{mk,t}\left(\varepsilon_{k,t},\lambda_{a,t}\right) = v_{mk,t} + \frac{1}{2}\frac{\left(y_{k,t} - v_{mk,t}\right)^{2}}{y_{k,t}} + \lambda_{k,t} \tag{13}$$

After substituting from Eqs. (13) and (12), the expected gain from secession, $\Delta_{k,t}$ can be rewritten in the following manner:[12]

$$\Delta_{k,t} = E_t\left[\frac{1}{2}\frac{\left(v_{m,t} - v_{mk,t}\right)^{2}}{y_t} + \frac{1}{2}\left(y_{k,t} - y_t\right)\left(1 - \frac{v^{2}_{mk,t}}{y_k y_t}\right)\right] + \lambda_{k,t} \tag{14}$$

The first term in Eq. (14) reflects the differences in income distributions between the union as a whole and region *k*. The greater the difference, the greater the incentive for the region to leave. Note that the incentive to secede increases with the absolute difference: even the poor region can gain from seceding because it can implement its preferred fiscal policy in that case. The second term captures the difference in tax base: the higher the region *k*'s mean income compared to the union's mean income, the greater the incentive to secede. Finally, the last term captures the cost of secession, which is always negative by assumption.

For the relatively rich region, therefore, the first two terms are both positive. If secession were costless, the rich region would always want to secede. For the poor region, the first term is positive but the second term is negative so that this region may prefer continued integration even if secession were possible at no cost. It is, however, possible that the poor region would prefer to secede, for example, if its mean income is only slightly lower than the union mean income (so that the positive tax effect is modest) but its income distribution is much more skewed than in the other region. In such a case, the benefit from being able to implement the region's preferred fiscal policy might outweigh the cost of losing the net transfer from the richer region. The break-up of Czechoslovakia, instigated by Slovakia, the poorer country in the federation, may be an example of this (as discussed in the Introduction).

3.2. Effects of shocks

Next, I turn to the role played by the region-specific shocks. Voters in one or both regions may be induced to vote for secession either in response to the home region's shock or because of the other region's shock: either shock can raise or reduce the incentive for secession captured by the expected gain from secession, $\Delta k_, t$.

The following two assumptions help make the analysis tractable:

A1Region *a* is always richer than region *b*; this holds both for the median incomes as well as (weakly) for the average incomes: $uma_, t > um_, t > umb_, t$ and $ya_, t \geq yt \geq yb_, t$. This is not to say that shocks cannot be large enough to reverse the relative ordering of the two regions. Rather, it merely means that which ever region happens to be richer is labeled as region *a*. The implication is that region *a*'s median voter would prefer strictly lower extent of redistribution than the union median voter if she were pivotal, whereas the opposite is true for region *b* 's median voter: $\frac{v_{ma,t}}{y} > \frac{v_{m,t}}{y} > \frac{v_{mb,t}}{y}$.

A2The median income in either region does not exceed the union's average income: $umk_, t < yt$ (i.e. neither median voter would prefer $tt^{?} = 0$ if pivotal in the union). This assumption may be reasonable for many but not all fiscal unions: the median income in Luxembourg is probably greater than the average income in the EU or the Eurozone. I discuss below the implication of relaxing it.

Because the vote on secession takes place before the shocks are realized, the decision is based on the expectations of the current period's shocks which in turn depend on the realizations of previous period's shocks and their persistence, $E_t\varepsilon_{k,t} = \rho_k\varepsilon_{k,t-1}$ and $E_t\varepsilon_{-k,t} = \rho_{-k}\varepsilon_{-k,t-1}$. I consider the impact of the other region's shock first:

Proposition 1.

(a)*Assuming that the persistence parameter is positive, $\rho_{-k} > 0$, positive shock in the other region at time $t-1$ reduces the home region's incentive to secede at time t, a negative shock increases the incentive to secede.*

$$\frac{\partial \Delta_{k,t}}{\partial \varepsilon_{-k,t-1}} < 0$$

(b)*The effect is greater (in absolute value) for region a than for region b (ceteris paribus).*

Proof.

(a) Differentiating $\Delta_{k,t}$ with respect to $\varepsilon_{-k,t-1}$ while holding $\varepsilon_{k,t-1}$ constant yields:

$$\frac{\partial \Delta_{k,t}}{\partial \varepsilon_{-k,t-1}} = \left[\frac{1}{2}\frac{v_{m,t}-v_{mk,t}}{y_t} - \frac{1}{4}\frac{\left(v_{m,t}-v_{mk,t}\right)^2}{y_t^2} - \frac{1}{4}\frac{y_t^2-v_{mk,t}^2}{y_t^2}\right]\rho_{-k} \tag{15}$$

The RHS of Eq. (15) can be reduced to $\frac{1}{4}\frac{1}{y_t^2}\left(y_t - v_{m,t} + 2v_{mk,t}\right)\left(v_{m,t} - y_t\right)\rho_{-k}$. The second term in parentheses is negative for both regions by assumption A2. Given that I assume that the intertemporal correlation term is positive, the expression is negative for both regions. (b) Assumption A1 implies $u_{ma,t} > u_{mb,t}$, so that the absolute value of this expression is higher for region *a* than for region *b*. ■

The upshot of Proposition 1 is that for a given realization of the region's own shock, $\varepsilon_{k,t-1}$, either region is more likely to secede if the other region encountered a negative shock in the preceding period, $\varepsilon_{-k,t-1} < 0$. The intuition underlying this result is simple. For a given own shock, $\varepsilon_{k,t-1}$, a positive shock in the other region reduces the expected union tax rate (*tax rate effect*) and raises the expected level of government spending (*transfer effect*). The transfer effect increases consumption in both regions. The tax effect is different, though. The median voter in region *a* prefers a lower tax rate than the union tax rate by assumption A1. A positive shock in region *b* decreases the expected union tax rate, so that the expected disparity between region *a*'s preferred tax rate and the union tax rate shrinks. The transfer effect also implies that the incentive for region *a* to secede falls after a positive shock in region *b*. On the other hand, region *b*'s preferred tax rate is higher than the tax rate chosen by the union median voter. Thus, as the expected union tax rate falls, the expected disparity between the two tax rates widens even further. Hence, the tax effect and the transfer effect go in opposite directions for region *b*. The response of region *b* will therefore be smaller than the response of region *a*, even though the overall effect is unambiguously positive for both regions.

Without the assumption A2, the sign of Eq. (15) may be positive so that the home region would be more likely to secede after a positive shock in the other region. It also implies that the median voter of the richer region would prefer a zero tax rate if pivotal in the union. Both of these effects are rather counter-intuitive and difficult to rationalize, and therefore, I disregard this possibility.

Analyzing how the decision on secession is affected by the region's own shock is less straightforward. Differentiating $\Delta_{k,t}$ with respect to $\varepsilon_{k,t-1}$ while holding $\varepsilon_{-k,t-1}$ constant yields:

$$\frac{\partial \Delta_{k,t}}{\partial \varepsilon_{k,t-1}} = \left[-\frac{1}{2}\frac{v_{m,t}-v_{mk,t}}{y_t} - \frac{1}{4}\frac{\left(v_{m,t}-v_{mk,t}\right)^2}{y_t^2} + \frac{v_{mk,t}}{y_{k,t}} - \frac{v_{mk,t}}{y_t} - \frac{1}{2}\frac{v_{mk,t}^2}{y_{k,t}^2} + \frac{1}{4} + \frac{1}{4}\frac{v_{mk,t}^2}{y_t^2} \right] \rho_k \tag{16}$$

The sign of this expression is analytically ambiguous. Therefore, I consider first a simplified case:

Proposition 2.

If mean incomes before shocks are the same in both regions, i.e. $y_{a,t} = y_{b,t} = y_t$, *and assuming that the persistence parameter is positive,* $\rho_k > 0$, *then*:

(a)*A positive shock in region a will increase this region's incentive to secede. A negative shock in region a will reduce this region's incentive to split off:*

$$\frac{\partial \Delta_{a,t}}{\partial \varepsilon_{a,t-1}} > 0$$

(b)*The response of region b depends on the difference between the median income in b and the union's median:* $\frac{\partial \Delta_{b,t}}{\partial \varepsilon_{b,t-1}}$ *is positive for small* $(v_{mb,t} - v_{m,t})$ *and negative otherwise.*

Proof.

For $y_{a,t} = y_{b,t} = y_t$, Eq. (16) can be rewritten as follows:

$$\frac{\partial \Delta_{k,t}}{\partial \varepsilon_{k,t-1}} = \left[-\frac{1}{2}\frac{\upsilon_{m,t}-\upsilon_{mk,t}}{y_t} - \frac{1}{4}\frac{\left(\upsilon_{m,t}-\upsilon_{mk,t}\right)^2}{y_t^2} + \frac{1}{4}\frac{y_t^2-\upsilon_{mk,t}^2}{y_t^2} \right]\rho_k$$

$$= \left[\frac{1}{4}\left(y_t^2-\upsilon_{m,t}^2\right) + \frac{1}{2}\left(\upsilon_{mk,t}-\upsilon_{m,t}\right)\left(y_t-\upsilon_{mk,t}\right)\right]\frac{1}{y_t^2}\rho_k$$

The first term of the expression in the second line above is always positive. The second term is positive for region a and negative for region b ; this follows from assumptions A1 and A2. Hence, $\frac{\partial \Delta_{a,t}}{\partial \varepsilon_{a,t-1}}$ is positive, whereas $\frac{\partial \Delta_{b,t}}{\partial \varepsilon_{b,t-1}}$ can be either positive or negative. When $(\upsilon_{mb,t} - \upsilon_{m,t})$ is small in absolute value, the first term outweighs the second term, and the opposite is true for large $(\upsilon_{mb,t} - \upsilon_{m,t})$. ■

The result described in Proposition 2 again reflects the tax effect and the transfer effect. A positive shock in either region reduces the expected union tax rate and raises the expected transfer. In case of region *A*, the median voter's preferred tax rate is lower than the union's tax rate. After the shock, the expectations of both the union's tax rate and the region's tax rate fall. However, the region's own preferred tax rate falls by more, thus further increasing the difference between the two tax rates.[13] The transfer, on the other hand, rises in the wake of a positive shock. However, region *a*'s tax base $y_{a,t}$ rises by more that the union's tax base y_t. This implies that region *a* would enjoy a greater increase in the level of the transfer in case of secession. Both these effects make secession more attractive for region *a*.[14]

In region *b*, the median voter's preferred tax rate is above the union's tax rate. A positive shock results in the reduction of both the expected union's tax rate as well as the region *b*'s expected tax rate. The expectation of the region's preferred tax rate falls by more and the difference in this case thus shrinks. The transfer effect on region *b* is similar the effect on region *a* described above. Hence, for region *b*, the tax and transfer effects go in opposite directions. Depending on how different the two regional income distributions are from each other, the overall effect therefore can be positive or negative.

3.3. Persistence and correlation of shocks

The discussion so far has been a rather straightforward extension of Bolton and Roland's analysis, discussing how changes in the regional distribution of incomes (caused by region-specific shocks) alter the incentives for secession and thus induce the union to break up. Next, I consider how the stability of integration – and in turn the likelihood of disintegration – depends on the nature of shocks. So far, I considered only the response of each region to their own shock and to the shock affecting their union partner. Now I look at the specific properties of the shocks: their persistence over time and their correlation across regions.

Proposition 3.

Persistence: *Assume the union is a-priori stable, i.e. neither region would vote for secession in the absence of shocks:*

$$\Delta_{k,t}(\rho_k \varepsilon_{k,t-1}, \rho_{-k} \varepsilon_{-k,t-1}) \,|_{\varepsilon k,t-1=\varepsilon-k,t-1=0} \leq 0$$

Then, assuming the other region's shock is white noise, $\rho_{-}k_{,}t_{-1} = 0$, *for a positive value of own shock,* $\varepsilon k_{,}t_{-1} > 0$, *there is a value of the persistence parameter* $\overline{\rho}_k$ *such that* $\Delta k_{,}t(\rho k \varepsilon k_{,}t_{-1}, 0) \leq 0$ *for every* $\rho_k \leq \overline{\rho}_k$. *Similarly, assuming the home region's shock is white noise,* $\rho k_{,}t_{-1} = 0$, *for a negative shock in the other region,* $\varepsilon_{-}k_{,}t_{-1} < 0$, *there is a value of the persistence parameter* $\overline{\rho}_{-k}$ *such that* $\Delta k_{,}t(0, \rho_{-}k\varepsilon_{-}k_{,}t_{-1}) \leq 0$ *for every* $\rho_{-k} \leq \overline{\rho}_{-k}$. *If* $\overline{\rho}_k$ *and* $\overline{\rho}_{-k}$ *are less then one, then secession takes place if* $\rho_k > \overline{\rho}_k$ *and* $\rho_{-k} > \overline{\rho}_{-k}$, *respectively.*

Proof.

The expected gain from secession rises for $\varepsilon k_{,}t_{-1} > 0$ and/or $\varepsilon_{-}k_{,}t_{-1} < 0$ (and falls for $\varepsilon k_{,}t_{-1} < 0$ and/or $\varepsilon_{-}k_{,}t_{-1} > 0$). As follows from Eqs. (15) and (16), $\frac{\partial \Delta_{k,t}}{\partial \varepsilon_{k,t-1}}$ and $\frac{\partial \Delta_{k,t}}{\partial \varepsilon_{-k,t-1}}$ equal zero for $\rho k = 0$ and $\rho_{-}k = 0$, respectively. Hence, if both shocks are white noise, they do not affect the expected gain from secession and hence they do not undermine the stability of integration. If either shock is persistent, $\rho k > 0$ or $\rho_{-}k > 0$, then the following holds

$$\Delta_{k,t}\left(\rho_k \varepsilon_{k,t-1}, 0\right)\Big|_{\rho_{k,t-1}>0, \varepsilon_{k,t-1}>0} > \Delta_{k,t}\Big|_{\rho_{k,t-1}=\rho_{-k,t-1}=0}$$
$$\Delta_{k,t}\left(0, \rho_{-k} \varepsilon_{-k,t-1}\right)\Big|_{\rho_{-k,t-1}<0, \varepsilon_{-k,t-1}<0} > \Delta_{k,t}\Big|_{\rho_{k,t-1}=\rho_{-k,t-1}=0}$$

By continuity, $\Delta k_{,}t(\rho k \varepsilon k_{,}t_{-1}, 0) \leq 0$ ($\Delta k_{,}t(0, \rho_{-}k\varepsilon_{-}k_{,}t_{-1}) \leq 0$) holds for at least part of the interval $0 < \rho k \leq 1$ ($0 < \rho_{-}k \leq 1$). ■

The upshot of Proposition 3 is that if shocks are sufficiently short-lived, they will not give a sufficient incentive for either region to secede: the gain from seceding would be so small so as to be outweighed by the efficiency loss due to disintegration. On the other hand, when shocks are sufficiently persistent, they can bring the union down.

So far, I have been assuming that the regional shocks are fully independent of one another, i.e. each shock only affects incomes in one region. In open economies, this is unlikely to be the case: shocks have spillover effects because of trade, migration and investment flows, due to remittances from migrants or because of dividend payments on past investments. Therefore, I now consider the case when shocks have spillover effects.

Proposition 4. Correlation: *Positive correlation (spillover) of shocks reduces the probability of secession, whereas negative correlation increases that probability, taking the persistence of shocks as given.*

Proof. Assume shocks' effects are correlated in that there is a spillover between the regions so that individual incomes in region k also depend on the shock experienced by the other region, $\frac{\partial v_{ikt,}}{\partial \varepsilon_{-kt,}} = \gamma$. Then, for a given home-region's shock, the shock in the other region affects the median voter's expected gain from secession in the following manner:

$$\frac{\partial \Delta_{k,t}}{\partial \varepsilon_{-k,t-1}} = \left[\frac{1}{2}\frac{v_{m,t} - v_{mk,t}}{y_t} - \frac{1}{4}\frac{\left(v_{m,t} - v_{mk,t}\right)^2}{y_t^2} - \frac{1}{4}\frac{y_t^2 - v_{mk,t}^2}{y_t^2}\right]\rho_{-k}$$

$$+\left[-\frac{1}{2}\frac{v_{m,t} - v_{mk,t}}{y_t} - \frac{1}{4}\frac{\left(v_{m,t} - v_{mk,t}\right)^2}{y_t^2} + \frac{v_{mk,t}}{y_{k,t}} - \frac{v_{mk,t}}{y_t} - \frac{1}{2}\frac{v_{mk,t}^2}{y_{k,t}^2} + \frac{1}{4} + \frac{1}{4}\frac{v_{mk,t}^2}{y_t^2}\right]\gamma\rho_k$$

The first term corresponds to the expression for $\frac{\partial \Delta_{k,t}}{\partial \varepsilon_{-k,t-1}}$ when shocks are independent, as in Eq. (15), whereas the second term captures the spillover effect of the other region's shock (cf. Eq. (16)). As shown by Proposition 1, the term in the first brackets is negative, while according to Proposition 2 the term in the second brackets is positive (assuming *umb,t – um,t* is sufficiently small). Hence, if the spillover effects of shocks are positive, $\gamma > 0$, so that the shocks become ex post positively correlated, the second term mitigates the effect of the first term. On the other hand, if shocks are negatively correlated, both effects go in the same direction, thus increasing the probability of secession. ■

The last two propositions contrasts with the key insight of the OCA literature that is concerned with monetary integration. In that literature, only the correlation (symmetry) of shocks plays a role: currency unions are predicted to be viable if the shocks are positively correlated. The present paper adds another dimension: the persistence of shocks. In particular, fiscal unions can be stable even with negatively correlated shocks, as long as these shocks are sufficiently transient.

3.4. Discussion

A number of observations can be made about other factors underlying disintegration:

Risk sharing: Integration reduces the uncertainty about fiscal policy. Both the tax rate and the tax base are more volatile after secession than under integration. Integration thus helps smooth taxes and in turn reduces the volatility of disposable income and consumption. The potential benefits from risk sharing are at their greatest when shocks are negatively correlated and temporary.

Uncertainty: An increase in the variance of either shock, σk^2, increases the probability of disintegration, but only if the shocks are persistent. High variance increases the likelihood that a sufficiently large shock will occur to prompt one of the region to split off. This is likely to have happened in the case of Czechoslovakia (discussed earlier) and possibly also for other multi-ethnic unions in Central and Eastern Europe: the economic reforms implemented in the late 1980s and early 1990s were associated with a substantial increase in the volatility of asymmetric shocks as well as with changes in their inter-regional correlation and persistence.

Decentralization may destabilize integration arrangements if it decreases the spillovers of shocks between regions. For example, promoting the use of regional or minority languages – such as French in Quebec, Catalan in Catalonia, or Dutch in Flanders – restricts labor mobility across language boundaries (see Bartz and Fuchs-Schündeln, 2012). Similarly, regional policies promoting local firms can make the regions more vulnerable to asymmetric shocks if the regions are dominated by different industries. All these measures in turn reduce the spillovers of shocks across regions. Hence, the efforts to rescue troubled unions by increasing the autonomy of regions may prove futile, and federalization, or devolution, may prove to be a step toward the slippery slope of disintegration.

Size: Relaxing the assumption of regions being equally sized, and assuming (for simplicity) that the cost of secession is independent of size, the smaller region stands to gain more by seceding than the larger region. Given that the union's fiscal policy responds to the average shock, the larger region's shock affects the centralized fiscal policy more than the smaller region's shock. This implies that the smaller region is more likely to find itself preferring secession following a particular realization of either its own shock or the other region's shock. The relative size helps explain why disintegrations often involve the secession of a relatively small part of the original union, such as Slovakia breaking away from the Czech Republic, the Baltic countries from the Soviet Union or Slovenia and Croatia from the former Yugoslavia. Furthermore, allowing more than two regions in the model would be equivalent to asymmetric size. For instance, assume that there are three equally sized regions. From the point of view of each region, the decision on secession involves considering its own shock, and the aggregate shock in the rest of the union, with the rest of the union being twice the size of the home region.

4. CONCLUSIONS

In this paper, I seek to shed light on the reasons why unions that survived for decades or centuries suddenly unravel. While there are often many very diverse motives for secessionist movements, my focus is on fiscal policy and fiscal redistribution. On the one hand, inter-regional fiscal transfers provide insurance against asymmetric and region-specific shocks. In doing so, they help smooth consumption over time. However, fiscal redistribution typically requires that regions delegate control over tax setting and redistribution to a higher level of government and may end up with fiscal policy that deviates from their preferences. The net balance of costs and benefits of fiscal integration can, correspondingly, be positive or negative.

I show that two aspects region-specific shocks are crucial for the stability of fiscal unions: the correlation (symmetry) of shocks and their persistence. When the participating regions experience symmetric shocks, they do not have much incentive to quit (regardless of whether the shocks are temporary or persistent). Things become more complicated when shocks are uncorrelated or negatively correlated. The benefits of risk sharing can be substantial in this case. However, a sufficiently large and persistent shock can turn risk sharing into a long-term unidirectional transfer. Europe abounds with examples of this: former Czechoslovakia (where historically fiscal transfers flowed from the Czech Republic to Slovakia), Belgium (Flanders cross-subsidizing Wallonia), Germany (the West making massive fiscal transfers to the East), or the UK (where a major attraction of the Scottish independence has been the prospect of keeping the bulk of North Sea oil revenue, which at present accrue to the UK's centralized budget). Such transfers constitute redistribution caused by past shocks, not insurance against future ones. The reluctance with which these transfers are made, and the conditions, limitations, and safeguards attached to them, underscore the importance of political economy aspects of integration.

Importantly, fiscal unions may be politically unpopular also in the countries on the receiving end of fiscal transfers. The protests in Greece and Spain against austerity measures imposed from Brussels and Frankfurt demonstrate this; the break-up of Czechoslovakia, instigated by Slovakia, the poorer partner in the federation, is another example. Quitting the fiscal union allows the richer country to lower taxes and scale down redistribution. The poorer country can do the opposite, increase taxes and redistribute more. In both cases, the post-independence fiscal policy better reflects the preferences of the median voter: secession brings the government closer to the people, in the rich and poor country alike. Depending on other factors, such as, for example, the relative sizes of the countries, it can be the richer or the poorer region that elects to secede.

A number of potentially important considerations have been left out of the analysis. First, in the presence of continued uncertainty about future shocks, maintaining the fiscal union is associated with an option value of waiting which is likely to be positive. In particular, the temptation to secede, stemming from the past shocks, can be undone by future economic fluctuations. Assuming that secession is irreversible, countries therefore face a strong incentive to be cautious. This aspect of decision making under uncertainty has been analyzed extensively by Dixit and Pindyck (1994) and others.

Second, the incentive to secede would be different if the regions participating in a fiscal union could borrow to mitigate the adverse effects of negative shocks. In this case, the regions could engage in intertemporal rather than inter-regional insurance. The role played by financial markets is analyzed by Farhi and Werning (2013) who argue that the ability of regions to self-insure against asymmetric shocks diminishes the gains from fiscal integration. When considering the political economy implications, anything that makes regions less dependent on inter-regional transfers also diminishes their incentive to secede in the wake of particularly large shocks. Therefore, fiscal unions which allow the participating regions to self-insure in the financial markets will entail lower gains from integration but should also prove more stable over time.

Finally, unless both countries wish to secede, there is a potential for bargaining and side payments whereby one country agrees to compensate the other sufficiently to stop it from seceding. As Claeys and Martire (2014) argue using examples from Spain and Italy, side payments are often incorporated into fiscal federalism regimes in the real world. Harstad (2008) shows, however, that bargaining and side payments create an incentive for both regions to behave strategically. In particular, the secession-prone region is likely to appoint a negotiator who values integration less than the median voter, so as to extract maximum transfer from the other side (the outcome of the 2015 Greek election may be an illustration of this). While interesting and certainly worthwhile exploring, this would add an additional layer to the analysis. My model sheds light on factors that shape the underlying incentive to secede, leaving the strategic aspects of bargaining about secession aside.

REFERENCES

1. Aidt, T., Dutta, J., 2015. Fiscal federalism and electoral accountability. J. Public Econ. Theory (forthcoming).
2. Alesina, A., Perotti, R., 1998. Economic risk and political risk in fiscal unions. Econ. J. 108 (449), 989–1008.
3. Alesina, A., Spolaore, E., 1997. On the number and size of nations. Q. J. Econ. 112 (4), 1027–1056.
4. Alesina, A., Spolaore, E., 2003a. War, peace and size of countries. J. Public Econ. 89 (7), 1333–1354.
5. Alesina, A., Spolaore, E., 2003b. The Size of Nations. MIT Press, Cambridge, MA.
6. Alesina, A., Spolaore, E., Wacziarg, R., 2000. Economic integration and political disintegration. Am. Econ. Rev. 90 (5), 1276–1296.
7. Bartz, K., Fuchs-Schündeln, N., 2012. The role of borders, languages, and currencies as obstacles to labor market integration. Eur. Econ. Rev. 56 (6), 1148–1163.
8. Beetsma, R.M.W.J., Jensen, H., 2005. Monetary and fiscal policy interactions in a micro-founded model of a monetary union. J. Int. Econ. 67, 320–352.
9. Besley, T., Coate, S., 2003. Centralized versus decentralized provision of local public goods: a political economy approach. J. Public Econ. 87 (12), 2611–2637.
10. Bolton, P., Roland, G., 1997. The break up of nations: a political economy analysis. Q. J. Econ. 112 (4), 1057–1090.
11. Buyst, E., 2009. Reversal of Fortune in a Small, Open Economy: Regional GDP in Belgium, 1896-2000. Vives discussion paper 8. VIVES, KUL Leuven.
12. Claeys, P., Martire, F., 2014. "If you want me to stay, pay: A model of asymmetric federalism in centralised countries". mimeo.
13. Dixit, A.K., Londregan, J., 1998. Fiscal federalism and redistributive politics. J. Public Econ. 68 (2), 153–180.
14. Dixit, A.K., Pindyck, R.S., 1994. Investment Under Uncertainty. Princeton University Press, Princeton, NJ. Farhi, E., Werning, I., 2013. "Fiscal Unions." MIT, mimeo.

15. Fidrmuc, J., 2000. Political support for reforms: economics of voting in transition countries. Eur. Econ. Rev. 44 (8), 1491–1513.

16. Fidrmuc, J., Horvath, J., Fidrmuc, J., 1999. Stability of monetary unions: lessons from the break up of Czechoslovakia. J. Comp. Econ. 27 (4), 753–781.

17. Gal, J., Monacelli, T., 2008. Optimal monetary and fiscal policy in a currency union. J. Int. Econ. 76, 116–132.

18. Goyal, S., Staal, K., 2004. The political economy of regionalism. Eur. Econ. Rev. 48, 563–593.

19. Harstad, B., 2008. Do side payments help? Collective decisions and strategic delegation. J. Eur. Econ. Assoc. 6 (2-3), 468–477.

20. Hindriks, J., Lockwood, B., 2009. Decentralization and electoral accountability: incentives, separation and voter welfare. Eur. J. Polit. Econ. 25 (3), 385–397.

21. Le Breton, M., Weber, S., 2003. The art of making everybody happy: how to prevent a secession. IMF Staff. Pap. 50 (3), 403–435.

22. Lülfesmann, C., Kessler, A.S., Myers, G.M., 2015. The architecture of federations: constitutions, bargaining, and moral hazard. J. Public Econ. 124, 18–29.

23. McKinnon, R.I., 1963. Optimum currency areas. Am. Econ. Rev. 53, 717–725.

24. Mundell, R.A., 1961. A theory of optimum currency areas. Am. Econ. Rev. 51, 657–665.

2

THE POLITICAL ECONOMY OF POLICY INSTRUMENT CHOICE: THEORY AND EVIDENCE FROM AGRICULTURAL AND FOOD POLICIES

Johan Swinnen[1,2,3*], Alessandro Olper[1,4], Thijs Vandemoortele[1]

[1]LICOS Centre for Institutions and Economic Performance, Leuven, Belgium

[2]Department of Economics, University of Leuven, Leuven, Belgium

[3]Centre for Food Security and the Environment, Stanford University, Stanford, USA

[4]Department of Economics, Management and Quantitative Methods, University of Milano, Milan, Italy

ABSTRACT

We study the political economy of instrument choice with an application to agricultural and food policies. We present stylized facts on the choice of policy instruments and develop a political economy theory of instrument choice. The key predictions of the model suggest a rational explanation of instrument choice patterns, based on the trade-off between transaction costs and distortions of the policies, and internal and external political constraints. Our empirical analysis supports the main predictions of the theoretical model. The shift from distortionary to less distortionary instruments is positively influenced by institutional development, a country's net trade status, and the GATT/WTO framework.

Keywords: Public Policy, Political Economy, Instrument Choice, Agricultural and Food

1. INTRODUCTION

An extensive literature on the political economy of agricultural policies has developed over the past 20 years. Papers in this literature have attempted to provide an explanation for the stylized facts on agricultural protection, such as the widely observed increase in agricultural protection when an economy grows—see de Gorter and Swinnen (2002) [1] , Swinnen (2010) [2] and Anderson et al. (2013) [3] for reviews. Studies have attempted to provide an explanation for the stylized facts on agricultural protection, such as the widely observed increase in agricultural protection when an economy grows (Anderson and Hayami, 1986) [4] . Theoretical studies attempting to explain these and other facts have stressed the implications of organization costs on the political decision- making process (Gardner, 1987; Olson, 1990) [5] [6] , structural factors affecting the distributional effects of agricultural protection (Anderson and Tyers, 1988; Honma and Hayami, 1986; Swinnen, 1994) [7] -[9] , the relative income position of agriculture (Bullock, 1992; de Gorter and Tsur, 1991; Swinnen and de Gorter, 1993) [10] -[12] and political institutions like differences in electoral rules and the degree of democracy (Beghin and Kerallah, 1994; Swinnen et al., 2001; Olper, 2001; 2007; Olper and Raimondi, 2010) [13] -[17] .

These political economy studies of agricultural policy have focused primarily on explaining the level of policy intervention and less attention is paid to the explanation of the instruments used for intervention (de Gorter and Swinnen, 2002) [2] . This bias in focus is an important shortcoming of the literature. From a welfare perspective the key question should be why governments have introduced so many market distortions through agricultural policies. The distortionary effects of government interventions are equally dependent on the choice of the instrument as on the level of the intervention. Therefore the choice of instrument should be at least of equal concern as the intervention level. In fact, both the trade and agricultural policy literature and the policy debates have reflected this importance (e.g. Gardner 1983) [18] . In the policy world, the debate on the choice of instruments has been a very important element of policy discussions. The differences in distortionary effects is recognized by the WTO in the classification of agricultural policy instruments in green, blue and amber boxes—with the green box for non-trade distorting policies instruments. This distinction between the level of support and the extent of market and trade distortions is at the heart of some important policy reforms, such as those of the EU's Common Agricultural Policy (CAP) over the past two decades. In fact, one could argue that the issue of instrument choice was the key element of the CAP reform, more so than the level of support (Swinnen, 2008) [19] .

Surprisingly, this attention to instrument choice in the literature and the policy debate has not translated in similar attention in studies on the political economy of agricultural and food policies where most of the focus has been on explaining the level of intervention rather than its form. A possible explanation for this bias in focus is differences in the availability of good empirical data, resulting in some well-known and puzzling stylized facts on policy level but not on instruments.[1]

This paper contributed to filling this gap, first of all presenting such stylized facts, drawing on OECD data. The paper then proceeds to provide an explanation of these stylized facts.

The paper is organized as follows. In the next section we present stylized facts on instrument choice in agricultural and food policies. Then we develop a theoretical model and derive some key hypotheses. Afterwards we empirically test these hypotheses using an econometric study. The final section concludes.

2. INSTRUMENT CHOICE IN AGRICULTURAL POLICY

We first present some stylized facts on agricultural and food policy instrument choice in OECD countries over the past 25 years.[2]

Since 1986 the OECD calculates policy support given to agriculture. The total amount of support to agriculture is referred to as Producer Support Estimate (PSE).[3] The PSE data cover 28 countries, 12 of which are not OECD members, over the period 1986-2009 (Table A1). The OECD's calculation of policy support distinguishes between several instruments. For the purpose of our analysis it is convenient to combine the instruments into "market price support" (mps), "input subsidies" (is) and "direct payments" (dp). Their share in total support (PSE) is represented by mpsh, ish, and dpsh, respectively.

The first instrument, mps, includes all transfers through tariffs, price support and subsidies directly linked to agricultural production. These instruments are typically considered as being the most distortive. The second instrument, is, are input subsidies and cover a very heterogeneous set of measures, spanning from investment aids and labor subsidies to land protection programs. Finally, the third instrument, dp, includes fully decoupled and partially decoupled agricultural payments. These instruments are generally considered the least distortive.

In the 1980s, the most important instrument was mps. The share of market price support in total support was 82%, whereas the share of direct payments made up only 9%, and of inputs subsidies 9%. In the next two decades the share of market price support has declined and that of direct payments increased substantially (Table 1). By the late 2000s the former had decreased to 49% and the later increased to 38%. In contrast, the share of input subsidies remained about the same.

The choice of policy instrument is correlated with 1) the level of development; 2) the trade status, and 3) the GATT Uruguay Round Agreement on Agriculture (URAA). Figure 1 (left panel) illustrates a positive correlation between economic development and the use of direct payments and Figure 1 (right panel) shows a negative correlation with the export share. In addition, Figure 2 indicates that the shift from market price support to direct payments started in the early 1990s, which was the time of the conclusion of the URAA and has continued during the Doha WTO negotiations.

GATT/WTO rules distinguish between instruments according to their distortionary impact and limit the use of distorting measures while non-distorting measures are not regulated. More specifically, the WTO classifies agricultural policy instruments in green, blue and amber boxes—with the green box for non-trade distorting policies instruments (see Josling and Tangermann, 1999; Tangermann, 1999; Josling, 2000 for more details) [29] -[31] .

In summary, these empirical indications suggest that the choice of instruments is non-random. As stylized facts, we find that the choice of instruments is correlated with three factors: 1) a country's level of development; 2) the URAA and the Doha WTO negotiations; and 3) a country's trade status. We now develop a theoretical model to explain these stylized observations.

Table 1. Support by policy instrument based on OECD PSE database (Million US $).

	Average 1986-1988		Average 2007-2009	
	Value	*Share*	*Value*	*Share*
Market price support	195.839	0.82	125,215	0.49
Input subsidies	20.400	0.09	33,403	0.13
Direct payments	22.425	0.09	98,146	0.38
Total PSE	238,665	1.00	256.764	1.00
Percentage PSE	37		22	

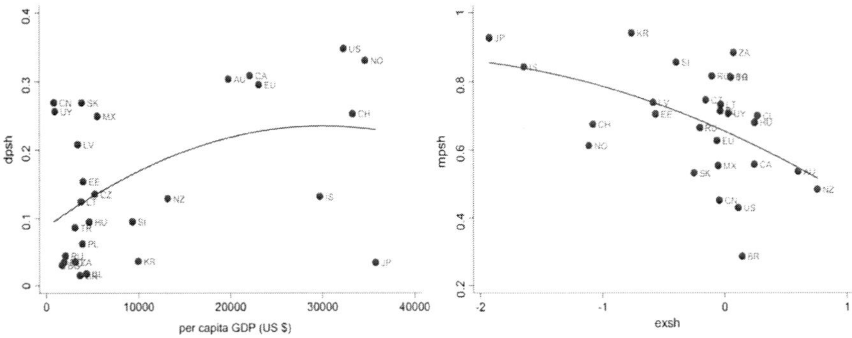

Figure 1. Relation between the share of decoupled (dpsh) and coupled (mpsh) transfers with the economic development (left panel) and the trade export share (right panel) in OECD.

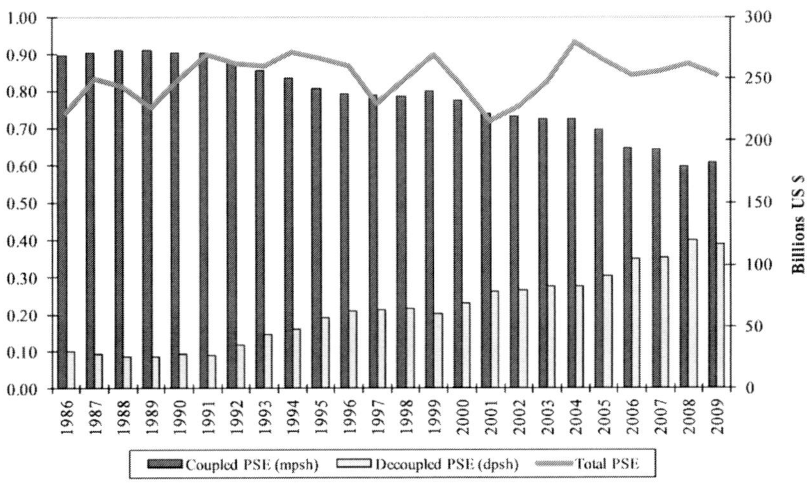

Figure 2. Evolution of total PSE (billions of US $) and the shares of coupled and decoupled transfers in OECD. (Source: own computation on PSE/CSE database).

3. THEORY

We use the same static framework as most models in the literature and consider the choice of governments between instruments in the absence of existing policies (see, e.g., Hillman and Ursprung, 1988; Foster and Rausser, 1993; Kono, 2006) [32] -[34] . We assume that governments have perfect information on the impact of the various policy instruments, so there is no room for policy obfuscation. Consider that for some reason, e.g. a dramatic decline in world market prices for agricultural products, the government introduces policies to support producers' incomes.

We assume that the government has two different policy instruments at its disposal (see Hillman and Ursprung, 1988; Rodrik, 1986; Coate and Morris, 1995) [21] [22] [32] to transfer income to producers: instruments t and s, which are assumed to have the following characteristics:

	Distortions	*Transaction costs*	*Impact on government revenue*
t	High	Low	Positive if net importing; Negative if net exporting
s	Low	High	Strongly negative

Policy t has low transaction costs but high costs of market distortions, and has a positive (negative) impact on government revenue if the country is a net importer (exporter). Policy s causes fewer distortions but is characterized by high transaction costs, and has a strongly negative impact on government revenue, independent of the country's trade status. Even if the country is a net exporter, the impact of instrument s on government revenue is more negative than instrument t's impact. One could think of tariffs vis-à-vis lump-sum transfers, or market price support vis-à-vis direct income support as examples of policies t and s, respectively.

As in Kono (2006) [34] , we assume that governments need both voter support and money to stay in power. Money can be raised both through interest-group contributions and through revenues from the implementation of policy instruments. Our assumptions imply a modified Grossman and Helpman (1994) [35] model of government decision-making where, in line with Maggi and Rodríguez-Clare (2000) [36] , the government maximizes a weighted sum of interest group contributions, policy revenues, and total voter support:

$$G(t,s)=C(t,s)+\omega^{R}(\alpha)R(t,s;\beta)+\omega^{V}V(t,s) \quad ,(1)$$

where G is government utility, C are the interest-group contributions, R measures the budgetary costs or revenues of the policy instruments, and V is total voter support. t and s are the income transfers of the two policy instruments, and ω^R and ω^V are the weights that the government gives to respectively revenue considerations and total voter support. β represents the trade balance of that country, and α is an inverse measure for a country's institutional development.

In developing countries—with relatively underdeveloped institutions—raising revenue through foreign trade taxes constitutes the single largest source of public revenue (Burgess and Stern, 1993; Rodrik, 1995; Bates and Block, 2010) [37] -[39] . The revenue motive is therefore more imperative in countries with less developed institutions. Since α inversely measures the country's institutional development, we assume that the weight attached

by the government to the revenue function increases with less developed institutions $\left(\frac{\partial \omega^R}{\partial \alpha} > 0\right)$.

As in Grossman and Helpman (1994) [35] , we assume that the interest group consists of active lobbyists that solicit income transfers from the government. For this purpose the interest group offers the government a schedule that lists the interest group's contributions as a function of the income transfers. The interest-group contributions $C(t,s)$ rise with the level of the income transfers $(C_t > 0; C_s > 0)$, but at a decreasing rate $(C_{tt} < 0; C_{ss} < 0)$.[4]

The policy revenue function $R(t,s;\beta)$, is assumed to be decreasing in policy instrument s $(R_s < 0)$, whereas the revenue impact of instrument t can be either positive $(R_t > 0)$ or negative $(R_t < 0)$, depending on the trade status of the country (respectively net importing or net exporting). We assume that $(R_s < R_t)$ to represent that instrument s has a highly negative impact on government revenue, even more negative than instrument t in the case of a net-exporting country. $b^t \alpha t$ is concave in the income transfers $(R_{tt} < 0; R_{ss} < 0; R_{ts} < 0)$. In line with the marginal impact of instrument t being respectively positive and negative for a net-importing and net- exporting country, the impact of an increase in the trade balance β, on instrument t's marginal revenue impact is negative, i.e. $R_{t\beta} < 0$. The negative revenue impact of instrument t is independent of the trade balance: $R_{s\beta} = 0$.

The function for total voter support, $V(t,s)$, is given by

$$V(t,s) = W(t,s) - b^t \alpha t - b^s \alpha s \qquad (2)$$

where the first term, $W(t,s)$, represents total voter welfare, and the second and third terms, $b^t \alpha t$ and $b^s \alpha s$, measure the total transaction costs related to each instrument. As before, α is an inverse measure for the country's institutional development. In an unfavourable institutional environment where institutions are underdeveloped and the administrative capacity is low, transaction costs are higher for the same amount of income transfer (Burgess and Stern, 1993) [37] . Since policy t involves lower transaction costs than policy s for the same amount of income transfer, we assume that $b^s > b^t \geq 0$. Hence $b^t\alpha t$ and $b^s\alpha s$ are the average transaction costs per unit of the income transfers t and s.

As both policy instruments are distortionary measures, $W(t,s)$ is decreasing in the income transfers $(W_t < 0; W_s < 0)$ at an increasing rate $(W_{tt} < 0; W_{ss} < 0; W_{ts} < 0)$. Instrument t is more distorting than instrument s, so $W_t < W_s$.

The equilibrium pair of income transfers (t^*, s^*) is determined by the first order conditions (FOCs):[5]

$$\begin{cases} G_t = C_t(t,s) + \omega^R(\alpha) R_t(t,s;\beta) + \omega^V W_t(t,s) - \omega^V b^t \alpha = 0 \\ G_s = C_s(t,s) + \omega^R(\alpha) R_s(t,s;\beta) + \omega^V W_s(t,s) - \omega^V b^s \alpha = 0 \end{cases} \quad (3)$$

Define $h = \frac{t}{t+s}$ as the share of policy t in the total income transfer. Comparative statics on the equilibrium $h^* = \frac{t^*}{t^*+s^*}$ for changes in the institutional development of a country, α, and the country's trade balance, β, yield the following two results.

Result 1: If $\frac{b^s}{b^t} > \frac{G_{ss}}{G_{ts}} > 1$ and $\frac{R_t}{R_s} > \frac{G_{ts}}{G_{ss}} < 1$: $dh^*/d\alpha > 0$.

Proof: See Appendix 1.

Result 1 implies that in countries with lower institutional capacity, where policy transaction costs are higher and the revenue motive is more important, ceteris paribus, the relative share of income transfer t^* is higher in equilibrium. Hence countries with less developed institutions (α higher) will apply relatively more distorting policies (h^* larger), provided that the transaction costs of the more distorting policy are sufficiently lower than that of the other policy $\frac{b^s}{b^t} > \frac{G_{ss}}{G_{ts}} > 1$, and that the less distorting policy has a sufficiently more negative impact on government revenue $\frac{R_t}{R_s} > \frac{G_{ts}}{G_{ss}} < 1$. The latter condition is always fulfilled if the more distorting policy has a positive impact on government revenue $(R_t > 0)$.

To illustrate this result, take the specific case of a net-importing country. In that case, $R_t > 0$, and the second condition is fulfilled. If in addition the more distorting instrument (t) involves no transaction costs, i.e. $b^t = 0$, the first condition holds as well. It is clear from Result 1 and the proof in Appendix 1 that in this specific case, an increase of the institutional capacity of a country (α lower) will always result in a higher relative share of the less distorting policy instrument s^* in equilibrium (h^* smaller). The result also holds under less strict conditions, which are discussed in Appendix 1.

Result 2: $\mathrm{d}h^*/\mathrm{d}\beta < 0$.

Proof: See Appendix 1.

Result 2 implies that if the trade balance of a country increases (β increase), the relative share of the more distorting policy in the total income transfer decreases (h^* decreases). For example, if for some exogenous reason a country's imports decrease, ceteris paribus, the country will shift to using the less distorting policy relatively more, although it involves relatively higher transaction costs.

4. EMPIRICAL EVIDENCE

To formally test whether our theoretical hypotheses are consistent with the observed evidence on instrument choices we use the share of market price support in total support (mpsh) as a proxy for the instrument t and the share of direct payments in total support (dpsh) as a proxy for the instrument s. As we explained in Section 2, the OECD data on instrument choice cover 28 countries over the 1986-2009 period.[6]

We proxy the institutional development and administrative capacity of a country by the real GDP per capita (gdppc), taken from the World Development Indicators. As an indicator of the trade status we use the net export share in total production (exsh), based on FAO data.[7] To capture the effect of international agreement we include a dummy variable, d_gatt. This dummy takes the value of 1 since 1995 (0 otherwise). 1995 was the first year of the GATT URAA implementation, which has introduced more constraints on the use of highly distortionary policy instruments like mps, than on lower distortionary instruments, like dp. In fact, fully decoupled policies which are not trade distorting are allowed under WTO principles.

As control variable and to account for path dependency and the persistence of policies, we include the level of the dependent variable in the previous period.

Finally, one may argue that from a conceptual point of view, the empirical model should also include the level of support (PSE). By including PSE as explanatory variable, one can analyze the relation between the policy level and instrument choice. However, there are two econometric reasons that render the inclusion of the level of support in our instrument choice equations problematic. First, PSE is endogenous, as the level of support is likely to depend itself on the policy instrument. Second, our explanatory variables, exsh, gdppc, and d_gatt, are also important determinants of the overall protection level. While the first problem could be solved potentially by using a simultaneous equation model, the second problem precludes finding good instruments for PSE in the mpsh and dpsh equations. We therefore do not include PSE in the regressions.

Summarizing, in what follows we will run the following empirical specifications:

$$mpsh_{it} = \alpha_0 + \alpha_1 mpsh_{it-1} + \alpha_2 gdppc_{it-1} + \alpha_3 exsh_{it-1} + \alpha_4 d\_gatt_{it-1} + \upsilon_{it}$$

$$dpsh_{it} = \beta_0 + \beta_1 mpsh_{it-1} + \beta_2 gdppc_{it-1} + \beta_3 exsh_{it-1} + \beta_4 d\_gatt_{it-1} + \eta_{it}$$

where α_1 and β_1 are expected to be positive; α_1, α_2 and α_3 are expected to be negative; and β_1, β_2 and β_3 are expected to be positive. We first run the regressions using a simple OLS estimator, and later will do robustness tests with alternative estimation techniques.

OLS regressions are reported in Table 2, with Columns (1) and (5) for mpsh and dpsh regressions, respectively. All the relevant variables have their expected signs and are statistically significant at the 95% level or more. Moreover, the adjusted R^2 of the models, ranging from 0.58 to 0.80, indicates a good explanatory power of the selected variables.

gdppc has a significant negative effect on mpsh, the share of market price support, a relation that turn into positive when the share of direct income support, dpsh, is considered. These results are consistent with our theoretical argument that countries with lower administrative capacity and lower institutional development have a preference for price support. Also in line with our hypothesis, the net export share has a significant negative effect on mpsh, and a positive and significant effect on dpsh.

The 1994 GATT Agreement as captured by the dummy d_gatt is significantly negatively correlated with mpsh, and positively with dpsh. These results are consistent with the argument that the GATT constraints exert an effect on instrument choices: mpsh declined on average after the implementation of the 1994 URAA, and dpsh increased. In all regressions the coefficients of the lagged value of the dependent variable are positive and strongly significant. The magnitude of the lagged coefficients, ranging from 0.66 to 0.86, confirm a strong level of persistency in instrument choice.

Table 2. Regression results.

Dependent variable	*mpsh*				*dpsh*			
Estimations method	OLS	LSDV	System GMM		OLS	LSDV	System GMM	
			One step	*Two step*			*One step*	*Two step*
	(1)	(2)	(3)	(4)	(5)	(6)	(7)	(8)
gdppc	−0.0018	−0.0107	−0.0035	−0.0036	0.0015	0.0085	0.0023	0.0027
	2.98^{***}	3.50^{***}	3.21^{***}	2.94^{***}	4.14^{***}	3.98^{***}	2.70^{**}	2.93^{***}
exsh	−0.0650	−0.0571	−0.1147	−0.1190	0.0132	0.0444	0.0195	0.0162
	5.51^{***}	1.28	5.06^{***}	4.78^{***}	1.45	1.77^{*}	1.19	1.01
d_GATT	−0.0511	−0.0472	−0.0882	−0.0871	0.0197	0.0273	0.0309	0.0274
	4.03^{***}	2.46^{**}	4.15^{***}	4.00^{***}	3.16^{***}	2.42^{**}	4.14^{***}	3.48^{***}
Lagged_mpsh(dpsh)	0.6608	0.4582	0.3950	0.4050	0.8038	0.5671	0.6930	0.6860
	13.99^{***}	8.29^{***}	4.83^{***}	4.72^{***}	19.01^{***}	8.82^{***}	7.58^{***}	7.62^{***}
Fixed effects	NO	YES	-	-	NO	YES	-	-
Observations	517	517	517	517	517	517	517	517
Countries	28	28	28	28	28	28	28	28
Number of instruments	-	-	27	27	-	-	27	27
F-statistics	82.4	78.7	-	-	152.6	197.8	-	-
Adjusted R^2	0.58	0.64	-	-	0.75	0.80	-	-
Test for AR(1): Pr > z	-	-	0.000	0.002	-	-	0.003	0.015
Test for AR(2): Pr > z	-	-	0.245	0.334	-	-	0.246	0.241
Hansen overid: Pr > chi^2	-	-	0.315	0.215	-	-	0.417	0.464

Notes: *t*-statistics based on clustered standard errors under coefficients. All regressions include also a constant term. The System GMM estimator is implemented in STATA using the xtabound2 routine, with the option collapse to limit the instruments proliferation. ***, ** and * p-value < 0.01, 0.05, 0.10 respectively.

Robustness Tests

We performed a series of additional robustness test. First, a potential problem in applying OLS to our specifi- cation is that the lagged dependent variable can be endogenous to the fixed effects in the error term, which gives the well know dynamic panel bias (see Roodman, 2009) [42] . A first step to deal with this is by removing the fixed effects from the error term, running the standard Least Square with Dummy Variables (LSDV) estimator. In doing so, we also control for any unobserved heterogeneity that are correlated with our explanatory variables.

The LSDV regression results are reported in Columns (2) and (6) for the mpsh and dpsh equation, respectively. As expected, the estimated coefficient of the lagged dependent variable is now lower in magnitude, but still strongly significant and has its expected sign in the two regressions. Generally speaking, all the OLS results are confirmed by the LSDV estimator, the only different being the effect of the trade status that now is estimated with less precision.

A potential problem with the (dynamic) LSDV estimator is that, when applied to a panel structure where N > T, namely the year dimension (T) is lower than the number of countries (N), it suffers of the so called Nickell bias, due to the endogeneity of the lagged dependent variable. To address this potential source of bias, the system GMM estimator proposed by Blundell and Bond (1998) [43] is used. This means estimating a system with the first-differences and the level equations, where the endogenous variables are instrumented by their level in the first-differenced equation and first-differenced instruments for the equation in level. Columns (3-4) and (7-8) report the results, considering both the one step and two step GMM option. As can be seen at the bottom of the columns, the Arellano-Bond tests for autocorrelation (AR1 and AR2), confirmed the presence of first order, but no second order, serial correlation, suggesting that the model dynamic is correctly specified. Moreover, the standard Hansen test confirms that in all cases our set of instruments is valid.[8]

The system GMM regressions strongly confirm our previous results, showing that the trade status and the level of development affected negatively the share of market price support and positively the share of direct payments, as well as the GATT dummy causes a shift from market price towards direct income support. Hence we can conclude that our results are very stable to different estimators.

5. CONCLUSIONS

In this paper we developed a theoretical political economy model to explain how various factors affect policy instruments choices. The theoretical model provides hypotheses on policy instrument use which are consistent with three stylized facts, i.e., 1) their correlation with the level of a country's institutional development; 2) their correlation with a country's net trade position; and 3) the impact of GATT/WTO rules. Moreover, the model explains these key observations with a rational choice political economy model without having to rely on imperfect information of policy effects or on theories of bureaucratic inertia and obstruction.

In the last part of the paper we econometrically tested these theoretical predictions using OECD data on instrument choice in agricultural policy. Our empirical analysis confirms the hypotheses and provides strong evidence that the shift from distortionary to less distortionary instruments is positively influenced by institutional development, the net trade status, and the GATT/WTO framework. Moreover, we also find evidence of strong persistency of policy instruments. The main empirical limitation of the paper lies in the difficulty to directly isolate the effect of institutions from the one of economic development, due to the high correlation between the two dimensions. Hence, future development should pay particular attention to this issue, for example by establishing the extent to which different political institutions, such as forms of government or electoral rules, affect differently the patterns of policy instrument choice.

ACKNOWLEDGEMENTS

The authors thank Jason Hartell and Goedele De Nolf for research assistance. This work was financially supported by the Research Foundation-Flanders (FWO), the European Commission and KU Leuven (OT, EF, and Methusalem projects).

REFERENCES

1. de Gorter, H. and Swinnen, J.F.M. (2002) Political Economy of Agricultural Policy. In: Gardner, B. and Rausser, G., Eds., Handbook of Agricultural Economics, 2B, 1893-1943.
2. Swinnen, J.F.M. (2010) The Political Economy of Agricultural and Food Policies: Recent Contributions, New Insights, and Areas for Further Research. Applied Economic Perspectives and Policy, 32, 33-58.
3. Anderson, K. and Hayami, Y. (1986) The Political Economy of Agricultural Protection: East Asia in International Perspective. Allen and Unwin, Sydney.
4. Anderson, K., Rausser, G. and Swinnen, J.F.M. (2013) Political Economy of Public Policies: Insights from Distortions to Agricultural and Food Markets. Journal of Economic Literature, 51, 423-477.
5. Gardner, B.L. (1987) Causes of U.S. Farm Commodity Programs. Journal of Political Economy, 95, 290-310.
6. Olson, M. (1990) Agricultural Exploitation and Subsidization: There Is an Explanation. Choices, 4, 8-11.

7. Anderson, K. and Tyers, R. (1988) The Pattern of Distortions to Agricultural Incentives. In: Maunder, A. and Valdes, A., Eds., Agriculture and Governments in an Interdependent World, Darthmouth, Aldershot, 175-186.

8. Honma, M. and Hayami, Y. (1986) Structure of Agricultural Protection in Industrial Countries. Journal of International Economic, 20, 115-129.

9. Swinnen, J.F.M. (1994) A Positive Theory of Agricultural Protection. American Journal of Agricultural Economics, 76, 1-14.

10. Bullock, D.S. (1992) Redistributing Income Back to European Community Consumers and Taxpayers through the Common Agricultural Policy. American Journal of Agricultural Economics, 74, 59-67.

11. de Gorter, H. and Tsur, Y. (1991) Explaining Price Bias in World Agriculture: The Calculus of Support-Maximizing Politicians. American Journal of Agricultural Economics, 73, 1244-1254.

12. Swinnen, J.F.M. and de Gorter, H. (1993) Why Small Groups and Low Income Sectors Obtain Subsidies: The "Altruistic" Side of a "Self Interested" Government. Economics and Politics, 5, 285-293.

13. Beghin, J.C. and Kherallah, M. (1994) Political Institutions and International Patterns of Agricultural Protection. Review of Economics and Statistic, 76, 482-489.

14. Swinnen, J.F.M., Banerjee, A.N. and de Gorter, H. (2001) Economic Development, Institutional Economy of Agricultural Protection. An Econometric Study of Belgium since the 19th Century. Agricultural Economics, 26, 25-43.

15. Olper, A. (2001) Determinants of Agricultural Protection: The Role of Democracy and Institutional Setting. Journal of Agricultural Economics, 52, 75-92.

16. Olper, A. (2007) Land Inequality, Government Ideology and Agricultural Protection. Food Policy, 32, 67-83.

17. Olper, A. and Raimondi, V. (2010) Constitutional Rules and Agricultural Policy Outcomes. In: Anderson, K., Ed., The Political Economy of Agricultural Price Distortions, Cambridge University Press, Cambridge and New York, 358-391.

18. Gardner, B.L. (1983) Efficient Redistribution through Commodity Markets. American Journal of Agricultural Economics, 65, 225-234.

19. Swinnen, J.F.M. (2008) The Perfect Storm: The Political Economy of the Fischler Reforms of the Common Agricultural Policy. CEPS Publications, Brussels.

20. Cassing James, H. and Hillman, A.L. (1985) Political Influence Motives and the Choice between Tariff and Quotas. Journal of International Economics, 19, 279-290.

21. Rodrik, D. (1986) Tariffs, Subsidies and Welfare with Endogenous Policy. Journal of International Economics, 21, 285-299.

22. Coate, S. and Morris, S. (1995) On the Form of Transfers to Special Interests. Journal of Political Economy, 103, 1210-1235.

23. Acemoglu, D. and Robinson, J.A. (2001) Inefficient Redistribution. American Political Science Review, 95, 649-661.

24. Tracy, M. (1989) Government and Agriculture in Western Europe 1800-1988. Harvester Wheatsheaf, London.

25. Josling, T. (2007) Distortions to Agricultural Incentives in the EU. Paper Prepared for the World Bank Project "Distortions to Agricultural Incentives".

26. Swinnen, J.F.M. (2009) The Growth of Agricultural Protection in Europe in the 19th and 20th Centuries. The World Economy, 32, 1499-1537.

27. Irwin, D.A. (2008) Antebellum Tariff Politics: Coalition Formation and Shifting Regional Interests. Journal of Low and Economics, 51, 715-741.

28. Williamson, J.G. (2003) Was It Stolper-Samuelson, Infant Industry or Something Else? World Tariffs 1789-1938. NBER Working Paper 9656.

29. Josling, T. and Tangermann, S. (1999) Implementation of the WTO Agreement on Agriculture and Developments for the Next Round of Negotiations. European Review of Agricultural Economics, 26, 371-388.

30. Tangermann, S. (1999) Europe's Agricultural Policies and the Millennium Round. The World Economy, 22, 115-1178.

31. Josling, T. (2000) New Farm Program in North America Their Treatment in the WTO: Discussion. American Journal of Agricultural Economics, 82, 775-777.

32. Hillman, A.L. and Ursprung, H.W. (1988) Domestic Politics, Foreign Interests and International Trade Policy. American Economic Review, 78, 729-745.

33. Foster, W.E. and Rausser, G.C. (1993) Price-Distorting Compensation Serving the Consumer and Taxpayer Interest. Public Choice, 80, 173-189.
http://dx.doi.org/10.1007/BF01047954

34. Kono, D.Y. (2006) Optimal Obfuscation: Democracy and Trade Policy Transparency. American Political Science Review, 100, 369-384.

35. Grossman, G.M. and Helpman, E. (1994) Protection for Sale. American Economic Review, 84, 833-850.

36. Maggi, G. and Rodríguez-Clare, A. (2000) Import Penetration and the Politics of Trade Protection. Journal of International Economics, 51, 287-304.

37. Burgess, R. and Stern, N. (1993) Taxation and Development. Journal of Economic Literature, 31, 762-830

38. Rodrik, D. (1995) Political Economy of Trade Policy. In: Grossman, G. and Rogoff, K., Eds., Handbook of International Economics, Volume 3, North Holland, Amsterdam.

39. Bates, R.H. and Block, S. (2010) Agricultural Trade Interventions in Africa. In: Anderson, K., Ed., The Political Economy of Agricultural Price Distortions, Cambridge University Press, Cambridge and New York, 304-331.

40. Brander, A.J. and Spencer, B.J. (1983) Strategic Commitment with R&D: The Symmetric Case. The Bell Journal of Economics, 14, 225-235.

41. Dixit, A.K. (1984) International Trade Policy for Oligopolistic Industries. Economic Journal, 94, 1-16.

42. Roodman, D. (2009) How to Do Xtabond2: An Introduction to Difference and System GMM in Stata. Stata Journal, 9, 86-136.

43. Blundell, R.W. and Bond, S.R. (1998) Initial Conditions and Moment Restrictions in Dynamic Panel Data Model. Journal of Econometrics, 87, 115-143.

NOTES

[1]This argument may apply more widely, while there have been some studies in the general literature on explaining instrument choice, in particular why governments chose inefficient policies to redistribute income or protect certain groups (e.g. Cassing and Hillman, 1985; Rodrik, 1986; Coate and Morris, 1995;

Acemoglu and Robinson, 2001) [20] -[23] , these studies are almost exclusively theoretical. Only recently have there been a few empirical studies on the determinants of instrument choice, including Kono (2006) [24] and Ederington and Minier (2006) [25] .

[2]For stylized facts on the historical evolution of agricultural policy instruments, see e.g. Tracy (1989) [24] , Josling (2007) [25] , Swinnen (2009) [26] ; on the historical evolution of trade policy, see e.g. Irwin (2008) [27] ; and Williamson (2003) [28] .

[3]Initially the PSE calculations were only for OECD member states but more recently also some other countries, such as China and Brazil, are covered. For countries not belonging to the OECD, the time coverage is not complete: the first year observation is around 1990-1992 and the last is 2007.

[4]Subscripts t and s denote partial derivatives.

[5]The Hessian matrix of the government's objective function is $H(G)=\begin{matrix} G_{tt} & G_{ts} \\ G_{ts} & G_{ss} \end{matrix}$. In order to obtain a global maximum and to perform comparative statics, this matrix must be negative definite. Since all the Hessian's elements are negative, i.e. $G_{tt}<0$, $G_{ts}<0$, and $G_{ss}<0$, the matrix is negative definite if $\det(H)=G_{tt}G_{ss}-G_{ts}^2>0$ (Winston, 2004). To secure uniqueness of the equilibrium and reaction function stability, in line with Brander and Spencer (1983) [40] and Dixit (1984) [41] , we assume that the own effects of the income transfers on marginal contributions, revenue, and total voter welfare exceed cross effects such that $G_{tt}<G_{st}$ and $G_{ss}<G_{st}$.

[6]In some cases, the PSE and the instruments share are negative: 13.3% of the observations have negative values for mpsh and 7.2% for dpsh. We dealt with this problem in three different ways. First, we recalculated mpsh and dpsh variables using absolute values of each instrument. Second, we ran the regressions excluding the negative values for mpsh or dpsh. Third, we ran the regressions with the subsample of the OECD member countries only, where there are no negative values. The model results are robust across these different samples.

[7]More specifically, exsh = (export value − import value)/production value.

[8]According to Roodman (2009), the instrument count does not exceed the number of groups and, to control for instrument proliferation that cause a weak Hansen test, we used the xtabond2 collapse option in STATA, instead of all available lags for instruments.

3

FDI REGULATORY REFORM AND POLITICAL BELIEFS: A POLITICAL ECONOMY APPROACH

Louis Jaeck[1,2*], Sehjeong Kim[3]

[1]College of Business and Economics, Department of Economics and Finance, United Arab Emirates University, Al Ain, United Arab Emirates

[2]CERGAM-CAE, Aix-Marseille University (AMU), Marseille, France

[3]Department of Mathematical Science, United Arab Emirates University, Al Ain, United Arab Emirates

ABSTRACT

This paper analyzes the setting of a reform towards liberalization of FDI policies as a political compromise pressured by the lobbying of a domestic lobby and a foreign MNC lobby. Using a common agency model of lobbying, we show that, under specific conditions, the interest group's influence is not distortive for a critical distribution of supporters over non-supporters of the reform. Also, our political economy framework shows that exogenous provision of information on the beneficial effects of FDI liberalization paradoxically weakens the reform process.

Keywords: Foreign Direct Investment, Lobbying, Common Agency, Beliefs, Political Economy

1. INTRODUCTION

In recent decades, multinational corporations (MNCs) have increased their foreign direct investment (FDI) activities worldwide and developing countries have been the main destination. FDI is the international flow of firm-specific asset such as production technologies, managerial and organizational practices, and trademarked brands. Usually, MNCs realize FDI through the establishment of new production facilities, or the merger and acquisition of an existing firm. The literature has traditionally distinguished two motives for FDI. Resource seeking FDI refers to firms willing to reduce production costs by relocating production to foreign countries abundant in necessary inputs, such as labor or natural resources. Market seeking FDI sees firms entering countries to produce goods and services for local sales. This strategy aims at reducing the burden of trade barriers and transportation costs. During the period between 1990 and 2013, the amount of FDI inflows had jumped from 35,000 to 77,000 million dollars and their share directed to the developing nations was 52% of global FDI inflows in 2013 (UNCTAD [1]). To explain such massive evolution in international economic flows, a vast literature has focused on how governments compete to attract FDI. Indeed, the democratization process occurring in the 1990s, with a large number of countries adopting free market economic policies, paved way for interstates competition to attract foreign investment. Indeed, FDI would yield infrastructure upgrading, promote technology transfer and improve managerial knowledge; those factors are of most importance to compete in global markets (Dunning [2]). FDI are also credited with boosting economic growth (Alfaro et al. [3]) and reducing unemployment (Spiezia [4] ; Vacaflores [5]). Such interstate competition has been witnessed mainly in developing countries as developed countries already exhibit high quality infrastructure, property rights protection and an educated work force, thus reducing the need for them to compete. Unsurprisingly, relaxing FDI regulation such as those on ownership, the creation of special economic zones, and lowering taxation on corporations have been widespread policies to attract FDI[1]. For instance, Kobrin [6] showed that during the period between 1992 and 2001, 95% of the 1086 individual policy changes either lessened restrictions on inflows of FDI or provided incentives to attract them.

However, interest groups' influence has been credited to be of great importance in shaping FDI policy changes. Using an original dataset of FDI regulation covering the period between 1962-2000 over 150 countries, 57 industries and 12 specific regulations that represent the most common barriers to FDI[2], Pandya [7] found that industries in which firms invest to gain market access such as service industries are more likely to be restricted, as powerful domestic producers lobby for protection. FDI policies and regulations may thus serve as a way to protect the national economy. So far, this theoretical debate has been investigated by political economists who focused on the interaction between FDI and trade policy. It started with the seminal argument that foreign firms try to circumvent protectionist barriers that impediment exports sales via setting up local production (Corden [8]). Other formulation refers to the quid pro quo FDI, where the motive for foreign investment is the pre-emption barriers that might otherwise be implemented (Baghwati [9])[3]. Dinopoulos and Wong [10] have shown that increased FDI by foreign entities will reduce protection threats against foreign imports in the host country. Quid pro quo investment is thus described as "indirect rent-seeking" via consensual policies (Hillman and Ursprung [11]). The quid pro quo investor seeks a liberal trade policy, and will eventually be deterred if trade liberalization does not occur. For instance, Zhao [12] has demonstrated how such investment is pre-empted if labor unions lobby a host country's government for protectionist policies. Similarly, Hillman and Ursprung [11] argue that such foreign investment could not take place if the foreign investor acquires a domestic monopoly firm. Confronting to import competition, the foreign investor supplying the domestic market may thus lobby for protection. The focus of this literature is whether the presence or threat of protection gives rise to FDI. On the other hand, other papers have studied how the presence of multinational firms affects the emergence of protection. In Hillman and Ursprung [16] 's model, domestic and multinational firms exposed to foreign competition lobby for protection in the jurisdictions where they have plants[4]. Contrary to Hillman and Ursprung [16] , Ellingsen and Warneryd [17] developed a model where the domestic industry lobby for less protection, as a high level of protection could attract more FDI aimed at avoiding trade barriers and thereby harming domestic firms.

Overall, this literature has focused on the political economy of the supply of FDI inflows which represents one dimension of FDI's politics. The political economy of FDI demand has been under-investigated, however. Scheve and Slaughter [18] have argued that FDI can increase the elasticity of labor demand in host countries, thus feeding job insecurity. Their finding suggests that individuals who perceive their jobs to be less secure may be less supportive of FDI. Preferences over international economic flows are complex and multidimensional. As such, they are not exclusively a function of the direct effects of economic flows, rather, they may the result of systematically biased political beliefs. For instance, relying on the Survey of Americans and Economists on the Economy from Harvard University, Caplan [19] argues that citizens would have an ''anti-foreign'' bias leading them to underestimate the benefits from free trade. Nevertheless, education would play a beneficial role in fostering the support for international economic flows. According to Hiscox and Hainmueller [20] , higher education encourages individuals to have more cosmopolitan preferences and provides the requisite economic literacy to appreciate the welfare gains to free trade. Similarly, relying on the annual public opinion survey conducted in 18 Latin American countries, Pandya [21] has empirically shown that more educated individuals are persuaded by the economic benefits of FDI, thus emphasising the importance of ideas in the formation of preferences for international economic flows[5].

In this paper, we seek to unify these two dimensions of FDI politics within the framework of the common agency model of lobbying (Grossman and Helpman [22]). Contrary to conventional political economy models that assume citizens are rationally ignorant of the functioning of the economy and the impact of economic policies (Converse [23] ; Page and Shapiro [24] ; Deli et al. [25]), we assume that the population exhibit heterogeneous political beliefs concerning international economic flows and in particular on the effects of FDI liberalization policies. In doing so, we fill a methodological gap highlighted by Rodrik [26] who insists on the necessity to account for ideas and beliefs in political economic modelling. The main contribution of the paper is to show that information provision related to the beneficial effects of FDI liberalization policies may paradoxically lead to less liberalization. This counter-intuitive result lies with the structure of the political economy setting and interdependence effects between lobbies' activities and the evolution of citizens' beliefs.

The paper is organized as follows: Section 2 presents the framework of our model in which we consider that society is not homogeneous with respect to citizens' beliefs over the effects of FDI liberalization policies. In Section 3, we develop the common agency model of lobbying. We analyze the setting of the reform in FDI policies as a political compromise pressured by interest groups. The latter are composed of a domestic industry lobby and a foreign MNC lobby that have opposed interests. They both lobby the government by offering political campaign contributions. In Section 4, we investigate the policy distortion resulting from interest groups' influence by comparing the equilibrium level of policy change with its socially optimal value. We show that interest groups' influence may not be socially distortive under certain conditions. Section 5 explores the exogenous effect of information provision on the equilibrium level of FDI policy change. The last section presents some concluding remarks.

2. THE MODEL

In this section we develop the assumptions of our basic economic model. We describe the utility functions and their arguments. In the spirit of Tagkalakis

[28] and Jaeck and Kim [29] , we formulate the unemployment equation as follows:

$$u = a(\ln w - \ln \pi) - \delta v \tag{1}$$

where u is the unemployment rate; w is the nominal wage; and π is the inflation rate. Note that $w - \pi$ represents the real wage. We assume that there is a level of FDI policies, $\overline{\varepsilon}$, that corresponds to the current level of FDI rules and regulations which is normalized to 1 so that its log is zero. Therefore, $v = v(\varepsilon) = \ln \varepsilon$ is a composite index that represents the strength of liberalization of FDI policies with $\varepsilon \in [1;+\infty[$ and $\partial v/\partial \varepsilon > 0$. Such indices consider FDI policies that affect foreign investors' market access[6]. The liberalization process is specified as a continuous variable; when v increases, the liberalization process becomes stronger. The parameter a measures the impact of the real wage, (a > 0) and δ measures the impact of FDI liberalization policies ($\delta > 0$). This latter assumption is supported by empirical evidence showing the positive impact of FDI in reducing the unemployment rate in Latin America (Vacaflores [5]), Central Europe (Radosevic et al. [30]), the Czech Republic (Dinga and Munich [31]) and in Italy (Spieza [4]). Therefore, the unemployment rate increases with the real wage ($w - \pi$) and decreases with the index v (i.e. deviation from the current state of rules and regulation of FDI; so if v = 0, no FDI liberalization policy is undertaken).

The population is composed of N citizens. Following Caplan [19] 's empirical contribution we assume that there are two types of citizens: those who believe in the beneficial effects of liberalization of FDI policies on reducing unemployment (informed citizens) denoted by N^i, and those who do not (misinformed citizens) denoted by N^m[7]. Alternatively, informed and misinformed citizens are assumed to hold correct and biased beliefs, respectively. Thus, the society is not homogenous with respect to citizens' beliefs over liberalization policies[8].

N represents the total population with $N = N^i + N^m$. To capture the impact of citizens' preferences for international economic flows on the political equilibrium, we assume that citizens' utility is essentially driven by the impact of FDI liberalization policies on the unemployment rate[9]. The representative utility function of an informed citizen is given by:

$$U^i = 1 - \{a(\ln w - \ln \pi) - \delta^i v\} \tag{2}$$

This representative informed citizen believes in the positive effects of liberalization on the level of unemployment. When the deregulation process increases, the unemployment rate decreases, and thus the utility increases. This is represented by $\partial U^i/\partial v > 0$. The term $\delta^i v$ may be interpreted as the citizen's belief over the effect of the liberalization process. We assume $\delta^i = \delta$, indicating that informed citizens have correct beliefs, $\delta^i v = \delta v$.

The representative utility function of a misinformed citizen is represented by:

The representative misinformed citizen does not believe in the beneficial effect of FDI liberalization policies leading to a misconception of the unemployment rate, with [10]. When FDI liberalization process increases, the unemployment rate

increases, and thus the utility decreases. This is represented by . However, it is assumed that external information related to the beneficial effects of liberalization policies, , compensates this bias. With, $\delta^m(1) = \delta^m > 0$ and $\partial \delta^m/\partial \mu < 0$. Thus, $\partial U^m/\partial \mu > 0$, everything else being equal[11].

3. THE POLITICAL PROCESS

In this section we develop the political model which is based on the common agency framework (Grossman and Helpman [22]). We characterize how interest groups' influence affect the political equilibrium. We consider two competing firms that operate in the service industry and produce the same good. The formation of the FDI policies easing market access in the home country is subject to the influence of interest groups. For methodological purpose, we first assumed that no external information on the beneficial effects of FDI liberalization policies is undertaken, therefore $\delta^m = \delta^m(1)$ is given. A domestic and a foreign MNC that belong to the home and foreign country, respectively, from distinct lobbies j, with j=d; f representing the domestic and foreign lobby respectively. Each lobby offers political contributions to the government. This money is for 'direct political influence' as it supports the electoral campaign for the reelection of an incumbent government[12]. As a reward, lobbies expect to obtain a better access to the legislator (Grossman and Helpman [22]). In our case, both lobbies are concerned with the degree of liberalization of FDI policies, $v(\varepsilon)$, but with opposed interests, and therefore, compete for influence. The domestic lobby supports a low level of liberalization as it seeks protection from competing foreign investors[13]. On the other hand, the MNC lobby supports more liberalization as it seeks market access. Following Olson [36] , we also assume that citizens (informed and misinformed) are too numerous to overcome the free-rider problem and as such they do not organize themselves into a lobby group. To examine how political contributions provided by lobbies affect the equilibrium level of FDI policies, we use a common agency model of lobbying (Grossman and Helpman [22]) which is a two-stage game. The timing of the game can be expressed as following: In the first stage, each lobby presents to the government a contribution schedule, s(v), which is contingent upon the level of FDI policies chosen by the government. In the next stage, the government sets the liberalization policy and collects the political contributions. Analyzing the determination of the political equilibrium requires first to define the aggregate welfare of each lobby j.

The domestic lobby's gross welfare function is represented by the domestic firm profit:

$$\pi^d = R^d(v) - c^d \tag{4}$$

where $R^d(v)$ is the total revenue with $\partial R^d/\partial v < 0$, and $c^d > 0$ the total cost function.

The MNC lobby's gross welfare function is represented by the MNC profit:

$$\pi^f = R^f(v) - c^f \tag{5}$$

where $R^f(v)$ is the total revenue with $\partial R^f/\partial v > 0$, and $c^f > 0$. We further assume that $c^f < c^d$ [14]. The relationship between $\partial R^d/\partial v < 0$ and $\partial R^f/\partial v > 0$ shows that an increase in the FDI liberalization process raises the profit of the MNC as it could expand its production, and reduces the one of the domestic firm as it loses market shares[15]. Each lobby sets up its contribution schedule so as to maximize its net welfare, which is the difference between the gross welfare and its contributions. Then, the government chooses the policy that maximizes a weighed sum of the aggregate social welfare and the received contributions. Following Grossman and Helpman [22] we assume that contribution schedules are globally truthful as they reflect everywhere the lobby's true welfare (Bernheim and Winston [40]). With this global truthfulness assumption, the political equilibrium is the solution of a program in which the government seeks to maximize an objective function, which is the sum of the aggregate social welfare W and the interest of the active lobbies. It is such that[16]:

$$Max_v\ G = \varphi^d \pi^d + \varphi^f \pi^f + W \tag{6}$$

The parameter $\varphi^j \in [0,1], j = d, f$ represents the interest group's ability to influence the policymaker. It depends on exogenously determined factors such as political skills. A higher value of φ^j means that the lobby j can better influence the government that puts a higher weight on the contribution offered by lobby j. We assume that interest groups can have different lobbying efficiencies and φ^d can be either greater or lower than φ^f. The social welfare function, W, exhibits three components: the informed citizen's welfare, the misinformed citizen's welfare, and the contribution received by the government respectively:

$$W = W^i + W^m + s^d + s^f \tag{7}$$

where W^i is the informed citizen's aggregate welfare equal to:

$$W^i = N^i U^i = N^i \left\{1 - \left[a(\ln w - \ln \pi) - \delta v\right]\right\} \tag{8}$$

And W^m is the misinformed citizen's aggregate welfare equal to:

$$W^m = N^m U^m = N^m \left\{1 - \left[a(\ln w - \ln \pi) - (1/\delta^m v)\right]\right\} \tag{9}$$

Differentiating Equation (6) with respect to v, we obtain the first-order condition of government optimization:

$$G_v = \varphi^d \pi_v^d + \varphi^f \pi_v^f + W_v = 0 \tag{10}$$

Here, G_v measures the government's marginal benefits from promoting FDI liberalization policies. The second-order condition requires that this variation is decreasing in v such that $G_{vv} < 0$. The relation in (10) contains a key characteristic of the model. Around the truthful equilibrium, a policy change induces a variation in each lobby's contribution that is exactly equal to the variation in this lobby's gross welfare.

In particular, a marginal increase in v induces variations in the domestic lobby and MNC's contributions by the amount of π_v^d and π_v^f, respectively. In what follows, we define respectively π_v^d and π_v^f as the domestic lobby and the MNC lobby's marginal willingness to contribute (MWTC) for a marginal change in the FDI liberalization process, v. In equilibrium, $\partial \pi^d / \partial v = \pi_v^d = \partial R^d / \partial v$

is negative, meaning that the domestic lobby is willing to offer less political contributions in exchange for a strengthening of the FDI liberalization process, as such policies reduce its total revenue. Also, $\partial\pi^f/\partial v = \pi_v^f = \partial R^f/\partial v$ is positive. This means that the MNC lobby is willing to increase its contribution when the FDI liberalization process strengthens as it could enhance the MNC to expand its production. Equation (10) shows that the political equilibrium level of FDI policy change is chosen as a compromise between political contributions from interest groups and social welfare.

4. POLITICAL EQUILIBRIUM POLICY

In this section, our primary focus is to compare the two equilibria (v^o) and (v^*). v^* is the socially optimal level of FDI policy change, which corresponds to an equilibrium when there are no direct lobbying. v^o is the equilibrium level of FDI policy change that results from the direct influence of lobbies. Analyzing the deviation between v^o and v^* will provide us with a better understanding of the distortion resulting from direct political influence. Using Equation (7) and rearranging, we first set out the socially optimal level of FDI policy change, which is the solution of the following first-order condition[17]:

$$W_v(v^*) = W_v^i(v^*) + W_v^{nm}(v^*) + \pi_v^d(v^*) + \pi_v^f(v^*) = 0 \tag{11}$$

with $W_v^i(v^*) = N^i[\delta(1/\varepsilon)] > 0$ and $W_v^m(v^*) = -\{(1/\varepsilon)N^m/(v)^2\delta^m\} < 0.$

The second order condition requires that $W_{vv} < 0$. Equation (11) shows that relaxing FDI regulations increases the informed citizen's welfare, decreases the misinformed citizen's welfare and increases (decreases) the MNC lobby's welfare and (the domestic lobby's welfare), respectively. The optimal level of FDI policy reform should balance the four factors. From (11) we get:

$$\pi_v^d(v^*) = -W_v^i(v^*) - W_v^m(v^*) - \pi_v^f(v^*) \tag{12}$$

To compare v^o and v^*, we evaluate Equation (10) at v^* and given the first order condition $W_v(v^*) = 0$ we obtain:

$$G_v(v^*) = \varphi^d\pi_v^d(v^*) + \varphi^f\pi_v^f(v^*) \tag{13}$$

In (13), with the second order condition $G_{vv} < 0$, if $G_v(v^*)$ is positive (negative), the equilibrium level of FDI policy change is higher (lower) than the social optimum. It is equal, and $v^0 = v^*$ when $G_v(v^*) = 0$. If $\varphi^d = 0, \varphi^f > 0$, then $G_v(v^*) = \varphi^f \pi_v^f(v^*) > 0$. When the MNC is the only one lobbying actively, the equilibrium level is higher than the optimal level. Similarly, if $\varphi^d > 0, \varphi^f = 0$, then $G_v(v^*) = \varphi^d \pi_v^d(v^*) < 0$. When the domestic lobby is the only one lobbying actively, the equilibrium level is lower than the optimal level. These results are expected. We consider the particular case where the two lobbies have the same political efficiency, such that $\varphi^d = \varphi^f$. Combining (12) and (13), we get:

$$G_v(v) = (\varphi^f - \varphi^d)\pi_v^f(v^*) + \varphi^d \left\{ -N^i [\delta(1/\varepsilon)] + \left[(1/\varepsilon) N^m / (v)^2 \delta^m\right] \right\} \quad (14)$$

From Equation (14), the following proposition shows the relationship between v^o and v^* when $\varphi^f = \varphi^d$:

Proposition 1: If the two lobbies have the same political efficiency ($\varphi^d = \varphi^f$), the equilibrium level of FDI policy change is equal to the optimal level if the ratio of informed over misinformed citizens equals a critical value A. These results hold everything else being equal.

From Equation (14), when $\varphi^d = \varphi^f$, the sign of $G_v(v^*)$ depends on the sign of $\left\{ -N^i [\delta(1/\varepsilon)] + \left[(1/\varepsilon) N^m / (v)^2 \delta^m\right] \right\}$. Therefore, we have $G_v(v^*) = 0$ for $(N^i / N^m) = 1/\delta^m \delta(v)^2 = A > 0$, and thus v^o equals v^*. The intuition behind proposi-

tion 1 is that in the case where $\varphi^d = \varphi^f$, when the level of policy change is optimally set, the marginal welfare effects of changing $v(W_v)$ is equal to zero, so the value of G_v depends on the two lobbies' MWTCs. From Equation (13), $G_v(v^*) = 0$ implies that $\pi_v^f(v^*) = \left|\pi_v^d(v^*)\right|$, the domestic lobby's MWTC for a marginal change in FDI liberalization policies equals the MNC one, resulting in the equilibrium level equals to its socially optimal level.

Corollary: The equilibrium level is higher than its socially optimal value if this ratio falls below the critical value A. It is lower than the optimal level if the ratio increases above A. These results hold everything else being equal.

When $\left(N^i/N^m\right) < A, G_v\left(v^*\right) > 0$ and thus $v^O > v^*$. Similarly, under v^* the government has to balance the impacts of strengthening the level of liberalization on informed citizens' welfare (W_v^i), on misinformed citizens' welfare (W_v^m) and on the contributions from the domestic lobby (π_v^d) and the MNC lobby (π_v^f). Since $W_v^i\left(v^*\right) > 0$, $W_v^m\left(v^*\right) < 0$, $\pi_v^d\left(v^*\right) < 0$ and $\pi_v^f\left(v^*\right) > 0$, the condition $W_v\left(v^*\right) = W_v^i\left(v^*\right) + W_v^m\left(v^*\right) + \pi_v^d\left(v^*\right) + \pi_v^f\left(v^*\right) = 0$ implies that when $\left|W_v^m\left(v^*\right)\right|$ increases under the influence of the growing number of misinformed citizens, either $\pi_v^f\left(v^*\right)$ must increase or $\left|\pi_v^d\left(v^*\right)\right|$ must decrease. The intuition is that because misinformed citizens and the domestic lobby have common interests as they both support the status quo towards strong FDI regulations, interdependence effects occur between these two groups. Given that strengthening the liberalization process would decrease the welfare of misinformed citizens, the government has an incentive to weaken the liberalization process. This would incentivize the domestic lobby to reduce its contribution for a marginal tightening of FDI regulation as it indirectly benefits from the change in the welfare of the misinformed. Comparatively, the domestic lobby contributes less than the MNC lobby for a marginal change in the FDI liberalization policies, resulting in a higher equilibrium level of liberalization. Similarly, when $\left(N^i/N^m\right) > A, G_v\left(v^*\right) < 0$ and thus $v^O < v^*$. The condition $W_v\left(v^*\right) = W_v^i\left(v^*\right) + W_v^m\left(v^*\right) + \pi_v^d\left(v^*\right) + \pi_v^f\left(v^*\right) = 0$ implies that when $\left|W_v^i\left(v^*\right)\right|$ increases under the influence of the growing number of informed citizens, either $\pi_v^f\left(v^*\right)$ must decrease or $\left|\pi_v^d\left(v^*\right)\right|$ must increase. Given that strengthening the liberalization process would increase the welfare of informed citizens who become a large number in the society, the government has an incentive to do so. Because informed citizens and the MNC lobby have common interests as they both support more FDI liberalization, interdependence effects might also occur between these two groups. This would incentivize the MNC lobby to decrease its contribution for a marginal softening of FDI regulation as it indirectly benefits from the change in the welfare of the informed.

Comparatively, the domestic lobby contributes more than the MNC lobby for a marginal change in the FDI liberalization policies, resulting in a lower equilibrium level of liberalization.

5. THE EFFECT OF INFORMATION PROVISION

In this section, we investigate the effect of an exogenous provision of information regarding the beneficial effects of FDI liberalization, μ, on the equilibrium level of FDI liberalization policy. We assume that such external information may come from different sources of the civil society such as think tanks for instance. Since $\mathrm{d}v^{O}/\mathrm{d}\mu = -G_{v\mu}/G_{vv}$, the sign of $\mathrm{d}v^{O}/\mathrm{d}\mu$ depends on the sign of $G_{v\mu}$ since $G_{vv} < 0$. By differentiating G_v with respect to, we obtain:

$$G_{v\mu} = \left\{\left(\partial\delta^{m}/\partial\mu\right)\left(N^{m}/\varepsilon\right)\right\}/\left(\delta^{m}\right)^{2}(v)^{2} < 0 \tag{15}$$

With $G_{v\mu} < 0$, we reach the following proposition on the effect of information provision on the level of FDI policy change. This proposition holds for any $\varphi^{j} \in [0,1]$.

Proposition 2: Information provision on the beneficial effects of FDI leads to weaken the FDI liberalization process.

The political effects of information provision on the stringency of FDI policies depend on the impact of information provision on G_v, the marginal benefit to the government arising from tightening the liberalization process. Here, the negative sign of $G_{v\mu}$ shows that the effect of information provision leads paradoxically to less liberalization of FDI policies. This is because the marginal benefits to the government increase when the liberalization process is weakened. The intuition lies with interdependence effects between lobby groups and citizen's welfare. Indeed, the increase in information provision compensates for the loss of misinformed citizens' welfare resulting from more liberalization, $\partial\left|W_{v}^{m}\left(v^{*}\right)\right|/\partial\mu = \left\{\left(\partial\delta^{m}/\partial\mu\right)\left(N^{m}/\varepsilon\right)\right\}/\left(\delta^{m}\right)^{2}(v)^{2} < 0.$

By analogy with proposition 1, this would incentivize the MNC lobby to decrease its contribution for a marginal softening of FDI regulation as it indirectly benefits from the change in the welfare of misinformed citizens.

Comparatively, the domestic lobby contributes more than the MNC lobby for a marginal change in the FDI liberalization policies, leading to less liberalization.

6. CONCLUSIONS

Recognizing that the political economy of FDI demand has so far received less attention as opposed to the study of FDI supply, this paper has proposed a challenging analysis seeking to unify these two dimensions of FDI politics. Using a common agency model of politics, we have proposed a modelling of a reform aimed at relaxing FDI policies that account for the impact of direct lobbying of a domestic lobby and a foreign MNC lobby which compete for influencing the FDI policy process affecting firms' market access. The domestic lobby supports a low level of liberalization as it seeks protection from competing foreign investors. On the other hand, the MNC lobby supports more liberalization at it seeks market access. Contrary to conventional political economy models, we have assumed that the population exhibits heterogeneous political beliefs over the effects of FDI liberalization policies.

Our general model has suggested interesting results under specific conditions. First, proposition 1 has shown that when interest groups have the same lobbying efficiency, the lobbies' influence is not necessarily distortive. Indeed, taking into account the heterogeneity of citizen's beliefs over the effects of FDI policies, the equilibrium level of policy change is equal to its socially optimal value for a specific distribution of informed over misinformed citizens. Although conventional results of common agency models of lobbying have demonstrated that interest groups' activities bias policy choices against unorganized stakeholders, our model shows that it is not always the case. This result lies with the structure of the political game where the two lobbies holding opposed interests may provide the same lobbying efforts. Second, we have shown that a change in the distribution of informed over misinformed citizens creates political distortions as the equilibrium outcome deviates from its socially optimal level. For instance, when the number of misinformed increases, we paradoxically observe a strengthening of liberalization of FDI policies. This counter-intuitive result has to do with interdependence effects that occur between the two groups who share a common interest, namely the domestic lobby and the misinformed. Second, our model has also accounted for the effect of exogenous provision of information on the beneficial effects of the liberalization of FDI policies. In extending proposition 1, proposition 2 has shown that the liberalization process is weakened when such provision occurs. This paradoxical outcome also results from interdependence effects between lobby groups and the evolution of citizens' beliefs. This theoretical result has important policy implications especially for education policies aiming at creating a support for FDI and international economic flows in general. Indeed, findings of the literature showing that educated individuals are persuaded by the economic benefits of FDI and support them, may not be transferred into more FDI liberalization depending on the structure of the political game of well-organized interests.

For further research, our model has, however, the following limitations and could be extended in many directions. First, we have considered a general index of FDI policies that affect foreign investors' market access. Further research would consider specific policies and integrate them into the industry's profit functions. In addition, developing an economic model that accounts for material sources of utility such as wages would enrich the realism of the model and bring interesting insights given the labor market effects of FDI. Then, testing our result would bring interesting insights into the empirical literature of the political economy of FDI. Finally, the high level of generality of our model allows us to apply it to other important political economy issues such as those related to labor market regulations.

ACKNOWLEDGEMENTS

We thank participants of Research Seminar at the Department of Economics and Finance, United Arab Emirates University, February 2016. We are also thankful for the UAEU support, Grants number G00001588. Finally we thank Mr. Shahabuddin Abdulrouf, Mr. Enayatulah Abdal Ghafoor and Mr. Hamid Tajjudin for their excellent research assistance.

CITE THIS PAPER

Jaeck, L. and Kim, S. (2016) FDI Regulatory Reform and Political Beliefs: A Political Economy Approach. Theoretical Economics Letters, 6, 1205-1218. http://dx.doi.org/10.4236/tel.2016.66114

REFERENCES

1. UNCTAD (2013) World Investment Report 2013: Trends and Determinants. United Nations.

2. Dunning, J. (1981) International Production and the Multinational Enterprise. Allen & Unwin, London.

3. Alfaro, L., Areendam, C., Sebnem, K. and Selin, S. (2004) FDI and Economic Growth: The Role of Local Financial Markets. Journal of International Economics, 64, 89-112.

4. Siepza, V. (2004) Trade, FDI and Employment: Some Empirical Evidence. In: Lee, E. and Vivarelly, M., Eds., Understanding Globalization, Employment and Poverty Reduction, Palgrave Macmillan, New York, 143-162.

5. Vacaflores, D.E. (2011) Was Latin America Correct in Relying in Foreign Direct Investment to Improve Employment Rates? Applied Econometrics and International Development, 11, 101-122.

6. Kobrin, S.J. (2005) The Determinants of Liberalization of FDI Policy in Developing Countries: A Cross-Sectional Analysis, 1992-2001. Transnational Corporations, 14, 67-104.

7. Pandya, S. (2007) Trading Spaces: Political Economy of Foreign Direct Investment Regulation, 1963-2000. PhD Dissertation, Harvard University, Cambridge, Mass.

8. Corden, W.R. (1974) Trade Policy and Economic Welfare. Claredon Press, Oxford.

9. Bhagwati, J.N. (1985) Investing Abroad. Esmee Fairbain Lecture, University of Lancaster, Lancaster.

10. Dinopoulos, E. and Wong, K. (1991) Quid pro quo Foreign Investment and Government Intervention. In: Koekkoek, K. and Mennes, C., Eds., International Trade and Global Development, Routledge, London, 162-190.

11. Hillman, A. and Ursprung, H. (1999) Foreign Direct Investment and Endogenous Protection with quid pro quo. Economics and Politics, 11, 1-12.

12. Zhao, L. (1996) The Complementarity between Endogenous Protection and Direct Foreign Investment. Economics and Politics, 8, 61-72.

13. Cooray, A., Tamazian, A. and Chaitanya Vadlamannati, K. (2014) What Drives FDI Policy Liberalization? An Empirical Investigation. Regional Science and Urban Economics, 49, 179-189.

14. UNCTAD (1996) World Investment Report 1996: Trends and Determinants. United Nations.

15. Bhagwati, J.N., Dinopoulos, E. and Wong, K.Y. (1992) Quid pro quo Foreign Investment. Proceedings of the Hundred and Fourth Annual Meeting of the American Economic Association, 186-190.

16. Hillman, A. and Ursprung, H. (1993) Multinational Firms, Political Competition, and International Trade Policy. International Economic Review, 34, 347-363.

17. Ellingsen, T. and Warneryd, K. (1999) Foreign Direct Investment and the Political Economy of Protection. International Economic Review, 40, 357-379.

18. Sheve, K.F. (200) Economic Insecurity and the Globalization of Production. American Journal of Political Science, 48, 662-674.

19. Caplan, B. (2002) Systematically Biased Beliefs about Economics: Robust Evidence of Content-Dependent Judgmental Anomalies from the Survey of Americans and Economists on the Economy. Economic Journal, 112, 1-26.

20. Hiscox, M.J. (2006) Through a Glass and Darkly: Attitudes towards International Trade and the Curious Effects of Issue Framing. International Organization, 60, 755-780.

21. Pandya, S. (2010) Labor Market and the Demand for Foreign Direct Investment. International Organization, 64, 389-409.

22. Grossman, G. and Helpman, E. (1994b) Protection for Sale. American Economic Review, 84, 833-850. [Citation Time(s):5]

23. Converse, P.E. (1964) The Nature of Belief Systems in Mass Publics. Critical Review, 18, 1-74.

24. Page, B. and Shapiro, R. (1992) The Rational Public: Fifty Years of Trends in Americans' Policy Preferences. University of Chicago Press, Chicago.

25. Deli, C., Michael, X. and Keeter, S. (1996) What Americans Know about Politics and Why It Matters. Yale University Press, New Haven.

26. Rodrik, D. (2014) When Ideas Trump Interests: Preferences, Worldviews and Policy Innovations. Journal of Economic Perspectives, 28, 189-208.

27. Leeson, P.T., Ryan, M.E. and Williamson, C.R. (2012) Think Tanks. Journal of Comparative Economics, 40, 62-77.

28. Tagkalakis, A. (2006) Labor Market Reforms in a Monetary Union. Oxford Economic Papers, 58, 655-680.

29. Jaeck, L. and Kim, S. (2014) The Impact of EMU Enlargement on Structural Reforms: A Political Economy Approach. International Advances in Economic Research, 20, 73-86.

30. Radosevic, S., Varblane, U. and Mickiewicz, T. (2003) Foreign Direct Investment and Its Effect on Employment in Central Europe. Transnational Corporations, 12, 53-90.

31. Dinga, M. and Munich, D. (2010) The Impact of Territorially Concentrated FDI on Local Labor Markets: Evidence from the Czech Republic. Labour Economics, 17, 354-367.

32. Saint-Paul, G. (2004) Why Are European Countries Diverging in Their Unemployment Experience. Journal of Economic Perspectives, 18, 49-68.

33. Jaeck, L. (2011) Information and Political Failures: To What Extent Does Rational Ignorance Explain Irrational Beliefs Formation? Constitutional Political Economy, 22, 287-301.

34. MacDonald, S.E. and Rabinowitz, G. (1993) Ideology and Candidate Evaluation. Public Choice, 76, 59-78.

35. Mac Culloch, R.J., Di-Tella, R. and Oswald, A.J. (2001) Preferences over Inflation and Unemployment: Evidence from Surveys of Hapiness. American Economic Review, 91, 335-341.

36. Olson, M. (1965) The Logic of Collective Action. Harvard University Press, Cambridge.

37. Insitute for Democracy and Electoral Assistance (IDEA) (2011) Political Finance Database.

38. Aidt, T.S. and Hwang, U. (2014) To Ban or Not to Ban: Foreign Lobbying and Cross-National Externalities. Canadian Journal of Economics, 47, 272-297.

39. Gawande, K., Krishna, P. and Robbins, M. (2006) Foreign Lobbies and US Trade Policy. Review of Economics and Statistics, 88, 563-571.

40. Bernheim, D. and Whinston, M. (1986) Menu Auction, Resource Allocation and Economic Influence. Quarterly Journal of Economics, 51, 1-31.

41. Aitken, B., Ann, H. and Lipsey, R.E. (1996) Wages and Foreign Ownership: A Comparative Study of Mexico, Venezuela, and the United States. Journal of International Economics, 40, 345-371.

42. Chari, A. and Nandini G. (2008) Incumbents and Protectionism: The Political Economy of Foreign Entry Liberalization. Journal of Financial Economics, 88, 633-656.

NOTES

[1]The literature has focused on spatial econometrics to explore the extent of competition in tax, environmental standards, economic policy reforms, bilateral investment treaties and labor standards. The reader may refer to Cooray et al. [13] for an excellent survey of this literature.

[2]The United Nations identifies sixty distinct policy measures that countries use to restrict FDI (UNCTAD [14]). Pandya restricts his analysis to the following: bans on foreign ownership, majority local ownership requirements, government monopoly, mandatory joint ventures, compulsory investment pre-screening, local content requirements, minimum exports quotas, discriminatory tax policy, caps on capital and profit repatriation, limits on access to foreign exchange, local employment minimums and mandatory local representation on boards of directors. Note that the first five policy instruments listed above restrict FDI by limiting foreign investors' market access. The remaining seven are regulations that apply to foreign and not to nationally-owned firms.

[3]See Baghwati et al. [15] for a survey.

[4]They show, however, that the presence of multinational firms in an industry may encourage trade liberalization under specific conditions.

[5]Surveys from 1995, 1998, and 2001 included the question: "Do you consider that foreign investment, in general, is beneficial or is it harmful for the economic development of the country?" The 1998 and 2001 surveys ask a different but related question: "Do you strongly agree, agree, disagree, or strongly disagree with the phrase: foreign investment should be encouraged?" The author also provides a comprehensive test of FDI's predicted effects on individual income. In support of Pandya [21] 's argument, Leeson et al. [27] have highlighted that ideas matter in shaping citizens' attitudes towards free market policies in the U.S. Relying on questions from the General Social Surveys that ask respondents their opinions about the government's relationship to the economy, they found that where think tank spending is higher, citizens have more "pro-mar- ket" attitudes toward economic policy.

[6]As an example, and building on Pandya [7] , we assume that FDI regulations subjected to the softening process are related to bans on foreign ownership, majority local ownership requirements, mandatory joint ventures, or compulsory investment pre-screening.

[7]Based on the Survey of Americans and Economists on the Economy from Harvard University, Caplan [19] found that citizens would have an "anti-foreign" bias leading them to underestimate the benefits from free trade. We

assume that such biased perception may also hold for the benefits of FDI liberalization policies.

[8]This assumption contrasts with the seminal standard assumption of citizens' rational ignorance that prevails in the public choice literature. The question of the origin of biased beliefs is left out of the paper. Biased beliefs may result from exposure to activist groups (Saint-Paul [32] ; Jaeck [33]) or ideology (MacDonald and Rabinowitz [34]).

[9]The assumption is in line with the seminal results of MacCulloch et al. [35] who showed that individual happiness increases when the unemployment rate decreases.

[10]This assumption is motivated by Caplan [19] 's empirical evidenced demonstrated an "anti-foreign bias" as well as Scheve and Slaughter [18] showing that individuals are less supportive of FDI if they perceive their jobs to be insecure.

[11]This assumption is motivated by Pandya's [21] study that relies on the annual public opinion survey conducted in 18 Latin American countries. Results clearly indicate that attitudes in favor of FDI increase with the level of education.

[12]IDEA [37] lists 41 countries with bans or other forms of restrictions on foreign donations to political parties. This includes the United Kingdom, France, Brazil, Canada, and Argentina. However, there are some examples of countries which do not impose bans such as Australia, Colombia, Denmark and Germany (Aidt and Hwang [38]). Gawande et al. [39]) have shown that foreign lobbies significantly impact the setting of tariffs and non-tariff trade barriers in the U.S. and that foreign activity may be welfare-enhancing.

[13]This assumption is in line with Pandya [7] 's results showing that industries in which firms invest to gain market access such as service industries are more likely to be restricted, as powerful domestic producers lobby for protection.

[14]Aitken, Harrison, and Lipsey [41] evidenced declining productivity for local firms competing with MNC as they face increased production costs due to greater labor demand.

[15]These assumptions are in line with FDI's negative effects for local firms such as loss of market share due to increased foreign competition (Chari and Gupta [42]).

[16]The objective function of the government without considering the global-truthfulness assumption would be as follow, $G = \varphi^d s^d + \varphi^f s^f + W$. If one considers the global-truthfulness property, the original objective function is re-written as Equation (6).

[17]When deriving the following condition, we use the relationship $s_v^d = \pi_v^d$ and $s_v^f = \pi_v^f$. This relationship occurs as a result of the global-truthfulness property of the contribution schedules.

4

POLITICAL CONNECTION, MANAGEMENT PROMOTION AND RISK TAKING ACTIVITIES

Qiaoyi Zhao[1], Suowen Wang[1], Chao Chen[2]

[1]Department of Accounting, Business School, Beijing Normal University, Beijing, China

[2]China Investment Corporation, Beijing, China

ABSTRACT

This paper investigates how political connection and management promotion affect chances of risk-taking activities, in order to offer theoretical support for state-owned enterprises to select optimal managers, and to maintain and increase their company values. Using the data of chairman of state-owned listed enterprises in Shenzhen securities market, we find that in state-owned listed enterprises, the shorter the pyramid of listed enterprises to ultimate shareholders is, the closer the political connection is, the more likely the chairman is to take up risk-taking activities for promotion. While for the same pyramid, the longer the tenure of chairman, the more chances of risktaking activities.

Keywords : Political Connection, Management Promotion, Firm Pyramid, Duration, Risk Taking Activities

1. INTRODUCTION

In China, the promotion of managers of state-owned enterprises is like the promotion of officials, whose hierarchy is very clear. A certain level of management in firms is equivalent to the appropriate level in government and managers may even be transferred to government departments. Therefore, if the manager of a state-owned enterprise has a good promotion prospects, he may have the opportunity to enter government departments, which shows political connection. We define political connection as the degree of relation between enterprise and government. Because each state-owned enterprise has many levels of subsidiaries, the shorter level is, the higher executive level is; the relation with government will be closer and the company will be more influenced by political factors. Because the Chinese government possesses the right to appoint chairman of a listed company, the chairman's political affiliation makes a difference. However, in state-owned listed enterprises, the higher executive level is, the more intense competition will be and the more difficult the promotion will be. Due to market conditions and their own characteristics, if managers simply do daily work to maintain its day-to-day operations, they can hardly have any outstanding performance to get the chance of promotion. So what is the influence the hierarchical system makes on managers' decisions? Will the managers of lower-level state-owned enterprises be more likely to do risk-taking activities to prove his management skills and enter government departments?

In addition, some managers' durations are very short and then they are transferred to other positions in many cases. It is easy to imagine that within a relatively short period, they just need to maintain its operating status. In contrast, for those with a longer duration, their own political promotion mostly depends on its businesses performance. So what difference would duration make on managers' decisions? For the same pyramid, will the manager with a longer duration be more likely to do risk-taking activities?

2. LITERATURE REVIEW

Firms face many kinds of risks during its operation and management. According to the theory of risk return theory, there is a reciprocal relationship between risk and return. Managers have two opposite choices based on the theory. On one hand, they do more risk-taking activities to get more profits. One the other hand, they accept less profits to reduce the risk. In other words, if a firm wants to get huge profits, it must take the risk of tremendous losses. So the firm has a motivation to do risk-taking activities.

The current studies on enterprises' risk-taking activities mainly focus on the factors influencing the risk-taking activities. The scholars analyzed the factors including the structure of managerial compensation, diversified and decentralized management of enterprises, corporate governance and the board structure and so on. Hoskisson et al. (1991) believed that limited diversification along with decentralized management could stimulate risk-taking activities of the managers [1] . Nonetheless, they also believed excessive diversification produced problems of control, in regard of which the managers tended to reduce risks. On the contrary, it increased the threat that the enterprise might be acquired. Hence the enterprise might restructure and pay more attention to diversification, and risk-taking activities thus would be induced. King and Wen (2010) supposed that solid creditor governance would result in that the enterprise undertakes more lower-risk investments like capital expenditure and undertakes less high-risk investments like research and development expenditure [2] . But solid shareholder governance would generate opposite effects, which meant encouragement of more risk-taking activities. Therefore, the final risk-taking activities of the managers depended on the result comprehensively determined by creditor governance and shareholder governance. Dong et al. (2010) thought that as a part of the managerial compensation, stock option payment would not have effects as it's expected to maximize the shareholders' benefits [3] . On the contrary, it might encourage the managers to harm the interests of the shareholders in order to maximize the value of these options. Their studies show that the stock option compensation of the managers can spur them to undertake risk-taking activities whose level is higher than the shareholders' expectation. Chen et al. (2006) concluded that the stock option payment of managers could spur them to undertake more risk-taking activities, from the analysis of banking [4] .

In the specific banking area, Konishi and Yasuda (2004) believed that the demand of capital adequacy ratio of Japanese banks prompted the managers to reduce risk-taking activities [5] . The relationship between shareholders' equity value and the risks of the bank was nonlinear. Initially, the risks decreased as the equity value of the fixed shareholders decreased. When the asset substitution benefit surpassed the managerial entrenchment benefit, the risks tended to increase. Delis and Kouretas (2010) found that the level of interest rates of most banks in Europe was negatively correlated with the risk-taking activities of the banks [6] . Low level of interest rates could spur the banks to undertake risk-taking activities. Pathan (2009) noticed that risk-taking activities of large banks in USA were positively correlated with powerful board, and negatively correlated with the manager's authority [7] , which was accordant with the previous conclusions of these two issues (Jensen and Meckling, 1976 [8] ; Merton, 1977 [9] ; Smith and Stulz, 1985 [10]).

Managers take adventures because of agency problems. In capital markets like the United States, agency problems were mainly reflected among the creditors, shareholders and managers (Jensen and Meckling, 1976). In China, state-owned enterprises are the mainstay of all enterprises. There is a double agency problem in stateowned enterprises that the managers are both company operators and appropriate level of government cadres. That is because the selection ways and means of the managers of state-owned enterprises in China are different from those of non-state-owned enterprises. They are not selected through the market, but by the government. The client (government) search for the hedging and added value of state-owned assets, while the agent (manager) work for their own wage, luxury consumption and leisure time. This will inevitably lead to conflicts between them. The agent's behavior is likely to eventually affect the benefit of its client in the absence of effective institutional arrangements. Dong Jun (2010) said some managers operated the state-owned enterprises as a step for political promotion, leaving the burden to investor agency and government [11] . Xu Chuanshen (2011) believed that it was the agency problem that made managers search for their own economic or political benefit, regardless of the stage of development and the actual situation of the firm itself, take the wrong business behavior, and eventually lead to damage to the value of the firm as a whole [12] .

In our special national conditions and economic system of China, the manager of state-owned enterprises not only plays a role of entrepreneurs, but also a government cadre with some political consideration. A manager tends to have more chances to get political promotion with a higher executive level, which means there is more contact with government. For example, a former chairman and general manager of China Huaneng Group, Li Xiaopeng, became a member of the Standing Committee in Zhejiang Provincial Committee and vice governor in 2008. A former general manager and party secretary of China Petrochemical Corporation, Su Shulin, was appointed vice governor and acting governor of Fujian Province in 2011. The degree of political connection has a certain impact on the enterprise. Chan et al. (2012) thought that politically-connected firms would display no financing constraints, whereas firms without connection would experience significant constraints [13] . Li et al. (2014) believed that there was a significant and positive relationship between political connections and the likelihood and extent of firm contributions [14] . Chen et al. (2014) concluded that share prices of politically connected firms would react with greater impacts than nonpolitically connected firms to announcements of identical political events [15] . And Houston et al. (2014) suggested that political connections could increase the value of US companies and reduce monitoring costs and credit risk faced by banks, which, in turn, would reduce the borrower's cost of debt [16] . However, what will political connection do with risk-taking activities? What's the influence the Chinese special system makes on the management of listed firms? Especially when competition is more intense and executive promotion is more difficult, will managers take more risk-taking activities for political promotion? Researchers all over the world rarely studied about this.

3. THE RESEARCH HYPOTHESES

There are large assets and wide distribution in the state-owned economy of China, which are related to the key sectors of the national economy. At present, the central owned state-owned assets are unified managed by the State-owned Assets Supervision and Administration Commission (SASAC), while SASAC authorizes some state-owned enterprises to do the specific investments in management. Each state-owned enterprise has many levels of subsidiaries. The shorter level is, the closer relations with SASAC, and it will be more influenced by political factors. The promotion of managers of state-owned listed enterprises is like the promotion of officials, whose hierarchy is very clear. A certain level of management in firms is equivalent to the appropriate level in government and managers may even be transferred to government departments. Therefore, if the manager of a state-owned listed enterprise has a good promotion prospects, he may have the opportunity to enter government departments. Moreover, if the firm ranks higher, the manager's level in government departments will be higher and his political future will be brighter.

Business managers will be promoted to upper level due to outstanding performance, but they are rarely leapfrog promoted. In addition, in state-owned enterprises, the higher executive level is, the more intense competition will be and the more difficult the promotion will be. And because of our special economic system, managers of state-owned enterprises are not only business managers, but also administrative cadres. When the client makes an assessment about the manager, the standard will be more complex, including both business management and political ideology. Therefore, due to market conditions and their own characteristics, if managers simply do daily work to maintain its day-to-day operations, they can hardly have any outstanding performance to get the chance for promotion. In order to get opportunities for promotion, managers need to try their best to prove management skills. It's hard to achieve better performance in a short time by the daily operation, while risk taking activity may be a crash and effective way.

Hypothesis 1: A manager tends to take more risk-taking activities if the pyramid of state-owned enterprise[1] to ultimate shareholders is shorter.

Every manager will be appointed for a certain period of time. Because of personal perspective and vision problems, there is often parallel transfer and rotation of cadres in China. So in state-owned enterprises, some managers' durations are very short and then they are transferred to other positions. In this case, if they simply do daily operations, the possibility of a big crisis and turbulence in business will be relatively small. Stable operation of the enterprise can let them go through this period steadily. But if they take adventures this time, they are likely to be just one step short of success. Therefore, they don't tend to do more risk-taking activities.

But for those managers with longer durations, they can get opportunities for promotion only by brilliant performance. Their advancement will be difficult because they must face competitions from within the firms and other state-owned enterprises outside the firms. If there are no outstanding achievements, they are likely to be left behind by others. Therefore, in order to achieve career success and get great economic and political benefit, they are likely to do more risk-taking activities.

It is not to say that managers with longer durations are more likely to take adventures. Managers' promotions are different with different levels. Therefore, relatively speaking, for the same pyramid, more risk-taking activities will be done by managers with longer durations to get better performance.

Hypothesis 2: For the same pyramid, a manager tends to take more risk-taking activities if his duration is longer.

4. STUDY DESIGN

4.1. Model and Variable

This paper discusses the relationship between management promotions and risk-taking activities using the following as our basic regression:

$$\begin{aligned}\text{Risktaking} = {} & \beta_1\text{Rank} + \beta_2\text{Tenure} + \beta_3\text{Rank}\times\text{Tenure} + \beta_4\text{Age} + \beta_5\text{Own} + \beta_6\text{Com} \\ & + \beta_7\text{ROE} + \beta_8\text{Size} + \beta_9\text{Lev} + \beta_{10}\text{Grow} + \beta_{11}\text{V} + \beta_i\sum\text{Inds} + \varepsilon \end{aligned} \tag{1}$$

where Risktaking is the adventures for the enterprise. Because it's difficult to measure, we use its outcome in this paper, which is the standard deviation of return on assets (ROA) divided by the mean value of ROA within the period of managers (Laeven and Levine, 2009 [17]). To avoid the influence of outliers, we winsorize observations of the top and bottom 5% for all financial data.

Rank is management promotions, decided by the rank of firms which tells the political connection[2]. Unlike other countries, because of our special economic system, there are some special limitations in promotions. First of all, in China, the promotion of managers of state-owned enterprises is like the promotion of officials, whose hierarchy is very clear, including leading roles of divisions, departments and ministries. In the administrative hierarchy, business managers will be promoted due to outstanding performance, but they are rarely leapfrog promoted. And if the executive level is higher, there will be more intense competition and managers need to make greater efforts. Due to market conditions and their own characteristics, if managers simply do daily work to maintain its day-to-day operations, they can hardly have any outstanding performance to get the chance for promotion. Therefore, in order to get opportunities for promotion and higher payment, managers of state-owned enterprises in higher executive level need to prove their management skills and tend to do more risk-taking activities. In China, there is hierarchy problem between state-owned listed enterprises and their ultimate controller, the State-owned Assets Supervision and Administration Commission (SASAC). Generally speaking, the shorter the pyramid of listed firms is to SASAC, the higher executive level is, the closer the political connections are. Instead, the lower executive level is, the lower degree of political connections are[3]. In our special national conditions and economic system of China, the manager of state-owned enterprises not only plays a role of entrepreneurs, but also a government cadre with some political consideration. For example, a former chairman and general manager of China Huaneng Group, Li Xiaopeng, became a member of the Standing Committee in Zhejiang Provincial Committee and vice governor in 2008. A former general manager and party secretary of China Petrochemical Corporation, Su Shulin, was appointed vice governor and acting governor of Fujian Province in 2011. For the time being, if the state-owned enterprise ranks higher, the manager's political future will be brighter, so he will have more power to make firm perform better. In contrast, if the state-owned enterprise ranks lower, the chance of advancement will be relatively small. Therefore, in different executive levels of state-owned enterprises, the same agency problem makes managers act differently. In other words, because the promotion to managers of their own value realization degree differs between man and man, or we can say that because the result of their risk-taking behaviors is different to promotions, managers of different levels will have different preferences. Therefore, the relationship between the state-owned listed enterprises and nation reflects managers' administrative level and political connections. Shorter pyramid means closer relationship with government and managers' chance of promotion may be greater. A firm's level means the relationship with its ultimate controller, according to Sun Zheng, Yu Xuhui (2007) [18] , and Xia Donglin, Zhu Song (2008) [19] .

Tenure is chairman's duration, using year as the unit. Parts of less than one year are measured as one year. We use chairman's duration in the annual financial reports of listed corporations before 2006.

Each company makes an assessment of advancement combined with its specific circumstances. Although different companies have different detailed assessment systems, each system basically contains manager's age, tenure, personal qualities, job performance, organizational leadership skills and work experience. This paper also controls the influence of managers of their own characteristics and firm's characteristics. Age is chairman's age, using the figure in the annual financial reports of listed corporations of 2006. Own is chairman's equity ratio, using the average number of shares at the end of the year divided by total shares during chairman's term of office. Com is the payment of chairman, using the natural logarithm of chairman's average payment during his term. ROE is the rate of return on common stockholders' equity of listed companies, using the average value of ROE in the chairman's term. Size is company size, using the natural logarithm of the average of total assets at the end of each year. Lev is the debt level, using the average debt asset ratio in the chairman's term. Grow is the increase rate of main business revenue. V is the ultimate controller's shareholding ratio. Inds are the industry dummy variables, using 12 dummy variables excluding the financial sector according to industrial classification standard of China Securities Regulatory Commission (CSRC).

4.2. Samples and Data

This paper selected the annual report data from 2001 to 2008 of listed corporations controlled by central and local SASAC in Shenzhen Stock Exchange[4]. And as the manager, it took chairman as the research object[5]. Chairman's age (Age), industry (Inds) and company's level (Rank), which indicates the length of the control chain, were decided by the annual report in 2006, while others were decided by the average record in the chairmen's term of office. Financial data (including ROE, Size, Lev, Grow and V) was extracted from Wind database. And chairman's duration (Tenure), equity ratio (Own) and payment (Com) were from Resset database.

Since this article only uses the data of state-owned listed enterprises in Shenzhen securities market, financial and ultimate controller's data of some samples were missing. Our final samples were 108 listed firms.

5. EMPIRICAL ANALYSIS

5.1. Descriptive Statistics

Table 1 is a descriptive statistics of the regressor variables. Enterprise's adventure (Risktaking) shows an aver age value of −0.28, and there is a marked difference between the maximum value and the minimum value. The average value being a negative number means that major fluctuations may happen to the company's profitability because of its adventure activities, which, as a result, will have a negative impact on the operation of the company. There are also some differences in the rank of state-owned enterprises (Rank) in the sample. The minimum rank value is 1, which means that the company is directly led by SASAC, indicating a high degree of political connections, while the maximum value is 4, showing that the company, under the indirect leadership of SASAC, is a third-tier subsidiary of a state-owned enterprise, and that it's less politically connected. The administrators' tenures (Tenure) vary from 4 years to 1 year, and the median falls on 2.26 years. The ages of the chairmen of the board range from 35 to 69, with an average of around 50. Gaps also exist in the payment of chairmen (Com) and the equity ratio (Own). The marked differences in the company size (Size), the ultimate controller's equity ratio (V), and the capacity of revenue growth (Grow) of the sample enterprises all have a certain impact on the engagement in risk-taking activities.

Table 1. Descriptive statistics of the sample.

Variable	Sample size	Average value	Standard deviation	Minimum value	Median	Maximum value
Risktaking	108	−0.280	1.750	−5.208	0.295	2.103
Rank	108	2.250	0.597	1	2	4
Tenure	108	2.833	0.555	1	3	4
Age	108	50.296	6.929	35	50	69
Com	108	12.072	1.216	7.600	12.300	14.420
Own	108	0.001	0.455	0	0	0.047
ROE	108	0.010	0.267	−1.613	0.047	0.827
Size	108	21.415	0.932	18.944	21.351	24.458
Lev	108	0.535	0.229	0.047	0.555	1.950
Grow	108	0.170	0.264	−0.279	0.125	2.038
V	108	36.731	14.797	12.160	33.760	82.120

5.2. Correlation

Table 2 shows the correlation coefficient matrix of regressor variables. Both the Pearson and Spearman correlation coefficients do not exceed 0.5, indicating that there is no severe collinearity problem.

Table 2. Correlation coefficient matrix.

Variable	Risktaking	Rank	Tenure	Age	Com	Own	ROE	Size	Lev	Grow
Risktaking		−0.047	0.133	0.037	0.037	−0.035	0.364	−0.058	−0.088	0.067
Rank	0.007		−0.110	−0.121	−0.095	0.037	−0.028	−0.130	−0.169	0.024
Tenure	0.049	−0.070		0.285	0.145	−0.022	0.019	0.070	0.072	0.149
Age	0.047	−0.085	0.255		0.082	0.054	0.080	0.084	−0.110	0.084
Com	0.062	−0.116	0.107	0.057		0.131	0.275	0.302	−0.033	0.115
Own	−0.176	−0.029	0.032	−0.085	0.124		0.040	0.031	0.105	0.025
ROE	0.371	0.044	−0.037	−0.008	0.058	−0.045		0.337	−0.274	0.500
Size	−0.027	−0.141	0.106	0.099	0.345	0.067	0.136		0.058	0.249
Lev	−0.111	−0.174	−0.076	−0.127	0.007	0.113	−0.121	−0.032		0.056
Grow	0.131	0.075	0.111	−0.045	0.016	−0.070	0.203	0.068	0.122	
V	0.096	0.072	0.155	−0.061	−0.028	−0.113	0.056	−0.009	−0.181	0.038

Note: left lower is the correlation coefficient of Pearson, while upper right is the correlation coefficient of Spearman.

5.3. Regression Analysis

Table 3 is the result of multiple regression. Model 2, based on Model 1, takes further control on the enterpriselevel features, and inspects the probability for chairman to get promoted, as well as the company's risk-taking activities. Model 3 removes the samples of listed companies that are directly controlled by the local organs relevant to the SASAC. Model 4 analyzes the samples whose control levels are above 2 separately.

Whether or not the company's basic characteristics are under control, both Model 1 and Model 2 show that the regression coefficient of rank is significant negative, which means that the political relevancy (Level) characterizes higher probability of promotion, and the company is more likely to take up risk-taking activities so as to improve its performance and the opportunity for promotion. Hypothesis 1 is validated. The coefficient of Rank × Tenure is significantly positive at the 0.10 level. In other words, among the listed companies of the same level, the longer the tenure of the chairman, the more chances of risk-taking activities. The reason is obvious: a shorter term often indicates an official's transition period, during which the official has no momentum to conduct risk-taking only to destroy his/her prospect. But in a longer term, the chairman, getting no promotion, may choose risk-taking to improve performance for higher recognition. So far, Hypothesis 2 is validated.

Table 3. The probability for chairman to get promoted and company's risk-taking activities.

Variable	Symbol	Model 1	Model 2	Model 3	Model 4[a]
		All	All	Rank > 1	Rank > 2
Rank	−	**−3.209***	**−3.410***	**−3.616***	**−2.149***
		(−1.76)	**(−1.81)**	**(−1.91)**	**(−1.95)**
Tenure	+	−2.276	−2.427	−2.795	
		(−1.57)	(−1.63)	(−1.54)	
Rank × Tenure	−	**1.129***	**1.169***	**1.329****	**0.642*****
		(1.81)	**(1.82)**	**(2.03)**	**(4.18)**
Age	−	0.001	0.003	0.002	−0.052
		(0.01)	(0.12)	(0.07)	(−1.45)
Com	−	0.051	0.088	0.079	0.002
		(0.36)	(0.60)	(0.52)	(0.01)
Own	−	**−0.673***	−0.581	−0.544	3.735
		(−1.94)	(−1.63)	(−1.51)	(0.95)
ROE	+	**2.323*****	**2.315*****	**2.253*****	**12.691*****
		(3.69)	**(3.53)**	**(3.38)**	**(3.49)**
Size	?		−0.151	−0.200	−0.560
			(−0.81)	(−1.03)	(−1.56)
Lev	?		−0.667	−0.702	2.492*
			(−0.89)	(−0.92)	(2.14)
Grow	?		0.174	0.217	0.765
			(0.26)	(0.31)	(0.33)
V	?		0.010	0.012	−0.018
			(0.82)	(0.97)	(−1.06)
Inds		Control	Control	Control	Control
Sample size		108	108	102	30
R^2		0.300	0.319	0.339	0.807

[a]The tenure variable is automatically removed in regression due to collinearity issues. ***, **, and *denote significant at the 0.01, 0.05, and 0.10 level, respectively.

After removing the samples of listed companies that are directly controlled by the local organs relevant to the SASAC, Model 3 still shows a significant negative influence at the 0.10 level in the coefficient of Rank, mean ing that to a certain degree, the company's risk-taking activities depend on the promotion of chairman, and the more chances to get promoted, the more likely to improve operating performance through risk-taking. For administrators of the same rank, the longer their tenure are, the more momentum to take part in risk-taking to get promoted. So the coefficient of Rank × Tenure at the 0.10

level is significantly positive. Thus, Hypothesis 1 and Hypothesis 2 are further verified.

The coefficient of rank in Model 4 is significantly negative, while the coefficient of Rank × Tenure is significantly positive, which suggests that when there are more promotion chances for chairman, the state-owned listed enterprises are more likely to carry out risk-taking activities. In some listed companies at a certain level, the tenure can result in differences in chairmen's performances, especially their risk-taking behavior. Again, Hypothesis 1 and Hypothesis 2 are proved to be true.

5.4. Sensitivity Testing

Since the government emphasizes on the rejuvenation of talented cadres, many administrators above 60 have to retire from the leading post. Although they may still be nominal chairmen of the companies, in fact, they don't actually take charge of the operation administration and investment decisions. As a result, we decide to carry out another regression analysis after removing the factor of chairman of state-owned enterprises above 60, referring to Model 5 of the Table 4. The regression results of Model 5 show that after removing the data of chairmen above 60, the shorter the state-owned enterprise's rank is, the more likely the chairman would take up risk-taking activities, which can be seen that the coefficient of Rank is significant negative, supporting Hypothesis 1. And among state-owned enterprises of the same level, the longer the chairman's tenure is, the greater the chances are for them to take risk-taking activities, which supports Hypothesis 2 again. Model 6 takes a further sensitivity test on the age factor after the remove of the elements whose ages are above 50. Still, the coefficient of Rank is significant negative, and the coefficient of Rank × Tenure is significant positive, so Hypothesis 1 and 2 are proved to be true.

Results from Model 5 and Model 6 also reveal that the shareholding ratio of chairman has an obvious inhibiting effect on the risk-taking possibility, that is to say, the coefficient of own is significantly negative, which do not consist with the conclusion made by Eisenmann (2002) [20] and Chen et al. (2006) through their research. Their research found out that the administrators' shareholding and share option would lead to more risk-taking activities with the purpose to make more personal fortune. However, in China, this is often the case when "money" and "promotion" cannot be obtained at the same time. Under such circumstances, companies with high shareholding ratios would reduce risk-taking activities to seek stability and to avoid risks, because the chairmen

Table 4. Sensitivity testing

Variable	Model 5	Model 6	Model 7	Model 8
	Age < 60	Age < 50	Ownship > 0	Ownship = 0
Rank	**−3.794***	**−3.081***	0.632	**−6.829****
	(−1.84)	**(−1.70)**	(0.34)	**(−2.43)**
Tenure	−2.546	−2.271	0.862	−4.887
	(−1.42)	(−1.58)	(0.53)	(−1.27)
Rank × Tenure	**1.282***	**1.076***	−0.322	**2.413****
	(1.74)	**(1.73)**	(−0.50)	**(2.51)**
Age	−0.086	0.040	−0.026	0.006
	(−1.15)	(1.21)	(−0.99)	(0.16)
Com	0.320	0.116	0.242	−0.005
	(1.30)	(0.77)	(1.58)	(−0.03)
Own	**−0.611***	**−0.566***	**−0.746*****	
	(−1.83)	**(−1.66)**	**(−3.51)**	
ROE	**4.546*****	**2.304*****	**1.633*****	**6.076*****
	(3.73)	**(3.66)**	**(3.87)**	**(2.92)**
Size	−0.003	−0.195	−0.389*	−0.289
	(−0.01)	(−1.06)	(−1.89)	(−1.11)
Lev	−0.341	−0.582	−1.043	−0.635
	(−0.39)	(−0.80)	(−1.08)	(−0.63)
Grow	−0.010	0.127	−0.015	−0.579
	(−0.01)	(0.19)	(−0.02)	(−0.62)
V	0.026	0.010	−0.008	−0.009
	(1.45)	(0.87)	(−0.57)	(−0.46)
Inds	Control	Control	Control	Control
Obs.	52	97	39	69
R^2	0.632	0.355	0.813	0.394

Note: ***, **, and * denote significant at the 0.01, 0.05, and 0.10 level, respectively.

can gain fairly great return on equity through stable management. Having no stock rights may bring more attention to their careers.

Given the impact shareholders of administrators have on the company's risk-taking activities, Model 7 and Model 8 conduct tests respectively on share holding companies and those are not. Model 7 shows the regression result of the companies where chairmen have shares. The coefficients of both Rank and Rank × Tenure are nonsignificant, in other words, the chairman, with shares in hand, may cut down the risk-taking activities in order to retain stability. On the other hand, if the chairman has no shares of the listed company, then he would need more stimulus from identity recognition, such as status, so he/she will have more motives to pursuit "career". Therefore, in the regression result from Model 8 where there are no stock rights samples, the coefficient of Rank is significantly negative at the 0.05 level, while the coefficient of Rank × Tenure is significantly positive at the same level, in accordance with the result of the entire sample. So Hypothesis 1 and 2 are verified.

Therefore, no matter we use the whole data, take control on the enterprise-level features, remove the samples of listed companies that are directly controlled by the local SASAC, or only analyze the samples whose control levels are above two, Hypothesis 1 and Hypothesis 2 are proved to be true. Besides, after removing the factor of chairman of state-owned enterprises above 60 or 50, we find that the shareholding ratio of chairman has an obvious inhibiting effect on the risk-taking possibility, which indicates that chairmen with high shareholding ratios may reduce risk-taking activities to seek stability while having no stock rights may bring more attention to their careers. In addition, Hypothesis 1 and 2 are also verified, which means the shorter the pyramid of listed enterprises is, the more likely the chairman is to take up risk-taking activities and for the same pyramid, the longer the tenure of the chairman, the more chances of risk-taking activities.

6. CONCLUSIONS

Taking chairman of state-owned listed companies as a study object, we find that in state-owned enterprises, the shorter the company level is, the higher its administrative level is; and the greater its political relevance is, the bigger the administrator's political benefits will be once he/she gets promoted. So the administrators of stateowned companies with shorter level will have a preference for risk-taking activities. At the same time, in stateowned companies of the same level, the administrators with shorter tenures are likely to be transitional ones, and they would adopt actions that can avoid risks. On the contrary, the administrators with longer tenures, in order to get further promotion, will prefer to carry out risk-taking activities to achieve expected outstanding performance. The above analysis explains that when political connection is strong, the managers of state-owned enterprises will make decisions referring to not only market standard, but also political risk and return. To some extent, the problem of corporate governance structure is prominent. SASAC is in charge of state-owned enterprises and at the same time plays the regulator's role, which shows a defect of system that needs to be improved. Managers of state-owned listed enterprises do not fully follow the market rules for management, which makes the resources of the whole society fail to get reasonable allocation and use.

The chairman's personal behaviors are directly relevant to the company's benefit because of the agent issue. Therefore, for those companies, when it comes to choosing appropriate administrators according to different developing periods and situations, as well as decreasing agent cost and maximizing company values, it is of great importance to study the relationship between the promotion of the chairman and the company's risk-taking activities. Existing researches pay little attention to the effects the administrator have on company's risk-taking activities, and this article provides relevant empirical evidence. Promotion is an encouragement for managers. Under China's special economic system, SASAC generally appoints managers whose political performance is more prominent as the chairman of state-owned enterprises. However, state-owned enterprises, especially central enterprises have already involved in technology, products and fields, which are extremely complex and diverse. And the requirements for leader's quality are comprehensive. This situation makes the management system of state-owned enterprises distorted. In addition, the managers who take their own political career into consideration, often subject to state-owned assets management department, and their short-sighted behaviors are prominent. So the decision-making errors may cause loss of state-owned assets, which is the cause for the lack of existing regulatory system. Therefore, the research on the relationship between promotion of chairman and company's risk-taking activities would offer theoretical support for state-owned companies of different types, sizes and developing periods to select optimal managers, and to maintain and increase their company values.

At present, because of the political connection system of state-owned enterprises in China, the development of enterprises experience significant constraints. On one hand, some managers of state-owned enterprises would like to take up more risk-taking activities in order to achieve political gains, but corruption problems caused by these adventures have become increasingly prominent at the same time. On the other hand, some managers choose to take conservative business decisions in order to avoid political risk, which makes a lot of resources of state-owned enterprises be idle and wasted. This paper studying on political connection and risk-taking activities provides a realistic requirement for the reform of state-owned enterprises.

The object of this research is currently limiting the behaviors of the chairmen of state-owned firms, and having no reference to other administrators' behaviors, so further study is needed. Besides, this research doesn't include non-state-owned enterprises, so omissions are inevitable. Further study can expand the range of sample, conducting further research on the relationship between the promotions of the chairmen of the non-state-owned companies and their risk-taking activities.

ACKNOWLEDGEMENTS

The research is supported by the Fundamental Research Funds for the Central Universities, Beijing Normal University, Beijing, China (Grant#2012WYB35), the National Natural Science Foundation of China (Grant# 71302023) and Beijing Higher Education Young Elite Program (#YETP0298).

REFERENCES

1. Hoskisson, R.E., Hitt, M.A. and Hill, C.W.L. (1991) Managerial Risk Taking in Diversified Firms: An Evolutionary Perspective. Organization Science, 2, 296-314.
2. King, T.H.D. and Wen, M.M. (2010) Shareholder Governance, Bondholder Governance, and Managerial Risk-Taking. Journal of Banking & Finance, 35, 512-531.
3. Dong, Z.Y., Wang, C. and Xie, F. (2010) Do Executive Stock Options Induce Excessive Risk Taking? Journal of Banking & Finance, 34, 2518-2529.
4. Chen, C.R., Steiner, T.L. and Whyte, A.M. (2006) Does Stock Option-Based Executive Compensation Induce Risk-Taking? Analysis of the Banking Industry. Journal of Banking & Finance, 30, 915-945.
5. Konishi, M. and Yasuda, Y. (2004) Factors Affecting Bank Risk Taking: Evidence from Japan. Journal of Banking & Finance, 28, 215-232.
6. Delis, M.D. and Kouretas, G.P. (2010) Interest Rates and Bank Risk-Taking. Journal of Banking & Finance, 35, 840-855.
7. Pathan, S. (2009) Strong Boards, CEO Power and Bank Risk-Taking. Journal of Banking & Finance, 33, 1340-1350.
8. Jensen, M.C. and Meckling, W.H. (1976) Theory of the Firm: Managerial Behavior, Agency Costs and Ownership Structure. Journal of Financial Economics, 3, 305-460.
9. Merton, R.C. (1977) An Analytic Derivation of the Cost of Deposit Insurance and Loan Guarantees. Journal of Banking and Finance, 1, 3-11.
10. Smith, C.W. and Stulz, R.M. (1985) The Determinants of Firms' Hedging Policies. Journal of Financial and Quantitative Analysis, 20, 391-405.
11. Dong, J. (2010) The Principal-Agent Problem of State-Owned Assets Management. Property Rights Guide, 12, 34-36.

12. Xu, C.C. and Yan, J.W. (2011) Study on the Principal-Agent Problem of State-Owned Enterprises. Economic Review, 1, 92-95.

13. Chan, K.S., Dang, V.Q. and Yan, I.K. (2012) Chinese Firms' Political Connection, Ownership, and Financing Constraints. Economics Letters, 115, 164-167.

14. Li, S., Song, X. and Wu, H. (2014) Political Connection, Ownership Structure, and Corporate Philanthropy in China: A Strategic-Political Perspective. Journal of Business Ethics, 1-13.

15. Chen, C.M., Ariff, M., Hassan, T. and Mohamad, S. (2014) Does a Firm's Political Connection to Government Have Economic Value? Journal of the Asia Pacific Economy, 19, 1-24.

16. Houston, J.F., Jiang, L., Lin, C. and Ma, Y. (2014) Political Connections and the Cost of Bank Loans. Journal of Accounting Research, 52, 193-243.

17. Laeven, L. and Levine, R. (2009) Bank Governance, Regulation and Risk Taking. Journal of Financial Economics, 93, 259-275.

18. Sun, Z. and Yu, X.H. (2007) Separation of Powers and the Choice of Accounting Firms. Auditing Research, 6, 52-58.

19. Xia, D.L. and Zhu, S. (2008) Level of the Pyramid and the Performance of Listed Companies. China Management Magazine, 2, 120-129.

20. Eisenmann, T.R. (2002) The Effects of CEO Equity Ownership and Firm Diversification on Risk Taking. Strategic Management Journal, 23, 513-534.

NOTES

[1]In fact, the state-owned listed corporations are divided into central SASAC controlled firms and local SASAC controlled firms, of which the latter are lower than the former in administrative level. However, in personnel promotions, managers of central enterprises are appointed by Central Organization Department, while managers of local enterprises are generally appointed by local government. Therefore, even if the level is only 2, the managers of local state-owned enterprises and central state-owned enterprises are quite different in the administrative level, but the promotions are determined by respective departments of power. Business promotions depend on the political connections with the respective departments.

[2]Because the information of what managers did after their withdrawals from the enterprises is difficult to obtain, only that of some famous corporate executives is available. It is difficult to measure management promotions

directly. So it is a very strong hypothesis that we use political connection to measure promotion possibilities.

[3]"The lower executive level is, the lower degree of political connections are." This is a very strong hypothesis. Although there is no data, it is indisputable realistically.

[4]This article only looks into the relationship between career advancement and risk-taking activities of state-owned listed enterprises, so we exclude private listed companies and those whose ultimate controllers were unable to confirm.

[5]The chairman plays an important role when a Board's agreement is required. Although to a certain extent, general manager is also one of the administrators, when it comes to issues involving major risks and resolution, it still needs the Board of Directors to hold discussions and then make decisions. Therefore, this paper took chairman as the research object.

5

BUCHANAN CLUBS

Todd Sandler

Department of Economics, School of Economic, Political and Policy Sciences, University of Texas at Dallas, 800 W. Campbell Road, Richardson, TX 75080, USA

ABSTRACT

This article evaluates the contribution of James M. Buchanan's theory of clubs. At the outset, the article distinguishes club goods from pure public goods. Next, the article distills the basic mathematical structure of Buchanan's treatment of clubs. This is followed by some key variants of Buchanan clubs. More general formulations of club theory are also addressed. To demonstrate the wide-ranging importance of Buchanan clubs, the article indicates varied applications of club theory. The article's message is that club theory remains highly relevant today.

Keywords: Buchanan clubs, Club applications, Exclusion mechanisms, Public goods

1 INTRODUCTION

In his seminal article, "An Economic Theory of Clubs," Buchanan (1965) introduced the analysis of club goods to bridge the chasm between private and pure public goods. For private goods, consumption rivalry and exclusion are complete, while for pure public goods, consumption is nonrivalrous and exclusion is not possible.[1] Nonexcludability of nonpaying benefit recipients leads to the free-rider problem, which requires government provision of pure public goods. Buchanan (1965) envisioned clubs as a member-owned institutional arrangement for the provision of a club good that is subject to some rivalry in the form of congestion. Crowding or congestion involves a detraction in a club good's quantity or quality from increased utilization by the sharers—e.g., higher bacteria counts in swimming pools, longer queues at amusement parks, or slower transits on bridges. The presence of congestion means that the extension of user rights to another individual implies a nonzero marginal cost, which, in turn, justifies the need to restrict users or members. In contrast, there is no need to restrict the number of consumers for a nonrivalrous good, because society prospers from extending consumption to anyone who obtains a positive marginal benefit.

The origins of "club theory" predates Buchanan's (1965) seminal article. Tiebout (1956) put forward a "voting-with-the-feet" hypothesis, whereby a population partitions itself among jurisdictions so as to match individuals' tastes with local public good and taxation options. In a private good context, Wiseman (1957) formulated a club principle for sharing costs among users of a public utility, while Olson (1965) put forward the notion of exclusive groups for sharing an impure public good. For exclusive collectives, membership size must be determined for the shared good, but Olson (1965) never used the term, club. Finally, early studies of highway congestion and tolls (e.g., Mohring and Harwitz 1962) addressed the sharing of an impure public good, where tolls internalized congestion and effectively fixed membership in terms of toll-paying users. For the forerunners of club theory, the interface between the provision of the shared good and membership is not clear, because provision is exogenous, which is not the case for Buchanan clubs.

Buchanan's club theory holds an exalted place in the study of public choice for a number of reasons. First, club theory can serve as the theoretical foundation for jurisdictional design, because this theory can be made to capture the provision, membership, and partitioning decisions associated with the earlier Tiebout hypothesis (McGuire 1974; Pauly 1967). Tiebout's (1956) celebrated article did not provide a formal model for his insightful thought-experiment. Second, Buchanan's club theory emphasizes that public goods may, under key circumstances, be provided privately, so that public goods need not imply government provision. Third, club theory indicates that membership size or the number of sharers is an endogenous choice that is not independent of the provision decision. Fourth, the study of clubs can be applied to an amazing array of situations that include treaty formation, military alliances, wilderness areas, cities, roads, antibiotic use, the Internet, international organizations, and customs unions. In fact, the study of clubs impacts virtually every field of economics in some way—e.g., labor economics (labor unions), international economics (free-trade areas), urban economics (road provision), monetary economics (monetary unions), sports economics (the size of leagues), public finance (impure public goods), environmental economics (national parks and forest preserves), and health economics (public–private partnership for disease control).

Even though Buchanan's (1965) club article generated literally hundreds of articles (Sandler and Tschirhart 1980, 1997), he devoted only a single article to the topic, leaving others to model and analyze myriad refinements to the study of clubs. These refinements concerned the optimality of clubs, alternative institutional forms for clubs, the number of clubs, the composition of members, the form of the congestion function, the type of exclusion mechanism, and the financing of clubs. Buchanan deftly laid the foundation to club theory in a simple, but efficient framework, and then moved on.

The primary purpose of this article is to characterize the essential structure of the Buchanan theory of clubs. In so doing, I indicate how the simple structure of Buchanan clubs paved the way for myriad follow-up articles. Thus, this article presents many aspects of club theory, not captured in Buchanan (1965). A secondary purpose is to provide the reader with an appreciation of why club theory is still studied today.

The remainder of the article contains six sections. Section 2 distinguishes club goods from other public goods, to show how Buchanan addressed the chasm between private and pure public goods. In Sect. 3, the theoretical structure of Buchanan clubs is displayed. Key variants of Buchanan clubs are analyzed in Sect. 4, followed by a discussion of more general formulations in Sect. 5. Varied and broad-reaching applications are given in Sect. 6. Finally, Sect. 7 contains concluding remarks.

2 CLUB GOODS VERSUS OTHER PUBLIC GOODS

A club is a voluntary group deriving mutual benefits from sharing one or more of the following: production costs, the members' characteristics, or a good characterized by excludable benefits (Sandler and Tschirhart 1980). Buchanan (1965) focused on clubs that share a partly rivalrous public good, characterized by excludable benefits. Such goods are known as club goods.

There are a number of noteworthy reasons why club goods are different from pure public goods. First, the use of a club good is voluntary because sharers must join the club to receive the good's benefits, which are withheld from nonmembers. Despite fees, club members perceive a net gain from membership. For pure public goods, everyone within the range of spillovers automatically receives the good's benefit or cost. Second, the optimal number of sharers for club goods is finite unlike that of pure public goods, where everyone can be accommodated without crowding externalities. Clubs are, therefore, exclusive collectives. Third, for club goods, the disposition of nonmembers must be addressed. Multiple clubs form, where the population is partitioned into nonoverlapping identical clubs (McGuire 1974; Pauly 1967), or a single club forms, where leftover individuals do not consume the club good (Helpman and Hillman 1977). Fourth, club goods must possess an exclusion mechanism that is virtually costless, so that nonpaying individuals do not receive the good's benefits. This mechanism can collect tolls to finance the club good. In contrast, exclusion is not possible or desirable for a pure public good. Fifth, club goods involve a dual decision—the choice of provision and membership size. Only optimal provision is relevant for pure public goods. Sixth, unlike pure public goods, club goods are often optimally provided through congestion-internalizing tolls. In contrast, the Nash equilibrium associated with the private provision of pure public goods is typically suboptimal (Cornes and Sandler 1996). Seventh, club goods can be efficiently supplied through alternative institutional arrangements—e.g., member-owned clubs or for-profit firms.

Club goods do not represent all goods between the polar extremes of private goods and pure public goods. There is no linear scale between these two extremes, insofar as the properties of publicness really vary along two dimensions—rivalry and excludability. Moreover, club goods must possess some rivalry and sufficient excludability. Thus, public goods that are nonrivalrous but excludable—e.g., pay-per-view television programs—are not club goods, because the marginal cost of additional users is zero. As such, exclusion does not achieve efficiency (Sandler 2004). Public goods that are subject to crowding but cannot be excluded (e.g., some forms of information) are not club goods. This is also true of public goods whose exclusion cost overwhelms any efficiency gains, so that exclusion is not justified under current technological realties. Hence, club goods do not encompass all impure public goods, where benefits are partly excludable and/or partly rival. The key issue is that there exists a sufficiently inexpensive exclusion mechanism to charge users for the congestion that their use causes.

3 BUCHANAN CLUBS

3.1 Mathematical representation

The Buchanan (1965) model for clubs assumes two goods: a private numéraire good, *y*, and a club good, *X*. Club members possess not only identical tastes, but also the same resource or budget constraint. Each member utilizes the entire club good, so that $x^i = X$, where x^i is the *i*th member's club utilization. As such, each member's utilization of the shared good is fixed at its provision amount. There is costless exclusion, so that there is no transaction cost of any kind. In addition, there is no discrimination among members; hence, each member pays the same membership fee where club cost is shared among members. Clubs are replicable and partition the population into a set of clubs, each with the optimal number of members.

The utility function of member *i* is

$$U^i = U^i(y^i, X, s), \tag{1}$$

where $\partial U^i/\partial y^i = U^i_y > 0, \partial U^i/\partial X = U^i_X > 0$, and $\partial U^i/\partial s = U^i_s < 0 \text{ for } s > \bar{s}$. Thus, utility increases with the consumption of the private and club goods, but decreases after some membership level, s¯, with the number of members, *s*. Buchanan's formulation allows members to enjoy camaraderie up to point s¯s¯, but thereafter negative congestion externalities take over. This s¯ can be anything greater or equal to zero, depending on the club good. For example, rock concerts can be more enjoyable until a certain crowd level is obtained, but after this level, toilets become crowded, noise competes with the musicians, views become obstructed, and parking becomes more difficult. For some venues, this s¯ may be quite large, while for small intimate nightclubs, s¯ may be as few as 10 people.

The *i*th member's resource constraint is

$$F^i(y^i, X, s) = 0, \tag{2}$$

where $\partial F^i/\partial y^i = F^i_y > 0, \ \partial F^i/\partial X = F^i_X > 0,$ and $\partial F^i/\partial s = F^i_s < 0.$ the margin, members must expend more resources for increases in the private and club goods; however, members must spend less for a given level of the club good as membership increases. This follows because more members can share the cost of the provision of the club good.

Each member chooses $y^i, X,$, and *s* to

$$\max U^i(y^i, X, s) \text{ subject to } F^i(y^i, X, s) = 0. \qquad (3)$$

The resulting first-order conditions can be rewritten as a provision and membership condition:

$$MRS^i_{Xy} = MRT^i_{Xy}, \quad i = 1, \ldots, s \text{ (Provision) and} \qquad (4)$$

$$MRS^i_{sy} = MRT^i_{sy}, \quad i = 1, \ldots, s \text{ (Membership)}, \qquad (5)$$

where MRT^i_{Xy} is the *i*th member's marginal rate of substitution between the club good and the private good, and MRT^i_{Xy} is the *i*th member's marginal rate of transformation between these goods. The former is a ratio of marginal utilities, while the latter is a ratio of resource marginal cost terms. In (5), the MRT^i_{Xy} have similar interpretations for the trade-off between membership size and the private good. Each of these conditions has a straightforward interpretation. For provision in (4), each member equates the marginal benefit of the club good, evaluated in terms of the numéraire, to the marginal cost of the club good. In the membership condition, members equate the marginal cost of an added member, which is the marginal crowding cost (MRT^i_{Xy}), to the marginal benefit of an added member, which is the marginal reduced cost of membership (MRT^i_{Xy}). Both of these terms are negative in the relevant range past s¯s¯.

These conditions embody some essential features. If, at the margin, the club is self-financing, then the sum of the members' marginal payments ($\sum_{i=1}^{s} MRS^i_{Xy} = MRT_{Xy}.$) for provision must equal the club's marginal provision cost, MRT^i_{Xy}, so that the provision condition in (4) then implies the Samuelsonian provision condition for public goods:

$$\sum_{i=1}^{s} MRS^i_{Xy} = MRT_{Xy}. \qquad (6)$$

Full financing is achieved when MRTXy equals or exceeds average provision cost. The need to simultaneously satisfy both (4) and (5) indicates the dual decisions, mentioned in Sect. 2. That is, the optimal membership size, s∗, and the optimal provision, X∗, must be determined together. This stems from the provision and membership conditions containing both membership and the club good as arguments. By maximizing average net benefits for the representative member, the Buchanan model assumes away nonmembers, because replicable clubs accommodate the entire population. If the population size is denoted by *Pop*, then the number of replicable clubs is Pop/s∗Pop/s∗, which is assumed to be an integer. When the homogeneous population is fully accommodated in the set of clubs, the solution is the *core*, because no alternative configuration of clubs can form and do better for its members (Pauly 1967; Sandler and Tschirhart 1980). In his original paper, Buchanan (1965) did not make the connection with the core, which came later as the literature developed his notion of clubs.

3.2 Graphical representation

The provision and membership conditions can be displayed graphically, thereby giving the reader a better appreciation for their dual nature. In Fig. 1, we display the optimizing club good provision levels for two alternative membership values. If membership is s1s1, then B(s1)B(s1)denotes the total benefit per member for alternative provision levels, while C(s1) depicts the total cost per member for alternative provision levels. The concavity of the benefit curve captures diminishing marginal benefits to increased provision; the linearity of the cost line reflects constant marginal provision cost. For membership s1s1, optimal provision corresponds to X∗1, where marginal provision benefit (the slope of the *B* curve) equals marginal provision cost (the slope of the *C* curve), so that (4) is satisfied. If, however, membership size increases to s2s2, then the benefit curve shifts down, as shown in Fig. 1, so that, at each provision level, the reduced slope is due to increased crowding from enhanced membership and crowding. With more members, the cost line pivots down to C(s2) as each member needs to assume a smaller cost burden because there are more burden sharers. The optimal provision, associated with s2s2, is X∗2, where (4) is satisfied. Generally, as membership increases, the optimal provision level increases (Buchanan 1965), so that membership and optimal provision rise together. Later, we assume that they do so linearly for convenience.

Next, we depict the optimal club membership choice for two alternative provision levels in Fig. 2. We commence with the benefit and cost curves—B(X1) and C(X1) respectively—tied to provision level X1 as membership varies. The benefit curve has an inverted U-shape: camaraderie increases marginal benefit up to a certain membership size, followed by declining marginal benefit owing to crowding as membership surpasses this threshold. The cost curve is a rectangular hyperbola, as the given cost of providing X1 is spread over more members. As shown, the optimal membership s∗1s1∗ for this provision level is achieved when the corresponding margins are equated to

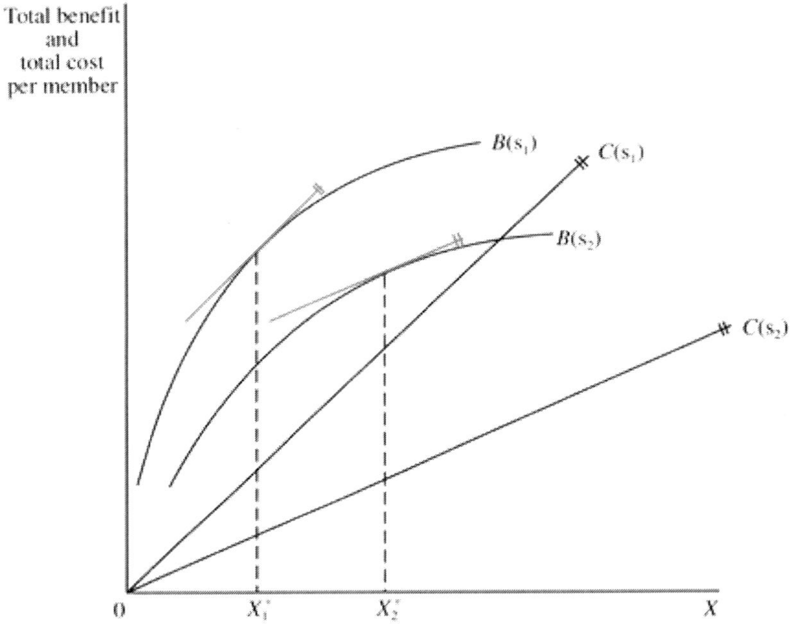

Figure 1. Optimizing club good provision levels for two alternative memberships

satisfy (5). An increase in provision to X2 shifts up the benefit curve, which is now flatter at any given membership. This flattening captures the reduced marginal crowding cost that greater provision entails—e.g., more highway lanes mean that the same traffic can flow with less congestion. For X2, the cost curve is displaced upward so that the slope has a larger absolute value at a given membership size. This follows because greater provision means that each member must assume a greater marginal cost burden. In Fig. 2, the optimal membership for X2 is s∗2, where (5) is again fulfilled. Optimal membership increases with augmented provision, whose relationship is assumed to be linear for simplicity in Fig. 3.

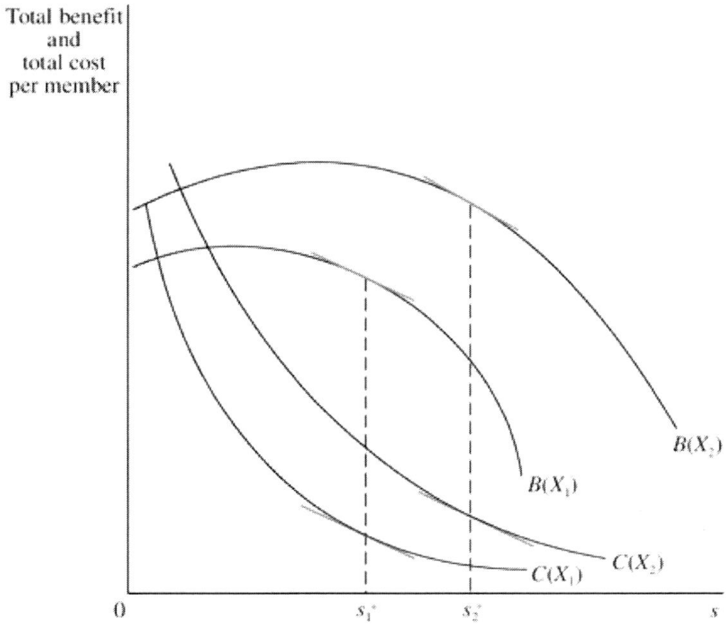

Figure 2. Optimizing club membership for two alternative provision levels

The four-quadrant Fig. 3 displays the club equilibrium for the two decision variables. Quadrant I depicts the optimal provision choice; quadrant II indicates the optimal membership choice; quadrant III transfer membership levels from the horizontal axis of quadrant II to the vertical axis of quadrant IV; and quadrant IV indicates stylized linear sopt and Xopt loci. These loci relate optimal *s* for alternative *X* levels, and optimal *X* for alternative *s* levels. Their relative slopes are consistent with stable club equilibrium at *E*, where the two curves intersect.

Figure 3 lends itself to comparative statics. Suppose, for example, a technological advance that reduces provision cost, which, in turn, lowers the cost curves in quadrant I without affecting the benefit curves. This would then imply a rightward shift (not shown) in the Xopt curve in quadrant IV, for which each membership size is now associated with a larger optimal provision level. This technological change also lowers and flattens the cost curves in quadrant II so that there is less need to spread cost over larger memberships. This, then, shifts soptsopt upward toward the horizontal axis in quadrant IV (not shown), so that each provision level is associated with a smaller optimal membership. In the new equilibrium, provision is apt to rise, while membership may rise or fall. The interface of the two decisions permit varied possibilities.

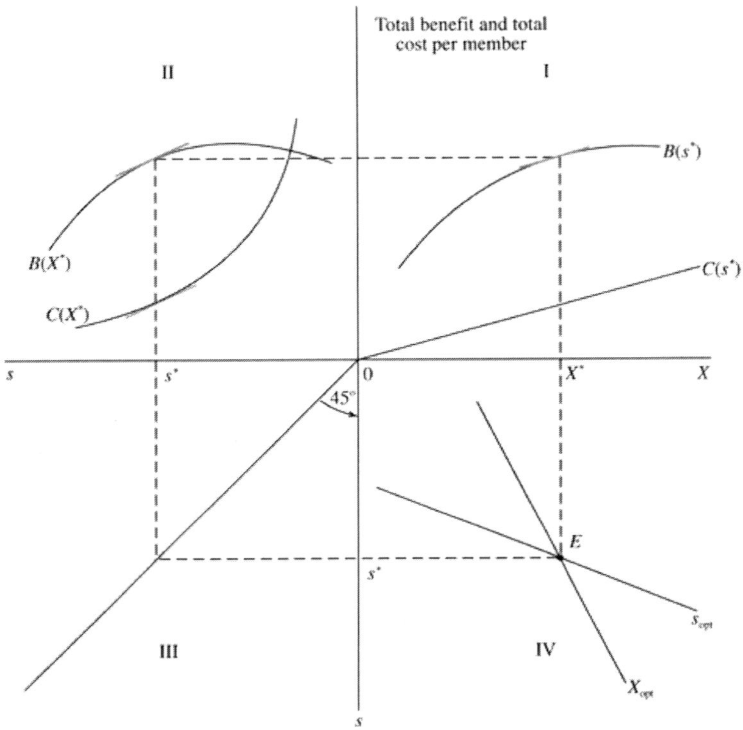

Figure 3. Homogeneous club equilibrium

4 SOME KEY VARIANTS OF BUCHANAN CLUBS

Buchanan (1965) presented a model that captures the essence of club theory, where the utilization rates of homogeneous members are fixed. The latter means that there is no rationale for distinguishing between membership fees and visitation tolls. In the ideal Buchanan club, each membership fee is *C*/*s* or the club's cost per member, thereby ensuring full financing. For homogeneous clubs, there are two important variants of the Buchanan club model.

The McGuire (1974) model is quite streamlined and has members choosing y^i, X, ,ands to

$$\max U^i(y^i, X) \text{ subject to } I^i = y^i + [C(X, s)/s], \qquad (7)$$

where Iili is the income of the *i*th member, the unit price of the private good is one, and C(·) is the cost of the club. This cost includes marginal provision cost, CX, and marginal crowding cost, Cs.[2] The simplest way to derive the provision and membership requirements is to substitute for yiyi in the utility function, using the budget constraint. Optimizing this transformed utility function with respect to *X* and *s* gives:

$$sMRS^{i}_{Xy} = C_X \tag{8}$$

and

$$(sC_s - C)/s^2 = 0 \quad \text{or} \quad C_s = C/s. \tag{9}$$

The provision condition in (8) is the standard Samuelsonian condition for public goods for identical individuals. Full financing of the club cost is embedded in the budget constraint in (7), where each identical member covers average cost of the club, *C*/*s*. In (9), the membership condition requires that marginal crowding cost, CsCs, equals this average cost.

There are some noteworthy things about the McGuire model. First, the membership condition captures the Tiebout (1956) representation, in which per person average cost is minimized for the shared good. This, however, assumes that Tiebout jurisdictions are either providing a single local public good or else a package of local public goods that can be treated as a single entity in terms of crowding and provision. Second, the McGuire representation gives a specific form to Buchanan's resource constraint, where the cost function serves two purposes and full financing is assumed at the outset. Third, the collection of communities is each of size s∗s∗, where $C_s = C/s$, is in the core, so long as s∗s∗ divides evenly into the population. If, however, population were heterogeneous, then homogeneous jurisdictions must form, where each homogeneous subset of the population is partitioned into communities of size, s∗isi∗, which equals the optimal club size for *i*-type individuals (Pauly 1967). Fourth, McGuire (1974) demonstrated that his clubs cannot optimally accommodate different types of individuals. This follows because members must utilize the entire quantity of the club good. To accommodate different tastes, utilization patterns of members must be allowed to differ, which comes with more advanced models (see, e.g., Sandler 1984; Sandler and Tschirhart 1984; Scotchmer and Wooders 1987). Without this accommodation, McGuire correctly indicated that clubs must be segregated with identical members. So what has started as an innocuous assumption has become an implication that could mistakenly direct policy to segregate clubs. In the real world, most clubs do not require members with the same tastes or use patterns—e.g., some drivers use a bridge twice a day, while others may use it on rare occasions. Fortunately, later work allowed for heterogeneous members—see Sect. 5—and did not imply segregation or identical use patterns.

The second variant of the Buchanan model is by Berglas (1976), who allowed for variable utilization or visits, *v*, by members. The representative homogeneous member chooses $y^i, v, X,$ ands to

$$\max U^i\left[y^i, v, c(X, sv)\right] \text{ subject to } sI^i = sy^i + C(X, sv), \tag{10}$$

where c(·) is the congestion function, which decreases with provision, cX<0, , and increases with total visits, csv>0.csv>0. In the budget constraint, C(·) denotes club cost, where CX>0is the marginal provision cost and Csv>0is the marginal maintenance cost. The latter implies that greater overall use necessitates more cleanup. In the utility function, a member's satisfaction goes down with increased congestion, so that Uic<0. There are now three relevant conditions associated with (10), which includes provision, toll, and membership. The provision condition is again the Samuelsonian public good requirement with slightly different notation than in (8). The toll condition is as follows:

$$C_{sv} - sc_{sv}MRS_{cy} = MRS_{vy}, \tag{11}$$

where the *i* superscript has been dropped from the *MRS* because everyone is identical.[3] In (11), the sum of marginal maintenance cost and marginal crowding cost $-sc_{sv}MRS_{cy}$) comprises the toll, *T*, which equals the member's marginal visitation benefit (MRSvy). Marginal crowding cost is summed over all members to internalize the crowding externality.[4] The membership condition is not independent of the visitation condition, because it equals the visitation condition multiplied by *v* on both sides (Cornes and Sandler 1996). Based on cost sharing in the budget constraint, the toll per visit is *C/sv*, where each member visits *v* times and pays *C/s* in total fees. The Berglas model adds two essential ingredients to Buchanan clubs: a congestion function and a visitation rate. These ingredients become more useful when heterogeneous members are allowed in subsequent articles. Berglas' concept of maintenance cost is also important because utilization may impose costs on members that go beyond congestion.

5 A DISCUSSION OF MORE GENERAL FORMULATIONS

5.1 Heterogeneous memberships

As an initial formulation of clubs, Buchanan (1965) was right to strip away complications by assuming homogeneous members. However, most real-world clubs—e.g., air traffic networks, Internet providers, communication systems, and those highlighted in Sect. 6—serve members, who possess dissimilar tastes and needs. These differences primarily manifest themselves in terms of varied utilization. An easy way to accommodate heterogeneous or "mixed clubs" is with a single club that serves a subset of the population, who are members (Artle and Averous 1973; Helpman and Hillman 1977; Sandler 1984). The optimal membership requirement distinguishes members from nonmembers; i.e., those individuals with the greatest willingness to pay join the club until membership charges outweigh membership benefits. This membership condition then distinguishes members from nonmembers.[5] The toll condition is the key new ingredient for mixed clubs. All members pay the same congestion-internalizing toll when crowding is anonymous,[6] but the total tolls paid by each member vary according to their revealed visits.

Consider Fig. 4 where Panel 1 displays the viewpoint of two members, *i* = 1, 2, and Panel 2 indicates the viewpoint of the club. The membership condition determines the number of members and, hence, the total number of visits, V∗V∗, where the final entrant's downward-sloping marginal benefit for visits (not shown) equals the marginal crowding costs (shown in Panel 2). In Panel 2, this intersection, corresponding to V∗V∗, then determines the toll, *T*, per visit. In Panel 1, two members' demands for visits (MRSivy,i=1,2)(MRSvyi,i=1,2) are displayed. Member 1 equates his demand to the equilibrium toll and makes v1v1 visits at a cost of v1Tv1T in tolls, while member 2 equates her demand to the equilibrium toll and makes v2v2 visits at a cost of v2Tv2T. Thus, *total tolls* are individualized based on revealed use. Consider a toll road. Drivers' use of the road determines membership in practice. That is, drivers who do not gain sufficient convenience will not pay for the toll road, opting instead for a less convenient free highway.

Next, consider multiple clubs with differentiated club goods, such as Internet providers with different download speeds. Internet users will partition themselves into these providers according to their tastes for speed. Once users are partitioned, taste differences can again be accommodated based on user charges for the quantity of data downloaded. The beauty of clubs is that exclusion forces preference revelation, while congestion charges or tolls provide a basis for financing the shared good.

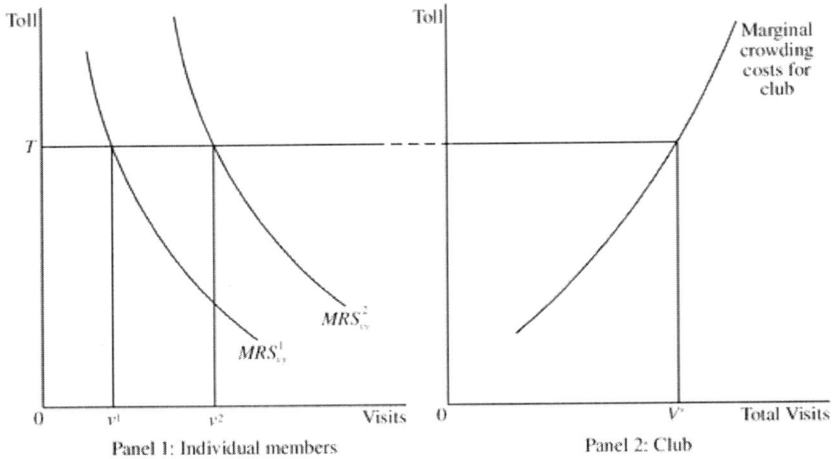

Figure 4. Individualized toll payments in a club

When members' attributes affect crowding, crowding is nonanonymous and tolls must be tailored to the user (DeSerpa 1977; Scotchmer 1997). Under these circumstances, club design becomes more difficult. Consider a learned society. Really smart or accomplished members may offer more positive externalities from their presence than any crowding that they cause, so that their membership fee or toll may be negative, resulting in a subsidy! Most members of the society have to pay tolls because their crowding dominates. In *some* clubs, the refinement of the notion of a visit may be a more practical means to account for nonanonymous crowding. Consider a golf course where some golfers cause more crowding per round than others. If the unit of utilization (a round of golf) were redefined by the number of strokes taken, then crowding becomes essentially anonymous. This follows because the number of strokes is a better indicator than a round of golf of the crowding externality that one golfer imposes on other golfers. Golf courses can also cater to different skilled players by their toughness of play (e.g., length of holes, width of fairways, and the number of hazards), where presumably the better golfers will play (join) the harder courses. Thus, even nonanonymous crowding can sometimes be circumvented through provision decisions (i.e., club goods tailored to the members' attributes) or finer utilization measurement. In the golf example, this circumvention does not work for, say, Tiger Woods, for whom other golfers would pay dearly to have on their course.

5.2 Congestion function

In the Buchanan (1965) article, the congestion function was just the identity map applied to the number of members. The congestion function can, however, assume many forms to capture the nature of a particular shared good. For example, it can depend on the average utilization rate, which is the total number of visits divided by provision. The actual form of the congestion function is important for at least two reasons: (1) it helps determine the toll and (2) it affects whether efficient tolls can self-finance optimal provision of the club good (Oakland 1972; Sandler 1982). By affecting the amount of marginal crowding cost, the congestion function influences the toll. For highways, a congestion function that is homogeneous of degree zero in total utilization and provision is associated with tolls that self-finance efficient provision[7](Cornes and Sandler 1996, 272–277.). If the congestion function depends on the average utilization of the club good, then this function is homogenous of degree zero and self-finance results. If congestion is not homogeneous of degree zero, then crowding-internalizing tolls may collect too little or too much to finance the club good (Oakland 1972; Sandler and Tschirhart 1980).

The form of the congestion function is important in urban economics when designing cities, infrastructure, and highways. Civil engineers can design highways that allow for better traffic flows, where a given amount of cars and trucks can be accommodated with less crowding. For airports, the spacing of take-offs and landings can make for a more favorable congestion relationship. The design of health clinics also determines the length of the queue or the resulting crowding. Since the congestion function may be tied to the amount of provision, we again see how provision and tolls are a dual decision.

The ability to monitor and charge for congestion is tied to the exclusion mechanism. These mechanisms can allow for fine exclusion, where each visit is monitored and a toll levied, or coarse exclusion, where only a membership fee is charged (Helsley and Strange 1991). Coarse exclusion results in inefficiency, since members will visit until their marginal benefit from visiting is driven to zero (Berglas 1976). Fine exclusion does not result in inefficiency, because per visit tolls internalize the associated congestion cost for every visit. In practice, clubs may resort to coarse exclusion if the transaction cost associated with fine exclusion more than offsets the efficiency gain.

5.3 Institutional forms of clubs

Buchanan (1965) only considered member-owned and operated clubs. There is, however, no reason why firms cannot provide clubs—e.g., movie theaters and athletic clubs. Many toll roads are now provided by private firms. Berglas and Pines (1981) demonstrated that firms in a competitive industry can also achieve the same equilibrium as a set of Buchanan replicable clubs, where population is a integer multiple of the optimal club size, s∗s∗. For simplicity, potential members are again assumed to possess the same tastes and endowments. Each firm maximizes its profit subject to a utility constraint for the members. The profit is the difference between revenues from tolls minus the cost of club provision and maintenance, while the utility constraint requires members to achieve at least the same utility, U∗U∗, as with a member-owned club.[8] The firm's optimization results in the same provision, toll, and membership conditions, previously associated with (10) (Cornes and Sandler 1996, 395–397). In the firm's problem, each member pays a per visit toll equal to C/sv.

There is also the possibility of government-provided clubs. For example, the federal government provides national parks, and state governments supply state parks. In many such cases, an entrance or user fee is charged. When crowding causes permanent degradation to the park, admittance is stopped for the day. For some popular national parks, a lottery system is now used during peak periods to limit degradation. If the government can charge congestion-internalizing tolls, then a government can also provide and manage club goods efficiently. At the local level, governments often rely on property taxes to finance the club good. These taxes may not really reflect crowding and utilization, thereby creating inefficiency. As an institutional alternative, government-managed clubs fail when they do not properly internalize crowding. Unlike other institutional forms, government-managed clubs may face more pricing or membership constraints—e.g., the use of coarse exclusion or the requirement to serve everyone (i.e., a public-access requirement).

There are other institutional form questions concerning clubs. For example, is there a difference between for-profit and not-for-profit clubs in terms of efficiency? This question has not been fully addressed but hinges on two considerations: (1) differences in transaction cost and (2) differences in internalizing the crowding externality. In the literature, there is no transaction cost distinction between for-profit clubs and member-owned clubs even though differences surely exist. Also, the ability of these clubs to distinguish between utilization rates may also differ according to institutional form, since member-owned clubs may favor coarse over fine exclusion. Another institutional question concerns multiproduct clubs, where multiple club goods are shared by the same membership. The notion of economies of scope[9] looms large in the analysis of such clubs (Brueckner and Lee 1991). Multiproduct club theory could serve as a better foundation for the Tiebout hypothesis, since jurisdictions offer an array of shared goods—e.g., highways, city hall, fire department, and police force. With economies of scope, the need to minimize average cost per member will lose its sway because this is a single-product concept and does not account for cost interaction among club goods. Moreover, shared club goods may appeal to different subsets of members (residents), which results in the need for efficiency trade-offs. A third institutional question involves distinguishing between different classes of members—e.g., first-class and coach passengers on an airplane. In some ways, this issue can be subsumed in the notion of a multiproduct club, where the classes of services are effectively different club goods, where different fees distinguish the two classes of services and members are partitioned between the classes. This example offers an important insight: the study of clubs can be pushed forward by combining insights and methods from earlier models.

6 APPLICATIONS OF CLUB THEORY

Perhaps, the greatest testimony of the importance of Buchanan's analysis of clubs is reflected in the many and varied applications of the theory. This section provides a small sampling of these applications, most of which involve extensions to Buchanan's original formulation to allow heterogeneous tastes and complex congestion and cost relationships.

Although jurisdictional design (Tiebout 1956) predated Buchanan's (1965) study on clubs, the latter article provided the theoretical foundation for this design (McGuire 1974). In so doing, many questions were raised including whether individual choice would necessarily internalize the crowding externality as people voted with their feet to find their ideal tax/public good package. Problems may arise because an individual's decision to join a jurisdiction did not always account for the crowding consequences that this choice imposed on the existing residents of the jurisdiction. Another question concerned the need for homogeneous jurisdictions because everyone consumed the same provision package. The partitioning of the population among a set of nonoverlapping jurisdictions resulted in a pioneering application of game theory to the study of public goods, since the notion of the core became relevant (Pauly 1967).

Another key application of club theory involved highway pricing, provision, and financing (Mohring and Harwitz 1962; Vickrey 1969). The reason why tolls can be used to provide highways efficiently is because any transit, beyond some minimal level of use, has a nonzero marginal cost owing to crowding. Thus, the practice of exclusion can serve to internalize an externality. The real question then becomes whether this toll can self-finance optimal provision without the need for subsidies. As mentioned earlier, this question hinges on the forms of the congestion and cost functions. If, for example, the cost function displays decreasing cost, then marginal cost financing will not fully cover the club good's cost and a two-part tariff is needed to make up the difference (Sherman 1967). One part is the user toll and a second part is a membership fee to cover the shortfall. The two-part tariff is particularly germane to urban transportation systems—e.g., commuter trains—where scale economies are present.

Club theory is also applicable to recreation areas. For a given wilderness capacity or area, Fisher and Krutilla (1972) determined membership size to equate the associated marginal cost and marginal benefit from the experience. These authors then focused on joining the membership and capacity (provision) decision along the lines of Fig. 3. Cicchetti and Smith (1973) later determined the optimal utilization or membership for low-density, fixed-capacity wilderness areas by adjusting for congestion in the form of trail encounters. These authors used questionnaires, distributed to hikers, to ascertain the congestion relationship and the setting of user fees.

Artle and Averous (1973) investigated the telephone system as a club good. Their theoretical representation maximized the net benefits of both subscribers and nonsubscribers, thereby deriving the Pareto optimality conditions for a single economy-wide club. The telephone system is a particularly interesting club since it possesses not only negative crowding, but also positive network externalities. Both of these opposing externalities must be taken into account when ascertaining membership, toll, and provision (Squire 1973; von Rabenau and Stahl 1974). Network externalities require membership well beyond that when there are just crowding externalities.

Olson and Zeckhauser (1966) introduced military alliances as sharing a pure public good—i.e., deterrence. This representation may have applied to the early years of NATO, when allies relied on deterrence primarily provided by US strategic weapons (Sandler and Hartley 2001). In contrast, Sandler (1977) described a conventional alliance as a club, for which protecting a potential front or perimeter is a club good, subject to the thinning of forces (Sandler and Forbes 1980). As such, club principles can be applied to ascertain the optimal alliance size and user fees. For NATO, shared defense gave rise to joint products in the form of purely public deterrence, impurely public front protection, and ally-specific benefits (e.g., disaster relief and putting down local unrest).[10] Sandler (1977) derived optimality conditions in light of these joint products. Membership restriction and tolls are only relevant for shared protection. Without joint products, optimality hinges on the share of excludable benefits. As this share approaches one, optimality is more assured as markets and thinning charges force preference revelation for country-specific and excludable impure benefits, respectively. Thus, club principles can be applied to some components of joint products.[11]

A novel club application involves the International Telecommunications Satellite Organization (INTELSAT), which is now a private company that links much of the world in an external communication network. Originally, the system consisted of geostationary satellites positioned some 22,300 miles over the equator. At that altitude, satellites remained essentially fixed over a point on the earth's surface. Sandler and Schulze (1981) showed how to allocate geosynchronous orbits and its complementary electromagnetic bandwidth in a club arrangement that accounted for two crowding phenomena: (1) signal interference owing to transmissions and (2) satellite collision owing to satellite drift. User tolls, based on signals sent and received, internalize the first externality, while fees for "parking spaces" in geostationary orbit internalize the second externality. User revenues finance the system and its upgrades. The provision decision concerns the number of satellites and their communication capacity.

Intergenerational clubs apply to a wide range of club goods—e.g., antibiotics, the stratospheric ozone layer, cities, planet Earth, cathedrals, and national parks. Multiple generations of members share the club good, which is subject to atemporal crowding and intertemporal depreciation. Depreciation implies the degradation of the club good due to use—e.g., bridge or airplane fatigue. If a toll is to self-finance the intergenerational club good, then the toll must internalize both crowding and depreciation. Maintenance now assumes an intertemporal dimension because it involves repairs to extend the shared good's lifetime. Also, membership span needs to be determined. Sandler (1982) demonstrated that self-financing now requires bonds, equities, or some leveraged combination of the two, which are supported through toll collection. Myopic toll collection becomes a relevant concern along with suboptimal maintenance. The latter arises because maintenance is purely public to the members, thereby leading to free-rider concerns. This worry may be internalized when members realize that, when they sell their ownership share to the next generation, inadequate maintenance will result in lower resale values.

Club theory even has a place in the modern analysis of terrorism. Sandler et al. (1983) characterized commando squads, used to address terrorist incidents, as providing crisis management and damage-limiting capabilities, whose benefits are excludable and subject to crowding. These squads can be provided by a collective of at-risk countries, which then charge for their deployment to specific terrorist events. Moreover, commando squads can be optimally positioned around the globe to allow for reasonably fast arrival for specific incidents. Sharing such squads provide cost savings to governments by eliminating duplicate squad that may be engaged infrequently. Despite this economic rationale, most governments maintain their own squads. From the terrorist's viewpoint, terrorist groups (e.g., Hezbollah and Hamas) may supply excludable club goods (e.g., health care, education, and social welfare) to recruit suicide bombers to hit hardened targets (Berman and Laitin 2008). These terrorist groups utilize these club goods to eliminate potential defection of bombers, whose families would be subsequently excluded from the goods' benefits. Would-be bombers are showered with club benefits, which can include camaraderie and prestige.

Canals, interregional highways, and power grids are a few examples of regional club goods (Estevadeordal et al. 2004). Initial provision of such regional club goods poses a problem, because a regional collective must form and possess the means to provide an expensive good. In some instances, these goods may be financed by regional collectives that draw funds from leading regional nations, regional development banks, the World Bank, and customs unions. Repayment of loans can come from congestion-internalizing tolls. The rise of regionalism makes these regional club goods of greater importance.

Treaties for common pollution problems are clubs. Earlier, the stratospheric ozone layer was described as an intergenerational club good. Thus, the Montreal Protocol and its amendments provide a club good to ratifying nations (Congleton 1992; Murdoch and Sandler 1997). At a regional level, treaties limiting acid rain represent regional clubs. Murdoch et al. (1997) investigated the ratification and adherence to the Helsinki and Sofia Protocols regarding sulfur and nitrogen oxides pollutants, respectively. Both of these pollutants display deposition rivalry as particles drift downwind. Nations that receive greater shares of these depositions have been shown to be more willing to ratify the treaty (Murdoch et al. 1997).

7 CONCLUDING REMARKS

A Buchanan club is a decentralized, voluntary organization sharing an impure public good that is excludable and congestible. In its ideal form, clubs operate without transaction cost and can be replicated to partition a homogeneous population. Because all members possess the same tastes and endowments, no centralized control is needed. Buchanan's (1965) stripped-down formulation captured the essence of clubs and served as an ideal platform for myriad extensions.

Buchanan's (1965) theory of clubs offered a number of seminal ideas. First, this theory showed that club goods can be privately supplied, provided that nonmembers can be costlessly excluded. Second, club goods concerned two interrelated choices that involve membership and provision. As club theory was extended, more interrelated decisions became relevant (e.g., the number of clubs). Third, clubs permit preference revelation through visits that can be monitored; hence, *total toll* charges can differentiate among members' tastes. That is, heavier users paid more in total tolls, but everyone paid the same toll per visit. Fourth, Buchanan's club framework provided for the first explicit marrying of game theory and the study of public goods. Fifth, club theory offered a theoretical foundation for jurisdictional design. Sixth, club principles are applicable to myriad goods.

Technology and innovations are continually providing more club goods. Noteworthy recent examples include the Internet, flight paths, satellite television, the international space station, and reusable suborbital spacecraft. Other club goods, unimaginable today, will come to dominate our lives. In addition, technology will continue to reduce the cost of exclusion, thereby satisfying the crucial costless exclusion assumption in the Buchanan (1965) article. For example, toll booths are no longer required on highways owing to remote ways to count passages and to charge accordingly. Some nonexcludable public goods will become club goods due to technological advances in monitoring. As such, the realm of club goods will grow as a subset of public goods. As clubs become more prevalent, new problems will surface and have to be addressed. These problems include the dynamic growth of membership over time. Another problem involves the need for surge capacity to accommodate members during peak usage. Currently, this can be addressed through tolls that vary based on usage rates. Nevertheless, there will be times of gridlock or when members are denied entry. Only a couple of articles have addressed this issue (see, e.g., Sandler et al. 1985).

Except for work on fine versus coarse exclusion, the institutional form of clubs has not been analyzed. Moreover, member-owned and firm-owned clubs are treated as having the same transaction cost. Thus, there are many areas of clubs that can use further investigation.

FOOTNOTES

1 A good's benefits are nonrival when a unit of the good can be consumed by one individual without detracting, in the slightest, from the consumption opportunities still available for others from the same unit. Nonrivalry means that the marginal cost of extending the good's benefits to another consumer is zero. If the benefits of a good are available to all once the good is supplied, then its benefits are nonexcludable.

2 Subscripts denote partial derivatives.

3 $MRS_{cy} = U^i_c / U^i_y$ and $MRS_{vy} = U^i_v / U^i_y$.

4 MRScyMRScy is negative because crowding reduces utility.

5 The sequence of joiners should be based on their willingness to pay, with those with greater willingness to pay joining first. That is, the joining sequence is ordered by the willingness to pay.

6 Crowding is anonymous when each visit causes the same congestion regardless of the visitor. That is, the attributes of the visitor do not affect the amount of crowding.

7 Homogeneous of degree zero means that equal proportional changes to total utilization and provision do not alter the level of congestion.

8 Each firm faces the following problem: $\max[svT - C(X, sv)]$ subject to $U[I - vT, v, c(X, sv)] \geq U^*$.

9 Economies of scope arise when providing two or more club goods jointly in the same club is less expensive than supplying them in separate clubs owing to shared common costs.

10 Joint products also apply to "green clubs," where members receive excludable reputation benefits for participating and pure public benefits from generating environmental improvements (van't Veld and Kotchen 2011).

11 Another joint-product example with purely public, impurely public, and country-specific private benefits is the Amazon jungle (Sandler 2004). For example, the sequestration of carbon and the housing of unique species are purely public, while ecotourism is a club good. Harvested fruits and nuts are private benefits.

ACKNOWLEDGMENTS

The author profited from comments from an anonymous referee and Roger Congleton on earlier drafts. Sandler's research was partly supported by the Vibhooti Shukla endowment.

REFERENCES

1. Artle, R., & Averous, C. P. (1973). The telephone system as a public good: Static and dynamic aspects. The Bell Journal of Economics, 4, 89–100.
2. Berglas, E. (1976). On the theory of clubs. The American Economic Review, 66, 116–121.

3. Berglas, E., & Pines, D. (1981). Clubs, local public goods and transportation models: A synthesis. Journal of Public Economics, 15, 141–162.

4. Berman, E., & Laitin, D. D. (2008). Religion, terrorism and public goods: Testing the club model. Journal of Public Economics, 92, 1942–1967.

5. Brueckner, J. K., & Lee, K. (1991). Economies of scope and multiproduct clubs. Public Finance Quarterly, 19, 193–208.

6. Buchanan, J. M. (1965). An economic theory of clubs. Economica, 32, 1–14.

7. Cicchetti, C. J., & Smith, V. K. (1973). Congestion, quality deterioration, and optimal use: Wilderness recreation in the Spanish Peaks primitive area. Social Sciences Research, 2, 15–30.

8. Congleton, R. D. (1992). Political institutions and pollution control. The Review of Economics and Statistics, 74, 412–421.

9. Cornes, R., & Sandler, T. (1996). The theory of externalities, public goods, and club goods. New York, NY: Cambridge University Press.

10. DeSerpa, A. C. (1977). A theory of discriminatory clubs. Scottish Journal of Political Economy,24, 33–41.

11. Estevadeordal, A., Frantz, B., & Nguyen, T. R. (Eds.). (2004). Regional public goods: From theory to practice. Washington, DC: Inter-American Development Bank and Asian Development Bank.

12. Fisher, A. C., & Krutilla, J. V. (1972). Determination of optimal capacity of resource-based recreational facilities. Natural Resources Journal, 12, 417–444.

13. Helpman, E., & Hillman, A. L. (1977). Two remarks on optimal club size. Economica, 44, 293–296.

14. Helsley, R. W., & Strange, W. C. (1991). Exclusion and the theory of clubs. Canadian Journal of Economics, 24, 888–899.

15. McGuire, M. C. (1974). Group segregation and optimal jurisdictions. Journal of Political Economy, 82, 112–132.

16. Mohring, H. D., & Harwitz, M. (1962). Highway benefits: An analytical review. Evanston, IL: Northwestern University Press.

17. Murdoch, J. C., & Sandler, T. (1997). The voluntary provision of a pure public good: The case of reduced CFC emissions and the Montreal Protocol. Journal of Public Economics, 63, 331–349.

18. Murdoch, J. C., Sandler, T., & Sargent, K. (1997). A tale of two collectives: Sulphur versus nitrogen oxides emission reduction in Europe. Economica, 64, 281–301.

19. Oakland, W. H. (1972). Congestion, public goods, and welfare. Journal of Public Economics, 1, 339–357.

20. Olson, M. (1965). The logic of collective action. Cambridge, MA: Harvard University Press.

21. Olson, M., & Zeckhauser, R. (1966). An economic theory of alliances. The Review of Economics and Statistics, 48, 266–279.

22. Pauly, M. V. (1967). Clubs, commonality, and the core: An integration of game theory and the theory of public goods. Economica, 34, 314–324.

23. Sandler, T. (1977). Impurity of defense: An application to the economics of alliances. Kyklos,30, 443–460.

24. Sandler, T. (1982). A theory of intergenerational clubs. Economic Inquiry, 20, 191–208.

25. Sandler, T. (1984). Club optimality: Further clarifications. Economics Letters, 14, 61–65.

26. Sandler, T. (2004). Global collective action. New York, NY: Cambridge University Press.

27. Sandler, T., & Forbes, J. F. (1980). Burden sharing, strategy, and the design of NATO. Economic Inquiry, 18, 425–444.

28. Sandler, T., & Hartley, K. (2001). Economics of alliances: The lessons for collective action. Journal of Economic Literature, 39, 869–896.

29. Sandler, T., & Schulze, W. (1981). The economics of outer space. Natural Resources Journal,21, 371–393.

30. Sandler, T., Sterbenz, F., & Tschirhart, J. T. (1985). Uncertainty and clubs. Economica, 52, 467–477.

31. Sandler, T., & Tschirhart, J. T. (1980). The economic theory of clubs: An evaluative survey. Journal of Economic Literature, 18, 1481–1521.

32. Sandler, T., & Tschirhart, J. T. (1984). Mixed clubs: Further observations. Journal of Public Economics, 23, 381–389.

33. Sandler, T., & Tschirhart, J. T. (1997). Club theory: Thirty years later. Public Choice, 93, 335–355.

34. Sandler, T., Tschirhart, J. T., & Cauley, J. (1983). A theoretical analysis of transnational terrorism. American Political Science Review, 77, 36–54.

35. Scotchmer, S. (1997). On price-taking equilibrium in club economies with nonanonymous crowding. Journal of Public Economics, 65, 75–88.

36. Scotchmer, S., & Wooders, M. H. (1987). Competitive equilibrium and the core in club economies with anonymous crowding. Journal of Public Economics, 34, 159–173.

37. Sherman, R. (1967). Club subscriptions for public transport passengers. Journal of Transportation and Economic Policy, 1, 237–242.

38. Squire, L. (1973). Some aspects of optimal pricing for telecommunications. The Bell Journal of Economics, 4, 515–525.

39. Tiebout, C. M. (1956). A pure theory of local expenditures. Journal of Political Economy, 64, 416–424.

40. van't Veld, K., & Kotchen, M. J. (2011). Green clubs. Journal of Environmental Economics and Management, 62, 309–322.

41. Vickrey, W. S. (1969). Congestion theory and transport investment. The American Economic Review, 59, 251–260.

42. von Rabenau, B., & Stahl, K. (1974). Dynamic aspects of public goods: A further analysis of the telephone system. The Bell Journal of Economics, 5, 651–659.

43. Wiseman, J. (1957). The theory of public utility price—An empty box. Oxford Economic Papers,9, 56–74.

6

SOURCES AND LEGITIMACY OF FINANCIAL LIBERALIZATION

Brian Burgoon[a], Panicos Demetriades[b], Geoffrey R.D. Underhill[c]

[a]Department of Political Science, Universiteit van Amsterdam, OZ Achterburgwal 237 1010 DL, Amsterdam, The Netherlands

[b]Department of Economics, University of Leicester, University Road, Leicester, UK, LE1 7RH

[c]Department of Political Science, Universiteit van Amsterdam, OZ Achterburgwal 237, 1010 DL, Amsterdam, The Netherlands

ABSTRACT

This article seeks to clarify how we understand domestic and international sources of globalization and specifically how we explain financial liberalization across countries. The article also develops our understanding of the underlying legitimacy of financial liberalization. We debate e.g. Abiad and Mody (2005) and others who have found political factors to have little impact on financial openness. Using the same data undergirding such conclusions we argue, in contrast, that even a slight broadening of the political variables employed in the model and much closer attention to "input" and "output" aspects of the political legitimacy of financial liberalization over time reveal a more central role for politics in shaping liberalization. Input legitimacy involves the representation of stakeholders in initial and ongoing decisions to liberalize, while "output" legitimacy concerns liberalization's distributional consequences and management thereof over time. Several empirical measures of domestic-national and international political factors plausibly influence such aspects of legitimacy and are found to play a significant role in shaping liberalization, suggesting legitimation politics to be more important to financial openness than existing studies have typically acknowledged.

Keywords: Financial openness; Liberalization dynamics; Financial regulation; Political legitimacy; Political variables; Financial reform

1. INTRODUCTION

Recent public intervention to stabilize the financial system in the wake of the crisis of 2007–9 and the emerging sovereign debt turmoil in Europe have led to concerns about the equity and efficiency of the international financial system and even to challenges to financial openness itself. These all remind us that although the benefits of financial openness may be considerable, global financial openness remains politically fragile and contested. Understanding the causes and dynamics of financial openness has increased in importance as reforms concerning the nature and regulation of the financial system are debated both nationally and internationally. Political economists therefore have strong reasons to conduct ongoing research into the origins and political underpinnings of financial openness as a key face of economic globalization. An important contribution to the literature is Abiad and Mody's (2005) study of the sinews of financial liberalization. The study[1] is based on a rich dataset of policy measures of financial openness, its possible causes and ongoing dynamics – capturing regulatory barriers underlying more downstream financial flows and going beyond existing measures of current and capital account openness.

Their explanation of the timing, pace, and extent of financial reforms and consequent origins of financial openness also stands out as remarkably apolitical. Their core argument and empirical findings highlight how increasing-returns become locked-in through learning effects. The initial step to liberalization is difficult and is typically sparked by economic shocks, but this policy breakthrough yields information and footholds for deepening liberalization over time which are related to the spatial dynamics of "catching-up" with the most liberalized countries in their region. Many plausible political factors which some previous studies found to have played an important role in shaping financial globalization – such as left-right partisanship or democratic institutions – play little role in their account and are found to have little influence on the particular measures of financial liberalization in the wide range of countries and time-periods covered by the study.

In this article we seek to consider more deeply the role that politics might play in shaping financial liberalization. We do so by slightly broadening the range of political variables considered, focusing on how national policy choices on financial liberalization might be significantly shaped by domestic-national and international factors that underlie the "input" and "output" aspects of the political legitimacy of financial openness. Input legitimacy concerns the involvement of and acceptance by stakeholders of a policy area in the decision to liberalise. Output legitimacy concerns the substantive effects of such policy change on the perceived interests of stakeholders, whatever their involvement and acceptance of the policy change. These factors turn out to influence significantly and directly the chances that governments may liberalize their financial markets, and also may do so indirectly by influencing the domestic learning and catch-up dynamics emphasized by Abiad and Mody and others.

With respect to input legitimacy, we find both domestic and international sources of legitimacy relevant to liberalization. These domestic political factors are two-fold. First, shifts to (as opposed to levels of) Left governments significantly decrease chances of liberalization. And second, both changes and incidence of Left government affect liberalization in ways strongly mediated by democratic representation: different levels of democracy affect the policy options and credibility concerns of parties, such that at low levels of democracy, moves to and incidence of Left governments tend to significantly decrease chances of liberalization, while in more democratic settings this negative effect of Left representation disappears. The international political factors relevant to input legitimacy and which affect financial openness involve the overall international level of voter support for free-market enterprise, international openness, and internationalism generally, and voter support for (post-) Communist parties, Marxist ideology, and international closure. Liberalization is significantly more likely when the international, extra-national *zeitgeist* supports free-market openness and less likely to the extent that it supports anti-market closure. Finally, both the domestic and international input-legitimacy factors may also mediate the learning-based lock-in and catch-up dynamics—as changes to left government have less negative effects as *ex ante* financial openness increases, and as international voter-support for free markets significantly increase the spurring effects of catch-up.

With respect to output-related legitimacy, we find that financial liberalization is more likely in combination with domestic and international spending programs that help address the internal distributional costs and risks of financial markets.

Building on the "Polanyian" idea that systems of compensation might increase political support for international openness, we find that some aspects of the public economy and not others increase financial liberalization: various measures of total spending have modest influence. But some features of social spending, particularly health spending, which provides in a developing-country context more generalized indemnification of risk than social security expenditures, spur liberalization. We also find that international sources of compensation – measured as bilateral developmental assistance, multilateral development assistance, and technical assistance – may not only involve conditionality that demands liberalization but also tend to help address social policy risks beyond domestic assistance. In any event, such "social insurance from without" tends to significantly increase the chances of financial liberalization. There is some modest evidence that domestic, though not international, sources of compensation may decrease catch-up behavior.

We develop these points in five sections, building on the empirics of Abiad and Mody's study. The first lays out the basic findings of that study with respect to the "non-role" of politics. The second section introduces a simple framework focused on input and output legitimacy of liberalization, and introduces the empirical specification to illustrate that framework. A third section then considers discusses how domestic left partisanship and democracy and international embrace of free markets are possible sources of input legitimacy. A fourth section then considers specifications focused on domestic spending and international aid as sources of output legitimacy. A fifth section, then, discusses robustness of the results to alternative measures of liberalization, alternative estimators, and different datasets. The findings, in any event, suggest the value of a research agenda to open up the range of political variables considered in relation to financial openness and to its longer-run political underpinnings.

2. NON-POLITICAL EMPIRICS ABOUT EXTERNAL SHOCKS, LEARNING AND CATCH-UP

Abiad and Mody's study of their financial openness data[2] has few theoretical commitments to a view that politics don't much matter, but their own argument and discussion of possible political conditions, and certainly their empirical analysis, all yield such a conclusion. Their main theoretical and empirical commitment is to the view that financial liberalization is difficult and a rare event, tending to be possible only with the impulse of exogenous economic shocks such as hyperinflation, recessions, or IMF-conditionality. Once begun, however, the expectation and empirical findings are that the early stages of liberalization are marked by increasing-returns that can get locked-in through a kind of learning effect, while at later stages liberalization reaches a kind of saturation point and yields diminishing marginal returns. Such a pattern they expect to follow an inverse-U pattern. They also expect and find that this lock-in learning dynamic is conditioned by a range of other conditions, not just the starting point of liberalization but also by existing levels of economic development and a range of external conditions such as currency crises. Finally, they follow the lead of other scholars who have given attention to spatial dependence (Simmons and Elkins, 2004 and Franzese and Hays, 2006), and expect that polities will tend to try to catch up with the financial openness of their region's most open polity. Abiad and Mody make sense of these developments in apolitical terms, as national reform embedded in the regional liberalization sensitize policymakers to the economic benefits of financial integration by yielding information and material benefits for deepening liberalization over time.

Mainly as a backdrop to these arguments, Abiad and Mody largely dismiss the role of many plausible political factors that previous studies have found to play an important role in shaping financial globalization. They consider particularly the role of left, right or center governments. Abiad and Mody anticipate that Left governments and executives might be more opposed to liberalization than right ones, on grounds that the former disproportionately represent losers from globalization. But they also anticipate that left governments might also have more political credibility to pursue such reforms than their right-party counterparts, on grounds that such reform can be more credibly sold as in a nation's rather than a party's interest. Their empirical investigation, however, shows consistently the result that presence of left or right (as opposed to center) governments tend not to matter in shaping changes in financial openness – neither directly influencing change nor interacting with various crisis conditions or *ex ante* financial openness. Such is the empirical fate of a range of other political conditions, especially institutional characteristics like quality of democracy and legislative fragmentation; these factors get discussed at the margins of the theoretical treatment and are in any event found to be empirically insignificant in shaping liberalization.

These findings go very much against the gist of a number of other studies into financial liberalization, including quantitative studies of capital account liberalization and openness. They go against, for instance, the findings of Quinn and Inclan (1997) that left partisanship – a la Stolper and Samuelson – interacts with levels of economic development, such that left partisanship spurs liberalization in developing countries but thwarts it in richer countries. It also goes against the many other studies of financial globalization that focus on a range of more or less elite struggles among economic sectors of finance, bureaucratic struggles, historical accidents, and spill-overs from other areas of economic and political globalization (e.g. Sobel, 1994, Laurence, 2001, Garrett, 2001 and Helleiner, 1994).

Consistent with Abiad and Mody's account, pursuing various specifications closer to these previous studies tend also to suggest partisanship matters less in the short-term changes on this particular measure of financial openness on this particular set of countries and years. For instance, left partisanship does not interact with various measures of economic development or factor endowments – and we considered a range of measures of capital-labor ratios, labor productivity, capital productivity, and GDP per capita, all as proxies for factor profile that might mediate the influence of partisanship. None of these measures yields consistently significant results. And in fact the consistent pattern is, though usually statistically insignificant, in the direction opposite Stolper-Samuelson expectations: higher levels of development tend to make left government more rather than less likely to liberalize finance. In any event, Abiad and Mody's findings on the non-importance of partisanship have a reasonable basis, even beyond their estimation approach.

Such findings raise important questions about the role of politics in financial liberalization, with important implications for our understanding of the longer-run policy dynamics of liberalisation. And such dynamics are, of course, in greater need than ever of study in light of the recent global financial crisis. If Abiad and Mody are correct, then liberalisation is a path which is difficult and often painful to stumble upon, but its positive nature becomes clear once the process has begun as the benefits of openness are increasingly manifest. Stimulated by shocks, policy-makers taking the correct initial technical decision to reform through liberalisation link up with the locomotive of learning, and policy is on track. If liberalisation has its origins in specific political conditions, however, then not only the explanation of its origins must be altered, but also our understanding of the longer-run dynamics of openness. We know that markets are dynamic and that they imply a range of adjustment costs and benefits for constituencies over time. The conditions which yielded decisions to begin an initial policy of liberalisation may not be the same as the long-run conditions taking policy further or rendering it sustainable in the long term. So this apparently obvious issue – does financial openness have political origins? – is nontrivial to understanding the relationship between the openness of financial systems and their governance.

From a perspective sensitive to the role of politics in financial liberalization – informed by but beyond the existing political conditions looming large in other studies of financial openness – there are a great many blind spots in the Abiad and Mody study. There is little discussion of the political or economic costs and benefits of liberalization, or of its distributional consequences, something many other studies have highlighted (Bergh and Nilsson, 2010). And it is certainly unclear from their analysis that all paths leading to liberalisation are the same, or that liberalization's end results are the same, particularly in distributional terms; after all, case and econometric research reveals that each move along the continuum between financial repression and openness seldom takes place in the same way, even in the wake of the same crisis (Underhill and Zhang, 2003). Even though similar forces may be at work, there is considerable cross-national variation in the experience of crisis and liberalisation, especially in terms of the political compromises produced, and national experiences admit of variation over time (Moran, 1990 and Coleman, 1996). Furthermore, little is said of the longer-run political costs of financial instability plausibly linked to openness itself, despite a considerable literature linking market liberalisation to increased market volatility (Prasad et al., 2007, Bhagwati, 1998 and Arestis and Demetriades, 1999). For the present purposes, however, perhaps the most obvious blind spot is the rather thin treatment of what "politics" may actually mean, as the political variables they address are simple notions of overt left-right orientation of government and parliamentary vs. presidential regime type (c.f. Lai, 2010). There is little attention to the deeper phenomena of constituency rivalry and interest politics, and how these might play out in relation to initial liberalisation and over time.

3. INPUT AND OUTPUT LEGITIMACY IN THE POLITICS OF FINANCIAL LIBERALIZATION

Our focus here is on articulating empirically a simple framework for understanding such more complicated notions of politics, concentrating on what can be termed the "input" and "output" legitimacy of financial liberalization, and on national-domestic and international factors that help constitute such legitimacy. Such a legitimacy framework has roots in political-economic study of European and global economic governance (Scharpf, 1999, Held, 1997 and Porter, 2001). And the sinews of legitimacy are clearly applicable to (proximately) national political decisions to liberalize finance, beyond the kinds of political factors articulated in the Abiad and Mody study and elsewhere.

Input legitimacy concerns the involvement of and acceptance by stakeholders in policy-making. In the case of financial opening, this means the involvement of and acceptance by stakeholders in policy "decisions" to liberalize financial regulations. Such input legitimacy encompasses a great many features of policy choice, most obviously the active or passive involvement or formal representation of various stakeholders to liberalization, whether they be workers, firm owners, citizens and any other national individuals or socio-economic groups. This representation can be captured by broad levels of democracy in a nation-state, implying at least passive involvement of stakeholders. But it might also involve more direct involvement in a policy decision – as opposed to de facto decision-making by bureaucrats unfettered by democratic accountability. Input legitimacy might involve, particularly in democratic settings, less direct and formally protected representation through partisan orientation of governments. And finally, input legitimacy involves a general embrace or popularity of a particular policy change, both domestically within a given polity or internationally in the broad world opinion surrounding such change.

Output legitimacy concerns the substantive effects of such policy change for the perceived interests of stakeholders, whatever their involvement and acceptance of the policy change. Such legitimacy is often more relevant than input-legitimacy to the longer run sustainability of the outcomes produced by liberalisation. But it is also relevant to the shorter-term actual introduction of financial liberalization (or reversals). Relevant to such output legitimacy are all downstream effects, real and perceived, of financial openness actually implemented as policy – hence, the relevance of growth, unemployment, inequality, poverty, and actual or perceived degree to which these are affected by financial openness. In our reckoning, however, many *ex ante* policy conditions can clearly be expected to foster output legitimacy – most obviously government and social policies that address the equity concerns of stakeholders potentially affected by financial liberalization.

These kinds of political factors relevant to such input and output legitimacy are, we believe, worth exploring in any empirical or theoretical account of financial liberalization. We provide that exploration by discussing and empirically illustrating such factors, where we can see both national-domestic and international sinews of input and output legitimacy underlying financial liberalization. Fig. 1 maps our investigation and results across the two kinds of legitimacy and levels of governance.

	Input Legitimacy	Output Legitimacy
International Level	International Voter support for *Net free-market internationalism*	Foreign Aid (multilateral, bilateral)
Domestic Level	A Left Government Left Government × Democracy	Social Policy Compensation (e.g. health spending)

Figure 1. Sources of legitimacy of financial openness at different levels of governance.

We develop all of these political sinews of input and output legitimacy through further empirical study of Abiad and Mody's measures of financial governance. We do so by building on a benchmark specification from Abiad and Mody's (2005) analysis (their Table Eight, column four, p.80) that takes account of country-specific effects and disturbances, and of how existing levels of financial regulation (interacted with policy measures) may influence the lock-in effects of learning. That baseline specification takes the following form:

equation(1)

$$\Delta FL_{it} = \theta_1 FL_{it-1} + \theta_2 FL^2_{it-1} + \theta_3 FL_{it-1} * Y_{it-1} + \theta_4 (Reg.-leader_F L_{it-1} - FL_{it-1}) + \theta_5 Shocks_{it} + \theta'_6 Ideology_{it} + \theta'_7 Structure_{it} + \varepsilon_{it} \quad (1)$$

where financial liberalization (ΔFL_{it}) is the first-difference of the composite of financial openness[3]; FL_{it-1} measures *ex ante* levels of financial openness (and its square); $FL_{it-1}{}^{*}Y_{it-1}$ captures possible interaction with development level; (*Reg.lead_* $FL_{it-1}{}^{*}Y_{it-1}$) gauges catch-up pressure of trailing the region's most liberalized polity; *Shocksit*captures various external shocks (recession, high inflation, IMF participation, and banking and BOP crises); *Ideologyit* captures particularly influence of Left, Center or Right ruling governments or executives, and their first year of office; and *Structureit*captures influence of existing trade openness and interest rates.[4] This specification addresses possible panel-wise correlation of errors and heteroskedasticity by including country dummies and country-wise clustering of robust standard errors[5]; and the inclusion of lagged levels of financial openness not only gauge learning and lock-in dynamics but also help address possible temporal correlation and heteroskedasticity. With respect to estimator, our benchmark follows Abiad and Mody's consideration of the capped interval of possible liberalization and of discrete shifts in levels of liberalization. Such specification choices, of course, are all open to criticism, and indeed Huang (2009) has recently criticized Abiad and Mody's ordered logit specification for, among other things, treating liberalization as involving substantively equal, discrete steps at both early and late stages of possible liberalization, and found Abiad and Mody's results fragile in the face of combining OLS estimation with (other) corrections for panel-wise and temporal correlation and heteroskedasticity.

Because we are concerned to show the broader role of politics even where Abiad and Mody's empirics and data suggest a modest role, we begin with their original data and specification. But we consider and discuss alternative specifications that broadly replicate our baseline results. We present these results by adding to the benchmark model summarized in Eq. (1), first the factors that influence 'input' legitimacy, and secondly adding those factors relevant to 'output' legitimacy. We then turn (in Section 5) to whether the results are robust to other specifications.

4. INPUT LEGITIMACY

domestic partisanship and democracy and global embrace of free markets.

Our discussion of political sinews of input legitimacy is summarized in Table 1 below. To clarify the role of factors relevant to input legitimacy, Column (1), based on Eq. (1), summarizes the estimation we take as the benchmark and point of departure. The most important results, well discussed in the Abiad and Mody piece, are that there does seem to be a lock-in learning effect, captured in this specification by the significant positive effect of lagged levels of financial openness for further changes in openness, and where the square of that lagged level is significantly negative – suggesting the inverse-U relationship of early increasing returns at lower levels of liberalization and saturation at higher levels of liberalization. Also noteworthy is the significantly positive interaction between GDP per capita (on PPP basis) and lagged liberalization, suggesting that desired liberalization is higher among richer countries. Furthermore, the "catch-up" parameter – measured as the difference between the level of financial openness of the region's most liberalized financial system and the country's own level of openness – is modestly significantly positive, suggesting that the chance of liberalization increases to the extent that a country lags behind regional liberalizers. Finally, balance-of-payments currency crises positively affect chances of liberalizing, while banking crises and levels of US interest rates tend to reduce such chances. Key for us, however, is that left or right governments (with center governments as the excluded category) have no significant influence on chances of liberalization.

4.1. Shifts in government

Our first example of how conditions relevant to input legitimacy might matter more than this benchmark suggests involves how left, right and center governments on issues of economic intervention generally influence chances of liberalization. Significantly, however, their empirical study only specifies government form as the incidence of left, right or centrist government. Yet, partisanship of governments might also matter to policy changes by virtue of the actual *change in power* from one to another government form. The idea, here, is that a shift in government can extra political stimulus and power for the new government taking over, yielding short-term changes in financial

Table 1: Input legitimacy and financial liberalization.

	(1)	(2)	(3)	(4)	(5)	(6)	(7)	(8)
	Benchmark	Δ Government	ΔGovernment* finance.open.	Government* Democracy.	Governmentt* Democ.dummy	Voter Net free-market Int'lism	Voter Free-market Int'lism	Catchup* Net free-mrkt.
Leftist Government$_{it}$	−0.092			−1.561**	−2.467***	0.051	−0.100	−0.112
	(0.354)			(0.790)	(0.788)	(0.378)	(0.354)	(0.414)
Rightist Government$_{it}$	−0.091			0.122	−0.090	−0.035	−0.118	−0.002
	(0.349)			(0.395)	(0.581)	(0.322)	(0.345)	(0.318)
Δ Left government$_{it}$		−1.261***	−2.266***					
		(0.411)	(0.495)					
Δ Right government$_{it}$		−0.569	−0.778					
		(0.425)	(0.606)					
ΔLeft * FL$_{it-1}$			3.498***					
			(1.181)					
ΔRight *Financ.openness$_{t-1}$			1.638					
			(1.217)					
Democracy (PolityIVscore)$_{it}$				−0.022				
				(0.028)				
Left * Democracy (Polity)$_{it}$				0.183*				
				(0.095)				
Right * Democracy (Polity)$_{it}$				−0.011				
				(0.043)				
Democracy dummy (1=Polity>0)$_{it}$					−0.896**			
					(0.369)			
Left * Democracy dummy$_{it}$					2.681***			
					(0.842)			
Right * Democracy dummy$_{it}$					0.241			
					(0.655)			
Net free-market internationalism$_t$						3.745***		0.869
						(0.706)		(1.524)
Free-market internationalism$_t$							0.015**	
							(0.007)	
Net free-market intism. * Catchup$_{it}$								6.092**
								(2.549)
Financial openness (FL$_{it-1}$)	6.662***	6.485***	6.373***	6.876***	7.371***	3.245**	6.129***	3.844**
	(1.583)	(1.612)	(1.704)	(1.625)	(1.699)	(1.628)	(1.678)	(1.583)
Financial openness sq. ((FL$_{it-1}$)^2)	−9.763***	−9.974***	−9.850***	−9.745***	−10.100***	−9.082***	−9.555***	−8.405***
	(2.641)	(2.583)	(2.573)	(2.605)	(2.571)	(2.630)	(2.634)	(2.464)
FL$_{it-1}$ * Y$_{it-1}$	0.000**	0.000**	0.000**	0.000**	0.000**	0.000	0.000**	0.000
	(0.000)	(0.000)	(0.000)	(0.000)	(0.000)	(0.000)	(0.000)	(0.000)
Catch-up (Reg.lead. FL$_{it-1}$ - FL$_{it-1}$)	2.070*	1.871	1.899	2.416**	2.698**	−1.144	1.599	−0.496
	(1.242)	(1.269)	(1.266)	(1.192)	(1.194)	(1.388)	(1.334)	(1.425)
Currency Crisis$_{it}$	0.454*	0.442*	0.434*	0.425*	0.432*	0.462*	0.442*	0.454*
	(0.233)	(0.243)	(0.245)	(0.232)	(0.237)	(0.248)	(0.236)	(0.246)
Banking Crisis$_{it}$	−1.014***	−1.054***	−1.057***	−1.076***	−1.096***	−0.946***	−0.973***	−0.988***
	(0.344)	(0.361)	(0.361)	(0.359)	(0.363)	(0.344)	(0.342)	(0.354)
Recession$_{it}$	−0.035	0.051	0.004	−0.056	−0.077	0.101	−0.029	0.111
	(0.373)	(0.373)	(0.382)	(0.383)	(0.391)	(0.385)	(0.372)	(0.381)
High Inflation$_{it}$	−0.429	−0.432	−0.457	−0.274	−0.239	−0.503	−0.455	−0.658
	(0.634)	(0.648)	(0.637)	(0.643)	(0.637)	(0.673)	(0.646)	(0.685)
First Year in Office$_{it}$	0.250			0.260	0.263	0.307	0.279	0.334
	(0.271)			(0.279)	(0.282)	(0.275)	(0.277)	(0.269)
IMF program$_{it}$	0.370	0.379	0.390	0.372	0.369	0.271	0.356	0.277
	(0.266)	(0.261)	(0.257)	(0.262)	(0.255)	(0.288)	(0.270)	(0.297)
US Interest Rate$_t$	−0.089**	−0.098**	−0.092**	−0.104**	−0.106**	−0.119***	−0.096**	−0.117***
	(0.044)	(0.042)	(0.043)	(0.049)	(0.047)	(0.042)	(0.043)	(0.042)
Openness$_{it}$	0.010	0.011	0.011	0.010	0.009	0.013	0.010	0.014
	(0.010)	(0.010)	(0.011)	(0.011)	(0.010)	(0.010)	(0.010)	(0.010)
Fixed effects	Yes	Yes	Yes	Yes	Yes	Yes	Yes	Yes
Year dummies	No	No	No	No	No	No	No	No
Observations	805	805	805	794	794	805	805	805
Wald χ^2	1.24e+07	8.8e+05	1.13e+07	1.26e+07	5.76e+07	4.13e+07	7.09e+08	2.07e+07
Log likelihood	−730.1	−725.9	−722.7	−723.1	−721.7	−718.4	−728.5	−714.4

Notes: The dependent variable is the change in the Financial Liberalization Index. Robust standard errors are in parentheses, adjusted for clustering by country. Fixed effects for 35 countries not shown but highly jointly significant.
*** denotes significance at the 1-percent level; ** denotes significance at the 5-percent level; * denotes significance at the 10-percent level.

regulation. Indeed, Abiad and Mody anticipate this possibility when they discuss the "'new government' or 'honeymoon' hypothesis," such as Krueger's finding based on case research that one of the most important conditions for liberalization is that a new government comes to power (Krueger, 1993). Although Abiad and Mody also cite reasons to think that shifts in power might not spark reform, as new governments delay painful policies until they have consolidated power (c.f. Haggard and Webb, 1993), the theoretical plausibility and case histories supporting the "new government" suggest that shifts in government may matter as much as, or in any event distinct from, incidence of government. These possibilities lead Abiad and Mody to consider a dummy for first-year-of office of a government, in addition to partisanship of government. But this specification doesn't address the possibility that different governments might differ in their first year of office.

Taking account of such developments in the empirical investigation involve, most simply and minimally, considering how first-differences of partisanship affect first-difference changes in financial regulation.[6] Table 1's column (2) summarizes the results of testing this possibility, by substituting *ΔLeft* and *ΔRight* for *Left and Right*, respectively. Our general expectation is that – possible Stolper-Samuelson effects notwithstanding – a shift to left governments (captured by a positive one in first differences) should decrease the chance liberalization while a shift away from left governments to either centrist or right governments (captured by a negative one in first-differences) should increase the chance of liberalization. One might also hypothesize that the opposite pattern ought to emerge with changes in right government control.

The results summarized in column (2) capture how this is broadly what one finds for changes in left partisanship, though not significantly for changes in right partisanship – both, as in the incidence models, having effects that can be discerned relative to shifts towards centrist governments. The shift to left governments, in particular, significantly decreases the chances that a polity will liberalize. Substantively, this effect can be captured by counterfactual estimates of how moving from no left government to a shift to left government affects predicted changes in openness, holding other parameters at their means. Such a shift increases the likelihood of a reduction of openness by 5.6 percentage points (from a probability of .024 to a probability of .08), and of there being no change by 6.7 percentage points (from probability .795 to .862), and *decreases* the chance of liberalization (a little or a lot) by 11 percentage points (from a probability of .177 to .067).

Column (3) suggests, further, that shifts to left governments might have effects mediated by *ex ante* financial openness. In particular, the individual coefficient for first-difference in left government suggests that at levels of full closure of financial markets (a score of 0 on the Abiad and Mody scale), a shift to left government predicts a significant reduction of chances of liberalization, on a scale roughly double for that just reported for column (2). But as financial openness becomes greater, this negative effect significantly declines – becoming insignificant once a country reaches a level of financial openness equivalent to .52 liberalization on the rescaled 0 to 1 measure of openness (0 being full closure and 1 being full openness).

4.2. Left government and democracy

Columns (4) and (5) consider a second aspect of input legitimacy, where the incidence of left government appears to significantly interact with levels of democracy in shaping chances of liberalization. As Abiad and Mody report, levels of democracy as well as partisanship generally appear to be insignificant predictors of liberalization. But levels of democracy might well alter the calculations of political parties in the kinds of policies they pursue, and this alteration might play out differently for left than for right or center parties – all net of economic development and other conditions.[7] And it's also possible that democratization might play out differently in different partisan settings – though government color tends to vary more than levels of democracy as an institution.

Although intuition and previous theory suggests offsetting possibilities, we anticipate a broadly positive interaction – with democracy making effects of left partisanship less negative or more positive. On the one hand, to the extent that left governments are more likely to oppose liberalization to help constituents (a pattern that holds for the shifts to left governments), then one might expect democratization to create stronger electoral incentives to act in such ways, as governments are more likely under democratic institutions to be held accountable for their actions. On the other hand, left governments might tend to oppose financial liberalization because of state control over finance and financial institutions, in which case democratization ought to be more neutral. And, perhaps most importantly, there is also the possibility that democratization will diminish the incentives left parties have to protect financial markets. Democratization brings with it voice for constituents that might unleash other ways of serving constituents (e.g. providing compensation provisions), might also make it more likely that left governments take action in a national interest connected to non-working-class constituents. Finally, the contracting and transaction-costs literature suggests that left parties will in more democratized setting be less likely to oppose liberalization and might be more successful in supporting liberalization than their right counterparts, because they are likely more credible in supporting the spread of markets in light of their ideological bent (Cukierman and Tommasi, 1998).

Both columns (4) and (5) consider the various possibilities focusing on levels of democracy interacted with simple levels, or incidence, of left and right governments (center governments as the excluded category). Column (4) specifies democracy by taking the Polity IV measure of 10-point autocracy and 10-point democracy, with levels of democracy ranging from complete autarchy (– 10) to complete democracy (10). Column (5) specifies democracy more roughly, taking a value of 1 for all country-years where the above Polity score is above 0. As both specifications make clear, democratization significantly mutes the tendency of left governments to oppose financial liberalization. Net of economic development as well as all other controls, lack of democracy creates conditions under which left governments tend to significantly oppose liberalization, and as levels of democracy rise this negative effect becomes weaker, such that at medium to high levels of democracy left parties are no longer associated with less financial liberalization or more closure.

Focusing on the substantive effects suggested by the estimation in column (5), in non-democratic settings (with a polity score of 0 or negative) moving from a year without left government to a year with left government leads to an increased chance of some financial closing (negative change in financial openness index) by 4.6 percentage points (from .0138 to .0313 probability), and of zero change in financial openness by 12.8 percentage points (from a predicted probability of .697 to .825), and lowers the chance of financial liberalization by 14.6 percentage points (from a probability of .29 to a probability of .143). However, under more democratic settings (where polity scores are higher than zero), moving from no left to left government predicts in the net a decrease in the chance of reversal by 11.2 percentage points (from a predicted probability of .123 to .026) and of no change by 2.5 percentage points (predicted chance of .824 to .804), and an increase in the chance of liberalization by 13.7 percentage points (from a probability of .034 to .171). Such conditionally positive effects of left government, however, are only significant for the middle third of the full distribution of country-year variation in incidence of left government.

In any event, these patterns suggest that democratization – perhaps the most obvious and general measure of input legitimacy –tends to diminish how much left governments oppose liberalization. Even if partisanship and democracy appear to have few direct effects, thus, their interaction suggests that democracy is conditional good news for the chances of liberalization.

4.3. International support for free-market internationalism versus protectionist closure

The final set of estimations in Table 1 concern the broad subjective embrace versus rejection of free market openness or internationalism, versus support for anti-capitalist regulation or closure. Both the domestic and *international* level of such embrace and rejection gauge the domestic thinking of a polity relevant to its subjective acceptance or rejection of financial liberalization in particular. These all capture the possible input legitimacy of financial reforms being explained – net of the kinds of institutional and partisanship conditions relevant to such legitimacy. While domestic measures are most obviously relevant to such input legitimacy, international voter support or rejection for free market ideas is also relevant by capturing the general ideological climate that likely influences a broad polity's tastes for financial liberalization – the tastes of the broad public as well as elites. Indeed, a recent study by Quinn and Toyoda (2007) finds that international levels of voter support for (post-) Communist parties tends to significantly decrease the chances that a polity introduces capital account liberalization, while international voter support for free-enterprise capitalism tends to increase chances of liberalization.

Unfortunately, we have insufficient information to measure the levels of citizen support for free-market internationalism versus regulatory intervention and protectionism – not least because a number of country-years in the sample are non-democratic where polls or party information are lacking – something further research may partially redress. But building on the technique Quinn and Toyoda (2007) use to gauge the influence of international ideology, we can find measures of international levels of voter support for free-market internationalism versus anti-capitalist closure. Such voter support can be gauged using the Comparative Manifesto Project (CMP) dataset, which provides salience measures of party "support" for a range of substantive policy issues, based on content analysis of the party programs of political parties on a range of substantive policy issues for 25 countries since 1945.[8] Based on the share of a party's program stating a position supporting or opposing free markets or capitalism, one can then judge what this means for voters by multiplying the platform scores by the percentage of votes the relevant party received in the election. One can then take the yearly averages for the inferred voter positions for all the countries in the sample to gauge the general international climate on issues – position-taking that gauge input legitimacy from without.[9]

Relevant to the input legitimacy of financial liberalization are a number of parameters in the CMP dataset. Providing a more encompassing measure of support for markets than Quinn and Toyoda develop, we focus on a measure of net support for international free markets encompassing the following elements: *Free enterprise* (per401 in the CMP dataset); *Protectionism: Negative* (per407); *Protectionism: Positive* (per406); *Controlled Economy* (per412); *Nationalisation* (per413) (See Appendix A.1, Klingeman et al., 2006). From these elements we construct a composite representing support for free-market internationalism in the net: *net free-market internationalism=(per401+per407)-(per406+per412+per413).* We then multiply the party-year scores by the percentage of votes gleaned in the relevant election, to generate each polity's support for net free-market internationalism per country-year. Since elections are not held yearly, we construct a 5-year moving average for each country-year to ensure that every country is in the estimates of yearly-varying voter positions. The final step is to calculate the average for the whole international system by taking the un-weighted average for all 25 countries per year. This gives us the average international support for net free-market internationalism. Fig. 2 shows how this measure of voter support is quite volatile across years, but tends in general to rise – broadly in line with rising levels of financial openness in the net.[10]

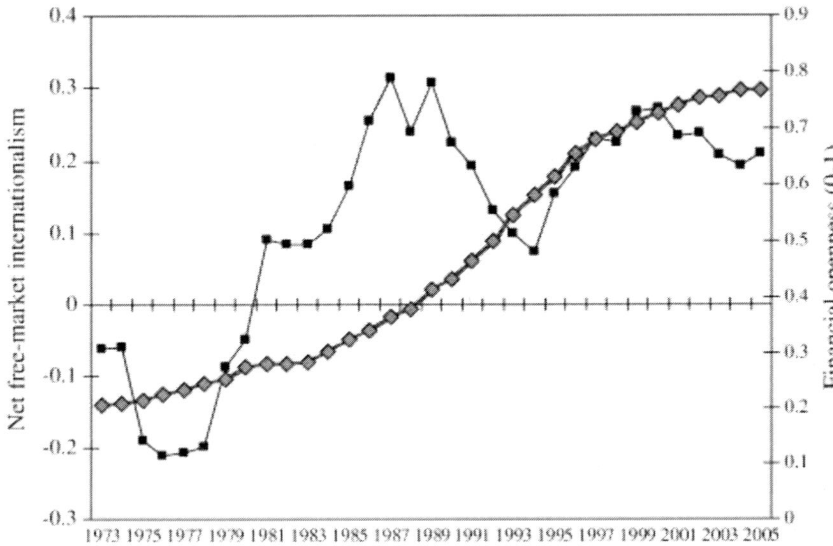

Figure 2. *Net free-market internationalism* of voters, and Financial openness.

Sources: Comparative Manifestos Project dataset (own calculations); Abiad and Mody, 2005 and Abiad et al., 2008 (own calculations).

We also considered a range of alternative measures of support or opposition to free markets and/or internationalism using the same technique applied to other elements of the CMP dataset. These include: each of the above components separately; support and opposition to international organizations and internationalism, without making explicit reference to political-economic openness (per108-per109); support for Marxist ideology (per404); and support for post-communist parties. And we also considered alternative measures of international support for or opposition to free-market internationalism, including use of raw scores of party proportions on these issues; or weighting the scores by share of parliamentary seats rather than votes.

Although the results are virtually identical regardless of the particular measure one uses, columns (6) through (8) in Table 1 show the results for *net free-market internationalism.* Columns (6) and (7) show how this measure of international voter support for free-market internationalism – measured first in the net (as specified above) and as absolute support for free enterprise and free trade (per401+per407) – correlates significantly positively with changes in financial openness. Significantly, we can also see in both specifications that the presence of these external voter sentiments tends to reduce the influence of the catch-up dynamic emphasized in the Abiad and Mody study. But column (8) in any event shows that the international voter support for free-market internationalism also interacts significantly with this catch-up dynamic: at low levels of prevailing support for free-market internationalism, countries that lag far behind the regional leader in financial openness are not likely to be significantly spurred to pursue financial liberalization; but at high levels of such internationalism, the urge to catch up becomes significantly more positive.

Substantively, in any event, the effects of international voter embrace of free-market internationalism are actually quite modest. If we consider the model in column (6), and counterfactually predict the change in chance of liberalization as we move from the 25th to the 90th percentile in the sample-distribution's variation in *net free-market internationalism* (from a score of – 2.66 to 33.6), we see a decrease in the chance that a country reverses course on financial openness by 1.4 percentage points (from .033 to .018 probability of reversal), and a decrease by 7.5 percentage points in the chance of no liberalization (from .82 to .745 probability), and an increase of 8.5 percentage points in the chance of liberalization (from a probability of .16 to a probability of .24). All these effects, however, are significant at a .05 level throughout the sample distribution. And they are robust not only to alternative estimators discussed below, but also to the exclusion of the US interest-rate dummy (another yearly-varying variable) and to use of other measures of support or opposition to free market internationalism.

5. OUTPUT-LEGITIMACY AND FINANCIAL LIBERALIZATION: DOMESTIC AND INTERNATIONAL COMPENSATION

In addition to such a range of domestic and international sinews of input legitimacy, we can also explore domestic and international sinews of output legitimacy. Among the many possibilities are those relevant to providing compensation for or mitigation of distributional costs and risks of economic openness generally and financial liberalization in particular. Such involves extension of the quite-established view that the provision of some kinds of policy compensation can help foster support for international economic openness (Polanyi, 1944, Ruggie, 1983, Rodrik, 1997 and Bretschgera and Hettichb, 2002). In studies of international trade openness this has been most fully investigated in the context mainly of public opinion surveys, but also some work on party manifestos (Hays et al., 2005, Burgoon, 2009 and Mayda et al., 2007). But there is also some qualitative work to support the claim with respect to financial economic openness(e.g. Bordo et al., 1999). Our final set of thoughts on the politics of financial liberalization considers how and whether both national and international sources of such compensation make a difference to financial openness. Table 2 summarizes the results.

Table 2. Output legitimacy and financial liberalization.

	(1)	(2)	(3)	(4)	(5)	(6)	(7)	(8)
Government consumption $_{it-1}$	0.010							
	(0.043)							
Social security transfers $_{it-1}$		11.185						
		(9.203)						
Health expenditures $_{it-1}$			50.045***					
			(13.841)					
Total social transfers $_{it-1}$				26.554**				
				(12.274)				
Bilateral aid received $_{it-1}$					2.971*			
					(1.588)			
Multilateral aid received $_{it-1}$						3.140**		5.504***
						(1.311)		(1.531)
Total aid received $_{it-1}$							2.612***	
							(0.844)	
MultiLaid$_{it-1}$ * Catch-up$_{it}$								−4.150
								(3.544)
MultiLaid$_{it-1}$ * FL$_{it-1}$								−1.635
								(3.060)
Leftist Government$_{it}$	−0.085	−0.146	−0.257	−0.343	−0.298	−0.220	−0.288	−0.229
	(0.368)	(0.471)	(0.484)	(0.520)	(0.447)	(0.450)	(0.448)	(0.450)
Rightist Government$_{it}$	−0.079	0.154	0.172	0.092	−0.098	−0.018	−0.057	−0.015
	(0.360)	(0.453)	(0.433)	(0.477)	(0.426)	(0.428)	(0.428)	(0.430)
Financial openness (FL$_{it-1}$)	6.601***	8.094***	8.527***	8.623***	5.598***	5.374***	5.007***	5.245***
	(1.575)	(2.336)	(2.459)	(2.407)	(1.973)	(1.864)	(1.907)	(2.019)
Financial openness sq. ((FL$_{it-1}$)^2)	−9.720***	−9.636***	−9.904***	−9.748***	−7.970***	−7.699***	−7.838***	−7.600***
	(2.593)	(2.907)	(3.011)	(2.902)	(2.640)	(2.629)	(2.665)	(2.628)
FL$_{it-1}$ * Y$_{it-1}$	0.000**	0.000	0.000	0.000	0.000**	0.000**	0.000**	0.000**
	(0.000)	(0.000)	(0.000)	(0.000)	(0.000)	(0.000)	(0.000)	(0.000)
Catch-up (Reg.lead FL$_{it-1}$ - FL$_{it-1}$)	2.063*	2.853*	3.076*	2.956**	3.426**	3.343**	3.035**	3.424**
	(1.234)	(1.512)	(1.583)	(1.477)	(1.427)	(1.388)	(1.389)	(1.413)
Currency Crisis$_{it}$	0.447*	0.517	0.406	0.451	0.297	0.364	0.346	0.382
	(0.231)	(0.319)	(0.331)	(0.326)	(0.276)	(0.283)	(0.276)	(0.287)
Banking Crisis$_{it}$	−1.017***	−0.950**	−1.051***	−1.096***	−0.991**	−0.976**	−1.000**	−0.979**
	(0.346)	(0.389)	(0.371)	(0.360)	(0.402)	(0.414)	(0.411)	(0.412)
Recession$_{it}$	−0.022	0.517	0.499	0.532	0.310	0.300	0.327	0.294
	(0.362)	(0.376)	(0.352)	(0.360)	(0.414)	(0.417)	(0.417)	(0.419)
High Inflation$_{it}$	−0.450	−1.115	−1.234	−1.134	−0.925	−0.940	−0.829	−0.953
	(0.599)	(0.727)	(0.819)	(0.765)	(0.904)	(0.903)	(0.915)	(0.906)
First Year in Office$_{it}$	0.254	0.068	0.066	0.049	0.287	0.302	0.273	0.289
	(0.269)	(0.328)	(0.328)	(0.324)	(0.331)	(0.332)	(0.331)	(0.334)
IMF program$_{it}$	0.362	0.033	0.051	0.011	0.339	0.346	0.296	0.353
	(0.272)	(0.302)	(0.301)	(0.304)	(0.311)	(0.305)	(0.315)	(0.306)
US Interest Rate$_t$	−0.089**	−0.068	−0.052	−0.059	−0.108**	−0.104**	−0.107**	−0.100*
	(0.044)	(0.045)	(0.049)	(0.047)	(0.053)	(0.052)	(0.052)	(0.052)
Open$_{it-1}$	0.010	0.006	0.009	0.004	0.021*	0.021*	0.021*	0.021*
	(0.010)	(0.013)	(0.012)	(0.014)	(0.011)	(0.012)	(0.011)	(0.012)
Fixed effects	Yes	Yes	Yes	Yes	Yes	Yes	Yes	Yes
Year dummies	No	No	No	No	No	No	No	No
Observations	805	575	575	575	626	626	626	626
Wald χ^2	9.3e+06	1.4e+06	9.3e+06	6.5e+05	6.2e+05	2.1e+06	1.5e+06	1.6e+06
Log likelihood	−730.1	−517.0	−511.7	−513.3	−520.1	−520.3	−518.8	−520.1

Notes: The dependent variable is the change in the Financial Liberalization Index. Robust standard errors are in parentheses, adjusted for clustering by country. Fixed effects for 35 countries not shown but highly jointly significant.
*** denotes significance at the 1-percent level; ** denotes significance at the 5-percent level; * denotes significance at the 10-percent level.

5.1. Domestic social policy compensation

Columns (1) through (4) consider the role of various measures of domestic government spending on financial liberalization. Although some have argued that all faces of the public economy are relevant to addressing the individual-economic social risks of economic openness, others have emphasized how not all faces of government spending are equally relevant to such risks (Rodrik, 1997 and Burgoon, 2001). The four estimations consider these possibilities by focusing on four measures of government spending, more or less targeted at particular issues relevant to the risks of openness. All are measured as spending as a share of national GDP, and all are lagged by one year to address the time it takes for polities to respond to the potential insurance-effects of such "compensation" and to address possible endogeneity.

Column (1) focuses on government consumption, a measure that has the best coverage, but excludes the many social transfer programs clearly relevant to the risks of openness (PWT 6.2). Perhaps this is why the effect is insignificant, though positively signed as expected. A somewhat better measure is total government spending or revenue, which includes such transfers, but also includes many other government spending programs many of which are irrelevant to – or perhaps even likely to undermine – support for financial liberalization (Kugler et al., 2002).[11] Although the results are not shown, this measure also yields positive but statistically insignificant results.

Columns (2) through (4) consider measures of the spending that come somewhat closer to the social policies often thought relevant to social risks of openness. Unfortunately, measures of social policy with reasonable coverage of the country-years in the Abiad and Mody dataset are hard to find, and we can only unearth quality measures for social security transfers and for public health expenditures. The former might be expected to have direct relevance for risks of economic openness, but in developing countries such transfers are often heavily skewed to public pension programs and targeted at employees in the formal, public economy. As such, they often do little to indemnify more generally vulnerable workers in more exposed sectors from the risks of financial or other kinds of economic openness. Column (2) shows the effect of such transfers, and following expectation we can see that the effects are positive but statistically insignificant.

Health spending, on the other hand, has often been providing stronger and more evenly dispersed benefits for workers in both developing countries, but also developed countries (as the current debate in the US lays bare). Higher public spending on such health, hence, might have a more meaningful compensatory effect for workers facing the vagaries of open financial markets. Columns (3) shows that measures including such health expenditures do, indeed, significantly increase the chances of financial liberalization. And column (4) shows that the positive effect of combined spending on health and social security transfers tends also to statistically significantly increase financial liberalization. The substantive effects of such spending, based on the model in column (3), appear to be rather substantial. Moving from the 25th to the 75th percentile in the sample distribution of health spending – the equivalent of moving from a setting where a country spends .71 percent of GDP on health benefits to one where it spends 2.54% of GDP on such benefits – decreases the chance that a country will undergo a reversal of financial openness by 3 percentage points (probability of .053 to .024), and also decreases the chance by 8.6 percentage points of there being no change in such openness. And such an increase in health spending predicts an increase of 11.5 percentage points in the chance that a government liberalizes (probability .103 to .218).

5.2. Foreign aid received

Columns (5) through (8), finally, suggest that the role of compensation in increasing the output legitimacy of financial liberalization may extend not only to some domestic social spending, but also to the levels of aid assistance that a country might receive from international sources. Such aid may come with strings attached that might be relevant to financial openness regardless of their substantive, compensatory effects: if aid is made conditional upon economic changes such as financial market opening, then we would expect the effect of aid to positive. But it is also plausible that international aid of various kinds, whether or not it comes with conditionality, may well play some compensatory role, as it were substituting for the shortcomings of domestic social policy compensation in less developed countries. Both bilateral initiatives of many Northern economies, particularly European countries, and multilateral-aid initiatives channeled through the European Union or World Bank auspices, have explicitly focused on a range of programs that provide direct (health programs) and indirect (infrastructure programs) social insurance role for those facing risks of economic openness. If so, one might hypothesize that, net of conditionality conditions, external compensation might also increase chances of financial liberalization.

Columns (5) through (7) show that due either to the compensatory or other roles such aid might entail, higher levels of bilateral aid (Column 5), multilateral aid (Column 6), and combined-multilateral-bilateral aid (Column 7) tend to significantly increase financial liberalization. All three measures are expressed as shares of GDP, and all are lagged by one year to try to address possible endogeneity and (even harder to address) the possibility of conditionality (OECD-DAC, 2011). As can be seen from the coefficients, all three have a positive, modestly statistically-significant effect on changes in financial openness. And as can be seen by the coefficients, which can be directly compared because they are in the same units, this effect is strongest for multilateral aid. Substantively, however, the effects are quite modest. Moving from the sample's 50th to the 90th percentile in multilateral aid received – equivalent of moving from a level of aid at .07 percent of GDP to a level of 12.6 percent of GDP – decreases the chance of reversal by .8 percentage points (from .025 to .017 probability) and of no change by 4.5 percentage points (from .84 to .796 probability), and increases the chance of liberalization by 5.3 percentage points (.135 probability to .188 probability of liberalization).

Interestingly, such positive effects of foreign aid received for liberalization appear not to be mediated by varying levels of *ex ante* financial openness or of catch-up dynamics (degree to which a country lags-behind lead-liberalizer of its region). As was also clear from the previous columns in Table 2, foreign aid also does not tend to have effects at the expense of the general catch-up effect, suggesting simply that this aspect of foreign influence might matter more than the spatial effects of lagging-behind regional leaders. But as Column (8) shows, foreign aid received does not significantly interact either the catch-up parameter or with *ex ante* liberalization. Higher aid levels do tend to diminish rather than increase the catch-up dynamic, though not significantly. And the interaction with lagged financial openness is virtually null. What this all suggests is that foreign aid may well be a significant force in spurring liberalization, though not in ways sensitive to either existing openness or other regional influences.

6. ROBUSTNESS AND SENSITIVITY CHECKS

To consider whether the results summarized in Table 1 and Table 2 are artifacts of method and measurement, we conducted a range of robustness and sensitivity checks. Table 3 summarizes the results of what we consider to be the most important of these checks. Each of the six columns summarizes the results of a particular estimation approach, focusing on how a number of the key measures of input and output legitimacy affect financial liberalization as modeled using that approach. Within any given estimation approach (for each column), we report key results from six different regressions (all based on the benchmark model from Table 1 and Table 2 denoted in the first column). The included controls and measures of all key right-hand-side variables are the same as in Table 1 and Table 2, though these are not shown to conserve space. The full results (twelve tables, reflecting six alternative specifications of Table 1 and Table 2) are available in Supplemental

7. CONCLUSION

This article has sought to clarify how domestic and international political factors linked to input and output legitimacy of economic globalization help explain financial liberalization across countries and time. The motivation to do so has been dissatisfaction with findings suggesting that such liberalization has little to do with standard political variables. The main findings of our own investigation of their dataset are that both domestic and international sources of both input and output legitimacy of financial liberalization appear to matter significantly to the short-term decisions of polities to change financial openness. First, we find that shifts to left partisanship, and the interaction of left partisanship and democracy, are important domestic sources of input legitimacy, while international voter support for free-market internationalism, as opposed to anti-capitalist closure, are important international sources of input legitimacy. Second, we find that some targeted social policies – and not spending generally – constitute provisions of compensation that may be important domestic sources of output legitimacy that serve to sustain financial openness. And multilateral and bilateral aid might not only spur liberalization through the conditionality sometimes attached to such aid, but may also serve a compensatory role that constitute important international sources of output legitimacy again supporting financial openness.

These findings provide a partial corrective to apolitical explanations of financial liberalization. Our message, in this sense, is simply that politics matter more and differently than this interpretation would have us believe. However, the ongoing debate on the reform of the financial system reminds us that these findings may also be seen as more significant in terms of our understanding of the underlying political economy of financial liberalization if the benefits of the latter are to be preserved in a politically sustainable fashion. Our study into input and output legitimacy as a framework through which to understand such politics is at the least a reminder of a larger research agenda into the politics of globalization than the present study allows. We believe it important to consider the complex power-political interaction of a wide range of state and market actors in both formal and private fights on issues of economic governance – well beyond the kinds left-right partisan conditions discussed above. We also believe that features of democratic involvement or subjective support for more or less open markets are crucial to input legitimacy and go well beyond measures of broad democracy and international voter attitudes discussed above. More obviously, the sources of output legitimacy are much more complicated than the simple role of compensatory social and aid provisions highlighted above – involving the gamut of policies and non-hard law practices that might diminish the distributional costs and system risks of open markets. These policies and practices are particularly key if, post-crisis, we consider the long-term stability of openness and not just the short-term embrace the present paper has investigated. All such politics, relevant to both the short and long-term, both domestic and international aspects of input and output legitimacy, cannot be lightly dismissed as shaping the global economy. These findings have implications for how financial openness might be dealt with in the aftermath of the 2007–9 financial crisis.

ACKNOWLEDGEMENTS

The authors gratefully acknowledge the funding support of the World Economy and Finance Research programme of the Economic and Social Research Council of the United Kingdom ('National and International Aspects of Financial Development', grant no. RES-156-25-0009), and also funding support under the European Commission's 7th Framework Research Programme, Theme Socio-economic sciences and humanities ('Politics, Economics and Global Governance: The European Dimensions' (PEGGED), Grant Agreement no. 217559). The authors are also indebted to a number of colleagues who provided support and challenging commentary on earlier versions of the manuscript. The regular seminars organized in the context of the ESRC project named above, especially the Amsterdam seminar in October 2007 and Cyprus in May 2008, were invaluable in this regard and we thank all participants who contributed so constructively to the discussion. In particular we wish to thank Stijn Claessens and Badi Baltagi in this regard. Our thanks are also due for comments from Henry Laurence as discussant on our panel at the September 2009 meetings of the American Political Science Association in Montreal. Of course our colleagues cannot be held responsible for shortcomings and the authors accept full responsibility for any remaining weaknesses.

REFERENCES

1. Abiad, A., Mody, A., 2005. Financial reform: what shakes it? what shapes it? The American Economic Review 95 (1), 66–88.
2. Abiad, A., Detragiache, E., Tressel, T., 2008. A new database of financial reforms. IMF Working Paper. WP/08/266.
3. Arestis, P., Demetriades, P., 1999. Financial liberalization: the experience of developing countries. Eastern Economic Journal 25/4, 441–457.
4. Bennett, D.S., Stam, A., 2008. EUGene version 3.202 [Computer Software]. http://www.eugenesoftware.org/2008.
5. Bergh, A., Nilsson, T., 2010. Do liberalization and globalization increase income inequality? European Journal of Political Economy 26 (4), 488–505.
6. Bhagwati, J., 1998. The capital myth: the difference between trade in widgets and dollars. Foreign Affairs 77 (3), 7–15.
7. Bordo, M., Eichengreen, B., Irwin, D., 1999. Is globalization today really different than lobalization a hundred years ago? NBER Working Paper. W7195.

8. Bretschgera, L., Hettichb, F., 2002. Globalisation, capital mobility and tax competition: theory and evidence for OECD countries. European Journal of Political Economy 18 (4), 695–716.

9. Burgoon, B., 2001. Globalization and welfare compensation: disentangling the ties that bind. International Organization 55 (3), 509–553.

10. Burgoon, B., 2009. Globalization and backlash: Polanyi's revenge? Review of International Political Economy 16 (2), 145–177.

11. Coleman, W.D., 1996. Financial Services, Globalisation, and Domestic Policy Change: a comparative study of North America and the European Union. Macmillan Press, London.

12. Cukierman, A., Tommasi, M., 1998. Credibility of policymakers and of economic reforms. In: Sturzenegger, F., Tommasi, M. (Eds.), The Political Economy of Reform. MIT Press, Cambridge MA, pp. 329–347.

13. Franzese, R., Hays, J., 2006. Strategic interaction among eu governments in active labor market policy-making. European Union Politics 7 (2), 167–189.

14. Garrett, G., 2001. The causes of globalization. Comparative Political Studies 33 (6/7), 941–991.

15. Haggard, S., Webb, S., 1993. What do we know about the political economy of economic policy reform? World Bank Research Observer 8 (2), 143–168.

16. Hays, J., Ehrlich, S., Peinhardt, C., 2005. Government spending and public support for trade in the OECD. International Organization 59 (2), 473–494.

17. Held, D., 1997. Democracy and globalization. Global Governance 3 (3), 251–267.

18. Helleiner, E., 1994. States and the Reemergence of Global Finance: From Bretton Woods to the 1990s. Cornell University Press,

19. Ithaca NY. Heston, A., Summers, R., Aten, B., 2006. PWT 6.2. Penn World Table Version 6.2, Center for International Comparisons of Production, Income and Prices.

20. University of Pennsylvania. Huang, Y., 2009. The political economy of financial reform; are Abiad and Mody right? Journal of Applied Econometrics 24 (7), 1207–1213.

21. Klingeman, H.-D., Volkens, A., Bara, J., Budge, I., McDonald, M., 2006. Mapping Policy Preferences II: Estimates for Parties, Electors and

Governments in Eastern Europe, European Union and OECD 1945–2003. Oxford University Press,

22. Oxford. Krueger, A.O., 1993. Political Economy of Policy Reform in Developing Countries. MIT Press, Cambridge, MA. Kugler, Jacek, Feng, Yi, Zak, Paul J., 2002. Politics of fertility and economic development (POFED). NSF GRANT (No.: SBR-9730474) 1998–2001.

23. Lai, Y.-B., 2010. The political economy of capital market integration and tax competition. European Journal of Political Economy 26 (4), 475–487.

24. Laurence, H., 2001. Money Rules: The New Politics of Finance in Britain and Japan. Cornell University Press, Ithaca, NY. Mayda, A., O'Rourke, K., Sinnott, R., 2007. Risk, government and globalization: international survey evidence. IIIS Discussion Paper No.218.

25. Moran, M., 1990. The Politics of the Financial Services Revolution. Macmillan Press, London. Organization of Economic Cooperation and Development (Development Assistance Committee) database, . Accessed 6.5.2011 http://www.oecd.org/document/ 33/0,2340,en_ 2649_34447_36661793_1_1_1_1,00.html.

26. Polanyi, K., 1944. The Great Transformation: The Political and Economic Origins of Our Time. Beacon Press, Boston.

27. Porter, T., 2001. The democratic deficit in the institutional arrangements for regulating global finance. Global Governance 7, 427–439.

28. Prasad, E., Rajan, R., Subramanian, A., 2007. The paradox of capital. Finance and Development 44, 16–19.

29. Quinn, D., Inclan, C., 1997. the origins of financial openness: a study of current and capital account liberalization. American Journal of Political Science 41 (3), 771–813.

30. Quinn, D., Toyoda, A.M., 2007. Ideology and voter preferences as determinants of financial globalization. American Journal of Political Research 51 (2), 344–363.

31. Rodrik, D., 1997. Has Globalization Gone Too Far? Institute for International Economics, Washington, D.C.

32. Ruggie, J.G., 1983. International regimes, transactions, and change: embedded liberalism in the postwar economic order. International Organization 36 (2), 379–415.

33. Scharpf, F.W., 1999. Governing in Europe: effective and democratic? Oxford University Press, Oxford, UK.

34. Simmons, B.A., Elkins, Z., 2004. The globalization of liberalization: policy diffusion in the international political economy. American Political Science Review 98 (1), 171–189.

35. Sobel, A., 1994. Domestic Choices, International Markets: dismantling National Barriers and Liberalizing Securities Markets. University of Michigan Press, Ann Arbor, MI.

36. Underhill, G., Zhang, X. (Eds.), 2003. International Financial Governance Under Stress. Cambridge University Press, Cambridge, UK.

37. World Bank, 2001. Database of political institutions, version 3. World Bank, Washington, DC.

7

GORDON TULLOCK: ECONOMIC GADFLY

Dennis C. Mueller

University of Vienna, Vienna, Austria

ABSTRACT

This article discusses Gordon Tullock's impact on the economics profession and on public choice in particular. It measures this impact through his publications, his editorship of the journal *Public Choice*, and his association with the Center for Public Choice.

Keywords: Public choice, Rent seeking

Gordon Tullock may have been the brightest person I ever met. I say "*may* have," because some brilliant people can also be quite reticent, so that their brilliance does not immediately shine forth. This certainly was not the case with Gordon Tullock. Upon first meeting a young Gordon Tullock, one would immediately be peppered with a stream of questions testing one's economic knowledge. If one succeeded in disposing of one question, Tullock moved quickly on to another. There seemed to be no topic in economics, and many topics outside of economics, on which he could not hold forth. To engage him in conversation over lunch was to participate in an intellectual roller coaster. As Gordon Tullock aged, he began to slow down a bit and became less combative. In his prime, however, the quickness of his mind was both readily apparent and a bit overwhelming.

One of the definitions of gadfly in my *American Heritage Dictionary* reads (1967), "One who acts as a constructively provocative stimulus." "Provocative stimulus" is an apt characterization of Gordon Tullock, although one might argue that his stimuli were not always very constructive. I was asked to write about Tullock's "impulse to the field." In thinking about this topic, it occurred to me that Tullock's impulses were often not direct consequences of the logical arguments in one of his publications, but were a result of the provocative stimuli coming forth from him both through direct contact and on the printed page. This explains my choice for a title of this essay. It also explains why I do not exclusively focus on the impact of his research on the profession. The next section does, however, deal with this topic. The essay goes on the discuss Tullock's impacts via the Center for the Study of Public Choice (Sect. 2), the *Public Choice* journal (Sect. 3). Some final thoughts bring the essay to a conclusion.

1 THE IMPACT OF TULLOCK'S PUBLICATIONS

How does one measure the influence of a scholar on the profession, and more generally on the evolution of ideas in the areas of the scholar's interests? This question is particularly difficult to answer in the case of Gordon Tullock, since he wrote on such a wide variety of topics. Trained in law, he has many publications in this field. His *Trials on Trial* (1980a) won the first Leslie T. Wilkins Award from the Criminal Justice and Research Center in 1982, as an outstanding contribution to the fields of criminology and criminal justice. In 1992, he was awarded an Honorary Doctorate of Law by the University of Chicago. His impact on the fields of law and criminology appears to have been significant, but I am not knowledgeable enough in these areas to say very much. He became interested in social biology, and has several publications on this topic. Even his work in economics spans a broad spectrum—his first publication was a *Journal of Political Economy* article on hyperinflation in China (Campbell and Tullock 1954). His most significant contributions have been in the field of public choice, and here again the range of topics is wide—voting rules, representative government, federalism, bureaucracy, revolution—to name but a few of the most important areas in which Tullock worked. One can also list him as an important figure in political science. In 1996, he was elected a Member of the *American Political Science Review* Hall of Fame.

The sheer volume of Gordon Tullock's publications is astounding—20 some books and monographs authored or coauthored, 15 books edited or co-edited. The section of his *curriculum vitae* devoted to articles published in journals runs to 25 pages. Many of these articles were selected for republication by editors of collected volumes. Here again one must remark not only on the *length* of Tullock's publication list, but also on its breadth. Durden et al. (1991, pp. 192–93) list 125 scientific journals, which cited Tullock's publications as reported in the Social Science Citation Index as of 1991, and report that another 308 journals have at least one citation of his work. They identify 55.4 % of Tullock's research falling into the general area of economics, 11.3 % in law, 10 % in political science, 2.1 % in business and finance, and an astounding 21.2 % falling in still other fields like social biology.

Tullock's first major contribution to the public choice literature, "Problems of Majority Voting," (1959), for example, was republished four times, including in the prestigious American Economics Association volume edited by Kenneth Arrow and Tibor Scitovsky (1969), *Readings in Welfare Economics*. "The Welfare Costs of Tariffs, Monopolies and Theft" (Tullock 1967c) was republished five times including in one volume in which Tullock was a co-editor. These re-publications in volumes edited by a large number of different scholars, some highly distinguished, is certainly one form of recognition by the profession.

Another way to judge the impact of a scholar on the field is to see how often her or his research is cited by other scholars. Accessing Google Scholar on March 3, 2015, I found 19,200 entries under the name of Gordon Tullock. The 15 publications (not including edited volumes) cited the most were as follows[1]:

1. *The Calculus of Consent* (1962) hardback and paperback editions, written with James M. Buchanan, 9345 citations.
2. "The Welfare Costs of Tariffs, Monopolies and Theft" (Tullock 1967c), reprinted four times in volumes edited by others, 3411 citations.
3. "Efficient Rent Seeking" (Tullock 1980b), 2469 citations.
4. "An Empirical Analysis of Cross-National Economic Growth" (1989), written with Kevin B. Grier, 1163 citations.
5. *The Politics of Bureaucracy* (Tullock 1965), 1556 citations.

6. "Polluters' Profits and Political Response: Direct Controls Versus Taxes," (1975), written with James M. Buchanan, reprinted once, 812 citations.
7. *Toward a Mathematics of Politics* (Tullock 1967a), 727 citations.
8. "Problems of Majority Voting," (Tullock 1959), 503 citations.
9. "The Paradox of Revolution," (Tullock 1971), reprinted once, 425 citations.
10. *Autocracy* (Tullock 1987), 416 citations.
11. "A New and Superior Process for Making Social Choices," (1976), written with T. Niclaus Tideman, reprinted three times, 373 citations.
12. *The Economics of Special Privilege and Rent Seeking* (Tullock 1989), 372 citations.
13. "Why So Much Stability?" (Tullock 1981), reprinted twice, 358 citations.
14. *The Vote Motive* (Tullock 1976), 341 citations.
15. *Rent Seeking* (Tullock 1993), 327 citations.

In total, I counted almost 50 publications with a hundred or more citations. I find this a fairly impressive record. Many articles, even in prestigious journals, receive only a handful of citations. Some appear to have been read only by the journal's referees. Tullock's work has clearly attracted considerable attention from other scholars.

So I conclude that Gordon Tullock's impact on the profession, or better said the *professions* given his broad range of research topics, has been immense. Let me now play the role of curmudgeon and say that his impact could have been still greater had he devoted a bit more time formulating some of his ideas. One has the impression sometimes that he wrote as fast as he talked resulting in some of his publications failing to attract the attention that they might have.

Evidence in support of this assertion might be found by comparing Tullock's success with that of a few of the other founding fathers of public choice. Where Tullock wrote quickly and published an immense body of research, Mancur Olson's reputation rests on two or three books and a handful of seminal articles. Olson took great care in crafting his arguments, and thus his second major work, *The Rise and Decline of Nations,* appeared 17 years after his first major publication, *The Logic of Collective Action* (Olson 1965, 1982). Google Scholar reports 30,400 results for Olson. *The Logic* registered 28,785 citations, *The Rise and Decline of Nations* 8595, about the same number as *The Calculus of Consent.* Anthony Downs recorded 74,000 results in Google Scholar. His classic, *An Economic Theory of Democracy,* had 22,726 citations (Downs 1957). I would also list Kenneth Arrow as one of the founding fathers of public choice. His *Social Choice and Individual Values* had 14,888 citations (Arrow 1951, 1963). Interestingly, three of these classics—Olson's *Logic of Collective Action* and the books by Downs and Arrow—were their doctoral dissertations, works upon which each author presumably devoted a lot of time and effort.

Further support for the point I am making arises when one looks at the history of Tullock's most cited work after *The Calculus*—"The Welfare Costs of Tariffs, Monopolies and Theft" (Tullock 1967c). The significance of this piece did not occur to me, however, until I read Anne Krueger's (1974) *American Economic Review* article in 1974, where the term "rent seeking" first appears. As I read Krueger's article, I had a sense of *deja vu* and then it dawned on me that I had seen Krueger's rent-seeking analysis in Tullock's 1967 article. As noted above, Tullock's original rent-seeking paper received 3411 citations. Krueger's *AER* article, on the other hand, was cited 5864 times. In the 100 pages of citations to Tullock's "The Welfare Costs of Tariffs, Monopolies and Theft" in Google Scholar, I was able to identify only five that preceded 1974. It appears that most of the profession, like I, did not appreciate the importance of Tullock's contribution until *after* they read Krueger's article. One explanation for this is probably that the article first appeared in the *Western Economic Journal* (now *Economic Inquiry*), not regarded as a top journal in 1967. Brady and Tollison (1991, p. 145) mention that the article was rejected by the *American Economic Review, Economica,* and the *Southern Economic Journal* before being accepted at the *Western Economic Journal.* Tullock (2003, p. 5) stated that it was also rejected by the *Journal of Political Economy.* John Gurley, editor of the *American Economic Review* in 1966, gave this explanation for his decision, "You will no doubt note that the referee neglects your point regarding the amount of real resources devoted to establishing, promoting, destroying, etc., monopolies. However, I have noted it, and, while I think it is certainly valid, it does not appear significant enough (as a theoretical contribution) to overthrow the referee's recommendation" (Brady and Tollison 1991, p. 146). The referee misses the rent-seeking argument entirely, the editor recognizes it, but fails to see its importance. Another example of an obtuse referee and a callous journal editor, perhaps, but one might also argue that the paper might have enjoyed a better fate, if Tullock had taken a bit more care in crafting the arguments. How many additional citations would "The Welfare Costs of Tariffs, Monopolies and Theft" have received, if it had first appeared in the *American Economic Review*?

Another instance of Tullock's work having less impact than it should have had is the fate of his "The General Irrelevance of the General Impossibility Theorem," (Tullock 1967b). This paper demonstrated with a tortuous application of geometry that the area of the issue space in which cycling would occur shrinks as the number of voters increases. Arrow's celebrated impossibility result sinks into irrelevance as the size of the electorate expands. Tullock delivered the coup de grace to one of the most important contributions to the literature. Despite being published in one of the most prestigious economic journals, *The Quarterly Journal of Economics,* and despite its provocative title, the article did not spell the end to the literature devoted to the Arrow cycling problem. It records a respectable 227 citations in Google Scholar, but it is difficult to say that it changed the trajectory of the public choice literature. It is also worth noting that it anticipated the discovery of the uncovered set more than a decade later.[2]

Let me conclude this discussion of the impact of Tullock's published research by repeating that its impact was significant. If I am correct, however, its impact could have been even greater had Tullock devoted a little more time and care to expressing his arguments.

2 THE CENTER FOR THE STUDY OF PUBLIC CHOICE

In the 1960s, James Buchanan and Gordon Tullock were at the Thomas Jefferson Center for Political Economy at the University of Virginia. They both exited from the University of Virginia at the end of the 1960s and soon regrouped at the Virginia Polytechnic Institute and State University (VPI) in Blacksburg, Virginia. There they founded The Center for the Study of Public Choice. The Center occupied a charming old mansion on a hill in the center of the VPI campus.

In 1985 James Buchanan started an annual lecture series to which people from around the Washington area were invited and treated to a hopefully interesting lecture, cocktails, and a banquet. I was asked to give the first lecture and entitled it "The Virginia School," picking up a name Mancur Olson coined to describe the work of Buchanan, Tullock, and their followers (Mueller 1993). In it I made the point that it is important for the spreading of the ideas of a particular school—the Chicago school, the Cambridge (England) school—for the leaders of the school of thought to be located at a particular location, so that scholars interested in learning about their ideas can visit them. That is why, I argued, it was legitimate to talk about Chicago and Cambridge schools of thought, but not a Marxist school, since there was no place at which a distinguished group of Marxist scholars was gathered.

The existence of the Center for the Study of Public Choice made it legitimate to think of there being a "Virginia School" of thought. The Center soon became a Mecca for scholars interested in the fairly young field of public choice. Its list of visitors is both long and contains many prominent scholars, or at least people who would later become prominent scholars. For example, during the spring of 1973, when I was a post-doctoral fellow at the center, the Nobel Prize winner James Meade and his wife visited for 3 months.

Three other early visitors from Europe were Elisabeth Liefmann-Keil, Bruno Frey, and Peter Bernholz. They soon founded the European Public Choice Society. Elisabeth Liefmann-Keil was the society's first president, 1972–74, and she was followed as president by Peter Bernholz, 1974–81. As with its American counterpart, the European Public Choice Society began with meetings of no more than 20 or so participants. Today it is a thriving society with annual meetings attracting 350 or more participants—more than its American counterpart is able to attract at this time. A somewhat similar story explains the creation of the Japanese Public Choice Society by Professor Hiroshi Kato following a visit to the Public Choice Center in Blacksburg.[3]

With the help of Geoffrey Brennan, Roger Congleton and Robert Tollison, I have tried to put together a list of important visitors to the Center in both Blacksburg and Fairfax, to which the Center moved in the early 1980s. By visitor to the Center I mean someone who spent a period of time in residence there, not someone who only came and held a seminar and then immediately departed. The list is undoubtedly incomplete and I apologize to those persons I have omitted. It is nevertheless rather long and impressive (see Table 1).

The sheer number of visitors to the Public Choice Center over the years is astounding. Also noteworthy is the fact that an overwhelming majority of the visitors came from outside of the United States. They also possessed a diversity of professional interests—economics, philosophy, political science, sociology, sociobiology, and of course, public choice. This diversity made the Public Choice Center a very interesting, indeed exciting, place to visit.

Of course, all of these visitors did not come to the Public Choice Center simply because Gordon Tullock was there. In addition to Buchanan and Tullock, the Center has always contained several additional members, both senior and junior, working in public choice. Some of these, like Geoffrey Brennan, Roger Congleton and Robert Tollison, have become distinguished scholars in their own rights. But, particularly at its beginning, the incentive to visit the Public Choice Center would have mostly been to rub elbows with Buchanan and Tullock.

Table 1. Visitors to The Center for the Study of Public Choice

1. Kuniomi Akagi	71. Samuel Hollander	141. Werner Pommerehne
2. Coskun Can Aktan	72. James L. Hudson	142. David A. Reese
3. Hans Albert	73. Robert Hughes	143. David Reisman
4. Max Albert	74. Brooks Hull	144. Pill-Woo Rhee
5. Robert Albon	75. Lester Hunt	145. Rudolf Richter
6. Gary Anderson	76. William J. Hunter	146. Il-Seop Rim
7. Bunshiro Ando	77. Hirokuni Iijma	147. Jennifer Ruback
8. Thomas Apolte	78. Anthony de Jasay	148. Carlos Sabino
9. Omer Arasil	79. Bruno Jeitziner	149. Andras Sajo
10. Detlef Auf der Heide	80. Ali Kahn	150. Kenichi Sakakibara
11. Hakan Ay	81. Hiroyuki Kawanobe	151. Mustafa Sakal
12. George Ayittey	82. Chung-Ho Kim	152. Javier Salinas
13. Jordi Bacaria	83. Gebhard Kirchgässner	153. Pierre Salmon
14. Rina Battiato	84. Hartmut Kliemt	154. Vural Savas
15. Salvatore Enrico Battiato	85. Barbara Krug	155. David Schap
16. Sebastiano Bavetta	86. Hitoshi Kugenuma	156. Allan Schmid
17. Ingemar Bengtsson	87. Kazuyoshi Kurokawa	157. Dieter Schmidtchen
18. R. J. Bennett	88. David Laband	158. Friedrich Schneider
19. Uri Ben-Zion	89. Sanghack Lee	159. Marten Schultz
20. Beat Blankart	90. Martin Leschke	160. Noboru Sekiya
21. Gordon Brady	91. Shirley Letwin	161. Arthur Seldon
22. Royall Brandis	92. Peter Lewisch	162. Roger Sherman
23. Charles H. Breeden	93. Hans-Edi Loef	163. Francisco Garcia Sobrecases
24. Penelope J. Brook	94. Loren Lomasky	164. Karol Soltan
25. Pamela Brown	95. Fernando Toboso Lopez	165. Birgir Thor Solvanson
26. Eugenio Cerioni	96. Uskali Maki	166. Uriel Spiegel
27. Oh-Hyun Chang	97. Chrysoshomos Mantzavinos	167. Bernard Steunenberg
28. Young Back Choi	98. Jacob Markl	168. M. H. Tamaddon-Jahromi
29. Dennis Coates	99. Edward Lopez	169. Kiyokazu Tanaka
30. James Coleman	100. Elizabetta Marmolo	170. Sabri Tekir
31. Peter Coughlin	101. Paolo Martelli	171. Hiromi Teramoto
32. Dennis Coyle	102. John M. Mbaku	172. Manfred Tietzel
33. Michael A. Crew	103. Richard McKenzie	173. Eugenia Toma
34. Bibekanada Das	104. Nimai Mehta	174. Mark Toma
35. William R. Dougan	105. Antonio Menduina	175. Jan Tumlir
36. Isaac Ehrlich	106. William Mitchell	176. Akihito Udagawa
37. Jon Elster	107. Juan D. Montoro-Pons	177. Lazlo Urban
38. Ross Emmett	108. Hans Monissen	178. Viktor Vanberg
39. Domenico da Empoli	109. Peter Moser	179. Martin van Hees
40. Dominik H. Enste	110. Giafranco Mossetto	180. Ulrich Van Lith
41. Giuseppe Eusepi	111. Dennis C. Mueller	181. Andrea Villani
42. Roger L. Faith	112. Shigeto Naka	182. Stefan Voigt
43. David I. Fand	113. Manfred Neumann	183. Thomas Voss

Table 1 continued

44. Mary Farmer	114. Yew-Kwang Ng	184. Karl Warneryd
45. Susan K. Feigenbaum	115. Douglass North	185. Hannelore Weck-Hannemann
46. Mariateresa Fiocca	116. Robert Nozick	186. Wolfgang Weigel
47. Arthur A. Fleisher III	117. Rustem N. Nureev	187. Edwin West
48. Anthony Flew	118. Jiro Obata	188. Jack Wiseman
49. Cay Folkers	119. Yojiro Oiva	189. Ulrich Witt
50. Francesco Forte	120. Katsuyoshi Okui	190. Weiyun Xu
51. Paul Foss	121. Mancur Olson	191. Mayumi Yamamoto
52. Pedro Puy Fraga	122. Elinor Ostrom	192. Attila Yayla
53. Paul Fudulu	123. Vincent Ostrom	193. Akira Yokoyama
54. Juan Carlos Gamazo	124. Koshiro Ota	194. Tatsuo Yoshida
55. Richard Gamble	125. Taro Ozawa	195. Jesus M. Zaratiegui
56. Otto Gandenberger	126. Fabio Padovano	
57. Enrique Garcia-Ayavirl	127. Karl-Heinz Paque	
58. Ernst Gellner	128. Jose Casa Pardo	
59. Vladimir Gligorov	129. Min Jeong Park	
60. Brian L. Goff	130. Glenn Parker	
61. David Gow	131. Ross Parrish	
62. Christa Gruenwald	132. John Passmore	
63. Anand Gupta	133. Sandra Peart	
64. Alan Hamlin	134. Laura Pennacchi	
65. Bernd Hansjurgens	135. Hartmut Picht	
66. Hiroo Harada	136. Alberto di Pierro	
67. Ann Harper-Fender	137. Ingo Pies	
68. Jac Heckelman	138. Jonathan Pincus	
69. David Henderson	139. Yakir Plessner	
70. Arye Hillman	140. Charles Plott	

Some of these visitors took part in the week-long Liberty Fund workshops that were held at the Center during the summers in the early years

What effect did they, and in particular Gordon Tullock, have on the visitors to the Center? Can we observe epiphanies in some visitors to the Public Choice Center? If so, was it James Buchanan or Gordon Tullock, or perhaps both together, who caused the transformations? I assume that the answers to these questions is in some cases "yes," and that one might be able to identify the persons whose research paths were altered by a visit to the Center either by a careful examination of their research, or by extensive interviews. I have not conducted either. But given his personality and mode of conduct, any visitor to the Center for even one week would have had to interact with Gordon Tullock. Some of these interactions undoubtedly left some visitors angry or repulsed. Some visitors must have felt overwhelmed, and some almost certainly left with an altered perspective on the field of public choice and some different ideas about where their research should be directed.

3 THE PUBLIC CHOICE JOURNAL

In the 1960s, while James Buchanan and Gordon Tullock were at the Thomas Jefferson Center for Political Economy at the University of Virginia. They organized a meeting of a small group of the pioneers working in what at that time was a novel area of research—the application of the methodology of economics to the study of political institutions. The papers presented at that meeting were published by the Thomas Jefferson Center in 1966 under the title, *Papers on Non-Market Decision Making* with Gordon Tullock as the editor.

Upon returning to Virginia, Buchanan and Tullock not only established *The Center for the Study of Public Choice* at VPI, they also founded a new journal to replace *Papers on Non-Market Decision Making*. Since Gordon Tullock had edited its predecessor, I suppose it was natural that he should edit the new journal, *Public Choice.* I also suspect that Buchanan did not wish to take on the time-consuming task of editing a journal.

Gordon Tullock was the editor of *Public Choice* until 1991, 25 years if one counts *Papers on Non-Market Decision Making* as the journal's forerunner. At least during the initial years of the journal's existence, Tullock appears to have been not only the only editor of *Public Choice*, but also its sole referee. One would submit a paper, and within a week receive an editorial decision from Gordon Tullock. If the paper was accepted for publication, it was typically accepted without a request for revisions. Ah, those were the days!

During the early years of the *Public Choice* journal's existence, it was one of the few journals that was receptive to this line of research. Since Tullock essentially decided what articles would appear in the journal, he can be said to have had a significant impact on the field's development through his editorship of the journal. Brady and Tollison (1991, p. 146) observe that Tullock as editor of *Public Choice* "took chances, he printed controversial papers, he was interested in ideas, and he depended on competition among scientists to straighten things out in the long run. This editorial policy...resulted in a number of important advances in economic theory and public choice..." Durden et al. (1991) assess the impact of the *Public Choice* journal under Tullock's (1966) editorship, and list the most important articles published in it while he was editor.

Gordon Tullock, as editor of *Public Choice*, was not adverse to publishing his own work in the journal. Sometimes these contributions might have been aptly subtitled, "ruminations on an interesting question in public choice." One such rumination was "Why So Much Stability?" (Tullock 1981). The problem of cycling under the simple majority rule has been a central issue in public choice from its very beginning when Arrow published his famous impossibility theorem. Indeed, if one counts Condorcet as the founder of public choice, it has been around for more than 200 years. The literature is replete with proofs of theorems showing that equilibria using the simple majority rule are extremely unlikely. Yet legislatures do not seem to go around in circles when they make decisions using the simple majority rule. Why not? This was the question posed by Tullock in this somewhat provocative article. One of the answers to the question was given by Tullock himself in 1967 as discussed above (Tullock 1967b). Tullock begins by reiterating the argument of his earlier contribution, but then goes on to offer still other possible answers in this 1981 article, mostly having to do with the stability of logrolling coalitions. The importance of this article for the development of public choice is not so much the answers Tullock gave to the question of stability, but its posing of the question itself. Numerous articles and books have appeared since 1981, which have wrestled with this question.[4] Two articles appeared in *Public Choice*, which offered alternative theoretical explanations for the question posed by Tullock (Niemi 1983; Hill 1985), and a third presented an empirical test for the existence of cyclical majorities (Stratmann 1996). "Why So Much Stability?" is Tullock's thirteenth most cited work, 358 times according to Google Scholar. Here, as so often in his career, Gordon Tullock opened up a very important, one might say controversial line of research.

In "Efficient Rent Seeking" (Tullock 1980b), Tullock introduced a formula for calculating the probability of a participant's success in a rent-seeking contest. This formula became the workhorse for modelers of rent seeking, which explains why this article is the third most frequently cited publication of Gordon Tullock. Tullock also discussed problems of equilibria in rent-seeking contests in this article, and this too motivated future research. Two articles directly stimulated by this article appeared in a mini-symposium on efficient rent seeking published 5 years later in *Public Choice* (Corcoran and Karels 1985; Higgins et al. 1985). Tullock again used his prerogative as editor to make a small contribution to the debate, in which he described the literature on efficient rent seeking as a bog out of which scholars like those just mentioned and Tullock himself were struggling to emerge (Tullock 1985). He closed his short contribution with the observation that his "role in this controversy is to watch people trying to get out of the swamp and then push them back in" (Tullock 1985, p. 262). As with his ruminations about the stability of political outcomes, Tullock's thoughts concerning the efficiency and equilibria of rent-seeking contests are more interesting for the work they provoked than for the answers Tullock reached.

Resuming my role of curmudgeon, I again would say that these interjections into *Public Choice*, which *certainly* stimulated others to think and write about the issues raised, might well have had an even greater impact had Tullock devoted a bit more time to developing his arguments. "Why So Much Stability," for example, is a 13 page article without any divisions into sections dealing with specific topics and questions. It is more or less a stream of insightful consciousness. In the end, Tullock summarizes his theoretical explanation for why there is so much stability with the statement that "the stable outcomes that are observed...represent equilibria because the conditions needed to produce motion from some initial or intermediate positions appear to be more severe than has been generally assumed" (Tullock 1981). This answer to the stability question has, to my knowledge, not been adopted by most of the profession.

4 FINAL THOUGHTS

There is a word in German that is used to describe something or some person as extremely unique—*einmalig*. I can think of no better word to use to characterize Gordon Tullock. Anyone who spent even a few hours with Gordon Tullock probably has never forgotten the experience. I was fortunate enough early in my career to have spent a full year in his presence, and down through the years to have crossed paths, and sometimes swords with him many times. Although it is difficult to pinpoint turning points in my research as a result of conversations with Gordon Tullock, these conversations certainly affected the way I looked at questions in public choice.

While she was still alive I, and I think many other economists, expected that Joan Robinson would be the first woman to win a Nobel Prize in economics. The fact that she did not receive a Nobel Prize is probably explained by fear on the part of members of the committee that decides on the prizes that she would do something outlandish to embarrass the committee, when the prize was announced or in Stockholm at the awards ceremony. In her later years, Joan Robinson was anything but politically correct.

I suspect that a similar explanation accounts for Gordon Tullock not receiving the Nobel Prize. The prize is supposed to be awarded for particularly important and original contributions to economics. Typing the words "rent seeking" into Google Scholar on March 26, 2015 brought up "about 673,000 results." The concept of rent seeking has to be regarded as one of the most significant developments in economics over the last half century. Thus, the introduction of the concept of rent seeking would seem to warrant a Nobel Prize. Gordon Tullock, gadfly, maverick, enfant terrible, was probably too politically incorrect, even in his more mellow later years, for the Nobel Prize committee to risk awarding him the prize. The Nobel Prize committee would appear to have been of the view that Gordon Tullock was *too einmalig.*

FOOTNOTES

[1]Durden et al. (1991) present a much longer list of Tullock's publications along with the numbers of citations in the Social Science Citation Index as of 1991.

[2]See discussion and references to the literature in Mueller (2003, pp. 236–41).

[3]See, discussion by Professor Akihito Udagawa, who was also greatly influenced by his visit to the Center. http://publicchoice.info/Buchanan/files/udagawa.htm, accessed Dec. 3, 2013.

[4]See, for example, Mueller (2003, pp. 114–26).

REFERENCES

1. Arrow, K. J. (1951). Social choice and individual values, New York: Wiley, rev. ed. 1963.
2. Arrow, K. J., & Scitovsky, T. (Eds.). (1969). Readings in welfare economics. Homewood, IL: Richard D. Irwin.
3. Brady, G. L., & Tollison, R. D. (1991). Gordon Tullock: Creative maverick of public choice. Public Choice, 71, 141–148.
4. Buchanan, J. M., & Tullock, G. (1962). The calculus of consent. Ann Arbor, MI: University of Michigan Press.
5. Buchanan, J. M., & Tullock, G. (1975). Polluters profits and political response: Direct controls versus taxes. American Economic Review, 65, 139–147.
6. Campbell, C., & Tullock, G. (1954). Hyper-inflation in China, 1937–40. Journal of Political Economy, 62, 237–245.
7. Corcoran, W. J., & Karels, G. V. (1985). Rent-seeking behavior in the long run. Public Choice,46, 227–246.
8. Downs, A. (1957). An economic theory of democracy. New York: Harper & Row.

9. Durden, G. C., Ellis, L. V., & Millsap, S. W. (1991). Gordon Tullock: His journal and his scholarship. Public Choice, 71, 171–196.

10. Grier, K. B., & Tullock, G. (1989). An empirical analysis of cross-national economic growth. Journal of Monetary Economics, 24, 259–276.

11. Higgins, R. S., Shughart, W. F, I. I., & Tollison, R. D. (1985). Free entry and efficient rent seeking. Public Choice, 47, 247–258.

12. Hill, J. S. (1985). Why so much stability? The impact of agency determined stability. Public Choice, 46, 275–287.

13. Kruerger, A. O. (1974). The political economy of the rent-seeking society. American Economic Review, 64, 291–303.

14. Morris, W. (Ed.). (1967). The American heritage dictionary of the English language. New York: American Heritage Publishing Co.

15. Mueller, D. C. (1993). The 'Virginia School' and public choice. In D. C. Mueller (Ed.), The public choice approach to politics (pp. 431–442). Aldershot: Edward Elgar Publishing Limited.

16. Mueller, D. C. (2003). Public choice III. Cambridge: Cambridge University Press.

17. Niemi, R. G. (1983). Why so much stability? Another opinion. Public Choice, 41, 261–270.

18. Olson, M, Jr. (1965). The logic of collective action. New Haven, CN: Yale University Press.

19. Olson, M, Jr. (1982). The rise and decline of nations: Economic growth, stagflation and social rigidities. New Haven, CN: Yale University Press.

20. Stratmann, T. (1996). Instability of collective decisions? Testing for cyclical majorities. Public Choice, 88, 15–96.

21. Tideman, T. Niclaus, & Tullock, G. (1976). A new and superior process for making social choices. Journal of Political Economy, 76, 1145–1159.

22. Tullock, G. (1959). Some problems of majority voting. Journal of Political Economy, 67, 571–79, reprinted in K. J. Arrow, T. Scitovsky (1969), pp. 169–178.

23. Tullock, G. (1965). The politics of bureaucracy. Washington, DC: Public Affairs Press.

24. Tullock, G. (Ed.). (1966). Papers on non-market decision making. Charlottesville, VA: Thomas Jefferson Center for Political Economy.

25. Tullock, G. (1967a). Toward a mathematics of politics. Ann Arbor, MI: University of Michigan Press.

26. Tullock, G. (1967b). The general irrelevance of the general impossibility theorem. Quarterly Journal of Economics, 81, 256–270.

27. Tullock, G. (1967c). The welfare costs of tariffs, monopolies and theft. Western Economic Journal, 5, 224–232.

28. Tullock, G. (1971). The paradox of revolution. Public Choice, 11, 89–100.

29. Tullock, G. (1976). The vote motive. London: Institute for Economic Affairs.

30. Tullock, G. (1980a). Trials on trial: The pure theory of legal procedure. New York: Columbia University Press.

31. Tullock, G. (1980b). Efficient rent seeking. In J. M. Buchanan, R. D. Tollison, & G. Tullock (Eds.), Toward a theory of the rent-seeking society (pp. 97–112). College Station, TX: Texas A&M Press.

32. Tullock, G. (1981). Why so much stability? Public Choice, 37, 189–205.

33. Tullock, G. (1985). Back to the bog? Public Choice, 46, 259–263.

34. Tullock, G. (1987). Autocracy. Dordrecht: Kluwer Academic Publishers.

35. Tullock, G. (1989). The economics of special privilege and rent seeking. Dordrecht: Kluwer Academic Publishers.

36. Tullock, G. (1993). Rent seeking. London: Edward Elgar Publishing.

37. Tullock, G. (2003). The origin rent seeking (sic). International Journal of Business and Economics, 2, 1–8.

8

GORDON TULLOCK AND EXPERIMENTAL PUBLIC CHOICE

Arthur Schram

[1]Center for Research in Experimental Economics and Political Decision Making CREED, Amsterdam School of Economics, University of Amsterdam, Amsterdam, The Netherlands

[2]Robert Schumann Center for Advanced Studies, European University Institute, Florence, Italy

ABSTRACT

In this paper, I discuss Gordon Tullock's views on Experimentation in Economics, his own research experiment, and his influence on the field of experimental public choice. I argue that Tullock can credibly claim to have been an early supporter of the method and that his work is cited more often than that of other public choice scholars active in the same period. His work on rent seeking forms the basis of an extensive experimental literature and studies on trust, demand revelation and voter turnout have been strongly influenced by Tullock's work.

Keywords: Gordon Tullock, Experiments, Public choice

1 INTRODUCTION

Gordon Tullock has been recognized as having had an important influence in the development of economics in general and of experimental public choice in particular (Houser and Stratmann 2012). His influence on research in this field can easily be deduced from the grand number of studies that build on his work. This note, therefore, provides a brief overview of the subfields in experimental public choice that build on Tullock's work.

Of course, the fact that experimental research is grounded in Tullock's contributions is neither a necessary nor a sufficient condition to conclude that he embraced experimentation as a fruitful research method for economics. For this, one needs to go back and search his work for views on this matter. In this note, I also discuss the results of such a search. Hence, the aim of this note is to discuss both, Tullock's views and his influence on experimental public choice.[1]

For decades, Tullock yearly attended the meetings of the European Public Choice Society. I have known him since I started attending these meetings in 1985. In the early 1990s, papers using data from laboratory experiments started to appear at these meetings and since then I have had the pleasure of entertaining many lively discussions with Tullock about the experimental method. He has often expressed support for using experiments to study questions in public choice and was keen on emphasizing that he had been one of the early proponents of the method. On various occasions, Tullock would make statements like "Arthur, you're doing the right thing. I've always said that experiments are very suited to study economic phenomena. I was saying so even before Vernon Smith became famous". One of the things I will show in this note is that such statements are verifiably true.

To do so, the next section presents a selection of quotes from Tullock's extensive body of work that relate to his opinion on experiments in economics. Subsequently, I will address the question of whether experimental economists refer to Tullock's work. For this purpose, Sect. 3provides some simple statistics. Section 4 discusses an experiment that Tullock himself organized and Sect. 5 provides a brief overview of literatures in experimental public choice that build on Tullock's work. Finally, I quote in Sect. 6 a few experimental papers that explicitly support or reject ideas developed by Tullock.

2 WHAT DID TULLOCK SAY ABOUT EXPERIMENTS?

To provide an overview of what Tullock has said over the years about experiments in economics, it is useful to move backward in time.[2] However Tullock's views on experiments had developed over the decades, they cumulated in him designing and running an experiment, which he published in Tullock (1999). This experiment will be discussed in Sect. 3.

Fifteen years prior to this work, Tullock had already embarked on an experimental project. In Tideman and Tullock (1976), he and his co-author had presented a new method for collecting funds for public goods that made revelation by consumers of their true valuation of the good a dominant strategy (thus avoiding the free-riding problem). This publication sparked vivid discussions, culminating in a special issue of *Public Choice* in 1977, dedicated to the topic. Tullock quickly saw that experiments provided a way to let data speak to these discussions. Though he and Tideman embarked on the project together, Tullock in the end was not involved in its completion. Yet, Tideman (1983) emphasizes:

> "This research grew out of Gordon Tullock's suggestion that experiments with the demand-revealing process were needed" (p. 387)

In the same period, in 1979, the first of a series of yearly edited volumes called *Research in Experimental Economics* appeared, edited by Vernon Smith (Smith 1979). Tullock (1980a) presents a very positive review of this volume. He writes:

> "I have been biased in favor of experimental work in economics and other social sciences, since I first advocated them in the *Organization of Inquiry*. It seems to me that this is a research tool which we have tended to ignore, and which should have received a good deal more resources than it has." (p. 253)

Tullock's claim to have advocated experiments as early as 1966 (which is when the *Organization of Inquiry* appeared) is substantiated by a closer look. In this book, Tullock draws analogies between research in the sciences and the social sciences. In doing so, he naturally arrives at the conclusion:

> "There are numerous areas [in economics] where experiments could be run with the full knowledge of the subjects and where considerable knowledge could be obtained." (p. 139)

In his elaboration of this issue, Tullock arrives at a description of the interaction between experimentation and theory that was remarkably insightful for the time and predicted various future developments in the field of experimental economics. Consider, for example, Tullock's argument:

> "Experiments, necessarily, are set up in terms of hypotheses, theories, and Weltanschauungen. If these initial intellectual presuppositions of the experiments are in a primitive condition as they were in the natural sciences several 100 years ago, then the initial experiments are likely to simply indicate difficulties in the theories being tested, but not to lead to any solution of these difficulties." (p. 139)

This nicely describes the role early experiments played in analyzing game theoretic predictions based on rational self-interested players. For example, the highly cited paper[3] by Güth et al. (1982) provided strong evidence of the problems with this standard theory but was not very insightful as to how to resolve these problems.

The *Organization of Inquiry* goes on to argue:

> "As time goes by, however, new theories which explain various experimental results will be developed; these in turn will be tested by experimentation. This will lead to the invention of new theories, and the eventual outcome, we can legitimately hope, will be a much clearer perception of the social reality." (p. 139)

Again, this is predictive of the development of the literature. For example, in response to the results of Güth et al., new theories of social preferences were developed (e.g. Fehr and Schmidt 1999; Bolton and Ockenfels 2000) that aimed to better predict such outcomes. These were subsequently subjected to experimental testing (e.g., Charness and Rabin 2002; Engelmann and Strobel 2004), which led to renewed theories, etc. This booming literature is an example of precisely the kind of process that Tullock described in 1966 in the quotes above.

In the same book, Tullock also showed a keen understanding of the experimental methodology. In fact, he argues for methods that since have become standard in the literature. First, in line with the above analysis of the interaction between theory and experiments, Tullock recognized the important role that experiments can have as tests of economic theories:

> "We prefer to depend on theories which are subject to deduction and experimental testing rather than on those which are "verified" solely by our perception of a pattern." (p. 100)

A rough estimate shows that over 50 % of the experiments published in economics test theories (Schram 2005).

Second, in experimental economics, repetition (and replication) is often argued to be one of its main advantages. Tullock foresaw this merit of the method:

> "... [a general result requires that] an experiment has been repeated several times, and a given result has been obtained." (p. 92)

> "The difference between observation and experiment turns on whether the investigator does or does not have control of the repetition of the reported events." (p. 123)

> "These problems fortunately do not arise in the case of experiments, which can normally be repeated at will." (p. 123)

Third, in experimental economics, decision-based compensation is seen as a prerequisite for creating an environment that is informative for the discipline (cf. fn 1). In chapter VII of the *Organization of Inquiry* Tullock does argue in favor of financial compensation of participants in an experiment, but is only thinking of a flat hourly fee. This is one example where he did not foresee how a major methodological issue would develop.[4] He did, however, foresee a second major norm. In experimental economics, deception of subjects is fundamentally banned (in fact, no journal in economics would publish a paper in which participants are incorrectly informed). The reason is given in a textbook by Davis and Holt (1993):

> "Most economists are very concerned about developing and maintaining a reputation among the student population for honesty in order to ensure that subject actions are motivated by the induced monetary rewards rather than by psychological reactions to suspected manipulation. Subjects may suspect deception if it is present." (p. 23)

A very similar argument was given by Tullock, 27 years earlier:

> "[In psychology experiments] the explanation given the subject is frequently simply a "cover" designed to conceal the real experiment from him. Unfortunately, this fact is getting around; experimental subjects may develop a considerable degree of sophistication which will make them systematically distrust the psychological experimenter." (p. 92)

All in all, Tullock's verbal claim to be an early supporter of the field of experimental economics is corroborated by statements he made in early publications, most notably in the *Organization of Inquiry* (1966). Remarkably, he foresaw many of the discussions on experimental methodology that would follow in subsequent decades.

3 DO EXPERIMENTALISTS USE TULLOCK'S WORK?

Given his early interest in experiments, a next question is whether experimentalists are interested in Tullock. A crude measure for this is the number of times Tullock's work is cited in experimental papers. First, I consider in Fig. 1 the number of papers in the leading field journal *Experimental Economics*[5] that cite Tullock and compare this to citations to a set of other leading scholars of Public Choice.[6]

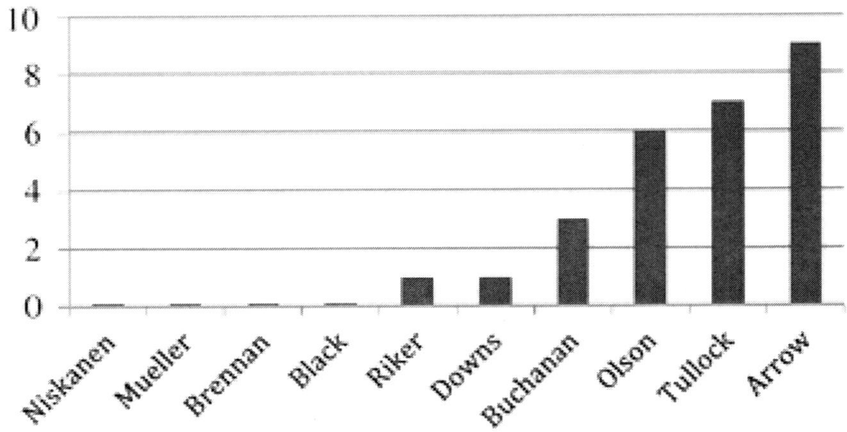

Figure 1. Cites in Experimental Economics. *Notes* Bars show the number of papers in *Experimental Economics* that cite the author concerned. The authors considered are William Niskanen, Dennis Mueller, Geoffrey Brennan, Duncan Black, William Riker, Anthony Downs, James Buchanan, Mancur Olson, Gordon Tullock, and Kenneth Arrow

Figure 1 shows that these public choice scholars are rarely cited in *Experimental Economics* (in total, <6 % of the papers ever published there cite any of these authors). Of those cited, Tullock is second only to Kenneth Arrow in the number of times his work is cited.[7] Of the seven citations, four were to the so-called Tullock (rent-seeking) contests to be discussed below.

For a more general (and even more crude) overview, Fig. 2 shows the number of hits in Google Scholar when searching for the author's name in combination with the term "laboratory experiment". Once again, Tullock is amongst the most cited public choice scholars.

All in all, it appears that experimental economists rarely cite public choice scholars, but when they do Tullock is amongst the most cited.

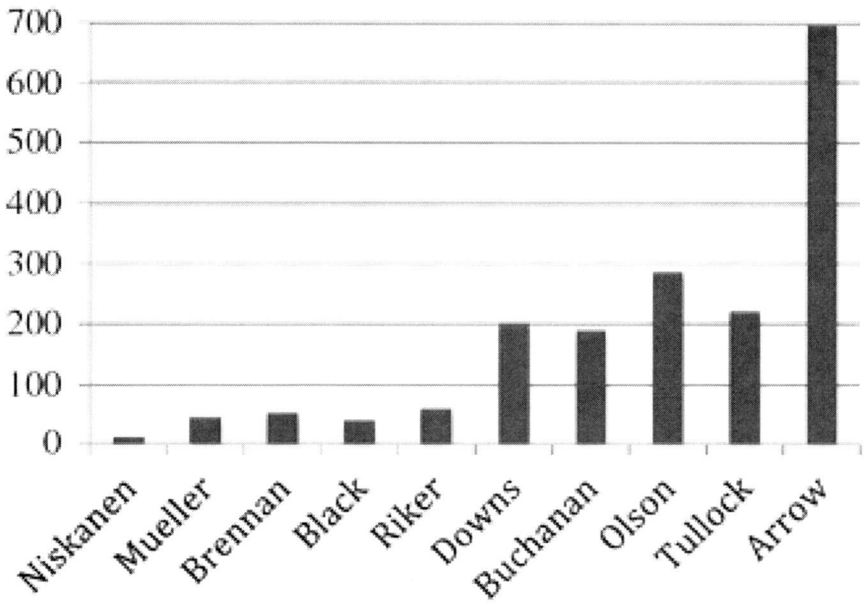

Figure 2. Google Hits. *Notes* Bars show the number of hits when searching in Google Scholar (on Sept 25, 2015) for the combination "first-name last-name" and "laboratory experiment" (e.g., "Gordon Tullock" "laboratory experiment"). The authors are depicted in the note to Fig. 1

4 HAS TULLOCK DONE EXPERIMENTS?

Given his early interest in experiments, it comes as no surprise that Tullock eventually designed and ran an experiment, which was published in Tullock (1999). In this experiment, subjects participate in prisoners' dilemmas (PD). This was a 'risky' endeavor because experiments on social dilemmas like the PD were already very common by that time, and much was already known about how efficient cooperation is affected by a variety of variables. It would seem hard at the time to come up with a novel insight. A much cited literature review by John Ledyard (1995) explicitly lists factors that have been shown to positively or negatively affect efficient cooperation.

Tullock was unsatisfied with this literature, in particular because he felt that the external validity of most of the games studied in these experiments was very low. In his view, the 'real world' was very different than the laboratory world typically used. In his words, most interactions outside of the laboratory "do not involve prisoners". In particular, Tullock (1999) lists three problems with the standard design: In the laboratory environment,

1) participants are chosen by the experimenter, while in the world outside of the laboratory, people choose their own partners to interact with;
2) communication is usually not allowed, while communication is a crucial part of human interaction in the 'real world';
3) pairs of participants are typically fixed whereas outside of the laboratory, people can leave partners for others if they are unsatisfied with the way things are going.

In such 'traditional' experiments substantial levels of (efficient) cooperation is typically observed in early rounds, but free-riding increases with repetition.

To address these problems, Tullock designed an experiment that deviated in three important ways from much of the prior literature. His experiment involved a group of players in a room that could form pairs, while three or four remained unpaired on the sideline. Pairs could communicate and individually decide on their strategies in a PD. This was repeated ten times. If anyone was unsatisfied with the course of events in their pair, they were free to break up and pair up with one of the sidelined participants. The results were certainly noteworthy. Of the ten pairs in this experiment, seven cooperated throughout the ten rounds. In aggregate more than 97 % of the decisions were to cooperate.

This cooperation level is remarkable and serves to make the main point of the paper. It must be said, however, that on some dimensions, the experiment falls short of the state of the art in the late 1990s. First, the paper neglects some important papers that had already appeared. For example, the strong effect of communication on cooperation had already been documented in Ledyard's 1995 review. Also, the effect of endogenous partner choice had already been observed in various papers, including Orbell and Dawes (1993) and Hayashi and Yamagishi (1998). Second, the paper does not fulfill the standards set in the experimental economics literature at the time. In particular:

- it fails to develop a benchmark of the 'standard environment', to which Tullock's environment can be compared;
- compared to the standard case, there are multiple changes (partner choice, communication, and the possibility of re-pairing);
- Tullock combined data collected at two different locations (Tucson, Arizona and Arlington, Virginia) without testing for subject pool effects;
- the number of observations (10 pairs) is very low.

I strongly suspect, however, that the only goal of the paper was to make a point about the validity of the standard experiments. In that respect, it achieves what it set out to do.

5 WHAT EXPERIMENTAL FIELDS BUILD ON TULLOCK'S WORK?

There are various research areas that could be captured under the umbrella of 'experimental public choice' (Schram 2003). These include studies on the voluntary provision of public goods (including work on the tragedy of the commons); rent-seeking contests; trust; demand revelation; and voting (e.g. the turnout paradox and spatial voting). One could argue that Tullock has influenced each of these area's, but his impact was perhaps least for the public goods literature. For the other areas, I briefly provide an overview of Tullock's influence.[8]

5.1 Rent seeking

Rent seeking is an area where Tullock's (1967a) work founded a complete experimental field. Rent seeking refers to the situation where welfare losses occur because resources are (unproductively) used in an attempt to obtain government-controlled rents. Tullock (1980b, 1998) shows how, in equilibrium, a situation can occur where the aggregate sum allocated by players exceeds the value of the rent. This so-called over-dissipation and the circumstances under which it can occur has been the topic of many experiments. Tullock's influence on this experimental rent-seeking literature (which extends to studies on all-pay auctions and raffles) is wonderfully described in Houser and Stratmann (2012). In their words:

> "Tullock's hypothesis regarding rent-seeking was seminal to a literature of experiments." (p. 212)

Experimental studies mostly provide support for the Nash (i.e., Tullock) prediction of over-dissipation, when the model predicts so. Moreover, as predicted by the theory, such over-dissipation decreases with the level of players' risk aversion.[9]

5.2 Trust

There is an extensive experimental literature on trust and its role in economic interactions (for seminal examples, see Fehr et al. 1993 or Berg et al. 1995). However, few experimentalists realize Tullock's (1967b) early and important contribution to the study of trust. In this short note, Tullock argues that a PD only involves trust, if it is played sequentially. This is another paper discussed extensively by Houser and Stratmann (2012). In their words:

> "Tullock's early realization was exceptionally forward-looking and foreshadowed the flourishing of trust game research in experimental economics that would only begin to appear more than two decades later." (p. 212)

Indeed, the importance of trust is now well recognized, and the fact that Tullock noted this as early as 1967 is remarkable at the least. For more details, see Houser and Stratmann (2012).

5.3 Demand revelation

In 1976, Tullock and Nick Tideman published a theoretical paper in the *Journal of Political Economy* in which they describe a mechanism that uses Clarke taxes to create a dominant strategy of demand revelation for a public good (Tideman and Tullock 1976). This publication led to a lively academic discussion that culminated in a special issue of *Public Choice* (1977) –initiated by Tullock himself– dedicated to the mechanism. More details about this mechanism –which they dubbed the 'demand revealing process'– and the subsequent debate are given in Tideman's contribution to this issue.

As mentioned before, Tideman (1983) presents the results of a field experiment that started as a joint project with Tullock and intended to test the theoretical properties of the mechanism. He invited a set of college fraternities to apply the mechanism in making decisions about their fraternity. The paper reports support for the mechanism. The design allows for compensation for participation. It does not, however, induce values for the outcome of the decision making process. As a consequence, this experiment does not allow for a test of whether the demand revealing process leads to truthful revelation of preferences for the public good.

An experiment by Attiyeh et al. (2000) does allow for such a test. In this experiment, values are induced and the data allow one to compare subjects' expressed demand to their known value for the good. The results provide no support for truthful revelation. Only a small minority of the subjects reports their true value, even though doing so is a dominant strategy. Only one theoretical prediction is supported by the outcome of this experiment. This is that the Clarke taxes paid ought to decrease with increased group size. The Attiyeh et al. experiment provides evidence that this is indeed the case.

5.4 Voter turnout

Tullock's contribution to the literature on voter turnout is an elaboration of Anthony Down's (1957) turnout paradox. In short, this paradox confronts the high levels of voter turnout at mass elections with the observation that for most voters the expected value of the vote will be lower than the costs of casting it (due to the extremely low probability that any individual vote will be decisive for the outcome). In his *Towards a Mathematics of Politics* (1967c) Tullock extends this basic theory and provides arguments why people may turn out after all.

Two elements stand out in this analysis. First, Tullock introduced game-theoretic arguments into the discussion by noting that the negative expected net benefits of a vote no longer hold if they make everybody abstain. If nobody else casts a vote, any single voter is decisive for the outcome and the paradox no longer holds. Tullock rightfully notes (p. 110) that one needs to determine the theoretically predicted turnout level by determining the strategic equilibrium amongst the voters. Such an equilibrium analysis did not appear in the literature until Palfrey and Rosenthal presented their analysis of the participation game in 1983. Second, Tullock stressed the important role that information and social pressures have in the turnout decision.

Both elements have been investigated. Such experiments typically apply the participation game in the laboratory (e.g., Großer and Schram 2006, 2010; Levine and Palfrey 2007). By and large, experimental studies show that turnout is predicted quite well by a quantal response equilibrium (McKelvey and Palfrey 1995).[10] The results also show that –as predicted by Tullock– information and social pressure are important determinants of the decision to cast a vote.

5.5 'Missing' experiments

There are at least three areas of Tullock's research that I would have expected to yield more experimental work. The first is on external effects and collective choice. In the *Calculus of Consent*, Buchanan and Tullock (1962) discuss the relationship between the existence of external effects and the extent of collective decision making. A question one can address experimentally is when and why subjects choose specific collective institutions to solve problems with external effects? There is an abundant literature showing that subjects in public goods games are willing to punish (at a cost to themselves) free riders in a public good environment (e.g., Fehr and Gächter 2000). Though a recent paper (Markussen et al. 2014) analyzes the choice between formal sanction regimes and informal sanctioning, there is certainly room for much more experimental work in this area.

The same holds for Tullock's (1969, 1974) work on the economics of crime. Though some papers have appeared that utilize laboratory experiments to study 'criminal' activity (e.g. van Winden and Ash 2012), and in particular tax evasion (e.g., Gërxhani and Schram 2006), the Tullock approach to studying criminal activity in terms of (expected) costs and benefits provides a framework that is very suited for further experimental analysis.

Finally, Tullock is well known for analysis of logrolling, i.e., vote trading in legislatures and its effect on government spending (Tullock 1959; Buchanan and Tullock 1962). This is another environment that lends itself for experimental testing. Yet, though various experimental studies on strategic voting have appeared, I know of only two on vote trading: McKelvey and Ordeshook (1980) and a recent working paper by Casella and Palfrey (2015).

6 EXPERIMENTAL RESULTS ON TULLOCK'S IDEAS

In search of explicit experimental validation or rejection of Tullock's ideas, I have found only three experimental papers that explicitly relate their results to theoretical views put forward by Tullock.

First, in the previously mentioned study by Markussen et al. (2014) on formal and informal sanctioning, the authors observe that their result that participants often prefer not to install formal sanctioning coincides with Buchanan and Tullock's views:

> "To be sure, Buchanan and Tullock wrote half a century ago that'The existence of external effects of private behavior is neither a necessary nor a sufficient condition for an activity to be placed in the realm of collective choice' (1962, p. 57)." (p. 303)

Note, however, that these authors argue that the reason for their results lies in social preferences; a view that seems hard to reconcile with Buchanan and Tollock's ideas.

Second, as mentioned above, Atitiyeh et al. (2000) found in their laboratory analysis of the demand revelation process that:

> "... Tideman and Tullock's argument that, simply from the rules of the pivot mechanism, the Clarke taxes ought to fall, per capita, was supported in our experiments."

Recall, however, that the authors found very little evidence of truthful demand revelation in their data.

Third, Potters et al. (1998) conclude from their rent-seeking experiments:

> "We find substantial evidence for the predictive power of the [Tullock] rent-seeking model, particularly if one allows for the fact that people sometimes make mistakes or are confused about what to do." (p. 783)

This support for the model has been replicated in many experiments on rent seeking.

7 CONCLUDING DISCUSSION

All of the contributions to this special issue provide evidence of the incredible width and creativity of Gordon Tullock's scholarship. His work has influenced a large variety of research programs within economics, political science, biology and law. In this note, I have tried to show his influence in the field of experimental economics.

In particular, I have tried to show that Tullock was one of the early supporters of using experimental methods to address research questions in economics. In the end, his interest in the method led to the publication of one paper where he used an experiment to make a point. His influence on the field is much more substantial than this, however.

Tullock's work has inspired experimental studies of rent seeking, trust, the demand-revelation process and voter turnout. His exceptional scholarship provides scope for many more experiments that can build on his work.

FOOTNOTES

1 Throughout this note, I will use the term "experiment" as it is commonly understood in the economics literature. This refers to data collection in a controlled (laboratory or field) environment that is structured in a way that allows one to derive causal relations between the variables of interest. A typical experiment in economics induces values to outcomes (and pays participants accordingly) to create a true (micro-)economic environment (Smith 1976).

2 Note that Vernon Smith published a first experimental paper in 1962, but that the method did not really catch on until the 1970s.

3 3462 citations in Google Scholar (Oct 1, 2015).

4 In fact, the development was already going on at the time. Roth (1995) argues that there was already a tendency to use performance-based incentives by the end of the 1950s.

5 *Experimental Economics* published its first issue in 1998. The numbers underlying Fig. 1were measured in September 2015, over a total of 486 papers in 64 issues of the journal.

6 The choice of "leading scholars" is admittedly arbitrary. The author made a first selection and adjusted this following comments at the Tullock Memorial Conference at GMU in October 2015.

7 It should be noted that the large majority of citations to Kenneth Arrow in the experimental literature refers to the Arrow–Pratt measure of risk aversion, which is not really public choice.

8 Tullock's work also had an influence on the development of neuro-economics, a field closely related to experimental economics (Houser and Stratmann 2012).

9 For more details, see Houser and Stratmann (2012).

10 The quantal response equilibrium can be interpreted as an extension of Nash equilibrium that allows for noisy decision making.

ACKNOWLEDGMENTS

I thank Roger Congleton and the other organizers of the Tullock memorial conference for the opportunity to develop and present this work and Klarita Gërxhani, Jens Großer and two anonymous reviewers for useful comments.

REFERENCES

1. Attiyeh, G., Franciosi, R., & Isaac, R. M. (2000). Experiments with the pivot process for providing public goods. Public Choice, 102, 95–114.
2. Berg, J., Dickhaut, J., & McCabe, K. (1995). Trust, reciprocity, and social history. Games and Economic Behavior, 10, 122–142.
3. Bolton, G., & Ockenfels, A. (2000). ERC: A theory of equity, reciprocity, and competition. The American Economic Review, 90(1), 166–193.
4. Buchanan, J., & Tullock, G. (1962). The calculus of consent: Logical foundations of a constitutional democracy. Ann Arbor: University of Michigan Press.

5. Casella, A., & Palfrey, T. (2015). Trading votes for votes: A decentralized matching algorithm. Working paper, Columbia University.

6. Charness, G., & Rabin, M. (2002). Understanding social preferences with simple tests. The Quarterly Journal of Economics, 117(3), 817–869.

7. Davis, D., & Holt, Ch. (1993). Experimental economics. Princeton: Princeton University Press.

8. Downs, A. (1957). An economic theory of democracy. New York: Harper and Row.

9. Engelmann, D., & Strobel, M. (2004). Inequality aversion, efficiency, and maximin preferences in simple distribution experiments. The American Economic Review, 94(4), 857–869.

10. Fehr, E., & Gächter, S. (2000). Cooperation and punishment in public goods experiments. The American Economic Review, 90(4), 980–994.

11. Fehr, E., Kirchsteiger, G., & Riedl, A. (1993). Does fairness prevent market clearing? An experimental investigation. The Quarterly Journal of Economics, 108(2), 437–459.

12. Fehr, E., & Schmidt, K. (1999). A theory of fairness, competition, and cooperation. Quarterly Journal of Economics, 114(3), 817–868.

13. Gërxhani, K., & Schram, A. (2006). Tax evasion and income source: A compara-tive experimental study. Journal of Economic Psychology, 27(3), 402–422.

14. Großer, J., & Schram, A. (2006). Neighborhood information exchange and voter participation: An experimental study. American Political Science Review, 100(2), 235–248.

15. Großer, J., & Schram, A. (2010). Public opinion polls, voter turnout and welfare: An experimental study. American Journal of Political Science, 54, 700–717.

16. Guth, W., Schmittberger, R., & Schwarze, B. (1982). An experimental analysis of ultimatum bargaining. Journal of Economic Behavior and Organization, 3, 367–388.

17. Hayashi, N., & Yamagishi, T. (1998). Selective play: Choosing partners in an uncertain world. Personality and Social Psychology Review, 2, 276–289.

18. Houser, D., & Stratmann, Th. (2012). Gordon Tullock and experimental economics. Public Choice, 152(1), 211–222.

19. Ledyard, J. (1995). Public goods: A survey of experimental research. In J. Kagel & A. Roth (Eds.), The handbook of experimental economics (pp. 111–194). Princeton: Princeton University Press.

20. Levine, D., & Palfrey, Th. (2007). The paradox of voter participation? a laboratory Study. American Political Science Review, 101(1), 143–158.

21. Markussen, Th, Putterman, L., & Tyran, J.-R. (2014). Self-organization for collective action: An experimental study of voting on sanction regimes. The Review of Economic Studies, 81(1), 301–324.

22. McKelvey, R., & Ordeshook, P. (1980). Vote trading: An experimental study. Public Choice,35(2), 151–184.

23. McKelvey, R., & Palfrey, Th. (1995). Quantal response equilibria for normal form games. Games and Economic Behavior, 10, 6–38.

24. Orbell, John M., & Dawes, Robyn M. (1993). Social welfare, cooperators' advantage, and the option of not playing the game. American Sociological Review, 58(6), 787–800.

25. Palfrey, Th, & Rosenthal, H. (1983). A strategic calculus of voting. Public Choice, 41, 7–53.

26. Potters, J., de Vries, C., & van Winden, F. (1998). An experimental examination of rational rent-seeking. European Journal of Political Economy, 14(4), 783–800.

27. Roth, A. E. (1995). Introduction to Experimental Economics. In J. H. Kagel & A. E. Roth (Eds.), Handbook of experimental economics (pp. 3–109). Princeton: Princeton University Press.

28. Schram, A. (2003). Experimental public choice. In C. Rowley & F. Schneider (Eds.), Encyclopedia of Public Choice, (pp. 96–104). Dordrecht: Kluwer Academic Publishers. Revised version appeared in 2008.

29. Schram, A. (2005). Artificiality: The tension between internal and external validity in economic experiments. Journal of Economic Methodology, 12(2), 225–238.

30. Smith, V. (1962). An experimental study of competitive market behavior. Journal of Political Economy, 70(2), 111–137.

31. Smith, V. (1976). Experimental economics: Induced value theory. American Economic Review Papers and Proceedings, 66(2), 274–279.

32. Smith, V. (Ed.). (1979). Research in experimental economics. Greenwich: JAI Press Inc.

33. Tideman, N. (1983). An experiment in the demand revealing process. Public Choice, 41, 387–401.

34. Tideman, N., & Tullock, G. (1976). A new and superior process for making social choices. Journal of Political Economy, 84(6), 1145–1159.

35. Tullock, G. (1959). Some problems with majority voting. Journal of Political Economy, 67, 571–579.

36. Tullock, G. (1966). The Organization of Inquiry. Durham, NC: Duke University Press. Page numbers based on online version at http://oll.libertyfund.org/titles/1555.

37. Tullock, G. (1967a). The welfare costs of tariffs, monopolies and theft. Western Economic Journal, 5, 224–232.

38. Tullock, G. (1967b). The prisoner's dilemma and mutual trust. Ethics, 77, 229–230.

39. Tullock, G. (1967c). Toward a mathematics of politics. Ann Arbor: University of Michigan Press.

40. Tullock, G. (1969). An economic approach to crime. Social Science Quarterly, 50(1), 59–71.

41. Tullock, G. (1974). Does punishment deter crime? The Public Interest, 14, 103–111.

42. Tullock, G. (1980a). Book review of "Research in Experimental Economics" (Vol. 1 by V. Smith (Ed.), JAI Press Inc., Greenwich, 1979); Public Choice, 35(2), 253.

43. Tullock, G. (1980b). Efficient rent seeking. In J. Buchanan, J. Tollison, & G. Tullock (Eds.), Toward a theory of the rent-seeking society (pp. 153–179). College Station: Texas A&M University Press.

44. Tullock, G. (1998). The fundamentals of rent-seeking. In A. Owens & C. Rowley (Eds.), The lock luminary 1(2).

45. Tullock, G. (1999). Non-prisoner's dilemma. Journal of Economic Behavior and Organization,29, 455–458.

46. van Winden, F., & Ash, E. (2012). On The behavioral economics of crime. Review of Law and Economics, 8, 181–213.

9

RENT SEEKING AND THE ECONOMICS OF CORRUPTION

Toke S. Aidt

Faculty of Economics, University of Cambridge, Sidgwick Avenue, Cambridge CB3 9DD, UK

ABSTRACT

The paper studies the influence of Tullock (West Econ J 5:224–232, 1967) and the rent-seeking literature more generally on the study of corruption. The theoretical corruption literature with its emphasis on principal-agent relationships within government and rent creation by corruption politicians has largely, but not entirely, overlooked that contestable rents encourage unproductive use of real resources in seeking these rents. As a consequence, the literature underestimates the value of corruption control and the cost of corruption itself.

Keywords: Rent seeking, Corruption Bribes

1 INTRODUCTION

For the modern reader, it is quite an eye-opener to go back and read Gordon Tullock's paper "The welfare costs of tariffs, monopolies, and theft" published in 1967 in the Western Economic Journal (now Economic Inquiry). The paper is very short and to the point, uses a few simple diagrams, and does not exhibit a single equation or a statistical table of any kind. Yet, it contains one of the most powerful new insights emerging from twentieth century economic thought, laid out clearly towards the end of the paper. The insight, of course, is that the social cost of government policy (monopoly, transfers, regulation, etc.) is much greater than suggested by the calculation of Harberger triangles and deadweight cost. The source of the extra cost is the contesting of rents created by the policies by potential beneficiaries expending real resources. This, along with Tullock's (1980) paper on "Efficient rent seeking" started a huge literature on rent seeking—the term coined by Krueger (1974) for the activities described by Tullock.[1]

The purpose of this paper is to discuss the influence of the rent-seeking literature on the study of the economics of corruption. The terms "rent seeking" and "corruption" are often used interchangeably. Closer inspection of the academic literature, however, reveals that the two literatures have proceeded in parallel to a surprisingly large extent. I shall argue that this is unhelpful and that both the rent-seeking and the corruption literature can benefit from each other.

The rest of the paper is organized as follows. Section 2 develops a taxonomy that helps set the stage for the rest of the analysis. Section 3 provides a brief overview of the theoretical corruption literature. Section 4 evaluates the influence of the rent-seeking literature on the study of corruption. Section 5 inquiries into the influence of the corruption literature on the study of rent seeking. Section 6 engages with the relationship between empirical research on corruption and rent seeking. Section 7 provides some concluding remarks.

2 THE CORE CONCEPTS, DEFINITIONS AND TAXONOMY

In this section, I briefly review the two main insights from Tullock (1967) and propose a general taxonomy that can help clarify the link between corruption and rent seeking.

2.1 The core ideas of the rent-seeking literature

It is useful, I think, to start by clarifying the main ideas and concepts, even if they are familiar to most readers. The rent-seeking literature embodies two core ideas, which can both be found in Tullock (1967). The insights are:

1. The missiles seek heat hypothesis: A contestable rent induces rent-seeking activities aimed at capturing the rent. These activities involve unproductive use of real resources and cause a social loss.

2. The invertability hypothesis: Rent-seeking costs are, by and large, unobserved but by applying contest theory and assumptions about the behaviour of rent seekers, the size of the social cost can be inferred from the value of the contestable rent.

Examples of contestable rents are abundant: assigning monopoly rights, protectionist trade policies, privileged budget allocations, income transfers, national resource rights, and so on. The distinguishing feature making a rent contestable is that *ex ante*—i.e., before it is assigned to any particular economic agent—it is up for grabs. This is what makes it rational for potential beneficiaries to expend resources in contesting rents.

Contestable rents differ from contestable profits, which trigger socially productive activities (Buchanan 1980). Contestable profits play an important and efficiency enhancing role in the allocation of resources in a capitalist market economy. Economic agents have an incentive to expand into markets with profits and to innovate to create profits; this improves resource allocation, expands output of the economy and increases aggregate welfare.

Many contestable rents are created and protected by government policy and government officials and politicians are *gatekeepers* who regulate who gains access to the rents. This is what Tullock had in mind. In this case, economic agents cannot contest the rent by shifting resources directly into production of the underlying good or service. Instead, they are motivated to invest time, effort and other real resources—to engage in rent-seeking activities—in attempts to secure either the initial assignment of the right to the rent or in ousting others from their position of privilege. These resources are employed unproductively but have social value in alternative employment.

All this is largely unobserved and certainly not recorded by any statistical agency and reported to the public. This makes it hard to know how large these loses really are. Fortunately, the second insight—the invertability hypothesis—can help: the social loss can be inferred through contest-models from the size of the contestable rent. It is, in other words, possible to "invert" the process and use the size of the observable rents to infer the unobserved social cost of rent seeking. A very extensive literature on rent dissipation, including Tullock's (1980) paper on efficient rent seeking, has subsequently demonstrated that the possible relations between the observable rent to the underlying rent-seeking expense are complex and contingent on many assumptions or influences.[2]

2.2 Definitions and taxonomy

In order to examine the influence that the two core insights from the rent-seeking literature have had on the corruption literature, the starting point must be to settle on definitions of what the two social phenomena are and to develop a workable taxonomy that can help us organize the material.

The standard definition of "rent seeking" is the quest for privileged benefits from government [see, for example, Hillman (2013)]. While there is general agreement on this definition, it has proved much harder to converge on a widely accepted definition of corruption.[3] An often used definition of corruption amongst economists is "sale by government officials of government property for private gain" (Shleifer and Vishny 1993) or situations where "the power of public office is used for personal gain in a manner that contravenes the rules of the game" (Jain 2001).

Taking these definitions at face value, it is clearly possible to have rent seeking without corruption and vice versa. If, for example, a government official is charged with allocating mobile phone licenses and the rules specify that he must select the company that makes the "most convincing case for efficient service delivery" and if he follows this rule to the best of his ability, then there is no corruption. Yet, there will be a lot of rent seeking. The mobile phone companies will expend vast resources on making their case for being the best for the job. Conversely, it is also possible to have corruption without rent seeking. Suppose, for example, that one of the companies pays a bribe to obtain the license without any checks on its ability to deliver the services efficiently (and no one else makes any effort to show their fitness for the job), then we clearly have a situation of corruption but without any real resources have been used unproductively in rent-seeking activities. This line of reasoning, however, gives the impression that corruption and rent seeking are entirely different social phenomena and *that* is misleading and unhelpful. The problem is that the definition of corruption used in the economics literature is too narrow.

It is more fruitful, as suggested by Lambsdorff (2002, p. 98), to employ a broader definition. Thus, let me define corruption as a special *means* by which private agents may seek to pursue their interest in competition for preferential treatment by government officials or politicians *and* where the "means" are valued by the recipient. The primary example of a "special means" is a bribe—a monetary payment in return for preferential treatment. The use of personal contacts (favouritism) according to the principle "you help me and I will help you" is another example.

This definition alongside the definition of rent seeking itself highlights an important consideration. It matters a lot from a social point of view, if the "means" of seeking preferential treatment involves the outputs or income from the production process or it involves the direct use of factors of production. In the first case, the available factors of production are employed to produce output and generate income to the factor owners, i.e., the economy is on the production frontier (maybe on a second best frontier, but nonetheless on the frontier). Some of the income thus generated may be used to seek rents and preferential treatment. This is the situation envisaged by much of the corruption literature. In the second case, factors of production, for example, labour, which could have been employed in production of output are deployed in the process of seeking rents—people who could become entrepreneurs become lobbyists. As a consequence, the economy produces below its production frontier and output and income is lost. This is the situation envisaged by the rent-seeking literature which is concerned with the efficiency losses due to unproductive use of resources in the quest for rents.

Using the definitions, corruption and rent seeking can be combined as instances of *influence-seeking activities*. Such activities can be distinguished along two dimensions: whether the gatekeeper who assigns the rent benefits from the influence-seeking activities and whether the influence-seeking activity involves a transfer of income (bribe) or unproductive use of resources. This gives rise to the two-by-two taxonomy in Table 1a and the illustrative examples in Table 1b.

Table 1. Taxonomy of influence-seeking activities

Means/gains	Gatekeeper does not gain	Gatekeeper gains
(a) General taxonomy		
Income transfer	Impure corruption	Pure corruption
Factor of production	Pure rent seeking	Impure rent seeking
(b) Examples of taxonomy		
Income transfers	Bribes with transaction costs	Bribes with no transaction costs
	Tirole (1992)	Rose-Ackerman (1975)
Factor of production	Advocacy, argumentation	Contestable bribery
	Tullock (1967)	Gradstein and Konrad (1999)

According to this taxonomy, pure corruption refers to the case where competition for preferential treatment is such that the gatekeeper benefits from the influence-seeking expenses/activities in the way of a costless income transfer from the beneficiary to the gatekeeper. Pure rent seeking refers to the situation in which competition for preferential treatment is such that the gatekeeper does not benefit from the influence-seeking expenses/activities, which represent unproductive use of factors of production. The case of impure corruption emerges if the income transfer is associated with a transaction cost such that the value of the income transfer to the gatekeeper is lower than the cost to those paying the transfer. Impure rent seeking emerges if the unproductive use of factors of production in seeking influence may, in fact, benefit the gatekeeper.

There are, of course, a whole raft of intermediate cases and many other distinctions can be made (corruption is restricted to a few competitors while rent seeking is open to all; corruption is not legal, while rent seeking is, etc.), but the two-dimensional taxonomy is, at the very least, helpful in clarifying the link between the rent-seeking and corruption literature. Most of the corruption literature is concerned with situations where the gatekeeper gains and the influence-seeking activity represents an income transfer. Bribery is the classical example of this which is often viewed as a costless transfer (e.g., Rose-Ackerman 1975; Lui 1985). In reality, even bribery is associated with transaction costs (e.g., Tirole 1992). This reduces the value of the bribe for the gatekeeper and in the limit, makes it worthless. The classical rent-seeking literature, including the examples given by Tullock (1967) and the analysis in Hillman and Samet (1987) and many other papers on rent dissipation is about pure rent seeking: real resources are being employed in seeking, say, a government-sponsored monopoly rent, which is assigned without any gain to the official who assigns it. However, it is possible to envisage cases in which the gatekeeper may gain. The literature on contest design, for example, engages with the possibility that the rent-seeking expense is, in fact, valued by the government official who assigns the underlying rent (Gradstein and Konrad 1999; Epstein and Nitzan 2015). This leads to what I call contestable bribery in Table 1b.

3 OVERVIEW OF THE CORRUPTION LITERATURE

The theoretical corruption literature has evolved along two main branches.[4] They are

1. The helping hand type of corruption: Corruption arises when a benevolent principal delegates decision making power to a non-

benevolent agent. The level of corruption depends on the costs and benefits of designing optimal institutions. Corruption is optimal.

2. The grabbing hand type of corruption: Corruption arises because non-benevolent government officials introduce inefficient policies in order to extract rents from the private sector. The level of corruption depends on the incentives embodied in existing (often suboptimal) institutions and policies. Corruption is not optimal.

The first branch of literature has its origin in the law and economics and in the organisational economics literatures, with classical contributions by Becker and Stigler (1974), Rose-Ackerman (1975), and Tirole (1992, 1994) and, more recent contributions, by Laffont and Guessan (1999), Acemoglu and Verdier (2000), Dabla-Norris (2002), and Dhami and Al-Nowaihi (2007) amongst many others. A typical "helping hand" scenario, which we shall use as a heuristic devise below, is environmental regulation. Un-internalised and socially harmful externalities provide a prima facie case for government intervention and a benevolent government would want to impose a correction. In practice, the task of doing so is delegated to a bureaucracy. The officials of the bureaucracy will amongst other things be tasked with checking that the polluting firms abide by the regulations. The problem, however, is that it is impossible for the government to monitor the officials perfectly. This leaves room for collusion between the firms and the officials. Any given official may agree to accept a bribe for not reporting violations of the regulations. Or the regulator may simply come to identify with the regulated firm. The benevolent government tries to avoid this by designing institutions (monitoring, wage structures, penalties) to maximise social welfare, but it is costly to design such institutions. It may, therefore, be optimal to accept a residual of corruption and rule violation. That is, corruption within this conception is, in fact, optimal in a second best sense.

The second strand of literature starts from the Tullock dictum "people are people" and does not assume any degree of benevolence in the conduct of the government. Examples of contributions to this literature include Shleifer and Vishny (1993), Bliss and di Tella (1997), and Aidt and Dutta (2008). A typical "grabbing hand" scenario, which we shall also explore below, is entry regulation. Suppose that there are no good welfare economics reasons for restricting entry into an industry. Yet, a corruptible government official or politician may nonetheless introduce a license system that restricts entry. The reason is that such regulation creates rents through artificial scarcity. As a consequence, potential producers in the industry is willing to pay a bribe to obtain a license. A leviathan-type politician would, then, issue the bribe maximising number of licences and collect the largest possible bribe income. In practice, however, institutional constraints may impose some limits of this sort of behaviour. The level of corruption depends on given institutional structures, culture, and history and is, in general, sub-optimal. Moreover, the *type* of corruption is endogenous to the political regime. Charap and Harm (2002) point out that this is a natural consequence of the predatory strategies that "rulers" operating under different constraints employ to extract rents from the economy. For example, in a dictatorship, a corrupt and low-paid bureaucracy, either of the competitive or monopolistic type, can at the same time help the dictator to maintain power and to extract rents from the economy. In contrast, in a functioning democracy, the preferred vehicle for rent extraction becomes interest group contributions to political campaigns.

4 THE INFLUENCE OF THE RENT-SEEKING LITERATURE ON THE STUDY OF CORRUPTION

We can use the two examples developed above to evaluate the influence of the rent-seeking literature on the study of the economics of corruption. In the "helping hand" scenario, a corruptible public official may share a rent with the firm that he is meant to regulate by accepting a bribe in return for turning a blind eye to environmental violations. The rent itself is created by asymmetric information and imperfect monitoring. There is a social loss involved because of socially undesirable environmental damage. This is, however, optimal given the costs and benefits of designing incentives. It is important for this conclusion that the information rent is *not* contestable and the influence-seeking activity—offering a bribe—is a pure transfer. It is also important that the bribe does not by itself involve a social loss, although one could imagine that transaction costs would reduce the value of the bribe received below the utility cost of paying it. Yet, the point remains that the receiver, the government official, values the bribe. In this type of model, influence seeking is limited to what I termed pure (or at worst impure) corruption in Table 1a. It is simply a transfer of resources from one set of agents to another. There is no social loss involved over and above the fact that public policy is distorted.

In the grabbing hand scenario, rents have to be created by the public official before bribes can be collected. This is done by introducing a license system which restricts entry to economic activity and creates artificial scarcity. This, by itself, involve a social loss. Yet, the public official has a private incentive to do this because he can extract some or all of the rent from the would-be producers who are willing to offer a bribe to be "assigned" the scarcity rent. Again, the bribe is a pure transfer between producers and public officials, and, given and take, transaction costs, it does not constitute a social loss in and by itself. Although the rent created by each licence is contestable, the structure of the contest is such that competition takes place through bribery. It does not involve any persuasion, advocacy or any other activity which would involve "burning" real resources with positive shadow prices and which might not benefit the public official personally in the process of seeking the rent conferred by the production licence.

The core insight from Tullock's seminal paper that these approaches (and the corruption literature more generally) have not taken up is the notion of "rent contestability". Consider the case of monopoly rents created by entry restrictions. Tullock (1967) points out that, if the monopoly rent is contestable, it will attract real resources, which he assumed was equal to its value. This adds the "Tullock rectangle" to the standard deadweight cost of monopoly. If, in contrast, the monopoly right were secured by paying the public official in charge a bribe, it would appear that the additional cost would vanish: the bribe is "just" a transfers from one party to another. However, this misses the point. Posner (1975) puts it like this: "It might seem that where monopoly is obtained by bribery of government officials, the additional loss of monopoly [the rent-seeking cost] would be eliminated since a bribe is a pure transfer. In fact, however, bribery merely shifts the monopoly profit to the officials receiving the bribe and draws real resources into the activity of becoming the official who is in the position to receive these bribes" (p. 82).[5]

This is a very important point which has been largely ignored in the corruption literature, but not entirely. Hillman and Katz (1987) take up the baton in their paper "Hierarchical structure and the social costs of bribes and transfers".[6] Their starting point is that agents who seek a rent may use bribery—transfers of income—to gain access to the rent. While these bribes do not (necessarily) involve any social loss, the bribe income stream may be contestable. This happens when bribe income is a prize that can be won through a contest for particular positions in government, i.e., the positions to which the bribes accrue are themselves contestable. In the environmental regulation scenario, for example, being appointed to oversee regulated firms may be open to many potential officials who all know that obtaining the appointment will allow them to extract bribes from the firms that they oversee. If so, a pure rent-seeking contest will follow and the resources employed in winning that contest may well be time and effort—factors of production that could be used productively. Consequently, the rent created by the corruption opportunity offered by asymmetric information and imperfect monitoring, not only represents a case of pure corruption. It also represents a case of pure rent seeking because the position in the government bureaucracy is a contestable rent. The situation becomes even worse when influence seeking takes place within a hierarchy in which lower-down officials pass some of the bribe income on to higher-up officials. In this case, each position becomes a contestable rent with an associated social cost of contestability (Hillman and Katz 1987). Another reason why the rent-seeking cost is likely to be large in this case is that the rents are *private*, i.e., the prize of obtaining a position in the hierarchy is a private revenue stream. Ursprung (1990) has shown that the distinction between private and public-goods rents is very important for the overall social cost. The degree of rent dissipation is much larger with private than with public-goods rents.

The point about contestability is also taken up in a sequence of studies of misallocation of talent and corruption, although the connection to the rent-seeking literature is not always made explicit. The general idea in this literature is that talented people can be employed as private sector entrepreneurs (or in some other productive job) or as government bureaucrats. Positions in the public sector offer corruption possibilities and government officials can benefit personally from the rents they control (created by, for example, collusion allowed by asymmetric information as in the example above). Controlling these rents is a contestable prize and agents will seek employment in the government sector to gain access to them. If the most talented people seek these jobs, there will be misallocation of talent: individuals who should have become productive entrepreneurs become rent seekers (in the sense of pure rent seeking) instead. The social costs of rent seeking is, then, the economic consequences of this misallocation of talent, which could be lower growth or income, plus, of course, the policy distortion created by bribery in the first place.

Murphy et al. (1991) develop this logic in a model of allocation of talent in which the government serves no particular purpose. However, government jobs offer the possibility to create and extract rents to the personal benefit of the holder of the job (which is their definition of corruption). The analysis emphasizes that talent is often general and talented individuals can be successful in many different jobs, including in jobs that offer pure corruption possibilities and in entrepreneurial jobs. More able people may be able to extract more rents, and if this advantage is sufficiently large, the most talented will seek jobs in the public sector *because* those jobs offer corruption opportunities. The social cost is too little innovation and lower economic growth [see also Murphy et al. (1993)].

The underlying premise of this analysis is that more able people are good at both rent seeking and productive activities. This appears plausible: many lobbyists are very clever, and could have put their talent to productive use in the biotech or some other frontier industry rather than use their abilities in the lobbying industry. However, this is not the only reason why corruption opportunities in the public sector can lead to misallocation of talent. Acemoglu and Verdier (1998, 2001) point to another more subtle mechanism. In their analysis, the government bureaucracy has a socially valuable purpose, namely to enforce contracts that support productive investment. This, however, creates corruption possibilities since individual bureaucrats may decide not to enforce a contract in return for a payment from the party that benefits. Anticipating this makes investment unprofitable *ex ante* and too little or no investment will be undertaken. The benevolent government may try to solve this problem by paying efficiency wages. This, however, generates a social cost because it attracts individuals to the public sector with no comparative advantage in that sector. The rent-seeking cost is indirect in this model: it is not so much the fact that government jobs offer corruption possibilities that is the source of the problem. Rather, it is the benevolent government's attempt to control corruption by paying above market wages that induces the misallocation of talent.

5 THE INFLUENCE OF THE CORRUPTION LITERATURE ON THE STUDY OF RENT SEEKING

While the corruption literature, leaving the exceptions noted above aside, could learn from the rent-seeking literature, it is not a one-way street. The rent-seeking literature can also learn from the corruption literature, or, at least, part of it.

Most importantly, the "grabbing hand" corruption literature emphasises rent creation: corrupt officials create rents which they extract for themselves via bribery. They do so by introducing artificial scarcity via licenses, permissions, cumbersome procedures, etc. In contrast, in the rent-seeking literature, the rents are often (but obviously not always) taken as given; they are there for "whatever reason". It is plain that the incentive of a public official to create artificial scarcity depends critically on whether he or she can subsequently benefit from the rent thus created. Government officials have little incentive to create rents if they cannot benefit from them (Hillman 2015). Bribery allows officials the maximum flexibility in capturing the rent they have created. As emphasized by Lambsdorff (2002), this makes corruption, understood as influence-seeking activities from which officials personally benefit, particularly harmful to society: corruption possibilities encourage rent creation. If, instead, rent creation triggers influence-seeking activities which do *not* directly benefit the official and may even be costly to him or her because it involves costly engagement with lobbyists and special interests, then the incentive to create the rent in the first place is decreased.

In short, corruption encourages rent creation because it allows the creator of the rent to benefit personally. To quote Tullock (1996, p. 8) in his discussion of corruption in nineteenth century China, "the official actually write the laws with the intent of being bribed to permit people to avoid carrying out the law." In contrast, if bribery for some reason becomes impossible or unattractive (e.g., because of better control structures) and, as a consequence, most rents will be contested in ways that do not benefit the official, then he or she might decide that it is time to repeal the regulation that generated the rent in the first place and be deterred from thinking up ways to create new rents. An implication, then, is that bribery is particularly harmful from a social point of view. It underlies the incentive for officials to create rents. This is socially harmful in itself because it involves creating artificial scarcity and this creates deadweight losses. On top of that, bribery and corruption more broadly maximise the risk of triggering costly contests related to obtaining the positions in government that enable the bribes to be collected.

While the consequences of the symbiotic relationship between rent creation and corruption has yet to be fully explored in the rent-seeking literature in general, the literature on contest design, initiated by Gradstein and Konrad (1999) and explored in Mealem and Nitzan (2015) amongst others, provides the foundation for a bridge between the two literatures. It studies how a contest might be designed if the "rent-seeking effort" is beneficial to the contest designer who then has an interest in maximising "effort". This incentive is particularly strong if the "effort" is a bribe transfer to the contest designer. A promising research programme would be to explore more deeply the interplay between corruption, rent creation and contest design.

6 THE EMPIRICS OF CORRUPTION AND RENT SEEKING

The past 30 years have seen a massive empirical research effort aimed at understanding the causes and consequences of (pure) corruption (see, e.g., Paldam 2002; Lambsdorff 2005; Svensson 2005; Treisman 2007; Aidt 2011a). This research agenda has been fuelled by cross country data on corruption perceptions and more recently by individual or firm level survey data on experienced corruption. These types of data have attracted a fair amount of critique and rightly so.[7] Yet, the empirical corruption literature clearly points to substantial economic costs of corruption. Mauro (1995), for example, finds a small negative growth effect and a large negative effect of corruption on investment. Subsequent research has shown that the growth effect interacts with the underlying quality of institutions (Aidt et al. 2008; Méndez and Sepúlveda 2006; Méon and Weill 2010) and that corruption has a detrimental impact on sustainable development (Aidt 2011b). Other studies have shown that corruption increases inequality (Gupta et al. 2002) and distorts fiscal and monetary policy and the composition of government spending (e.g., Mauro 1998; Hessami 2014; Dimakou 2015). Expenditure tracking studies undertaken in many countries have demonstrated how vast amounts of public resources intended for schools and other public spending programmes simply disappear and never reach the intended beneficiaries (Reinikka and Svensson 2004).

Unlike the study of corruption, empirical research on rent seeking can hardly be said to be booming.[8] The existing research efforts have partly been guided by the invertability hypothesis and partly by attempts to measure rent seeking costs directly. Krueger (1974), Posner (1975) and Cowling and Mueller (1978) pioneered the indirect method based on the invertability hypothesis. Krueger (1974) estimated that the welfare loss from trade intervention in India and Turkey in the 1960s was between 7 and 15 % of GNP. Posner (1975) estimated the rent seeking cost associated with monopoly regulation in the USA to be between 5 and 32 % of industry sales. Cowling and Mueller (1978) found that the total welfare cost of monopoly in the US and the UK, respectively, was 13 and 7 % of gross corporate product. These studies and others like them *assume* full rent dissipation. The theoretical literature on rent seeking contests shows that this assumption is only valid in special cases and that the degree of dissipation depends on the contest function, on risk preferences, on the nature of the prize being sought, and on many other features. Employing the full dissipation assumption is, therefore, likely to inflate the cost estimates. Lopez and Pagoulatos (1994) is a rare example of a study that estimates the degree of rent dissipation. They find, in an application to US trade policy, that 67 % of the value of the available rent is dissipated and estimate the total social loss of trade barriers in the US to be 12.5 % of the value of domestic consumption. Hazlett and Michaels (1993) also estimate dissipation ratios. They explore a natural experience induced by a cellular telephone licence lottery in the 1980s in the USA and find that the ratio was 31.2 % on average.

An alternative approach is to estimate the social cost of rent seeking simply by adding observable expenditures on rent seeking related activities up. A typical finding is that the actual money spent on lobbying (in the USA) is low relative to the value of the rents at stake—an observation Tullock (1988) himself made when he rhetorically asked why the total amount of resources going into politics appear to be small relative to the value of the prizes that can potentially be won.[9] Others have gone further than counting lobbying expenses and added more expenditures to the rent seeking bill (e.g., expenditures on advertising, on crime prevention, or on property rights disputes) or tried to estimate rent seeking costs from "excess" presence of certain types of economic activities in capital cities (e.g., sit-down restaurants). The estimates emerging from this type of research vary a lot in size, from 0.2 to 23.7 % of GDP (Del Rosal 2011, Table 2). The fundamental problem with this approach clearly is that it requires an up-front judgement about what constitutes rent seeking costs, and doing that objectively is hard, if not impossible.

The empirical rent-seeking literature suggests that rent dissipation is incomplete, and that the total rent seeking cost, therefore, could be a lot smaller than the value of the rents. In contrast, the empirical corruption literature points to substantial welfare costs of corruption and strongly suggests that corruption is a major obstacle to economic development. Of course, one could take the view that corruption costs in practise are correlated with rent seeking costs. However, doing so would diverge attention away from the very important task of quantifying the true cost of rent seeking. One way out of this conundrum is to base empirical research on rent seeking more firmly on rent seeking theory and to build structural models that can be matched to observable data on policy outcomes, campaign contributions, employment in the lobbying industry, etc. and in that way help us back out the true cost of public policy.

7 CONCLUSION

It is surprising that the corruption and rent-seeking literatures have not crisscrossed more than it appears to have been the case. After all, they are both concerned with what I have called influence-seeking activities and there is clearly scope for fruitful cross fertilization. The corruption literature, both the branch that focuses on principal-agent relationships within government and the branch that focusses on leviathan-type governments, has largely ignored the "missiles seek heat hypothesis" of rent seeking, i.e., the notion that the presence of contestable rents elicits socially costly activities aimed at winning the rents. The consequences of this are two-fold. First, the literature underestimates the value of corruption-control policies. The overriding objective of the law and economics and organisational economics literature on corruption is precisely to devise and evaluate such policies. A fruitful research project would be integrate the notion of contestable rents and the associated rent-seeking cost into the principal-agent models of corruption and to reconsider existing results about socially optimal levels of corruption. Second, the literature underestimates the social cost of corruption. Insofar as corruption is conceptualized as a costless transfer of income from one party to another, it may appear that corruption is a social problem only because it leads to policy distortions and because it leads to inequitable and unfair allocations of public resources and funds. The rent-seeking literature would insist adding Tullock rectangles on the debit side. We just need to quantify them.

FOOTNOTES

1The rent-seeking literature has been surveyed by Nitzan (1994), Tollison (1997), Congleton et al. (2008), Hillman (2013), and Long (2013 [2015]). The papers in Congleton and Hillman (2015) summarize the different dimensions of the rent-seeking literature.

2See, e.g., Hillman and Samet (1987) on all-pay auctions, Ursprung (1990) on rents as public goods, and Aidt and Hillman (2008) on rents that endure over time and may require re-contesting.

3Williams (2000) contains a collection of social science articles that dwell more deeply into the definitional issues.

4Aidt (2003) lists two additional categories, called efficient corruption and self-reinforcing corruption. For the purpose of evaluating the influence of the rent-seeking literature on the corruption literature, it is, however, sufficient to zoom in on the two main categories listed in the text. For other classifications, see Tanzi (1998), Rose-Ackerman (1999) or Jain (2001).

5Krueger (1974, pp. 292–293) makes a similar point.

6Hillman and Ursprung (2000) describe nested contests in which outsiders compete to be insiders who compete directly for rents. Political culture determines the openness of the contests to outsiders.

7See the critical discussion in Kaufmann et al. (2006).

8Del Rosal (2011) offers a critical survey of the empirical rent-seeking literature.

9Mixon (2002), for example, finds that interest group contributions related to obtaining social security funds in the USA amount to only 0.2 % of the value of the potential rents. Goldberg and Maggi (1999) estimate the weight given to social welfare relative to special interest groups in the setting of US trade policy. Their results suggest that the influence of special interests is very small, which, again, suggests that the welfare cost of rent seeking is of limited importance. Hillman and Ursprung (2016) discuss reasons why there appear to be less rent seeking and less rent dissipation than might be expected.

REFERENCES

1. Acemoglu, D., & Verdier, T. (1998). Property rights, corruption and the allocation of talent: A general equilibrium approach. Economic Journal, 108, 1381–1403.

2. Acemoglu, D., & Verdier, T. (2000). The choice between market failure and corruption. American Economic Review, 90(1), 194–211.

3. Aidt, T. S. (2003). Economic analysis of corruption: A survey. Economic Journal, 113, F633–F652.

4. Aidt, T. S. (2011a). The causes of corruption. Journal for Institutional Comparison, 9(2), 15–19.

5. Aidt, T. S. (2011b). Corruption and sustainable development. In S. Rose-Ackerman & T. Søreide (Eds.), International handbook on the economics of corruption (Vol. 2, pp. 3–51). Cheltenham: Edward Elgar.

6. Aidt, T. S., & Dutta, J. (2008). Policy compromises: Corruption and regulation in a democracy. Economics and Politics, 20(3), 335–360.

7. Aidt, T. S., Dutta, J., & Sena, V. (2008). Governance regimes, corruption and growth: Theory and evidence. Journal of Comparative Economics, 36(2), 195–220.

8. Aidt, T. S., & Hillman, A. L. (2008). Enduring rents. European Journal of Political Economy,164, 509–533.

9. Becker, G., & Stigler, G. (1974). Law enforcement, malfeasance and the compensation of enforcers. Journal of Legal Studies, 3, 1–19.

10. Bliss, C., & di Tella, R. (1997). Does competition kill corruption? Journal of Political Economy,105, 1001–1023.

11. Buchanan, J. (1980). Rent seeking and profit seeking. In J. M. Buchanan, R. D. Tollison & G. Tullock (Eds.), Towards a theory of the rent-seeking society (pp. 3–15). College Station, TX: Texas A&M Press. Reprinted in R.D. Congleton, A.L. Hillman & K.A. Konrad (Eds.) (2008), Forty years of research on rent seeking 1—The theory of rent seeking (pp. 55–67). Heidelberg: Springer.

12. Charap, J., & Harm, C. (2002). Institutionalized corruption and the Kleptocratic state. In G. T. Abed & S. Gupta (Eds.), Governance, corruption, economic performance, Chapter 6 (pp. 135–158). Washington, D.C.: The International Monetary Fund.

13. Congleton, R. D., & Hillman, A. L. (Eds.). (2015). Companion to the political economy of rent seeking. Cheltenham: Edward Elgar.

14. Congleton, R. D., Hillman, A. L., & Konrad, K. A. (2008). Forty years of research on rent seeking: An overview. In R.D. Congleton, A.L. Hillman & K.A. Konrad (Eds.) (2008), Forty years of research on rent seeking 1—The theory of rent seeking (pp. 1–42). Heidelberg: Springer.

15. Cowling, K., & Mueller, D. C. (1978). The social costs of monopoly power. Economic Journal, 88, 727–748. Reprinted in R.D., Congleton, A.L. Hillman & K.A. Konrad (Eds.) (2008), Forty years of research on rent seeking 2—Applications: Rent Seeking in Practice (pp. 67–88). Heidelberg: Springer.

16. Dabla-Norris, E. (2002). A game theoretical analysis of corruption in bureaucracies. In G. T. Abed & S. Gupta (Eds.), Governance, corruption, economic performance, Chapter 5 (pp. 111–134). Washington, D.C.: The International Monetary Fund.

17. Del Rosal, I. (2011). The empirical measurement of rent-seeking costs. Journal of Economic Surveys, 25(2), 298–325.

18. Dhami, S., & Al-Nowaihi, A. (2007). Corruption and the provision of public output in a hierarchical asymmetric information relationship. Journal of Public Economic Theory, 9(4), 727–755.

19. Dimakou, O. (2015). Bureaucratic corruption and the dynamic interaction between monetary and fiscal policy. European Journal of Political Economy, 40(Part A), 57–78.

20. Epstein, G. S., & Nitzan, S. I. (2015). Contestable policies. In R. D. Congleton & A. L. Hillman (Eds.), Companion to the political economy of rent seeking (pp. 53–72). Cheltenham: Edward Elgar.

21. Goldberg, P. K., & Maggi, G. (1999). Protection for sale: An empirical investigation. American Economic Review, 89(5), 1135–1155.

22. Gradstein, M., & Konrad, K. A. (1999). Orchestrating rent seeking contests. Economic Journal, 109 (458), 536–545. Reprinted in R.D. Congleton, A.L. Hillman & K.A. Konrad (Eds.) (2008), Forty years of research on rent seeking 1—The theory of rent seeking (pp. 571–580). Heidelberg: Springer.

23. Gupta, S., Davoodi, H. R., & Alonso-Terme, R. (2002). Does corruption affect income inequality and poverty? Economics of Governance, 3, 23–45. Reprinted in G. T. Abed & S. Gupta (Eds.), Governance, corruption, economic performance, Chapter 17 (pp. 458–486). Washington, D.C.: The International Monetary Fund.

24. Hazlett, T. W., & Michaels, R. J. (1993). The cost of rent-seeking: evidence from cellular telephone license lotteries. Southern Economic Journal, 59, 425–435.

25. Hessami, Z. (2014). Political corruption, public procurement, and budget composition: Theory and evidence from OECD countries. European Journal of Political Economy, 34, 372–389.

26. Hillman, A. L. (2013). Rent seeking. In M. Reksulak, L. Razzolini, & W. F. I. I. Shughart (Eds.), The Elgar companion to public choice (2nd ed., pp. 307–330). Cheltenham: Edward Elgar.

27. Hillman, A. L. (2015). Rent seeking as political economy. In R. D. Congleton & A. L. Hillman (Eds.), Companion to the political economy of rent seeking (pp. 10–16). Cheltenham: Edward Elgar.

28. Hillman, A. L., & Katz, E. (1987). Hierarchical structure and the social costs of bribes and transfers. Journal of Public Economics, 34, 129–142. Reprinted in R.D. Congleton, A.L. Hillman & K.A. Konrad (Eds.) (2008), Forty years of research on rent seeking 1—The theory of rent seeking (pp. 523–536). Heidelberg: Springer.

29. Hillman, A. L., & Samet, D. (1987). Dissipation of contestable rents by small numbers of contenders. Public Choice, 54, 63–82. Reprinted in R.D. Congleton, A.L. Hillman & K.A. Konrad (Eds.) (2008), Forty years of research on rent seeking 1—The theory of rent seeking (pp. 165–184). Heidelberg: Springer.

30. Hillman, A. L., & Ursprung, H. W. (2000). Political culture and economic decline. European Journal of Political Economy 16, 189–213. Reprinted in R.D., Congleton, A.L. Hillman & K.A. Konrad (Eds.) (2008), Forty years of research on rent seeking 2—Applications: Rent seeking in practice (pp. 219–243). Heidelberg: Springer.

31. Hillman, A. L., & Ursprung, H. W. (2016). The political economy of income distribution: Where are the rent seekers? Constitutional Political Economy (this issue).

32. Jain, A. K. (2001). Corruption: A review. Journal of Economic Surveys, 15(1), 71–121.

33. Kaufmann, D., Kraay, A., & Mastruzzi, M. (2006). Measuring governance using cross-country perceptions data. In S. Rose-Ackerman (Ed.), International handbook on the economics of corruption (pp. 52–104). Cheltenham: Edward Elgar.

34. Krueger, A. O. (1974). The political economy of the rent-seeking society. American Economic Review, 64, 291–303. Reprinted in R.D. Congleton, A.L. Hillman & K.A. Konrad (Eds.) (2008), Forty years of research on rent seeking 2—Applications: Rent seeking in practice (pp. 151–163). Heidelberg: Springer.

35. Laffont, J. J., & Guessan, T. N. (1999). Competition and corruption in an agency relationship. Journal of Development Economics, 60, 271–295.

36. Lambsdorff, J. G. (2002). Corruption and rent seeking. Public Choice, 113(1–2), 97–125.

37. Lambsdorff, J. G. (2005). Consequences and causes of corruption: What do we know from a cross section of countries?. Passau: University of Passau.

38. Long, N. V. (2013).The theory of contest: A unified model and review of the literature. European Journal of Political Economy, 32, 161–181. Reprinted in R.D. Congleton & A.L. Hillman (Eds.) (2015), Companion to the political economy of rent seeking (pp. 19–52) Cheltenham: Edward Elgar.

39. Lopez, R. A., & Pagoulatos, E. (1994). Rent seeking and the welfare cost of trade barriers. Public Choice, 79, 149–160.

40. Lui, F. T. (1985). An equilibrium queuing model of bribery. Journal of Political Economy, 93, 760–781.

41. Mauro, P. (1995). Corruption and growth. Quarterly Journal of Economics, 110, 681–712.

42. Mauro, P. (1998). Corruption and the composition of government expenditure. Journal of Public Economics 69, 263–279. Reprinted in G. T. Abed & S. Gupta (Eds.), Governance, corruption, economic performance, Chapter 9 (pp. 225–244). Washington, D.C.: The International Monetary Fund.

43. Mealem, Y., & Nitzan, S. (2015). Contest effort. In R. D. Congleton & A. L. Hillman (Eds.), Companion to the political economy of rent seeking (pp. 124–137). Cheltenham: Edward Elgar.

44. Méndez, F., & Sepúlveda, F. (2006). Corruption, growth and political regimes: Cross country evidence. European Journal of Political Economy, 22(1), 82–98.

45. Méon, P.-G., & Weill, L. (2010). Is corruption an efficient grease? World Development, 38(3), 244–259.

46. Mixon, F. G. (2002). Social security trust funds flows and the welfare cost of rent seeking. Applied Economics, 34, 975–979.

47. Murphy, K. M., Shleifer, A., & Vishny, R. W. (1991). The allocation of talent: Implications for growth. Quarterly Journal of Economics, 106, 503–530.

48. Murphy, K. M., Shleifer, A., & Vishny, R. W. (1993). Why is rent seeking so costly to growth? American Economic Review Paper and Proceedings, 83, 409–414. Reprinted in R.D. Congleton, A.L. Hillman & K.A. Konrad (Eds.) (2008), Forty years of research on rent seeking 2—Applications: Rent seeking in practice (pp. 213–218). Heidelberg: Springer.

49. Nitzan, S. (1994). Modeling rent-seeking contests. European Journal of Political Economy, 10, 41–60.

50. Paldam, M. (2002). The cross-country pattern of corruption: Economics, culture and the seesaw dynamics. European Journal of Political Economy, 18(2), 215–220.

51. Posner, R. A. (1975). The social cost of monopoly and regulation. Journal of Political Economy, 83, 807–827. Reprinted in R.D. Congleton, A.L. Hillman & K.A. Konrad (Eds.) (2008), Forty years of research on rent seeking 2—Applications: Rent seeking in practice (pp. 45–65). Heidelberg: Springer.

52. Reinikka, R., & Svensson, J. (2004). Local capture: Evidence from a central government transfer program in Uganda. Quarterly Journal of Economics, 119(2), 679–705.

53. Rose-Ackerman, S. (1975). The economics of corruption. Journal of Public Economics, 4, 187–203.

54. Rose-Ackerman, S. (1999). Corruption and government, causes, consequences and reform. Cambridge: Cambridge University Press.

55. Shleifer, A., & Vishny, R. W. (1993). Corruption. Quarterly Journal of Economics, 108, 599–618.

56. Svensson, J. (2005). Eight questions about corruption. Journal of Economic Perspectives,19(3), 19–42.

57. Tanzi, V. (1998). Corruption around the world, causes, consequences, scope, and cures. IMF Staff Papers, 45 (4), 559–594. Reprinted in G. T. Abed & S. Gupta (Eds.), Governance, corruption, economic performance, Chapter 2 (pp. 19–58). Washington, D.C.: The International Monetary Fund.

58. Tirole, J. (1992). Collusion and the theory of organization. In J. J. Laffont (Ed.), Advances in economic theory (sixth world congress Vol. 2). Cambridge: Cambridge University Press.

59. Tirole, J. (1994). The internal organisation of government. Oxford Economic Papers, 46, 1–29.

60. Tollison, R. D. (1997). Rent seeking. In D. C. Mueller (Ed.), Perspectives on public choice. A handbook (pp. 506–526). Cambridge: Cambridge University Press.

61. Treisman, D. (2007). What have we learned about the causes of corruption from ten years of cross-national empirical research? Annual Review of Political Science, 10, 211–244.

62. Tullock, G. (1967). The welfare cost of tariffs, monopolies, and theft. Western Economic Journal 5, 224–232. Reprinted in R.D. Congleton, A.L. Hillman & K.A. Konrad (Eds.) (2008), Forty years of research on rent seeking 1—The theory of rent seeking (pp. 45–53). Heidelberg: Springer.

63. Tullock, G. (1980). Efficient rent seeking. In J. M. Buchanan, R. D. Tollison, & G. Tullock (Eds.), Towards a theory of the rent-seeking society (pp. 97–112). College Station, TX: Texas A&M Press. Reprinted in R.D. Congleton, A.L. Hillman & K.A. Konrad (Eds.) (2008), Forty years of research on rent seeking 1—The theory of rent seeking (pp. 105–120). Heidelberg: Springer.

64. Tullock, G. (1988). Future directions for rent-seeking research. In C. K. Rowley, R. D. Tollison, & G. Tullock (Eds.), The political economy of rent seeking. Boston: Kluwer.

65. Tullock, G. (1996). Corruption theory and practice. Contemporary Economic Policy, XIV, 6–13.

10

THE IMPACT OF THE US POLITICAL PRESSURE ON RMB EXCHANGE RATE: AN EVENT STUDY ANALYSIS

Wei Guo[1,2]

[1]Department of Economics, College of Economics, Jinan University, Guangzhou, China

[2]Department of Credit Management, Guangdong University of Finance, Guangzhou, China

ABSTRACT

This paper takes the US as an example and uses event study approach to analyze the political events in which the US pressured RMB exchange rate between July 22, 2005 and March 31, 2016 as well as the outcomes of such actions, trying to reveal the influence of such events during the appreciation and depreciation period of RMB. The conclusions are as follows: 1) The pressure from the United States did not play a significant role in promoting RMB appreciation since only 53.4% out of 116 events between July 22, 2005 and March 31, 2016 were successful; 2) In various political events that aim at imposing pressure between July 22, 2005 and March 31, 2016, the US Congress had more significant influence on RMB exchange rate than the US administrative sectors; 3) Judging from the number of events, RMB exchange rate hasn't undergone obviously increased pressure from the US since its devaluation in 2014. However, unlike the situation in the appreciation stage, US administrative sectors were more influential than the Congress in the devaluation stage.

Keywords: Political Pressure, RMB Exchange Rate, Event Study

1. INTRODUCTION

After joining the World Trade Organization in 2001, China accumulates huge amounts of foreign exchange reserves through current-account surplus in foreign trade. After the exchange rate reform in July 2005, the current- account surplus has undergone even faster growth. Although the growth rate slowed down due to the international financial crisis between 2008 and 2011, the trend of surplus remained unchanged. According to the data from State Administration of Foreign Exchange (SAFE), China's current-account surplus reached 219.7 billion US dollars and the capital & financial account surplus reached 38.2 billion US dollars in 2014. From the perspective of balance of payments, China's current-account surplus implies losses to the corresponding accounts of trading partners such as the United States. These trading partners tend to balance the revenue and expenditure account through issuance of debts, which would further aggravate the imbalance of economic structure, especially in the context of an international financial crisis. Therefore, the fluctuation of RMB exchange rate became the focus of concern and debate among countries like the United States.

In 2001, an article titled "China's Cheap Currency" was published in "Financial Times" and triggered hot debates among the international public over the revaluation of RMB. Since then, RMB exchange rate became a hot field of research in the international community and academia. In 2002, the Vice Finance Minister of Japan, Haruhiko Kuroda, and his Deputy Masahiro Kawai published the article "It's the Time for Global reflation" in "Financial Times", pointing out that China is exporting deflation to the world and putting forward the "China threat" theory. At the G7 finance minister conference in February of the same year, Japan's Finance Minister Masajuro Shiokawa submitted a bill to express the hope that finance ministers and central bank governors from the other six countries could put pressure on China and urge the revaluation of

RMB. Masajuro Shiokawa accused the Chinese government of curbing the appreciation of RMB at the conference. He deemed the excessive undervaluation of RMB exchange rate as the direct cause of global deflation, demanding RMB appreciation by following the example of 1985 Japan-US "Plaza Accords". However, due to surpluses in the trade with China, Japan successfully got rid of continuing decline in the context of economic growth in Asia, which made it less imperative for Japan to call for revaluation of Renminbi. Since then, the United States became the major origin of pressure on appreciation of RMB. Especially after China surpassed Japan and became the largest origin of deficit for US in 2002, RMB exchange rate has aroused particular concern among American interest groups, congress and the government. Issues concerning exchange rate have also become an important means for US to push China in the new century. On the one hand, US administration officials like the President, Secretary of the Treasury and even the chairman of Fed have repeatedly stated that China needs to assume more responsibility in correcting global economic imbalances and pushing the unilateral appreciation of RMB through bilateral ("Strategic Economic Dialogue" (SED) and "Strategic and Economic Dialogue" (S&ED)) and multilateral (IMF and the G20) mechanisms. On the other hand, US congressmen frequently propose motions or bills regarding RMB exchange rate, aiming at creating linkage between RMB exchange rate and Sino-US trade. It oppressed substantial and rapid RMB appreciation by threatening to impose anti-dumping duties and countervailing duties; or justifying the anti-dumping duties and countervailing duties on goods imported from China by accusing China of withholding RMB exchange rate to obtain unfair competitive advantages. The most prominent event is that the US Senate passed the "Currency Exchange Rate Oversight Reform Act of 2011" in October 2011, demanding the US government to investigate whether the exchange rates of major trading partners were undervalued. Then it determined to impose punitive tariffs, aiming at pushing the appreciation of RMB.

According to the statistics, RMB has appreciated more than 25% against the US dollar since the reform of exchange rate system in 2005 until the end of 2013. Such substantial appreciation resulted from economic factors like strong economic growth over the years, continual accumulation of current-account surplus and inflows of foreign speculative capitals. But are there any political incentives other than economic factors behind the rapid appreciation of the RMB, especially the external political incentives from countries like US that force the appreciation of RMB all along? Some events seem to offer a clue to the answers. The first event is Paulson effect. Paulson effect refers to the phenomenon that former US Treasury Secretary Henry Paulson's three visits to China after assuming office triggered substantial appreciation of RMB three times. During Paulson's first visit in September 2006, the RMB exchange rate successively broke three integer marks—7.94, 7.93 and 7.92—in four days, which hit a new high. Between 14th and 15th December of the same year,

Paulson paid the second visit to China and led a delegation to carry out SED. The central parity rate of RMB exchange rate exceeded the 7.82 mark for the first time and reached the level of 7.8197. During the third visit to China, the RMB exchange rate approached the 7.74 mark and once again hit a new high since the reform of exchange rate system. The second event is the 2012 US presidential election. During the US presidential election in 2012, the final candidates Barack Obama and Romney successively condemned each other for adopting overly weak China policy. In the meantime, the yuan-dollar exchange rate underwent eight consecutive limits under great upward pressure. Although the Chinese government repeatedly stressed the independence of the RMB exchange rate policy and denied the impact of foreign political pressure on changes in the exchange rate. In an official declaration of foreign policy, such a statement is particularly necessary and understandable. However, from an academic point of view, we need to use economic methodology to further reveal the causes of external political pressure and the specific impact of impellent events on the RMB exchange rate. This paper takes U.S. as the primary pusher and uses event study approach to analyze the political events between July 22, 2005 and March 31, 2016 in which the United States put pressure on RMB exchange rate and outcomes of such actions, trying to reveal the influence of such events during the appreciation and depreciation of RMB.

2. LITERATURE REVIEW

In recent years, the scholars have tried different theories and empirical research methods to verify the relevance between RMB appreciation and external political pressure. Li Zenggang, Dong Liwa (2005) studied Renminbi exchange rate under framework of Two-Level Game, which indicates the issue of currency contains complicated political and economical factors, the decision of Renminbi exchange rate involves game between countries, game between interest groups, and game between interest groups and the government [1] . Xiao Ting and Wang Yan (2012) analyzed the Sino-US disputes over exchange rate from the perspective of evolutionary game theory [2] . They found that in the face of external appreciation pressure, the Chinese government's attitude towards RMB exchange rate experienced a transition from unchanged exchange rate, accelerated appreciation, slight appreciation and finally to the long-term and slow appreciation. Li Zilian (2011) constructed a panel data variable coefficient model which takes the RMB exchange rate against currencies of different countries as the explained variables and political variables including interest groups, election cycle, political parties and factions as well as the bills of US House and Senate as major explanatory variables. After empirical analyses on the data of United States, Japan, Britain, Germany and France between 1995 and 2009, the study concluded that: factors like interest groups, election cycle as well as political parties and factions contribute to the appreciation of RMB [3] . Han Huichao, Xu Kangning (2014 constructed a Pro-bit model to analyze "Exchange rate reform to promote fair trade act" from the U.S. congress in 2010, empirical result shows that pressures put on China for Renminbi appreciation is the consequence of game between interest groups, members of congress and voters [4] . Zhang Xin, Cui Yanjuan, Sun Gang (2015) started from the perspective of political games, studied the impact of foreign governments and the Chinese government on Renminbi exchange rate, they found that game between governments has significant influence on Renminbi exchange rate, since the foreign governments stay in the advantage positions in the game, the pressures put on Renminbi has significantly promoted the appreciation of Renminbi [5] . Zhu Mengnan et al. (2015) established a "Political Cycle Spillover Effect Model" by taking the US political cycle as the most critical political factor and analyzing the transmission mechanism between political cycle and RMB exchange rate. They conducted empirical analyses and found that: US political cycle has a direct short-term impact on the RMB exchange rate and such impact is mainly transmitted through capital flows and policy control; the RMB appreciation rate would show cyclical variations along with the US presidential election and mid-term election: the RMB appreciation rate would significantly decrease in the first year after the US President assumes office and undergo sharp increase in the first year after the mid-term election [6] . Inspired by events like "Paulsen effect", some scholars began to focus on different events that affect the fluctuation of RMB exchange rate through external political pressure. For example, Frankel & Wei (2007) collected news from mainstream US newspapers about the United States putting pressure on RMB and analyzed whether the US political pressure enhances the flexibility of RMB's daily return. The results indicated that the US political pressure showed no significant influence between July 1, 2005 and January 8, 2007 after other factors in the currency basket were controlled [7] . Liu and Laurent (2012) collected news concerning RMB from mainstream US newspapers and built some political indicators. They found that US political pressure and non-US political pressure had insignificant influence on RMB's daily return between July 2005 and May 2011; however RMB's conditional volatility is subject to external political pressure [8] . Liu Tao and Zhou Jizhong (2011) focused on investigating the effect of pressure from US Government and Congress. They used "classification event study" to investigate the impact of US political pressure on RMB appreciation between 2005 and 2010 and pointed out that: although the impact of US political pressure on RMB appreciation is generally insignificant, the impact would become more significant when RMB remains fixed or devaluates; the pressure from US legislation branches is more effective than that form governmental sectors [9]

The existing literatures studied the impacts on determination and fluctuation of RMB exchange rate from the perspective of game theory, domestic political factors of countries that impose pressure or external political events, which provides people with new angles to better understand the determination mechanism and fluctuation of exchange rate. However, the relevant researches still have some drawbacks for the lack of a mature research system during the development stage: Firstly, the existing literatures' definition of external events is unclear. The majority of studies adopt the classification of legislative and administrative sector without classification and analysis of specific sources within two sectors; secondly, most studies were simply focused on whether external political pressure caused the appreciation of RMB. They didn't study the devaluation period after February 2014 or analyze the existence and results of impellent events in such period. This paper attempts to overcome these shortcomings in the study. It firstly carries out rigorous and systematic definition and classification of the pressure from US; Secondly, it covers the depreciation period after 2014, observing whether the external political pressure remains when devaluation became the norm and the effects of such pressure.

3. EVENT STUDY APPROACH

"Event study" was first put forward by James and Dolley in 1933 when they were examining the price effects of stock splits. The principle is using event study approach to observe the impact of specific economic or political events on changes in stock price or stock yield, so as to explain part of the reasons why stock price or stock yield fluctuates in a short term. Subsequently, the scholars began to use it in economic and financial areas. In the studies on exchange rates, event study is mainly used to research the effects of governmental intervention in foreign exchange market on fluctuations of exchange rates. Scholars have adopted this method to observe the influence of governmental interventions in the exchange market (usually monetary sterilization events like buying or selling) on exchange rates. Neely (2005) [10] divided relevant literatures into three classes according to differences in the application of event study: time series event study, other event study methods and well-defined structure analysis event study. In recent years, the scholars are still trying different event study methods to research the effects of external political events on the RMB exchange rate. For example, Liu and Laurent (2012) applied the time series event study method; built some political pressure indicators that pressure RMB; used GARCH model to conduct empirical analysis of the external pressure's influence on RMB's daily returns and conditional volatility. Liu Tao (2011) adopted the "classification event study" which includes means like non- parametric sign test, paired sample test and predictive value test to investigate whether US political pressure pushes the appreciation of RMB.

Considering the difficulties in quantifying external political events; that the events are sporadic and clustered; and that varied types of events require specific classification and definition, this paper adopts the concept of "classification event study method" proposed by Liu Tao (2011) to distinguish from the "time series event study method" and highlight that the political events are complex in type and need more specific classification and definition. The specific steps are as follows: 1) Define the events, 2) Define the time window of events, 3) Define the criteria for successful events, 4) Make assessments of the successful events.

3.1. Define the Events

The definition of political events plays a very important part in researches on the impact of external pressure on RMB exchange rate and the extent of such pressure. However the existing literatures have had different definitions of political impellent events. Liu and Laurent (2012), searched headlines with the keyword "RMB appreciation" and "RMB exchange rate flexibility" in both Bloomberg and Reuters news database, included foreign dignitaries' comments relating to RMB in official and non-official occasion into the event statistics, and collected 213 events between May 30, 2011 and July 22, 2005; Hu Zaiyong (2013) modelled on the practice of Liu and replaced the Chinese databases. He searched the keyword "putting pressure" and "RMB" in the Chinese Biz Serial Database and Chinese Newspaper Resources Full-text Database, finding 256 events between August 31, 2011 and July 22, 2005 [11] ; While Liu Tao (2010) defined impellent events as the official, formal, and public pressure, including events such as US legislative branches' official motions and hearings, official high-level meetings, and the twice-yearly exchange rate policy report from Ministry of Finance. He captured 53 events between July 2005 and October 2010, all of which were divided into legislative and the administrative ones. This paper defines political impellent events as the official, formal, and public pressure including US Congress's motions and hearings with respect to RMB exchange rate, Sino-US heads meetings, US Treasury Secretary's visits to China, the release of reports on international economy and exchange rate policy, SED and S&ED Conferences, as well as China-US Joint Commission on Commerce and Trade (JCCT). It collected a total of 116 events between July 22, 2005 and March 31, 2016. Secondly, events like congress motions and hearings, the release of reports on international economy and exchange rate policy generally occur in one day; while events like Sino-US heads meetings, US Treasury Secretary's visits to China and Sino-US bilateral conferences usually last for a few days. This paper defines both of them as separate events. On the other hand, as for coincidence of events, (for example, the 2007 SED meeting, JCCT and the release of reports on international economy and exchange rate policy all took place between December 11th and 19th) this paper combines multiple events into an event period. A total of 107 events periods were finally obtained in this way.

3.2. Define the Pre- and Post-Event Windows

Define the time window of events means to set the length of event periods. The length of event periods would affect the accurate understanding of events' impacts on the exchange rate at a specific time. It may be difficult to fully capture the impact of events on exchange rate if the window is too short; if the window is too long, the coincidence of events may cause interference among events, which makes it impossible to observe the influence from a particular event. In the existing literatures, Rasmus Fatum & Michael m. Hutchison (2003) [12] , Pierdzioch & Stadtmann (2004) [13] and Liu Tao (2010) all used 2 days as the window length to avoid overlap. After observing 107 event periods during the sample period, this paper decided to take 2 business days when the RMB/USD exchange rate is released as the window length, that is, to contrast the exchange rate fluctuations 2 days before and after the event period during the evaluation of event effects, and require at least 2 pre-event (after-event) windows (4 bilateral exchange rate published days) between 2 separate events.

3.3. Define a Successful Event

In the studies of political pressure's influence on the RMB exchange rate, the successful event means that fluctuations of RMB exchange rate meet the expected effect of a political impellent event, which generally speaking, is the result of RMB appreciation. However, the changes in exchange rates are quite complex in reality and there're also various forms of successful events. Therefore, it is necessary to develop criteria of "success" before contrasting changes in RMB's daily return in the pre-event and after-event window to better observe the impacts of external political pressure on RMB. With reference to the success criteria proposed by Neely (2005), Rasmus Fatum and Michael M. Hutchison (2003), Marcel Fratzscher (2005) [14] , and Liu Tao (2010), this paper adopts the follows success criteria, see Table 1.

4. ANALYSIS OF THE ASSESSMENT RESULTS

This paper uses event study approach to assess the impact on RMB from US political pressure between 22 July 2005 and 31 March 2016. RMB's daily return is taken as the RMB exchange rate: $r_t = (\ln s_t - \ln s_{t-1}) \times 100\%$, s_t refers to the RMB/USD exchange rate. As for the subject of events, the political events are divided into those initiated by the legislative branches and by the administrative departments. The events initiated by legislative branches mainly include US Congress's motions and hearings in connection with RMB exchange rate ; while the events initiated by administrative departments include Sino-US heads meetings, US Treasury Secretary' s visits to China, reports on international economy and exchange rate policy, SED and S&ED Conferences, as well as China-US Joint Commission on Commerce and Trade(JCCT). The data sources of abovementioned events are listed in Table 2.

4.1. Results of Assessment on Classified Events

By applying the event study method and the definitions discussed above, political events from United States between 22 July 2005 and 31 March 2016 which concerning RMB exchange rate are classified and assessed in the following table, see Table 3.

Table 1. Success criteria of events.

Success criteria	RMB's daily return before and after the event	Explanation
Reversal	$\Delta S_{pre} > 0, \Delta S_{post} < 0$	Reversal means that RMB was devaluating before the event and switched to the state of appreciation after the event.
Smoothing	$\Delta S_{pre} > 0, \Delta S_{post} > 0 \text{ and } \Delta S_{post} < \Delta S_{pre}$	Smoothing means that RMB was devaluating before the event and the depreciation mitigated after the event despite the continued trend of depreciation.
Enlarging	$\Delta S_{pre} < 0, \Delta S_{post} < 0 \text{ and } \Delta S_{post} < \Delta S_{pre}$	Enlarging means that RMB was undergoing appreciation before the event. then the appreciation continued and enlarged after the event.

Table 2. Data sources.

Event	Data sources	Key words
Congress(motion)	https://www.congress.gov/ http://thomas.loc.gov/home/thomas.php	Exchange rate. currency. China. exchange rate manipulation. exchange rate intervention. undervalue currency
Congress(hearing)	Committee on Ways and Means, Committee on Finance websites: http://waysandmeans.house.gov/ http://www.finance.senate.gov/hearings	exchange rate, currency, China, exchange rate manipulation. exchange rate intervention, undervalue currency
Sino-US heads meeting	www.baidu.com	Sino-US heads meeting, US president's visit to China
US treasury secretary's visit to China	www.baidu.com	US treasury secretary's visit to China
Report on international economy and exchange rate policy	The U.S. Treasury Department's website: https://www.treasury.gov/Pages/default.aspx	Report to Congress on International Economic and Exchange Rate; International Economic and exchange rate report
SED, S&ED	The U.S. Treasury Department's website: https://www.treasury.gov/Pages/default.aspx	Strategic Economic Dialogue (SED); U.S. China Strategic and Economic Dialogue (S&ED)
JCCT	www.baidu.com	JCCT

SED (Strategic Economic Dialogue) was renamed as S&ED (Strategic and Economic Dialogue) in 2009.

4.2. Analysis of Assessment Results

4.2.1. General Analysis

See Figure 1. According to the definition of events in this paper, there were 116 events between July 22, 2005 and 31 March 2016 in which the United States put pressure on RMB, wherein 51 events were initiated by the US Congress and 65 events by US administrations. In exclusion of 2005 and 2016 with incomplete number of events, 2011, 2007, and 2010 are the most eventful years; four years with the highest success rates are respectively 2008 (75%), 2015 (66.67%), 2011 (60%) and 2013 (60%). 58 out of 107 event periods are in line with the "success" criteria, accounting for about 54.2% in the total number of events. It is worth noting the difference between events and event periods, part of the event periods contain two or more events. Since the influence of these events on RMB is inseparable from each other, they are included into one event period. However, there is a possibility that multiple events in the same event period successfully affected the RMB exchange rate. There are totally 62 independent events in this sample, which means at most 62 events could be successful from the viewpoint of event count. Nevertheless, the highest success ratio does not exceed 53.4%. The following statistics are all conducted in the way of event count for ease of classification, namely regarding all independent events in the successful event period as successful events. Therefore, there are totally 116 events during the sample period.

4.2.2. Analysis of Successful Events

See Figure 2. The successful events accounted for 56.9% in all events started by US Congress (29 out of 51 events succeeded) and 50.8% in those started by US administrations (33 out of 65 events succeeded). Among six categories of administrative political events, US Treasury Secretary's visits to China and the semiannual report on international economy and exchange rate policy released by US Treasury Department imposed more effective pressure on RMB. The success rate of US Treasury Secretary's visits to China was 57.1% (8 out of 14 events succeeded), while the success rate of report on international economy and exchange rate policy was as much as 68.4% (13 out of 19 events succeeded).

4.2.3. Analysis of Reversal Events

See Figure 3. Among all three standards of successful events, the "reversal"—RMB was devaluating before the events and switched to the state of appreciation after the event—is the most effective and persuasive event, so this paper also analyze the sources of reversal events. There're totally 28 reversal events during the sample period. US Congress and Administrations respectively started 14 events. "Reversal" accounted for 27.5% in all

Table 3. Results of assessment on classified events.

Serial No.	Event period	Nature of events	Successful or not	Success criteria
1	05-10-6	Congress	√	Reversal
2	05-10-20	Congress	√	Smoothing
3	05-11-21	Sino-US heads meeting	√	Enlarging
4	05-11-28	Report on international economy and exchange rate policy		X
5	06-2-16	Congress	√	Reversal
6	06-3-2	Congress		X
7	06-3-8~9	Congress	√	Smoothing
8	06-4-11	JCCT		X
9	06-4-18~21	Sino-US heads meeting		X
10	06-5-10	Report on international economy and exchange rate policy		X
11	06-9-19~28	US treasury secretary's visit to China/Congress		X
12	06-12-14~15	US treasury secretary's visit to China		X
13	06-12-19	Report on international economy and exchange rate policy	√	Enlarging
14	07-1-9	Congress	√	Reversal
15	07-1-23	Congress	√	Reversal
16	07-1-31	Congress	√	Reversal
17	07-2-12~28	Congress		X
18	07-3-7~8	Congress/US Treasury Secretary's visit to China		X
19	07-3-27~28	Congress	√	Reversal
20	07-5-9	Congress	√	Enlarging
21	07-5-16~23	SED	√	Smoothing
22	07-6-13	Congress		X
23	07-6-28	Congress	√	Reversal
24	07-7-16	Congress	√	Reversal
25	07-7-26~8-2	US treasury secretary's visit to China	√	Enlarging
26	07-12-11~19	JCCT/SED/Report on international economy and exchange rate policy		X
27	08-4-2~3	Congress/US treasury secretary's visit to China	√	Enlarging
28	08-5-16	Report on international economy and exchange rate policy	√	Reversal
29	08-6-17~18	SED		X
30	08-8-7~8	Sino-US heads meeting		X
31	08-9-16	JCCT	√	Reversal
32	08-12-4~10	Report on international economy and exchange rate policy/SED	√	Enlarging
33	09-1-13~14	Congress		X
34	09-4-15	Report on international economy and exchange rate policy		X
35	09-5-13	Congress	√	Smoothing
36	09-6-1~2	S&ED/US Treasury Secretary's visit to China		X
37	09-6-11	Congress		X
38	09-7-27~28	S&ED		X
39	09-10-15	Report on international economy and exchange rate policy	√	Reversal
40	09-10-29	JCCT		X
41	09-11-15~18	Sino-US heads meeting		X

42	10-3-17	Congress		X
43	10-3-24	Congress		X
44	10-4-8	S&ED		X
45	10-5-24~25	S&ED	√	Enlarging
46	10-6-10~17	Congress	√	Enlarging
47	10-6-23	Congress	√	Enlarging
48	10-7-8	Report on international economy and exchange rate policy	√	Reversal
49	10-7-30	Congress		X
50	10-9-15~29	Congress		X
51	10-10-24	US treasury secretary's visit to China	√	Smoothing
52	10-12-15	JCCT	√	Smoothing
53	11-1-18~21	Sino-US heads meeting		X
54	11-2-14	Congress	√	Reversal
55	11-4-6	Congress	√	Enlarging
56	11-5-9~10	S&ED		X
57	11-5-27	Report on international economy and exchange rate policy	√	Enlarging
58	11-6-16	Congress	√	Enlarging
59	11-6-21	Congress		X
60	11-9-13	Congress	√	Reversal
61	11-9-26	Congress	√	Reversal
62	2011-10-3~6	Congress		X
63	2011-10-11~14	Congress		X
64	11-10-18	Congress		X
65	2011-10-25~26	Congress		X
66	2011-11-2~3	Congress	√	Enlarging
67	11-11-21	JCCT	√	Reversal
68	11-11-25	Congress	√	Enlarging
69	11-12-6	Congress	√	Enlarging
70	11-12-12	Congress		X
71	11-12-16	Congress	√	Reversal
72	11-12-27	Report on international economy and exchange rate policy	√	Enlarging
73	2012-1-10~11	US treasury secretary's visit to China	√	Reversal
74	2012-2-13~17	Sino-US heads meeting	√	Reversal
75	12-2-29	Congress		X
76	2012-5-2~3	S&ED		X
77	12-5-25	Report on international economy and exchange rate policy	√	Smoothing
78	12-6-7	Congress		X
79	2012-8-15~16	Congress	√	Enlarging
80	12-11-17	Report on international economy and exchange rate policy	√	Reversal
81	12-12-5	US treasury secretary's visit to China		X
82	12-12-19	JCCT		X
83	2013-3-19~20	US treasury secretary's visit to China/Congress	√	Smoothing
84	13-4-12	Report on international economy and exchange rate policy	√	Enlarging
85	2013-6-7~8	Congress/Sino-US heads meeting	√	Smoothing

86	2013-7-10~11	S&ED		X
87	13-7-17	Congress		X
88	13-10-30	Report on international economy and exchange rate policy	√	Smoothing
89	2013-11-15~16	US treasury secretary's visit to China		X
90	2013-12-19~20	JCCT		X
91	14-1-15	Congress		X
92	14-4-15	Report on international economy and exchange rate policy	√	Reversal
93	14-5-13	US treasury secretary's visit to China	√	Smoothing
94	14-6-25	Congress	√	Reversal
95	2014-7-9~10	S&ED		X
96	14-10-15	Report on international economy and exchange rate policy		X
97	2014-12-16~18	JCCT		X
98	2015-2-10~12	Congress		X
99	2015-3-28~31	US treasury secretary's visit to China	√	Reversal
100	15-4-9	Report on international economy and exchange rate policy		X
101	15-4-29	SED	√	Smoothing
102	15-5-18	Congress	√	Reversal
103	2015-6-23~24	S&ED		X
104	2015-9-22~27	Sino-US heads meeting	√	Reversal
105	15-10-19	Report on international economy and exchange rate policy	√	Reversal
106	2015-11-21~23	JCCT	√	Reversal
107	2016-2-28~29	US treasury secretary's visit to China	√	Reversal

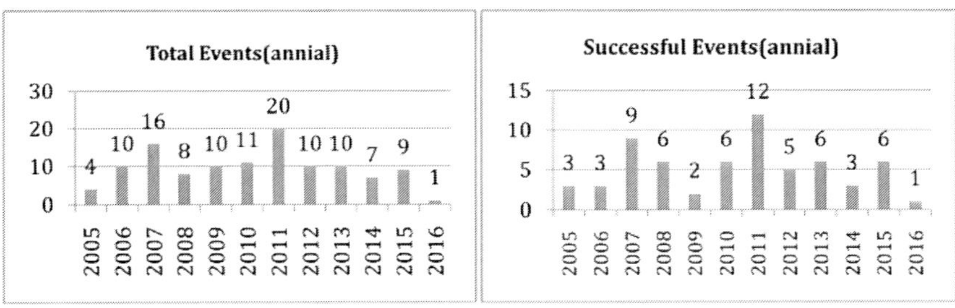

Figure 1. Total events and successful events from 2005.7.22 to 2016.3.31.

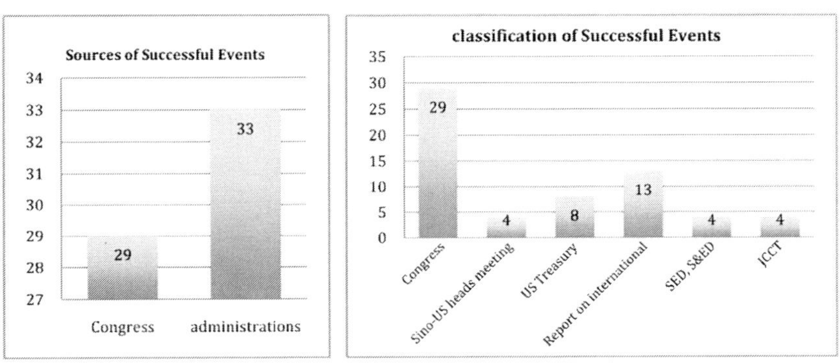

Figure 2. Sources of successful events, classification of successful events from 2005.7.22 to 2016.3.31.

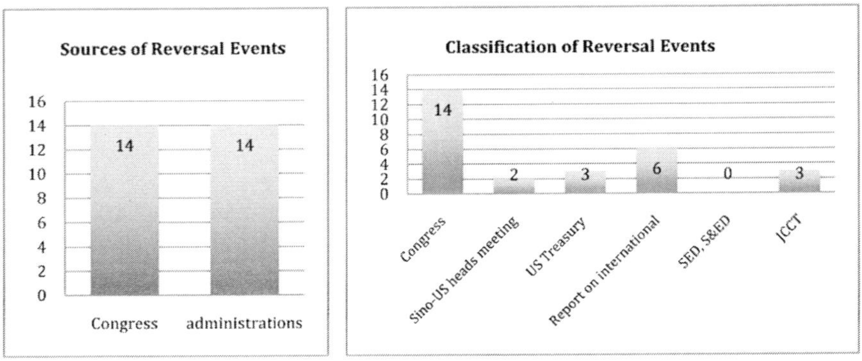

Figure 3. Sources of reversal events, classification of reversal events.

congress events (14 out of 51 events) and 21.5% in the administration events (14 out of 65 events). Furthermore, among six categories of administrative political events, US Treasury Secretary's visits to China and the semiannual report on international economy and exchange rate policy released by US Treasury Department showed a "reversal rate" of 31.6% (6 out of 19 events), while the pressure from JCCT showed a "reversal rate" of 30% (3 out of 10 events).

Generally speaking, the United States started a total of 116 events between July 2005 and March 2016 to pressure RMB, and 53.4% of these events succeeded in affecting RMB exchange rate; as for the subject of pressure, US congressional sectors played a more effective role in pressuring RMB exchange rate in comparison to administrative sectors; as for the pressure from administrative sectors, US Treasury Secretary's visits to China, the release of semiannual report on international economy and exchange rate policy, and the JCCT had relatively stronger effects on RMB exchange rate.

5. CONCLUDING COMMENTS

Firstly, the conclusions of this paper are similar to the study results of Frankel and Wei (2007), Liu and Laurent (2012), Liu Tao and Zhou Jizhong (2011) despite the extended length of sample period and improved methods to classify events. Since only 53.4% out of 116 events succeeded and merely 24.14% events achieved reversal effect (turned devaluation into appreciation), this paper similarly concludes that the pressure from United States does not play a significant role in promoting RMB appreciation.

Secondly, among various political impellent events, the US Congress had more significant influence on RMB exchange rate than administrative sectors.

Although US Congress usually plays the role of regulator in exchange rate policies, the impact of motions, bills proposed by both houses as legislatures and related hearings on RMB exchange should never be underestimated; as for the pressure from administrative sectors, the semiannual report on international economy and exchange rate policy, the JCCT and US treasury secretary's visits to China had relatively stronger effects on RMB exchange rate.

Finally, judging from the number of events, RMB exchange rate hasn't undergone obviously increased pressure from US since its devaluation in 2014. From the perspective of success rate, only 2015 showed a higher success rate of 66.67% among three years during the depreciation stage. It's worth noting that unlike the situation in the appreciation stage, US administrative sectors were more influential than the Congress in the devaluation stage; in the administrative events, US treasury secretary's visits to China and the release of semiannual report on international economy and exchange rate policy had more significant influence on RMB exchange rate.

REFERENCES

1. Li, Z.G. and Dong, L.W. (2005) The International Political Economics of Exchange Rate Determination. Journal of Guangdong University of Finance, No. 11, 44-51.
2. Xiao, T. and Wang, Y. (2012) An Analysis of US-China Debates on Renminbi Exchange Rate Based on the Evolutionary Game Theory. Southwest Finance, No. 3, 39-41.
3. Li, Z.L. (2011) Politics and Exchange Rate: Political Economics Analysis of RMB Appreciation. World Economics and Politics, No. 9, 136-160.
4. Han, H.C. and Xu, K.N. (2014) The Political Economics Analysis of US Pressure on Renminbi Exchange Rate. Contemporary Finance & Economics, No. 4, 5-13.
5. Zhang, X., Cui, Y.J. and Sun, G. (2015) Look from the Dual Exchange Rate of RMB Exchange Rate—Is China really a Currency Manipulator? Finance & Trade Economics, No. 7, 32-43.
6. Zhu, M.N., Zhao, Q. and Wang, Y.G. (2015) The Incentive of RMB Exchange Rate Fluctuation: Base on the Assessment of US Political Cycle's Spillover Effect. Management World, No. 4, 38-51.
7. Frankel, J.A. and Wei, S. (2007) Assessing China's Exchange Rate Regime. Economic Policy, No. 51, 575.

8. Liu, L. and Pauwels, L.L. (2012) Do External Political Pressures Affect the Renminbi Exchange Rate? Journal of International Money and Finance, 31, 1800-1818.

9. Liu, T. and Zhou, J.Z. (2011) Do External Pressures Promote the Appreciation of Renminbi? Base on the Assessment of US Impellent Events' Outcomes between 2005 and 2010. Journal of Financial Research, No. 11, 32-46.

10. Neely, C.J. (2005) An Analysis of Recent Studies of the Effect of Foreign Exchange Intervention. Working Papers 2005-030, Federal Reserve Bank of St. Louis.

11. Hu, Z.Y. and Liu, S.G. (2013) Do External Political Pressures Affect RMB/USD Exchange Rate? Studies of International Finance, No. 12, 26-34.

12. Fatum, R., Hutchison, M.M. (2003) Is Sterilized Foreign Exchange Intervention Effective after All? An Event Study Approach. Economic Journal, 113, 390-411.

13. Pierdzioch, C. and Stadtmann, G. (2004) The Effectiveness of the Interventions of the Swiss National Bank—An Event-Study Analysis. Kiel Working Paper No. 1160, Kiel Institute for World Economics, 229-244.

14. Fratzscher, M. (2008) Communication and Exchange Rate Policy. Journal of Macroeconomics, 30, 1651-1672.

11

CONSTITUTIONAL INTERESTS IN THE FACE OF INNOVATIONS: HOW MUCH DO WE NEED TO KNOW ABOUT RISK PREFERENCES?

Ulrich Witt Æ Christian Schubert

Max Planck Institute of Economics, Jena, Germany

ABSTRACT

In constitutional political economy, the citizens' constitutional interests determine the social contract that is binding for the post-constitutional market game. However, following traditional preference subjectivism, it is left open what the constitutional interests are. Using the example of risk attitudes, we argue that this approach is too parsimonious with regard to the behavioral foundations to support a calculus of consent. In face of innovative activities with pecuniary and technological externalities in the post-constitutional phase, the citizens' constitutional interests vary with their risk preferences. To determine what kind of social contract is generally agreeable, specific assumptions about risk preferences are needed.

Keywords: Constitutional preferences, Social contract, Original positionInnovation, Risk preferences

1 INTRODUCTION

In order to assess the legitimacy of constitutional rules from an individualistic perspective, Constitutional Political Economy makes frequent use of the device of the social contract. This device structures the comparative normative analysis of alternative constitutional rules, yielding conclusions as to which of them are conducive to mutually beneficial cooperation in the post-constitutional (market) game. Individuals participating at the process of constitutional deliberation are assumed to be situated such that they are induced to favor universal ("fair") over discriminatory rules. The rules stipulated in the social contract are then essentially determined by the "common constitutional interests" of the individuals concerned. Due to the fact, however, that most contributions to Constitutional Political Economy adhere to the methodological premise of "radical subjectivism" (Buchanan and Vanberg 2002), these interests are not materially specified. Rather, in general, a formal interpretation is advanced according to which "'improvement' is strictly defined in terms of what the individuals concerned themselves regard as "improvement" (Vanberg 2005, p. 26). Accordingly, the "good" is defined in an endogenous, procedural way, viz., as "that which emerges from agreement among free men, independently of intrinsic evaluation of the outcome itself" (Buchanan 1975, p. 167).

We will argue that this radical subjectivist stance (which corresponds to an analogous methodological position adopted in mainstream welfare economics) considerably weakens the operational power of Constitutional Political Economy. This is particularly true, if it is assumed that, after the constitution has been adopted, agents will play a market game in which innovations are possible. In face of an inherently risky novelty-generating game, individuals will reasonably anticipate that at any time some members of society will be risk-averse (and that they themselves will likely become more risk-averse over time), and their calculus of consent will reflect this. In such a situation, radical subjectivism on constitutional interests and preferences prevents practically relevant and normatively plausible (conjectural) policy conclusions. In order to be able to assess, from the viewpoint of the constitutional stage behind a "veil of ignorance", the likely impact of future commercial, institutional, or technological novelty on individual income, well-being, and the opportunities for mutually beneficial exchange, additional behavioral hypotheses are needed.

We will support our claim by drawing upon hypotheses about the individuals' risk attitudes and the systematic changes in them over an individual's life-span. This somewhat more "objective" (behavioral) approach would, we will argue, allow theorists interested in evaluating innovations on an individualistic basis to use the device of the (hypothetical) social contract for their purposes. Hence, our approach implies an enlargement of the informational base of the contractarian approach to welfare which may be seen as being analogous to the one advocated by scholars such as Sen (1979) in the realm of orthodox, quasi-utilitarian welfare economics. In the same sense as Sen's contributions, we suggest to follow the creed that "[t]he account of well-being must be tailored to the human frame: it must connect with what makes human lives go well, not the lives of ideal persons." (Qizilbash 1997, p. 263)

The paper is organized as follows. Section 2 surveys the way the social contract model is usually employed in Constitutional Political Economy. Distinguishing between so called "pecuniary" (market-mediated) external effects of innovations on the economic conditions of the citizens and "technological" (not market-mediated) externalities, we discuss in Sect. 3 the importance of making specific assumptions on individual risk attitudes first in regard to the pecuniary externalities. It turns out that the risk of negative pecuniary externalities—often deemed normatively irrelevant in Constitutional Political Economy (see, e.g., Vanberg 2006)—does affect the terms of the social contract. Section 4 elaborates on the analogous calculus of consent for the case of technological externalities. It is shown that unanimous consent is facilitated by including specific regulations on innovativeness in the social contract. Section 5 offers our conclusions.

2 DIFFERENT VERSIONS OF THE CONTRACTARIAN ARGUMENT IN CONSTITUTIONAL POLITICAL ECONOMY

As the contemporary heir to classical political economy, modern Constitutional Political Economy is essentially based on two conceptual pillars: First, it can be defined as applying "the methods...of modern economics to the study of the basic rules under which social orders may operate" (Brennan and Hamlin 1998, p. 401). Thus, it starts from the fundamental methodological distinction between the level of the "rules of the market game" and the level of single exchange acts within a given system of rules. It is focused on examining both the behavioral effects and the normative legitimacy of alternative rules by arguing that, due to their complexity and open-ended character, market outcomes can only be influenced "indirectly" by shaping the institutional arrangements that bring them about (Vanberg and Buchanan 1991). This focus on rules we will dub the *instrumental* position in the following.

Second, constitutional political economy is characterized by a distinctly *normative* position which is based on the principle of "normative individualism". According to this principle, only the real individuals' preferences or interests are accepted as genuine sources of value (Buchanan 1990).[1] It is presumed that a generally agreeable, supra-individual ("objective") source of normativity is absent so that it is only the voluntary bilateral exchange between consenting individuals which can be claimed to be able to generate legitimacy. The objects of exchange remain unspecified, as do the individuals' preferences. Related to this subjectivist creed, Constitutional Political Economy elaborates upon the Wicksellian idea of extending the concept of economic efficiency from the market sphere to the study of collective choice processes by applying the procedural logic of exchange acts, centering around the subjectively perceived *gains from trade* that turn up as gains from joint commitment in the realm of constitutional choice (Buchanan 1977; Buchanan 1991a).[2] As a consequence, the normative position held by Constitutional Political Economy is grounded on the device of the *social contract* that generalizes this idea to the level of collective (multilateral) exchange processes. The social contract is used as a tool to assess the legitimacy of specific constitutional rules, by allowing to test whether rational individuals would be willing to accept these rules, when placed in a "constitutional choice" situation.

The two conceptual premises have to be carefully distinguished. In principle, the instrumental focus on rules would also be compatible with an outcome-oriented utility maximization paradigm (with "outcomes" defined negatively or in pattern-based form). As regards the normative focus, the consensus-oriented gains from trade-paradigm could also be applied—practical difficulties notwithstanding—to alternative interventions at the level of single market transactions and outcomes. Let us have a closer look at the two pillars.

As to the first one, the focus on more or less abstract rules governing social interaction is usually justified by the fact that the post-constitutional market game can best be characterized as an open-ended evolutionary process, being constituted and driven by creative, inventive choices on the part of (at least some of) the individual market participants (Buchanan and Vanberg 2002). Consequently, specific future states and outcomes cannot be predicted, let alone deliberately be brought about. Since it is assumed that no value scalar exists independently of the choices made, the efficiency of outcomes can only be inferred in terms of the characteristics of the process from which they result, rather than in terms of the "welfare attributes" of the outcomes per se (Vanberg 2005). In other words, "the basis for any normative... judgment must be shifted from patterns of results to characteristic features of the institutional-structural parameters themselves" (Buchanan and Vanberg 2002, p. 124). Only rules and procedures can be "improved" in a meaningful sense. This hypothesis is derived from the epistemological assumption that, as a result of, say, cumulative "trial-and-error-learning" (Vanberg 2005, p. 37; see also Vanberg 1994), technological knowledge about the working properties of rules is more easily available than the much more specific knowledge about particular welfare effects of outcome-oriented interventions. Hence, it is assumed that even if detailed statements about the future course of events are impossible, the general working properties of alternative rules can be examined, as can the overall pattern of costs and benefits that they may generate over time. The resulting insights can then be used to inform choices among alternative constitutional regimes.

As to the second pillar, viz., the individualistic position on normativity, the use of the social contract plays a key role. It is somewhat more intricate. The historical predecessors of modern constitutional political economy—Hobbes in particular—had used this concept in order to demonstrate the idea that from the viewpoint of a situation of general social anarchy, it would be in the interest of everyone involved to enter into a general agreement to refrain from using violence against others and to accept a centralized state agency—the notorious *Leviathan*—in order to violently enforce the respective set of regulations. Put differently, everyone would reasonably assent to the multilateral exchange of behavioral constraints that is implied by such a mutual disarmament. By tapping general agreement as a source of legitimacy in its own right, Hobbes was able to move, in an "individualistic" spirit, beyond traditional objective approaches to normativity.

While retaining their predecessors' meta-ethical stance on norms and values, modern contractarians pursue more modest aims. Rather than deriving the legitimacy of the state in general, they use the social contract model to test the normative appeal of specific constitutional rules and to develop plausible statements as to their normative quality. This is reflected in the Pareto criterion or, equivalently, the criterion of *unanimity* which is often (wrongly, as it will turn out) held to be the only normative premise which the contractarian argument requires. Unanimity can be seen as the only criterion that is able to properly reflect the principle of normative individualism in the realm of collective choice. It is epitomized by the subjectively perceived mutual gains that people can reap when they exchange behavioral constraints by jointly committing themselves to rules (Buchanan 1991b, 81ff). These gains determine the "common constitutional interests" that constitute the only normative measuring rode which most authors in constitutional political economy accept.

The unanimity test is carried out by way of a thought experiment about how individual agents would decide within some artificially specified constitutional situation, the "original position". Hence, modern contractarians use the social contract device in a *hypothetical* sense, if often only implicitly. This is justified by the fact that, due to prohibitive transaction costs ("costs of collective decision-making" in Buchanan and Tullock's 1962 terminology), real consent is obviously unattainable in a complex society. If it were actually attainable, contractarians would not need to be consulted anyway. Using hypothetical agreement only implies, however, that the conclusions obtained cannot claim to be more than mere conjectural recommendations. For as already Hume (1748/1992) emphasized in his "On the Original Contract", fictitious contracts can only effectively bind fictitious individuals.[3] Consequently, any demonstration that some given rule would be agreeable to all individuals participating at a hypothetical vote on some social contract does not logically imply that the same rule would be agreed upon by real individuals under real circumstances. It does not carry with it genuine legitimizing force. Thus, such a demonstration can at best serve as one possible (ideally psychologically effective) contribution to the public deliberation that those real individuals concerned by the rule are engaged in when reasoning about and discussing alternative constitutional arrangements.

Such a contribution implies hypothetical imperatives, discerning which rules should turn out to be generally acceptable for the individuals, given some plausible hypothesis on those individuals' constitutional interests. Nonetheless, it is the real consent of these individuals only in terms of which the legitimacy of any proposed rule can be judged (a point emphasized by Vanberg 2005 and Buchanan 1991a, b among others). Hence, a careful distinction is required between the social contract's role as a *normative tool* (possibly one among many others) that may be based on more or less individualistic premises, and its role as a model for actual (ideally perfectly individualistic) procedures that eventually confer legitimacy on constitutional rules.

Given these clarifications about the status of contractarian conclusions, how exactly are these conclusions generated? Methodologically, the contractarian argument works like a deductive-nomological prediction (see Müller 2000, pp. 37–46, referring to Hempel and Oppenheim 1948). Given some universal law and a set of antecedent conditions, a singular statement (the *projectandum*) can be logically deduced. In the context of a contractarian argument, the universal law is represented by some behavioral hypothesis, usually a strict variant of the rational choice model. The set of antecedent conditions is represented by some assumptions about the individuals' utility functions, their informational endowments or their relative bargaining power. Individuals can, e.g., be assumed to aim at maximizing their personal utility, be mutually disinterested, be uncertain about their future position in society, but on the other hand to possess perfect technological knowledge about the working properties of alternative constitutional rules. From the behavioral hypothesis and the situational assumptions a (more or less general) statement follows logically as to what kind of rule those fictitious individuals would choose.

It is evident that any modification of the situational assumptions, say, about the set of admissible individual preferences, may alter the contractarian conclusions in a potentially fundamental way by shaping the set of possible welfare-increasing states that are accessible from the original position. That is why designing these assumptions involves (often only implicitly) genuine value judgments. There is consequently a wide variety of contractarian approaches that differ in terms of precisely those assumptions that concern both what individuals *want* and what they *know* in the original position. Following Sugden (1993), it is convenient to distinguish between "strong" and "weak" versions of the social contract model. The main difference concerns the respective theorist's ambition to purge the whole approach from any undesired positive (in particular psychological) and evaluative presuppositions deemed superfluous.

As to the strong variant, it is best exemplified by Buchanan's (1975) attempt to legitimize the modern liberal "rule of law" state with its protective and productive branches as emerging from a general consent among individuals living under conditions of a rule-less (hence, Pareto-inferior) "natural anarchy".[4] The exact conditions, including in particular the individuals' initial endowments, that prevail in this original position are deliberately left open, for any attempt to define them would invoke specific value judgments, and Buchanan wants to keep his approach "value-free" except for the unanimity criterion itself. Thus, according to this version of contractarianism, anything is deemed legitimate that individuals turn out to agree upon. Hence, this approach can be described as being based upon a "strongly individualistic" notion of justice (Müller 2000, pp. 49–50). As the conditions under which they agree are left unspecified, even agreements obtained under circumstances implying an extremely unequal bargaining power (such as a slave's acceptance of her master's rule) carry legitimizing force; consequently, Buchanan cannot exclude the possibility that a "fair" social contract would include slavery.

Due to the low level of specification, the resulting social contract approach has an extremely low degree of operational content. It cannot move beyond the observation that what is unanimously chosen by the individuals is Pareto-superior to the original position and pareto-optimal. No practical policy conclusions can be derived, as they would involve a choice between alternative Pareto-optima. Needless to say that *a fortiori*, this approach cannot "predict" the emergence of a complex liberal rule-of-law state, as Buchanan attempted to. Notice that the strictly Paretian approach to Welfare Economics suffers from exactly the same lack of operational content: Since the Pareto criterion can only define a "strict partial ordering" among the set of possible social states, it cannot discriminate between different points located on the Pareto frontier (Sen 1970, pp. 21–30). Again, the lack of operational content is due to the fact that only one, extremely abstract, value judgment is admitted to the analysis.

As regards the weak versions of the social contract model, they attempt to restrict the set of possible conclusions ("predictions") by constraining the set of admissible conditions within the original position. Only those constitutional choices are deemed to be "fair" that satisfy certain procedural fairness requirements. This principle is usually realized by introducing a "veil of uncertainty" (Buchanan and Tullock 1962) or "veil of ignorance" (Rawls 1971) that serves as a metaphor for artificially restricting the information available to the individuals in the original position. It is based on the presupposition that, when deliberating about alternative constitutional rules from behind a sufficiently "thick" veil, even rational and strictly self-interested individuals are forced to occupy a "moral" viewpoint, where "moral" is to be understood as implying universalisability. They are induced to judge rules from an impartial position, i.e., to figure out how they would evaluate a given rule if they would be in any of the social positions that are taken to be available in the post-constitutional stage. This then increases the chances that even self-interested individuals may agree upon a set of rules that truly are in their common "constitutional interest".

Within the set of weak social contract models, there is a second distinction to be taken into account between those approaches that interpret the veil (and the original position more generally) in an *empirical* way and those construing it essentially as a *normative* device. As regards the empirical variant, it is based on the assumption that in constitutional decision-making situations, individuals typically deliberate on rules that are relatively general, abstract and durable. Hence, their precise effects on particular welfare positions are hard to predict. This is a fact that prevents individuals from judging those rules from their own, narrowly conceived self-interest. It leads them to favor exactly those general rules that constitute the "just" constitutional market order that benefits everyone involved (Brennan and Buchanan 1985). Relatedly, Vanberg (2005, p. 31, italics added) sees the use of the veil construct as serving to clarify the question "what kinds of procedures for choosing rules are more likely than potential alternative procedures to result in the adoption of rules that are ... mutually beneficial," stipulating that "conjectures of this kind are about the *factual* working properties of procedures...for choosing rules rather than about subjective evaluations of the persons concerned." Based on these insights, hypotheses can be advanced as to how the "thickness" of the veil should be deliberately manipulated in order to increase "the prospect of achieving agreement" (Vanberg and Buchanan 1989, p. 54). While a thicker veil makes agreement on values ("interests") more probable, consensus on positive constitutional "theories" will be facilitated by making the veil sufficiently "thin" (ibid; see, however, Müller 1998 for a qualification of this assumption). Insights such as these would then serve as the basis for policy advice concerning the design of collective decision-making procedures.

For good reasons,[5] most contractarian approaches use the social contract in a normative sense, i.e., as a device that explicitly embodies a given set of value judgments. In particular, the veil of uncertainty or ignorance is employed as representing and effectively introducing some version of a moral impartiality requirement, by forcing even selfish individuals to adopt a neutral viewpoint with respect to the constitutional rules they are bargaining or deliberating upon. As Kliemt (2004) emphasizes, the original position needs to be modeled in such a way that it is "embedded" in a sufficiently rich ethical background in order to allow for meaningful and determinate conclusions. This approach implies, however, first, that the ambition to base constitutional advice on *purely* individualistic grounds is abandoned. Due to its extremely thin evaluative basis, accounts based on pure Normative Individualism prove unable to narrow the range of admissible conclusions sufficiently to avoid indeterminacy. External value judgments may also be necessary to avoid strong counterintuitive results, such as Buchanan's (1975) slavery contracts: The proposal by Vanberg (1986) to supplement Buchanan's strictly individualistic unanimity criterion by introducing a (necessarily non-individualistic) cost-based criterion of "voluntariness" that excludes any involuntarily concluded contracts from the evaluative space of his contractarian theory, exemplifies this normative approach. The second implication is that the ambition to develop a normative device that is universally applicable has to be abandoned, for the ethical basis that determines the original position's antecedent conditions will necessarily reflect the moral common sense of a particular cultural background (Pettit 1974). All this does however not pose a problem as long as the social contract model is not used as a legitimizing device in the sense explained above, but only as a normative tool.

These methodological presuppositions favor a weak (veil-centered) and normative social contract approach which, however, is still short in operational relevance. A way to make progress in this respect is to enrich the contractarian model with material hypotheses about human behavior as the backdrop of the individuals' constitutional interests. If the individuals anticipate to be playing a post-constitutional innovative market game, a straight forward example of such hypotheses are the human attitudes towards risk. Although the discussion of a behavioral foundation for constitutional political economy must be confined here to this example, we claim that such a foundation is a desideratum more generally. For if the antecedent conditions of the contractarian argument are left unspecified, the model can only generate an extremely thin partial ordering of social states and rules that does not allow to make any substantive statements about the content of the social contract.

It is true that, on the basis of the criteria of unanimity and voluntariness alone, the radical subjectivist stance on constitutional interests still arrives at a conclusion: from behind the "veil", individuals will unanimously agree to a set of constitutional rules that maximize their chances to engage in mutually beneficial exchange on the basis of whatever preferences they may have (Vanberg 2006). Such a conclusion would recommend all institutional arrangements that enlarge the scope of decentralized "systems competition". But even this conclusion already presupposes a specific preference for certain "basic goods" (such as liberty and individual responsibility) over others which cannot be taken for granted on empirical grounds (see Buchanan 2005). We do not deny the plausibility of the above conclusion for certain areas of constitutional rule-making; we just question its status as the only object of unanimous consent from behind a "veil of ignorance". In order to reach more concrete (hypothetical) statements as to the normative quality of constitutional rules, the traditional radical subjectivism on individual interests is not helpful.

3 CONSTITUTIONAL PREFERENCES AND RISK ATTITUDES: THE CASE OF PECUNIARY EXTERNALITIES OF INNOVATIONS

In this section we will discuss the need for more specific hypotheses about the preferences of the citizens when it comes to the calculus of consent about the terms of the social contract. More specifically, we focus here and in the next section in an exemplary fashion on the role that risk attitudes play for determining the interest component of the constitutional preferences (Vanberg and Buchanan 1989) of the participants in the social contract. The significance of risk attitudes results, we will argue, from the fact that human inventiveness and innovative action are characteristic features of the post-constitutional market game. The "discovery procedure" in which the market process results (Hayek 1978) does not necessarily produce outcomes that are to everyone's advantage. However, what forms the market game can take depends on the rules stipulated in the social contract concerning innovativeness, in short called the "innovation regime" here.

As explained elsewhere in detail, the regime may allow more or less innovativeness and/or discriminate between different forms of innovations, i.e. invoke more or less, and different forms of, regulations on innovations (Witt 1996). How the social contract is specified in this respect cannot be decided without making some assumptions about the citizens' risk attitudes. Hence, the need for more specific hypotheses about these attitudes. To lay out the argument, it is useful to first discuss in generic terms the consequences of market innovations and the potential risks they imply. Since the seminal work of Schumpeter (1934, 1942), innovativeness and innovations are seen as something beneficial and, hence, desirable in economics, an assessment that is now widely shared in public. The background of the Schumpeterian interpretation is the historical experience of a positive correlation between innovativeness on the one hand and economic growth on the other. Indeed, for the past two centuries, the correlation between innovations and a rising per capita income seems evident (Rosenberg and Birdzell 1986; Mokyr 1990).

However, innovations by definition mean newly implemented problem solutions which have not been tried before. For this reason, who profits from the beneficial effects of an innovation hinges not only on whose problems the innovation solves, but also on whether that problem solving triggers new problems elsewhere. There are obvious risks implied here. First, a rising per capita income usually does not (fully) reflect the social costs that innovations can incur on society (or on some of its members) in the form of negative technological externalities. Innovations can have unforeseen harmful effects on health and/or the environment. Second, it is only on average that innovativeness results in a growth of per capita income. Innovations regularly also produce losers among some participants in the market game—a fact Schumpeter (1942) already alluded to with the euphemistic formulation "creative destruction". These effects in the form of negative pecuniary externalities usually have to be born unevenly.

In view of risks like these implied by a post-constitutional market game with unregulated innovativeness some interesting questions arise. A first (normative) question is whether technological and pecuniary externalities should be considered equally relevant for the calculus of consent at the constitutional stage. A second (methodological) question is whether the calculus of consent regarding these risks should be based on material hypotheses about human risk attitudes. Following the considerations in the previous section, both questions will be answered in the affirmative here. The reason regarding the first question is that, in the eyes of the citizens who deliberate on the stipulations of the social contract behind a veil of ignorance, it does not matter whether a possible destitution to be faced later is technologically caused or caused by market forces. In both cases the citizens have to strike a balance between benefits and risks of innovations which they consider acceptable. The reason for the affirmative answer to the second question is that speculations about (hypothetical) calculi of consent that abstract from fundamentals of human nature seem rather artificial.

Concerning the citizens' information about what will happen in the post-constitutional market game, we assume that they do not know whether they will have a chance to become an innovator themselves and how innovation(s), be they their own or those of other market participants, will affect their well-being. With respect to the risk attitudes it seems reasonable to assume that the citizens not only know their own attitudes, but are also aware of the fact that risk preferences or, more generally, attitudes towards perceiving and taking risks, show a significant, inter-personal variance between individuals (a point also emphasized by Vanberg 2006). The empirical variance reflects genetically determined differences, cultural influences, and the state of individual experiences. Moreover, independent of the inter-personal variance at each point in time, risk preferences systematically change over time with increasing age. On average there is a greater inclination to take risks among juveniles and young, particularly male, adults. Beyond early adulthood, risk aversion grows with increasing age (see Rubin and Paul 1979 and the references given there).

For this reason it is almost certain that, both at the constitutional stage and in the post-constitutional market game, there will be participants who are already highly risk-averse or become so over their further life cycle. Given that these facts about risk attitudes are part of human nature, it seems straightforward that, in the calculus of consent at the constitutional stage, they are recognized. Two questions then arise: whose risk attitudes will determine the stipulations of the social contract regarding innovativeness, and what kind of stipulations will this be? Keeping to the unanimous consent criterion, each citizen has a veto right. Since citizens with more risk friendly preferences tend to tolerate more innovation risks, they always strike a more favorable balance between benefits and risks of innovations than less risk friendly agents. A (strategically motivated) veto by the former would therefore not be credible—it would hurt them more in their perception than it would hurt the risk-averse. Given that the balance between benefits and risks appears least favorable to the most risk-averse citizen, only this agent can exert a credible threat so that the stipulations of the social contract regarding innovativeness will hinge on what is agreeable to her or him.

Our approach differs in several respects from related contractarian models proposed by Vickrey (1945, 1960) and Harsanyi (1953, 1975) on the one hand and Rawls (1971) on the other hand. First of all, besides our emphasis on innovativeness, our model of the constitutional decision-making calculus does not include a representative agent, but rather a multitude of heterogenous agents. As regards the seminal accounts by Vickrey and Harsanyi (who introduced the expected utility calculus to model the choices of a representative "impartial observer" in the original position), we diverge from their assumptions about the "preference space". Both Vickrey and Harsanyi assume that the representative agent expects to occupy any of the conceivable post-constitutional positions with equal probability. This key postulate (based on the contentious Laplace rule) then leads to the prediction that the agent will rank outcomes in a utilitarian way. The conclusion critically hinges, however, on the fact that both authors refrain from imposing any structure on the individuals' preference space. While Vickrey takes agents to assess future positions according to their given constitutional preferences, Harsanyi assumes them to abstract from their own tastes and (using empathetic "extended preferences") to put themselves into the shoes of possible future selves. In contrast, we assume that in both the constitutional and the post-constitutional setting, the preference space is not completely open. Rather, some agents have and/or will have risk-averse preferences for certain.

As regards Rawls' (1971) model, this does make specific assumptions concerning the agents' risk attitudes—an approach we share. But, unlike Rawls who takes the agents to be perfectly ignorant about their *future* risk preferences, we assume some knowledge about human nature, i.e., about the general patterns of how these preferences develop in the course of one's life time. Furthermore, we claim that risk attitudes show a significant inter-personal variance, while Rawls assumes that behind the veil the agents are identically (and to an extreme extent) risk-averse. This assumption notwithstanding, Rawls considers the agents to be unable to form subjective estimates for the likelihood of occupying any conceivable position in the post-constitutional game, including the worst position. In contrast, we assume that agents are able to do this (see below). Accordingly, we do not share Rawls' view that the agents uniformly stick to the maximin criterion when judging alternative sets of rules and corresponding patterns of outcomes.

Since the stipulations of the innovation regime need to be differentiated with respect to the kind of potential negative externalities and the ways of coping with them, we focus in this section on market-mediated pecuniary externalities first. (For the discussion of technological externalities neglected here see the next section.) From his contractarian perspective Viktor Vanberg writes on the negative pecuniary externalities: "The very productivity of the 'game of the market' depends on its openness for the discovery of 'superior' products and production, and in agreeing to play the market game people accept the risk that their investments may be devalued by such discoveries. The productive advantage of the market game and this risk are two sides of the same coin. One cannot have the one without the other, *and fairness in playing the market game requires all players to accept this risk.* As the theory of rent-seeking shows, players may, of course, lobby governments for special privileges that allow them, at the expense of other players, to enjoy the benefits of the market's productivity while avoiding its accompanying risks" (Vanberg 2006, p. 207, italics added). Does such an assessment do justice to the underlying problem of risk preferences differing between the citizens?

Imagine an innovation that raises productivity and/or increases the quality of a commodity or service produced by one of the competitors in a market. If the demand side accepts the innovation (i.e. if the innovative offer is able to make customers better off), other competitors in the market regularly face problems for their business. They lose customers and orders, often with the consequence that labor has to be laid off. Expected returns from specific investments made earlier when the innovation was not yet known have to be given up for lost. This can mean losses of private wealth for capital owners or foregone expected income from human capital investments, if not even unemployment and loss of current income for members of the labor force. Under freedom of contract, the gains from an innovation succeeding in the market are always larger for the economy as a whole than what the competitors lose by the pecuniary externalities (see Witt 1987)—this being the very reason for the historical increases of average per capita income. Nonetheless, not knowing who will be winners and who will be losers of future innovations, the fact that such losses have to be born by some agents is highly relevant for risk-averse citizens who later have to accept the related stipulations in a social contract.

Let the citizens be indexed i = 1, ..., *n*. For expository convenience assume that, at the constitutional stage, i.e. behind a veil of ignorance, the calculus of consent can be represented as follows. The expected outcome of a "laissez faire" innovation regime (indicated by suffix lf) is given by a simple lottery $L(y_{lf}, p)$ in which an income y is earned with probability p, both incomes and probabilities being subjective estimates of the citizens (index suppressed subsequently). More specifically, the participants in the post-constitutional market game suffering from negative pecuniary externalities of the successful innovations of others are assumed to expect a low income y_l. In contrast, the income of those who do not expect to suffer the externalities can be assumed to have a significantly higher value y_h. Let the expectation of being a player in the post-constitutional market game who suffers from pecuniary externalities be given by the probability p and the expectation of the opposite event by 1-p. Hence, the income a member of society expects is

$$E(y_{lf}) = py_l + (1-p)y_h = y'_{lf}, \tag{1}$$

where y_{lf}' is the same amount of money obtained with certainty. Risk aversion then means that the utility $u(E(y_{lf}))$ derived from the expected income is strictly smaller than the utility $u(y_{lf}')$ derived from the sure income y_{lf}'. Put the other way round, for citizen j with the most risk averse preferences the inequality

$$CE\ (L(y_{lf},\ p))_j < y'_{lf} \tag{2}$$

holds, where $CE\ (L(y_{lf},\ p))_j = c_j$ denotes j's certainty equivalent of the lottery characterizing the "laissez faire" innovation regime, i.e. a sure income c_j.

Now imagine the only alternative innovation regime would be the opposite of unconstrained innovativeness, namely a regime requiring unanimous approval of any innovation by all parties affected by its possible negative pecuniary externalities. Abstracting from transaction costs and/or strategic maneuvering that may in practice hamper such a regime, there would be no innovations causing negative pecuniary externalities either because they would be vetoed or because those profiting from the innovation would have to pay compensations to the losers to obtain their approval. Since nobody would be made worse off, but some may be better off, by innovations, this regime can be dubbed a "Pareto" innovation regime (indicated by suffix p).[6]Compared to the "laissez faire" regime, a "Pareto" innovation regime considerably lowers the benefits accruing from innovative activities—and hence the incentives to undertake them. In fact, in the presence of transaction costs and/or strategic maneuvering, the "Pareto" regime is likely to result in a complete breakdown of innovative activities. All existing competitors would then be protected and the dynamic competitiveness of the markets would be grossly reduced, as would be technical progress and economic growth.

However, unlike under the "laissez faire" regime where gains and losses may be accumulating in a vastly uneven way among the citizens, there will be nobody suffering pecuniary externalities where others enjoy the high incomes that innovations make possible. Behind the veil of ignorance, all citizens can expect from a "Pareto" regime a low, but sure income y_p. Of course, compared to the expected income under the "laissez faire" regime the condition $y_p << E(y_{lf})$ holds. For a rational decision making on the stipulations of a social contract at the constitutional stage it then follows:

Proposition 1

At the constitutional stage, the most risk-averse citizen j consents to a social contract that stipulates a "laissez faire" innovation regime, if and only if

$$CE(L(y_{lf}, p))_j \geq y_p. \qquad (3)$$

To prove this, assume contrary to (3) that CE $(L(y_{lf}, p))_j < y_p$. Consenting to a "laissez faire" regime under that condition would mean that citizen j reveals a preference for a sure income $c_j < y_p$. Since no other motives have been assumed this would violate the rationality assumption. Hence, a rational risk-averse agent j consents to a "laissez faire" regime rather than a "Pareto" regime if and only if condition (3) is satisfied.

The "laissez faire" regime and "Pareto" regime may be extreme cases, but they are not unrealistic. A *grosso modo* positive (laissez faire like and, hence, risk friendly) attitude towards innovations as it is characteristic for the public opinion nowadays seems to be a rather recent phenomenon. For most of human history, public attitudes towards innovations were much less supportive of, if not hostile towards, innovativeness, at least in the sphere of production and trade. Indeed, there are historical examples of regulations that strongly resemble a "Pareto" regime. The guild systems in Europe and Asia, for instance, denied newcomers free access to the local markets (North 1981, Chap. 10, Jones 1988, Chap. 7). Higher authorities usually backed the enforcement of market closure so that potential newcomers had little, if any, room for mustering political power to fight their exclusion (cf. Ekelund and Tollison 1981, Chaps. 3 and 4). The institutional set-up of at least the European guild systems, which had a guild assembly as the collective decision making body, meant that collective consent was also necessary for innovations by guild members. Often unanimous approval was required before innovations could be introduced and practiced. Innovative cross-fertilization between different professional and/or regionally distinct guilds substantially bridled.[7]

"Laissez faire" and "Pareto" regimes are, of course, not the only possibilities. Indeed, with somewhat more complex innovation regimes it is even possible to soften condition (3) in proposition 1 without imposing constraints on innovativeness in the post-constitutional market game. One such possibility is, for instance, to combine a laissez faire regime with a tax financed social security system that guarantees to those suffering the pecuniary externalities an income never falling short of the subsistence level y_{min}. For such a "laissez faire with social security" regime (indicated by suffix s) the following can be established:

Proposition 2

Under certain conditions, the most risk-averse citizen j who is unwilling to consent to a "laissez faire" innovation regime, is willing to consent to a social contract that stipulates a "laissez faire with social security" innovation regime.

To demonstrate the conditions under which proposition 2 holds let us explore the "laissez faire with social security" regime more closely. Assume that a transfer payment $t = \max \{y_{min} - y_l, 0\}$ is guaranteed by the government so that a citizen's income will at least be y_{min} with certainty. Let t be financed by a tax T invoked on those not suffering the pecuniary externalities, i.e. on high income earners, where the tax revenue is always set equal to the size of the transfer payments (balanced budget condition). Hence,[8] $T = [p/(1 - p)]t$. The expected income then changes into:

$$E(y_s) = E(y_{lf}) + pt - (1 - p)\ T. \tag{4}$$

Note that under the balanced budget condition, the expected incomes $E(y_s) = E(y_{lf})$. Since the expected income in excess of the sure subsistence level is given by

$$\begin{aligned} E(y_s) - y_{min} = p \max\{y_l - y_{min}, 0\} + (1 - p)(y_h - y_{min} \\ - [p/(1 - p)] \max\{y_{min} - y_l, 0\}) \end{aligned} \tag{5}$$

the right hand side of Eq. 5 represents a lottery $L(y_{ex}, p)$ of its own. Accordingly, the certainty equivalent of the lottery $L(y_s, p)$ for citizen j can be expressed as a sum

$$CE(L(y_s, p))_j = y_{min} + CE(L(y_{ex}, p))_j > CE(L(y_{lf}, p))_j. \tag{6}$$

Despite the equality in the expected values of the income in Eq. 4, the inequality sign regarding the certainty equivalents in (6) holds, because of the sure income component y_{min} guaranteed by the government. Consequently, it is possible that the condition

$$CE(L(y_s, p))_j \geq y_p > CE(L(y_{lf}, p))_j$$

holds. Indeed, this is the necessary condition for proposition 2 to hold. In that case the most risk-averse member of society consents to a "laissez faire with social security" regime while, by condition (3) in proposition 1, that member will not consent to a "laissez faire" innovation regime.

As it appears, the question of what stipulations of the social contract regarding innovativeness can find unanimous consent depends on what is assumed about the specific risk preferences of the citizens. Different assumptions lead to strongly differing stipulations. From the fact that in many democracies a majority of voters show a rather consistent tendency towards endorsing social security transfer payments one may infer that these votes reveal a risk aversion. Many of these payments are indeed contingent on the occurrence of risks that are related to negative pecuniary externalities of large scale innovativeness.[9] Taken at face value, the majority thus seems to express a political preference for something like a "laissez faire with social security" innovation regime.[10] Yet, the preferences revealed by voting in the *post*-constitutional phase are one thing and the hypothetical reconstruction of the decision that would have been made behind the veil of ignorance another one. The very purpose of the constitutional choice calculus is to escape from the many biases expressed in factual voting turnouts due to partisan interests and strategic voting. Taking recourse to voting turnouts is therefore no option for deriving hypotheses about risk preferences.

We have argued that the diversity of risk attitudes and their systematic change over a life time are part of human nature. On the basis of this behavioral hypothesis it can be conjectured that, at all times, there are citizens who are already strongly risk-averse or anticipate to become so later. If this conjecture is true, it is likely that, under the unanimity rule, only rather protective innovation regimes for the post-constitutional market game will find consent. This may either be a regime that compensates for negative pecuniary externalities resulting from "creative destruction" by some kind of social security payments—a result that is not easily accommodated with the usual identification of the concept of "social security" with rent-seeking activities of interest groups. Or this may be an innovation regime like the "Pareto" regime that rules out such externalities, together with a large share of potential innovativeness.

4 CONSTITUTIONAL PREFERENCES AND RISK ATTITUDES REGARDING TECHNOLOGICAL EXTERNALITIES OF INNOVATIONS

Let us turn now to the constitutional preferences of the citizens regarding negative technological externalities of innovations and the corresponding question of what stipulations of the social contract are 'consentable'. To ease the analysis we will now abstract from the existence of pecuniary externalities. While in the case of negative pecuniary externalities where, under freedom of contract, the sum of private gains from an innovation being carried out always exceed the sum of private losses, in the case of negative technological externalities of an innovation this is different. The social costs can by far exceed the sum of the private gains of the agents profiting from an innovation. Moreover, these excessive costs often only turn out with a considerable time delay and may only then alert the affected agents or the society as a whole to the social costs that have to be borne.

Examples of such developments easily come to mind. In the 1950s asbestos was introduced into the markets as innovative material that was emphatically welcome where incombustible or fireproof products were needed. In the late 1970s it was discovered that dust particles from asbestos have a serious carcinogenic impact in humans. Another case is fluorocarbon. It was introduced and widely adopted as multi-purpose innovation serving as a lubricant, refrigerant, fire-extinguishing agent, insulator, and aerosol propellant. But then evidence was gradually emerging that it played a causal role in the Earth's stratospheric ozone layer depletion. Or take the example of nuclear power that was propagated, publicly welcomed, and heavily subsidized as the major innovation in energy technology in the 1960s. Its hazards were drastically experienced only later in power plant accidents in Three-Mile-Island and Chernobyl.

In terms of Coase's (1960) classical formulation of the problem of social costs, the inevitable risk of yet unknown negative technological externalities of innovations means that there are inherent, non-negligible transaction costs. These make it difficult, if not impossible, to rely on *ex ante* negotiations between an innovator who would cause the externality and those who would be affected as a way of efficiently internalizing the social costs. The social costs arising from innovations at later points in time, e.g., from damages to health or the environment, are therefore an object necessitating publicly enforced regulations. In the spirit of constitutional political economy, their agreeability can be assessed by comparison with the stipulations of a social contract that would find unanimous consent by the citizens at the constitutional stage.

By the same logic as in the case of pecuniary externalities, different stipulations in the social contract lead to different innovation regimes. These, in turn, are associated with differences in the risk and/or the extent of the damages. Since money income is no adequate measure for environmental and health damages, the negative externalities will be taken into account here by their effects on subjective well-being or utility. The best way in which regulations can cope with the harmful effects is to prevent them. Accordingly, innovation regimes can now be distinguished by the means they use to prevent innovations from developing negative technological externalities and the extent to which they succeed in doing so. One means would be a ban on (or injunction of) innovations—an "innovations ruled out" regime that suppresses technological externalities by suppressing innovations in the first place. (In a legal perspective, it is equivalent to granting every member of society a non-attenuated property right in an externality-free environment.) This regime can serve here as a benchmark for discussing the implications of different assumptions about risk preferences.

Other regimes use liability as a means (i.e. attenuate the mentioned property right). Such rules cannot make harmful effects and the corresponding losses in well-being undone. But they can create incentives for the innovator to recognize potential social costs as early and as seriously as possible and to internalize them in her or his decision making. Hence, liability rules can influence both the likelihood and the size with which social costs arise. Such regimes do not rule out innovations in toto, but differ with respect to how far they hold the innovator liable for any negative technological externalities. As will be explained in a moment in more detail, they range from a "no liability" regime at the one end via a "limited liability" regime to a "strict liability" regime at the other end of the spectrum.

Which of these regimes can be expected to (hypothetically) find unanimous consent at the constitutional stage, and under what conditions, has now to be clarified. Again there will be citizens who are, or anticipate to become, highly risk averse, and it is the consent of the most risk averse member to one of the innovation regimes that needs to be assured for the unanimously approved social contract. The calculus of consent can be modeled along similar lines as the risk preference model of the Eqs. 1–6. Yet, the different innovation regimes have to be assessed now by the impact they have on the level of well-being that can be reached as a result of innovations on the one hand and the loss of well-being due to their negative technological externalities on the other hand.

Let the level of well-being attainable by innovations that have no negative technological externalities be w_I. The level of well-being resulting if innovations do cause damages can be denoted by $w_I - w_D$. Again these variables and the probabilities for a damage to occuror not to occur, q and (1 - q) respectively, are taken to be the subjective estimates of member i (index suppressed subsequently). The expected outcome of the innovation regimes can then be represented by a simple lottery L(w,q). In the benchmark case of an "innovations ruled out" regime the lottery degenerates to a level of well-being w_{min} that, innovations and their potential hazards being absent, is taken to result with certainty.

In the light of the examples given above it is realistic to assume that the characteristics and the technological externalities of innovations are not instantaneously recognized in full. They are rather revealed only gradually. Those agents closer involved with the innovation are likely to notice problems earlier than others. The levels of well-being that a citizen can expect to attain when innovations are allowed is then likely to vary with the liability rules. Let the expected value under a "no liability" innovation regime (indicated by suffix nl) be given by[11]

$$E(w_{nl}) = q(w_I - w_D) + (1 - q)w_I. \tag{7}$$

Since in the absence of any liability the innovator is given no incentive to care about negative technological externalities of her or his innovation (except to the extent of the share she or he has to bear), it is not very likely that she or he will take much effort to (promptly) respond to emerging evidence of innovation-induced damages.[12] For this reason, the loss of well-being, w_D, that the citizens have to bear can become very large. Indeed, it can become so large that the expected contribution of an innovation to individual well-being turns negative.

This would be different if innovators are made liable in a strict and unlimited way for the social costs their innovations turn out to cause, i.e. under a "strict liability" innovation regime (indicated by suffix sl). A strong incentive would be given to proceed cautiously, to use emerging information as carefully as possible, and to react in a prompt and determined manner once externalities are discovered. Accordingly, a lower damage to well-being $w_D' < w_D$ would result. However, all care taken cannot prevent negative technological externalities to occur that, by the nature of novelty, cannot be anticipated at the time of carrying out the innovation. Even when stopped instantaneously, damages cannot be made undone. An innovator who is held liable, strictly and without limits, for any ill effects that may later be discovered evidently faces an uncontrollable risk of a potentially devastating loss. For any kind of risk taking attitude the threat of excessive damage claims will negatively impact the willingness to carry through an innovation. Yet with a significantly reduced innovativeness, the level of individual well-being which the citizens can reach as a result of innovations will also be reduced. Let the new level be $w_I' < w_I$. This reduction can overcompensate the damage reduction. If the expected value for the level of well-being under the "strict liability" innovation regime is denoted by:

$$E(w_{sl}) = q(w_I' - w_D') + (1 - q)w_I', \tag{8}$$

it is thus possible that $E(w_{sl}) < E(w_{nl})$.[13]

How can such an overcompensation be avoided without removing the incentive to react appropriately when negative externalities turn up? One way would be to delimit the innovator's liability to only those damages that he or she could have prevented by immediately taking appropriate measures, when the first hints to a damaging effect are discovered. Such a limited liability implies a principal-agent problem. Unlike the innovator, the public in the role of the principal is incompletely informed about both the occurrence of externalities and timely remedies. However, ex post the efforts taken by the innovator in the role of the agent can be observed and insufficient performance can be sanctioned. A credible threat of ex post sanctions creates incentives to take appropriate effort. The institutional solution to the principal-agent problem is, in legal terms, to apply a liability for negligence rule to the mastering of discovered externalities.

An institutional solution such as this means that the risk of unforeseen damages is not born by the innovator alone, but in part also by society as a whole. Assuming that the conditions to which her or his liability extends are indeed under the control of the innovator, such an innovation regime does not reduce the innovative efforts. Unlike under the "strict liability" regime, the level of well-being w_I will therefore not be reduced. As under the "strict liability" regime, however, the damage to well-being will be reduced to w_D'. Hence, the expected value for the level of well-being under a "limited liability" innovation regime in the specified sense (indicated by suffix ll) is given by

$$E(w_{ll}) = q\ (w_I - w'_D) + (1 - q)w_I. \tag{9}$$

In view of the Eqs. 7–9 it is obvious that, in terms of the levels of attainable well-being, the lottery $L(w_{ll})$ corresponding to the "limited liability" innovation regime dominates the lotteries $L(w_{sl})$ and $L(w_{nl})$ corresponding to the other two regimes. Accordingly, for all citizens independent of their risk preferences

$$CE(L(w_{ll}, q)) > CE(L(w_{sl}, q)) \text{ and } CE(L(w_{ll}, q)) > CE(L(w_{nl}, q). \tag{10}$$

Turning now to the calculus of consent of the most risk-averse citizen j regarding the negative technological externalities occurring only after innovations have been carried through the following can be shown to hold:

Proposition 3

The most risk-averse citizen j consents to a social contract stipulating an innovation regime other than "innovations ruled out", if and only if it is a "limited liability" regime for which

$$CE(L(w_{ll}, q))_j \geq w_{min} \tag{11}$$

The first claim in proposition 3 follows from the order relation (10). To prove the second claim assume that, contrary to condition (11), CE $(L(w_{ll}, q))_j = v_j < w_{min}$. Consenting to the "limited liability" regime under that condition would mean that member j reveals a preference for a sure level of well-being v_j smaller than the sure level w_{min} that can be attained under the "innovations ruled out" regime. Since no other motives have been assumed this would violate the rationality assumption. Hence, the rational most risk-averse agent j consents to a "limited liability" innovation regime if and only if condition (11) is satisfied.

To enforce a "limited liability" innovation regime a society must be able to create and support the necessary legal institutions. What one observes, however, are also publicly financed facilities for doing systematic research on potential hazards of existing and currently developing technologies. Since the corresponding knowledge that is being created has the features of a public good, its provision through contract research privately financed by an innovator would likely fall short of what is desirable. Moreover, research of this kind may be used by a publicly financed health agency or an environmental agency to implement state-of-the-art protective measures *ex ante*. By public authority these may be enforced as a standard by making innovations contingent on the agency's approval.[14] The probability of doing harm to health and/or the environment implied by innovations can thus be reduced. This does not necessarily reduce the economic benefits, nor does it, of course, mean that the yet unknown potential amount of damage to well-being will be lower, should a non-anticipated negative externality nonetheless occur. For expository purposes, the well-being variables w_I and w_D' can therefore be taken to be unaffected. However, the research and regulation activities come at a cost to the public that needs to be financed by raising a tax from each citizen which causes a corresponding reduction in well-being w_T.

Let us dub an innovation regime with these extensions a "limited liability with regulatory agency" regime (indicated by suffix lr). If the subjectively expected hazard reduction is represented by a probability ε, 0 < ε < q, so that q − ε = r, the expected value of well-being associated with such a regime is

$$E(w_{lr}) = r\,(w_I - w_D') + (1-r)w_I - w_T = E(w_{ll}) + \varepsilon w_D' - w_T. \quad (12)$$

On the basis of the assumptions underlying Eq. 12 it follows:

Proposition 4

If condition (11) is not satisfied and the most risk-averse citizen j is therefore unwilling to consent to a "limited liability" innovation regime, j will consent to a "limited liability with regulatory agency" innovation regime, if the certainty equivalent of the hazard reduction exceeds w_T sufficiently.

To prove proposition 4 consider the calculus of consent of the rational, risk-averse citizen j, who does not consent to the "limited liability" regime, because $CE\,(L(w_{ll}, q))_j < w_{min}$(proposition 3). This citizen will not consent to a "limited liability with regulatory agency" innovation regime either, if the certainty equivalents of the two lotteries representing the innovation regimes satisfy the condition CE $(L(w_{Ir}, r))_j \leq$ CE $(L(w_{II}, q))_j$. In view of Eq. 12 this is exactly the case, if the certainty equivalent of $\varepsilon\ w_D'$ is smaller than, or equal to, the sure amount w_T. Hence, for consent as stated in proposition 4 it is necessary, but not sufficient, that the difference between the certainty equivalent of the hazard reduction and the sure amount w_T is positive. The sufficient condition is that the difference becomes so large that

$$\text{CE}\ (L(w_{Ir}, r))_j \geq w_{min} > \text{CE}\ (L(w_{II}, q))_j$$

holds. This is the more likely, the less risk-averse j is, the greater j assesses the hazard reduction that is possible, and the lower the agency costs w_T.

As in the previous section, the two propositions derived here demonstrate that a legitimization of some particular innovation regime by means of a hypothetically reconstructed consent to corresponding stipulations of the social contract is only possible on the basis of specific hypotheses about the citizens' risk preferences. Again we have drawn here on the risk-related behavioral hypothesis derived from human nature that predicts the presence of citizens with strongly risk-averse preferences. If they do not even favor an "innovations ruled out" regime, unanimous consent is likely to result in something like a regime involving publicly financed agencies that regulate technological innovations—an institution sometimes considered incompatible with the idea of "a minimal state" in Constitutional Political Economy.

In the developed world, something like a "no liability" regime was prevailing during the early phases of industrialization. It was gradually turned into a "limited liability" regime and, with rising per capita real income, a slow conversion to a "limited liability with regulatory agency" regime developed. In more recent times, in some of the most prosperous countries even political preferences for partial "innovations ruled out" regimes become apparent, e.g. with respect to innovations in gene technology or cloning techniques. From the fact that a rising share of the citizens favor regulations, or even a partial ban, of innovations in their voting behavior it may again be inferred that there is considerable risk aversion. Yet, as already emphasized at the end of the previous section, these votes reflect *post*-constitutional preferences. They are not cast behind a veil of ignorance and can therefore not be accepted as unambiguous indicators of the true constitutional interests of the citizens.

5 CONCLUSIONS

In this paper we have attempted to show that its adherence to a strong form of preference subjectivism prevents Constitutional Political Economy from developing more definite statements about the normative quality of alternative constitutional innovation regimes. By a constitutional innovation regime we understand the stipulations of a hypothetical social contract regarding the conditions under which, in the post-constitutional market game, innovations are legitimate. It turned out to be implausible to presume that individuals, when situated behind a "veil of ignorance" with respect to the positions they will hold in the post-constitutional market game, will unanimously opt for a laissez faire regime, even when only pecuniary externalities are considered in isolation. Given their knowledge about their own risk attitudes and about the general human disposition to become more risk-averse in the course of one's life, they can rather be argued to opt for a regime that is supplemented by a social security net. In the case of negative technological externalities risk-averse preferences have been shown to favor a limited liability rule supplemented by publicly financed regulatory agencies. Both findings were reconstructed here from the rational calculus of the most risk averse citizen participating in constitutional decision-making.

FOOTNOTES

[1]Vanberg (2005, pp. 24–26) defines it, somewhat broader, as "the presumption that the welfare of the individuals concerned represents the relevant standard against which market and state are to be judged" and as prescribing that "the individuals involved must themselves be respected as the ultimate judges on what qualifies as 'good' or desirable in their social transactions and rule arrangements".

[2]"[I]ndividuals choose to impose constraints on their own behavior…as a part of an exchange in which the restrictions on their own actions are sacrificed in return for the benefits that are anticipated from the reciprocally extended restrictions on the action of others…" (Buchanan 1990, p. 4).

[3]See also Buchanan (1977), Kliemt (1986), Müller (2002) and Binmore (1994, p. 39), who argues that "(t)here is nothing about the circumstances under which people are hypothesized as bargaining in the original position that can justify the assumption that they are bound, either morally or in practice, to abide by the terms of a hypothetical deal reached in the original position." A similar argument has however already been made by Hobbes (see Hardin 1998, p. 647).

[4]Another case of a strong contractarian approach is Gauthier's (1986) rational bargaining-based model of morality.

[5]Evidently, apart from its questionable empirical assumptions (constitutional deliberation often involves quite specific rules) this approach runs into problems of circularity: it presupposes exactly what it purports to explain. When in the constitutional choice set only "general" rules are available, it is trivially clear that "general" rules will be agreed upon in the end. It may be argued, therefore, that the interpretation of the social contract (exclusively) in empirical terms is a nonstarter (Müller 2000, pp. 80–81).

[6]The "Pareto" regime implicitly presupposes that only those innovations are carried out that result in compensation payments not exceeding the income constraint(s) of the innovator(s), see Kerber (1993) for a discussion.

[7]It accords with its hostility towards, and a low pace of, innovativeness that the medieval European economy basically stagnated over the period 1500–1820, see Maddison (2001, Tables B.19 and B.22).

[8]For analytical convenience it is assumed that $y_h > T$.

[9]Their historical background has been the extreme inequality in the distribution of the innovation benefits during the industrial revolution, exposing large fractions of the population to pauperism, famines, and an extremely low life expectancy, see, e.g., the report in Engels (1968).

[10]If so, this would explain the majority vote despite the fact that the benefactors of the social security transfer payments form a comparatively small group endowed with little voting power. The alternative explanation in public choice theory, which interprets the social security transfer payments as a result of inefficiency causing rent-seeking activities (see Mueller 1993), has to refer to hypotheses that do not *prima facie* seem more plausible. It is claimed, e.g., that voters are negligent of the small burden placed on them by each single interest group privilege and therefore accept it. Or it is conjectured that the majority vote results from logrolling between many rent-seeking interest groups in the political process.

[11]For a level of well-being w_{nl}' attained with certainty for which $w_{nl}' = E(w_{nl})$ holds, risk aversion then again implies that $u(E(w_{nl})) < u(w_{nl}')$.

[12]In fact, it can even be argued that there is an incentive for the innovator to withhold a reaction in order to induce other citizens to pay her or him for discontinuing the innovation (see Schlicht 1996).

[13]Inserting Eqs. 7 and 8, this condition holds if $(w_I - w_I')/(w_D - w_D') > q$.

[14]An example is the admission procedure for new drugs practiced by the U.S. Food and Drug Administration. The approval by public authorities (which are

usually risk-averse) can be seen as a control against an overly risk-taking behavior of innovators regarding their liability.

REFERENCES

1. Binmore, K. G. (1994). Game theory and the social contract. vol I: Playing fair. Cambridge, MA: MIT Press.
2. Brennnan, G., & Buchanan, J. M. (1985). The reason of rules. Cambridge, MA: Cambridge University Press.
3. Brennan, G., & Hamlin, A. (1998). Constitutional economics. In P. Newman (Ed.), The new palgrave dictionary of economics and the law, vol. I (pp. 401–410). London: Macmillan.
4. Buchanan, J. M. (1975). The limits of liberty. Chicago: University of Chicago Press.
5. Buchanan, J. M. (1977). A contractarian paradigm for applying economic theory. In J. M. Buchanan (Ed.), Freedom and constitutional contract (pp. 235–242). College Station: Texas A&M University Press.
6. Buchanan, J. M. (1990). The domain of constitutional economics. Constitutional Political Economy, 1, 1–18.
7. Buchanan, J. M. (1991a). The Foundations of Normative Individualism. In Ders, The economics and ethics of constitutional order (pp. 221–231). Ann Arbor: University of Michigan Press.
8. Buchanan, J. M. (1991b). The economics and ethics of constitutional order. Ann Arbor: The University of Michigan Press.
9. Buchanan, J. M. (2005). Afraid to be free: Dependency as desideratum. Public Choice, 124, 19–31.
10. Buchanan, J. M., & Tullock, G. (1962). The calculus of consent. Ann Arbor: University of Michigan Press.
11. Buchanan, J. M., & Vanberg, V. J. (2002). Constitutional implications of radical subjectivism. Review of Austrian Economics, 15, 121–129.
12. Coase, R. H. (1960). The problem of social cost. Journal of Law and Economics, 3, 1–44.
13. Ekelund, R. B., Jr., & Tollison, R. D. (1981). Mercantilism as a rent-seeking society: Economic regulation in historical perspective. College Station: Texas A&M University Press.

14. Engels, F. (1968). The condition of the working class in England. Stanford: Stanford University Press.

15. Gauthier, D. (1986). Morals by agreement. Oxford: Oxford University Press.

16. Hardin, R. (1998). Modern contractarianism. In P. Newman (Ed.) The new palgrave dictionary of economics and the law, vol. II (pp. 645–651). New York: Stockton Press.

17. Harsanyi, J. C. (1953). Cardinal utility in welfare economics and in the theory of risk taking. Journal of Political Economy, 61, 434–435.

18. Harsanyi, J. C. (1975). Can the maximin principle serve as a basis for morality? A critique of John Rawls' theory. Amercian Political Science Review, 69, 594–606.

19. Hayek, F. A. (1978). New studies in philosophy, politics, economics and the history of ideas. London: Routledge.

20. Hempel, C. G., & Oppenheim, P. (1948). Studies in the logic of explanation. Philosophy of Science, 15, 135–178.

21. Hume, D. (1748/1992). Of the original contract. In T. M. Green & T. M. Grose (Eds.), David Hume-the philosophical work (pp. 443–460). Aalen: Scientia.

22. Jones, E. L. (1988). Growth recurring—economic change in world history. Oxford: Clarendon.

23. Kerber, W. (1993). Rights, innovations and evolution: the distributional effects of different rights to innovate. Review of Political Economy, 5, 427–452.

24. Kliemt, H. (1986). Individualism, libertarianism and non-cognitivism. Analyse & Kritik, 8, 211–228.

25. Kliemt, H. (2004). Contractarianism as liberal conservatism: Buchanan's unfinished philosophical agenda. Constitutional Political Economy, 15, 171–185.

26. Maddison, A. (2001). The world economy: A millennial perspective. Paris: OECD.

27. Mokyr, J. (1990). The lever of riches: Technological creativity and economic progress. Oxford: Oxford University Press.

28. Mueller, D. C. (1993). The public choice approach to politics. Edward Elgar: Aldershot.

29. Müller, C. (1998). The veil of uncertainty unveiled. Constitutional Political Economy, 9, 5–17.

30. Müller, C. (2000). Das vertragstheoretische Argument in der Ökonomik. Berlin: Duncker & Humblot.

31. Müller, C. (2002). The methodology of contractarianism in economics. Public Choice, 113, 465–483.

32. North, D. C. (1981). Structure and change in economic history. New York: Norton.

33. Pettit, P. (1974). A theory of justice. Theory and Decision, 4, 311–324.

34. Qizilbash, M. (1997). Needs, incommensurability and well-being. Review of Political Economy, 9, 261–276.

35. Rawls, J. (1971). A theory of justice. Cambridge, MA: Belknap Press.

36. Rosenberg, N., & Birdzell, L. E. (1986). How the west grew rich: The economic transformation of the industrial world. New York: Basic Books.

37. Rubin, P. H., & Paul, C. W. (1979). An evolutionary model of taste for risk. Economic Inquiry, 17, 585–596.

38. Schlicht, E. (1996). Exploiting the coase mechanism: The extortion problem. Kyklos, 49, 319–330.

39. Schumpeter, J. A. (1934). The theory of economic development. Cambridge, MA: Harvard University Press.

40. Schumpeter, J. A. (1942). Capitalism, socialism, and democracy. New York: Harper.

41. Sen, A. K. (1970). Collective choice and social welfare. Amsterdam: North-Holland.

42. Sen, A. K. (1979). Personal utilities and public judgments: Or what's wrong with welfare economics? Economic Journal, 89, 537–558.

43. Sugden, R. (1993). Rationality and impartiality: Is the contractarian enterprise possible? In D. Gauthier & R. Sugden (Eds.), Rationality, justice and the social contract (pp. 157–175). Ann Arbor: University of Michigan Press.

44. Vanberg, V. J. (1986). Individual choice and institutional constraints. Analyse & Kritik, 8, 113–149.

45. Vanberg, V. J. (1994). Cultural evolution, collective learning and constitutional design. In D. Reisman (Ed.), Economic thought and political theory (pp. 171–204). Boston: Kluwer.

46. Vanberg, V. J. (2005). Market and state: The perspective of constitutional political economy. Journal of Institutional Economics, 1, 23–49.

47. Vanberg, V. J. (2006). Human intentionality and design in cultural evolution. In C. Schubert & G. von Wangenheim (Eds.), Evolution and design of institutions (pp. 197–212). London: Routledge.

48. Vanberg, V. J., & Buchanan, J. M. (1989). Interests and theories in constitutional choice. Journal of Theoretical Politics, 1, 49–62.

49. Vanberg, V. J., & Buchanan, J. M. (1991). Constitutional Choice, Rational Ignorance and the Limits of Reason. Jahrbuch für Neue Politische Ökonomie, 10, 61–78.

50. Vickrey, W. S. (1945). Masuring marginal utility by reaction to risk. Econometrica, 13, 319–333.

51. Vickrey, W. S. (1960). Utility strategy, and social decision rules. Quarterly Journal of Economics, 74, 507–535.

52. Witt, U. (1987). How transaction rights are shaped to channel innovativeness. Journal of Institutional and Theoretical Economics, 143, 180–195.

53. Witt, U. (1996). Innovations, externalities and the problem of economic progress. Public Choice, 89, 113–130.

12

THE SOCIAL LIFE OF MEASUREMENT: HOW METHODS HAVE SHAPED THE IDEA OF CULTURE IN URBAN REGENERATION

Peter Campbell, Tamsin Cox & Dave O'Brien

[a]Department of Sociology, Social Policy and Criminology, University of Liverpool, Liverpool, UK;

[b]Policy and Research, DHA, Birmingham, UK;

[c]Department of Sociology, Social Policy and Criminology, University of Liverpool, Liverpool, UK;

[d]History of Art, Edinburgh College of Art, University of Edinburgh, Edinburgh, UK

ABSTRACT

Although 'culture-led regeneration' has been critiqued as both a concept and practice, it is clear that policy-makers continue to make efforts to use cultural activity of varying forms to achieve ends which could be (and are) described in terms of urban 'regeneration'. Whilst the idea of culture-led urban regeneration had gained considerable prominence in a range of policy by the early twenty-first century, many questions have remained over how exactly such 'regenerative' outcomes could be convincingly demonstrated, despite much activity to attempt such demonstration over the course of preceding years. The desire for convincing evidence can be seen in a continued, and increasing, focus on evaluation, and methods aimed at providing evidence of impact and outcomes. In light of the renewed political focus in recent years on 'proving' the effects and value of cultural activity, this paper considers the continuation of practice in this area, and asks what lessons, if any, have been learned in evaluative practice which seeks to demonstrate the regenerative effects of culture. In light of the continuation of apparently problematic practices, the paper seeks to delineate and account for what has been learned, and what has not.

Keywords: Culture-led regeneration; evidence; evaluation; cultural value; methods

INTRODUCTION

Understanding the relationship between social scientific methods and the social world has become a significant component of contemporary research work. Whilst the exact theoretical framework for such study has differing iterations (including performativity, the social life of methods, studies of calculation and valuation, or classificatory struggles), it is clear that an essential part of understand-ing the contemporary world is to understand the role of social science methods in the construction, existence and replication of that world. Indeed, Journal of Cultural Economy has been the forum for the discussion and development of this agenda, whether in a conceptual (Miller 2008; Butler 2010; Callon 2010; Helgesson & Kjellberg 2013; Law & Ruppert 2013) or applied (e.g. Marres & Weltevrede 2013; O'Brien 2016; Yarrow & Kranke 2016) form. In this context, this paper extends the social life of methods agenda to culture-led urban regeneration, a practice that has reshaped the urban environ-ment across many major towns and cities in the UK, along with urban sites across the rest of the world (most notably in Europe, North America, and South East Asia).

Using a review of the evidence base for the impact of culture-led urban regeneration policy, this paper argues that the methods of evidence gathering, more so than any of the social scientific results of this evidence gathering, have been crucial in the transmission of models of urban regeneration. In particular these models have spread across differing and distinct urban settings that would otherwise have little to render them comparable, and thus appropriate subjects for any form of policy transfer. As the era of formal urban regeneration policy comes to an end (O'Brien & Matthews 2015) the paper demonstrates the contingency of the idea of culture in urban regeneration, a contingency grounded in the social life of methods sustaining that idea. The paper develops a new approach to an otherwise crowded field of study (see Oakley & O'Brien 2016 for a recent summary of the extensive literature) by reframing the questions associated with culture-led urban regeneration around the role methods have played in the creation and continuance of that social and policy phenomena. In taking seriously the social life of methods for culture-led urban regeneration, aca-demic engagements critical of the use of culture in urban settings will find another front for resist-ance (Lees et al. 2007; O'Brien & Matthews 2015).

METHODS AND THEIR SOCIAL LIFE

This paper begins from the perspective that social science research methods are not separate from the social world, but rather they are a constitutive part of that world. This social life of methods perspec-tive develops the well-established concern with reflexivity within the contemporary social sciences. The social life of methods is summarised and elaborated by Law et al. (2011). They use the example of surveys of attitudes across differing European nations to show the interrelationship between methods and the social world. Methods are used within a context that is closely determined by the findings of the methods themselves. In the case of European attitudinal surveys, the idea of Europe itself is produced in close relationship to the survey method and helps to set the circum-stances for the activity of the survey. Thus there is a triple movement of survey practitioners and administrators, descriptions of social reality, and the institutional and organisational settings acting on and through the research.

One useful example here is contemporary class analysis, whether in the form of the Great British Class Survey (Savage et al. 2015) or classificatory struggles (Tyler 2015). Class in contemporary Britain is a reflexive set of categories, whereby a social scientific framework used to understand occupational relationships with labour markets (Goldthorpe & McKnight 2004) is also the site for powerful position taking for individual's descriptions of their identities (Savage 2000; Savage et al. 2015), and for revan-chist exercises of class power and politics (Tyler 2015). Class is, therefore, as much a technical social scientific tool as it is a lived reality of individuals and communities. Most crucially, it is difficult to sep-arate the social science of occupations, labour relations, life chances, and politics, from the use of class language within individual identity. A second example moves towards the case study of culture-led urban regeneration. O'Brien (2013) has shown how the cultural 'omnivore', itself a product of specific choices in survey instruments, has a powerful place within public policy for culture in the UK, repre-senting the 'ideal-type' consumer of state-sponsored culture. Those who do not fit this pattern are then sites for potential policy interventions to bring their consumption patterns closer to the survey-research produced omnivore (Miles & Sullivan 2012).

This approach has also prompted an engagement with a specific culture-led urban regeneration policy: Liverpool's 2008 European Capital of Culture. Here the findings of economic impact and community involvement, which for Cox and O'Brien (2012) were specific to a single time and place, were placed at the centre of future, general, public policy. Both methods, and their findings, in this work have a social life. It is here where a more detailed engagement with culture-led urban regeneration is most important.

Historical 'evidence' for the regenerative role of culture

There have been attempts to gather evidence on the socio-economic benefits of artistic and cultural activity for many years, at least from the 1970s, if not earlier (cf. Reeves 2002, p. 7; Gray 2007, p. 206; O'Brien 2013, p. 91). Clearly, however, the work of Myerscough (1988) in the late 1980s proved influential, for some serving to rectify an 'almost scandalous lack of empirical research into the oper-ation of the arts sector' prior to this point (Hughes 1989, p. 34). Moving through the 1990s, Gray (2007) identifies a move to focus on a range of instrumental outcomes for cultural activity, and as the 1990s ended, the New Labour administration in the UK epitomised governmental belief in the idea of 'cul-ture-led' urban regeneration, with an intensifying rhetoric around 'evidence-based policy' (Oakley 2008) and an emphasis on gathering 'data' of some form to support the arguments around culture's potentially regenerative role. Nevertheless, much research (e.g. Reeves 2002, p. 17; García 2004, p. 321; Oakley 2004, p. 72; Selwood 2006, p. 45; Gray 2006, p. 111; Lees & Melhuish 2015, p. 253) repeatedly notes a lack of robust evidence as we move into the first decade of the twenty-first century.

The persistence of a pattern?

Given a consistent identification of a lack of robust evidence from a range of research practice up to 2006, but a persistent use of social science (or 'social science-like') methods to prove the case for cul-ture, in 2014 a review was conducted specifically on recent research practice used to assess the role that culture plays in urban regeneration as part of the Arts and Humanities Research

Council's 'Cul-tural Value' project. Material was gathered in relation to cultural policy interventions that were expli-citly described as 'regenerative', or which belonged to a 'type' of intervention that is routinely described as 'regenerative', by searching academic sources and grey literature, and through consul-tation with the cultural sector. The review focussed mainly on data from the UK, but also drew on practice further afield, including significant European cultural regeneration programmes. In total, 151 relevant sources from the period 2006–2014, covering reports from cultural organisations, commissioned research, policy-makers, local government, academics, and media sources, were identified and analysed.[1]

Interestingly, Reeves' findings regarding the limitations of evidence produced by methods utilised in the 1990s to demonstrate the impacts of cultural practice (2002, p. 102; echoed by Evans & Shaw 2004), clearly persist in the evidence produced in more recent years. Indeed, in the last decade, near-identical critiques have consistently been made regarding, for example, the prevalence of ad hoc evaluations which cannot be drawn together to build a substantial evidence base (Ennis & Douglass 2011, p. 10), and evaluation which veers more towards advocacy and which thus cannot entertain the possibility of negative impacts (Belfiore 2006, p. 32). Ennis and Douglass (2011, p. 9) concluded that the highest quality evidence available does not allow the question of whether culture-led urban regeneration is successful to be answered.

It may well be asked, therefore, why after having been identified as problematic for so long, these issues persist. On a very basic sociological level, Schutz (1960, p. 214) argues that 'human activities are only made understandable by showing their in-order-to or because motives'. In this situation, it could be argued that evidence is gathered in similar ways over time, despite the problems noted above, in order to support the narrative around the role culture can play in urban settings, because this fits into a broader discourse on the nature of culture and economy (cf. Campbell 2014), and because a suite of research approaches have become entrenched in this field, structuring it into specific forms. The discussion below attempts to clarify the persistence of the range of motives and constrain-ing circumstances shaped by this broader field, based on a consideration of the material outlined above, and to demonstrate why the evidence base pertaining to the role of culture in urban regener-ation has thus become 'stuck' in a particular paradigm, and thus to reveal how and why the methods for evidencing the impact of culture-led urban regeneration have a specific and particular social life.

PERSISTENT EXPLANATIONS

A number of persistent explanatory factors can be suggested to account for the steadfast nature of critiques of evidence-gathering practice.

Short-term data cannot establish long-term outcomes

Methods are often employed on behalf of those organising a cultural event to enable impact to be demonstrated to funders and other stakeholders. This is usually a short-term necessity, and so research evidence is most often generated alongside specific programmes or events, and in close proximity to their operation. Once data has been generated, 'evidence' has done its job (for certain actors, at least). There is thus a mismatch between the timescale of methods used and outcomes sought. With reference to a range of developments around new cultural venues over the course of a decade, Hyslop argues that 'in most cases it is too early to judge the success of the long-term impact of these projects on the economic and social development of their communities' (2012, p. 153, emphasis added; see also Barnardo's 2005, p. 16; Ela Palmer Heritage 2008, p. 30; CABE 2008, p. 5). If evidence gathering is repeatedly linked only to time-limited interventions, evidence of long-term impact will, by definition, not be found.

Despite longstanding identification of this problem (Reeves 2002, p. 104; Evans & Shaw 2004, pp. 8, 57), however, it is notable that long-term study remains rare. García and Cox (2013, p. 19), for instance, find 'little to no research' into the long-term effects of the entire European Capital of Culture pro-gramme and, in relation to the limited amount of such research that is available, find that 'claims and evidence about medium to long-term effect varies considerably' (p. 24). Relatedly, the 2013 Centre for Economics and Business Research (CEBR) report to Arts Council England and the National Museum Directors' Council (2013, p. 88) finds that many studies do not even seek to establish a baseline from which future impact can be measured, or report findings only relating to a short period of time.

Whilst such short-termism can clearly lead to the lack of robustness in findings, it can also poten-tially serve a purpose by enabling more optimistic findings than may result from a long-term approach. Sharp (2007, p. 286), for instance, discusses how enthusiasm around the potential impact of cultural projects can initially be very high, but also outlines how this can easily change dramati-cally; a change uncaptured by short-term studies. Similarly, García and Cox (2013, p. 133) demon-strate that developments in physical infrastructure can be well-used during a major cultural programme, and that tourism levels can be boosted in the short-term, but that these changes – if measured – can prove unsustainable. This potential complexity is 'helpfully' reduced by brief studies which focus on initial 'good news', and inappropriately inflate the role that culture plays in broader regeneration. Once this evidence of 'success' has been achieved, often there is no political impetus to consider whether effects over the longer-term could or should be examined. Evans (2011, p. 6) suc-cinctly describes how this kind of practice will not enable us to adequately contextualise the size and nature of the role that cultural programmes may appropriately play in urban settings:

> The culture and regeneration story requires a historical analysis that also maps change and effects over a much longer time period, within which events form only a relatively small (financial and strategic) part. Investment in housing, retail, transport, education and local amenities are likely to have a more lasting legacy and impact. This will also be important in order to consider how culture might better contribute to the regeneration process, as opposed to simply being corralled into a 'festival event' or 'year'.

There is little evidence, however, of the adoption of such analysis. Also, whilst there is much that is specific about regeneration programmes using culture, it should be noted that this evidence deficit applies much more broadly. Ennis and Douglass pointedly state the continuing necessity for longer-term study, and the production of longitudinal data, without which 'it may not be possible to determine conclusively whether culture-led regeneration, or indeed any regeneration, works' (2011, p. 2, emphasis added). This form of study, however, may be increasingly unlikely in the context of a 'fast policy' world, in which 'rapid results', and positive results at that, are required (Van Heur 2010, p. 190).

Culture may be a low priority, or have limited resources

A further reason for an absence of longitudinal methods is likely to be the expense of carrying out such research. Belfiore (2002, p. 98) rightly notes the complexity and expense of such assessment (see

also Evans & Shaw 2004, p. 58; Ennis & Douglass 2011, p. 10), which is likely to be beyond the capa-bilities of all but the very largest institutions (Ela Palmer Heritage 2008, p. 30). Evans and Shaw's conclusions from 2004 (p. 21) specifically regarding economic impact thus still seem to apply a dec-ade on, and will likely persist:

> The level of primary survey research required to measure economic and distributive effects outside of the cul-tural project itself (and even here, distributive data is hard to capture) is felt to be prohibitive and hard to

> justify, unless motivated by a funding or other imperative – longitudinal studies of effects even more so.

To adequately back up the claims made for culture takes financial resources which, increasingly, the cultural sector does not have (Lees & Melhuish 2015, p. 256). Besides limited financial resources, we can also consider how limitations in terms of other forms of resource affect evidence-gathering prac-tices. Generating evidence of regeneration is an inherently difficult task, but it is also only one task amongst many for those working in the cultural field (Hesmondhalgh et al. 2015, for example, describe a proliferation of performance management indicators over recent years). For many cultural organisations, this kind of activity is also likely to be significantly outside the skills and capacities of the governance and administration of the organisation. The kinds of evidence sought regarding 'regeneration' can also often relate to outcomes that are not necessary a fundamental part of core operational or charitable objectives; evidence which can be used for advocacy may seem worth gen-erating, evidence which cannot may seem to be more limited in its 'use' to many organisations. Relat-edly, it is instructive to consider the following point from one of the reports reviewed regarding the competing pressures which apply not just to cultural organisations, but to potential external partners in research:

> The evaluation methodology was predicated on involving local authority data collection officers in gathering the quantitative data. Despite extensive efforts it proved impossible to ensure the involvement of the officers in gathering data to demonstrate the role of culture within regeneration. If Arts Council England is to pursue an emphasis on 'hard evidence' it may wish to consider making funding conditional on the involvement of such officers. (General Public Agency 2008, pp. 8–9)

The resources which evaluation can draw on to establish a firm case may, therefore, continue to be limited in a number of senses. Vickery (2007, p. 21) notes in the context of local authority practice how culture is a relatively low priority and, whilst it is certainly true that many recent regeneration initiatives have found a role for arts and culture as part of wider investment programmes, one key continuity in recent practice is the somewhat marginal position of cultural activity in such programmes.

Vickery (2007) also notes that up until the 1990s, urban regeneration was largely led by property development (p. 29), and that during the 1990s, the role of culture in urban regeneration was still often linked strictly to physical or spatial development, focussed mainly either on altering the design of the urban environment, or on installing public artworks (pp. 18–19). Recently, initiatives which can be identified as positing a role for culture in processes of regeneration include the Single Regen-eration Budget, which helped, for instance, to fund public art (Public Art Leicester 2005; Gateshead Council 2006), community music projects (Dhamak Beats 2012) and artists' studios (ACAVA 2014); the European Regional Development Fund, which has invested in the renovation and construction of new cultural facilities (European Commission 2013), business assistance for cultural enterprises (DCLG 2013) and a centre for carnival arts (UKCCA 2010); the New Deal for Communities, which, in certain areas, used arts and culture-related activities to attempt to tackle mental health inequalities (Blank et al. 2004); and the Housing Market Renewal scheme, which helped fund artists' studios (NFASP 2010), public art (Pendle Borough Council 2014) and artist-led participatory pro-jects (Media and Arts Partnership 2008; Arts Council England 2009). Whilst such initiatives fund cultural projects, and so propose that these may contribute in some way to wider regeneration goals, the peripheral position of this activity proves problematic in terms of dealing with the persist-ent evidence gap outlined above, as there remains typically little or no discussion of the role of cul-ture in relation to overall findings regarding regeneration (e.g. DCLG 2007; DCLG 2009; DCLG 2010; Audit Commission 2011; Leather et al. 2012). So long as culture remains a low priority in urban policy broadly speaking, we can therefore expect the evidence base available to reflect this

– with the 'social life' of the methods shaped by the level of importance given to such activity. It should also be noted that, even when an explicitly regenerative programme's focus is entirely cultural

– such as in the case of the European Capital of Culture programme – that the scale of investment is often still small in comparison with other activity seeking urban regeneration outcomes (Cox & O'Brien 2012, p. 97).

A lack of clarity in the terms of research

The circumstances delineated above may thus help us to understand the persistence of a lack of clarity about what research methods are actually attempting to achieve, and therefore how these achievements could be appropriately understood. Often the starting point of research is to position cultural activity as a known benefit with known effects, already revealed by previous evaluation prac-tice, which can thus be continued.

If, for instance, cultural activity aims to promote 'creative industries', what is the mechanism by which this will occur? Often, it seems as though this question need no longer be asked, even though Knell and Oakley (2007, p. 21) note that whilst discussion of creative industries has become promi-nent, funding of arts activity has often carried on in much the same manner as it did prior to this prominence, with links being assumed rather than made explicit. Correlation, of course, need not imply causation, and simply monitoring and reporting what happens at the same time as a cultural event does not necessarily provide us with evidence for what this event has itself achieved. By what means would creative industries be promoted, if indeed they would?

On this subject, specifically in relation to the recent years of the European Capital of Culture pro-gramme, García and Cox (2013, p. 142) point out a continued articulation of an assumed relation-ship between this programme and the development of creative industries, rather than any kind of clear planning to promote such a relationship. Again, when evaluating the achievements of culture, a search for 'good news' rather than an attempt to establish solid evidence seems to characterise prac-tice. Without the articulation of a mechanism by which culture has a role to play, evidence gathering can involve a 'sweeping up' of any available information that can add weight to the argument for the beneficial role of culture, veering away from research and towards advocacy. This leaves us in a pos-ition where a role for culture is asserted (e.g. New Economy 2013, p. 27), suspected (THRU 2013, p. 259), or where research proves to be merely descriptive rather than analytical (Markusen & Gadwa 2010, p. 382). By contrast, where a relationship seems to be established in a more concrete fashion – for instance, between the concentration of cultural institutions and house prices – the direction and nature of this relationship is not necessarily clear (CEBR 2013, p. 113).

Without clarity on how, and by what means, culture is expected to contribute to regeneration, most evidence produced will be of little relevance beyond its own specific context. In recent years, Evans (2011, p. 13) has astutely tackled this issue:

> Whilst there is no shortage of 'evidence', techniques and methods, how these relate – if at all – to the governance and regeneration regime, and where power over which and whose culture is 'invited to the festival' resides, is not apparent or at least not part of the evaluation or impact study process. The extent to which this accumu-lating evidence on the wider effects of hosting and delivering such mega-events has and may be used in the future to inform future events and both cultural and regeneration strategies, is at best marginal.

Nevertheless, such accumulation continues to occur.

Measurement is not always feasible

Clearly, many of the effects that cultural activity can have are difficult, if not impossible, to capture. This does not mean, however, that there is not room for improvement in practice in this area. In a review of 'evaluations by English RDAs [...] that deal with culture and regeneration', Ennis and Douglass (2011, p. 8) find that whilst evidence which is related to economic outcomes, such as num-ber of 'safeguarded jobs', can be firmly established, other areas are left to 'qualitative judgment'. They continue, echoing the points above,

> These qualitative assessments are in some cases little more than hopeful statements, lacking the specific evi-dence that has long been needed. For example, countless evaluations point to improved perceptions of a neighbourhood, but do not demonstrate how this connects to the long-term goals of regeneration. Similarly, projects are said to improve confidence amongst residents, based on small surveys taken shortly after the completion of the project. Since evaluations are generally carried out shortly after completion, there are none showing the long-term impact that really matters most for regeneration.

Labadi also notes (2008, p. 107) that qualitative data on the impact of regeneration schemes can be tainted by 'optimism bias', referring to one study where,

> the six people who agreed to be interviewed and had overall positive opinion of the scheme were all deeply involved in the regeneration and therefore could not really have the necessary critical detachment.

Again, the methods adopted to demonstrate regeneration impacts may veer too close to advocacy for cultural organisations for it to give an accurate picture of what has been achieved, seeking primarily to show positive impact rather than ascertain if it exists (e.g. General Public Agency 2008, p. 11; DC Research 2011, p. 2; LARC 2011, p. 9). There are many ways in which such practice could theoreti-cally be changed, but there is limited evidence from this review that these changes have taken place in recent years. For instance, Reeves (2002, p. 104) noted the lack of comparative studies, or the use of control groups to establish the effects of cultural activity over a decade ago. In the course of this research, we did not identify any evidence of such studies having taken place in the more recent past to provide evidence for the value of cultural activity, and broader problems with the evidence base in this area have been noted (Belfiore 2006; What Works Centre 2014). O'Brien (2013, p. 47) when discussing methods to assess the impacts of cultural engagement notes that 'there has been little progress over the past decade of evaluation and research', and Lees and Melhuish (2015, p. 243) note repeated difficulties with evaluating arts projects linked to forms of social regen-eration. Current methods of evaluation cannot acknowledge that the arts and culture are, as Gray (drawing on Gallie) puts it, 'essentially contested concepts' (2008, p. 212), and this may lead to an emphasis on a 'simpler' area in which to identify results – the economic.

An over-emphasis on the economic

The drive to demonstrate economic impact continues to shape research methods. The necessity of some economic component to urban regeneration – as well as a broader research agenda which emphasises the necessity of fostering 'economic competitiveness' (Belfiore 2015, p. 97) – also helps to explain evidence production skewed towards economic indicators and economic impact. Indeed, whilst non-economic impacts may be poorly established due to the difficulties outlined above, they may also be poorly established due to a lack of interest in such issues. The goals of those commissioning and funding cultural activity may not match those of cultural institutions, or indeed those of the wider public (cf. García 2005, p. 846; Holden 2007, p. 32; Shin & Stevens 2013, p. 644). In their discussion of the specific use of heritage-related programmes to achieve regen-eration goals, Ela Palmer Heritage note a lack of evidence relating to social impacts:

> The lack of requirement for social impact evaluation has stemmed from a focus on the economic impacts of regeneration, mainly concentrated on market value, job creation and the desirability of the area for business. (2008, p. 30)

This focus primarily on the economic may also be explained by the fact that, once economic matters are dealt with, social impacts continue to be either taken for granted or expected to naturally 'trickle-down'. Clearly this is controversial with respect to cultural programmes (Colomb 2011, p. 77, see also Evans & Shaw 2004, p. 58), as well as regeneration programmes more broadly (Jones & Evans 2008, pp. 72–73).

Even if figures relating to direct economic impact can be established, these can be difficult to dis-entangle from the impacts of other investments and programmes (Cox & O'Brien, 2012). What is perhaps more problematic, however, as O'Brien (2013, p. 12) points out, is that 'our choice of econ-omic valuation methods may then lead us to actually miss the importance of what it is we are attempting to value'. Nevertheless, the prevailing circumstances resulting in a reliance on economic valuation methods continue to intensify. This does not mean that there is not room for improvement in the methods applied in this area, however. In earlier reviews of methods used in this field, Reeves (2002, p. 42) noted the reliance on economic indicators but also the following problems:

- a reliance on narrow economic values and economic indicators considered inadequate for measuring 'dif-ficult-to-quantify' outcomes

- failure to take account of displacement and leakage of spending from the local economy
- failure to distinguish between distributional effects and aggregate income effects of arts spending

These criticisms can also be identified long before this list of Reeves (cf. Hughes 1989, p. 38), and continue to shape the research field. In considering a wide range of cultural research, Markusen and Gadwa argue that many studies,

> ... are plagued with unwarranted assumptions and inference problems. These include: 1) not adequately demonstrating that the arts are an export base industry; 2) treating all spending as new spending, as opposed to factoring out expenditures that would otherwise have been made elsewhere in the local economy; 3) not acknowledging that non-profit arts expenditures are directly subsidized by the public sector through both capi-tal and operations support; and, 4) failing to count the foregone tax revenues that non-profit status confers. (2010, pp. 380–381)

These points are also echoed in consideration of specific studies (e.g. Labadi 2008, pp. 28–29). Clearer guidance on how to appropriately apply such methods has become available in recent years, such as the English Partnerships 'Additionality Guide' (2008), and guidance is also available in the UK government's 'Green Book' on evaluation regarding leakage, deadweight and displacement (HM Treasury 2003, p. 53), but with the following caveat:

> In some cases, the best source of information for assessing additionality may be from those who clearly have an interest in the outcome of the decision. In these circumstances, the information and forecasts should be con-firmed by an independent source.

In recent cases relating to the cultural field (e.g. GHK 2009, p. 28), it is difficult to ascertain whether this has been attempted, but it seems rather that 'traditional' methods persist which do not heed such advice. Even studies which do take these issues into consideration somewhat can leave questions unanswered. For instance, English Partnerships (2008, p. 14) caution against assuming zero dead-weight when assessing interventions, but this assumption can be seen to be made in practice (e.g. Roger Tym and Partners 2011, p. 27). More often, though, it seems that issues such as these are simply not considered at all in extant research (CASE 2011, p. 63). A recent evidence review by the What Works Centre (2014) did not consider any studies attributing economic impact to cultural interventions as a result of visitor numbers, on the basis that the available studies were insufficiently robust, particularly in respect to identifying the net economic benefits of interventions. Continual inappropriate application of methods has led some economic impact figures to be characterised as no more than 'wild guesses' (Labadi 2008, pp. 34–35). If the adoption of more robust methods were to lead to a diminution of economic impact figures, however, then less robust methods may be favoured in order to increase the level of 'good news', or because they are simpler (and cheaper) to apply.

What should also be noted on this point, however, is that even if these factors were considered there is also robust criticism of the use of economic impact studies per se. Rushton (2015) argues that 'there are no insights to be gained, no policy implications' from such studies, which are 'expensive to produce, useless and forgotten as research'. Little, therefore, seems to have changed since Madden considered these techniques in detail in 2001 and found that, despite their prolifer-ation, 'nearly every economist who reviews "economic" impact studies of the arts expresses concern over the technological and practical limitations of the methodologies' (p. 165), agreeing that no pol-icy implications can be drawn from such studies (p. 161), which, indeed, are not designed to serve such a purpose, but which can be used to inappropriately overstate contribution to a local economy (p. 168). When it comes to the matter of what evidence can be used to make the case specifically for the role of cultural activity, the following point of Madden's is especially insructive:

> By their very nature, 'economic' impact studies are poor at accounting for intangibles. And it is worth pointing out that governments are prone to put intangible considerations before financial considerations. For example, governments often intervene to depress the drugs, prostitution and pornography industries despite their some-times substantial financial flow-on effects. (2001, p. 170)

Given their persistence, however, Madden's view that despite their inappropriateness in many ways, economic impact studies of cultural activity 'can be seen as a perfectly rational response to political demand' (p. 174) is also instructive, a point reinforced by Crompton (2006). As with a range of methods, we may not be led to a clearer understanding, but achieving such an understanding may not be the dominant goal of evaluation practice.

'When the legend becomes fact, print the legend'

The body of research regarding cultural regeneration thus seems particularly susceptible to the gen-eration of myths or legends (common in many areas of research, cf. Rekdal 2014), whereby a piece of data, often a figure or set of figures, becomes a 'known' truth, repeated in multiple sources, free of contextual information, and thus becomes a desired point of replication for future study. For instance, as a very brief illustration of the disconnect between evidence and its provenance, Arts Council England (2014, p. 19) note the 'estimated £10 million' contribution to the local economy of the Hepworth Wakefield – a figure sourced via Local Government Association's (LGA's) 2013 report. This second report gives limited information regarding the derivation of the figure (p. 6), but no further reference to enable the source of this information to be followed up. Further inves-tigation reveals that this figure seems to have been sourced from the gallery's annual report (Hep-worth Wakefield 2012, p. 80), which notes that the figure is based on '511,781 visitors' spending 'an average of £21' each. The caveats above regarding economic calculations clearly apply here, but this would not be clearly known from either of the initial reference points, which are likely to have a higher visibility, helping to perpetuate this figure as a 'known' truth. O'Brien (2013, p. 111) similarly demonstrates how a range of research on Liverpool's tenure as European Capital of Culture is 'debased' into a set of key headline figures, which help to form a 'mythology' around the nature of culture-led regeneration. If such 'mythologies' persist, then they themselves likely help to perpetuate the patterns of research identified above.

Where to next?

What can be seen in the case of evidence for culture-led urban regeneration, then, is the persistence in recent years of the utilisation of methods that continue to evince the problems identified in the field historically, and so a somewhat problematic social life for the methods used to justify cultural interventions in association with regeneration. As the underlying factors shaping evidence gathering persist, so too do the kinds of evidence produced. These methods thus help to constitute an object of study and a field of practice which, having been well established in the early 2000s, and found to persist in the early 2010s, is likely to continue for the foreseeable future, and perhaps intensify in its drive towards quantification. There also seems to be increasing enthusiasm (e.g. Markusen & Gadwa 2010, p. 382; Arts Council England 2014, p. 6) for the use of statistical analysis of secondary data to ameliorate some of the problems with evidence discussed above, perhaps inspired by recent enthusiasm for the concept of 'big data'. There is good reason to exercise caution here. The recent 2014 Arts Council review of evidence of the value of culture (p. 6) points to 'promising work using [...] logistic regression techniques', but the work referred to actually enables us to conclude relatively little from its statistical findings. Before methods move further in this direction, it may be wise to note Gorard's warning on the use of statistical analysis more broadly:

> The danger of spurious findings is a general one, and cannot be overcome by using alternative forms of regression [...] In fact, more complex methods can make the situation worse [...] Complex statistical methods cannot be used post hoc to overcome design problems or deficiencies in datasets. (2006, pp. 82–83)

This approach also raises the question of what can realistically be known with available secondary data. Whilst secondary data can deal with some of the problems around data gathering outlined above, the Culture and Sport Evidence (CASE) report into this very issue (2011) concluded that cur-rent data and methods were mainly helpful when considering business and property-related data (p. 71), and that current approaches still often do not effectively consider issues of economic displace-ment (p. 4), appropriate comparators (p. 17), or direct attribution to specific interventions (p. 80). When data is available to undertake such methods (which is rarely), only relatively large interven-tions can be adequately assessed. As such, this does not seem like a trajectory for research that will necessarily avoid the difficulties noted above.

In addition, given the conditions outlined above, it seems unlikely that broader factors constrain-ing the production of robust evidence on culture's role in regeneration will disappear. What is per-haps more pressing is whether the very idea of culture-led regeneration is one which has now reached its peak (Evans 2011, p. 15; Lees & Melhuish 2015, p. 243). Nevertheless, the importance of establishing a robust evidence base around these issues continues to have some prominence (Arts Council England 2014), and arguments around regenerative potential remain familiar:

> There are five key ways that arts and culture can boost local economies: attracting visitors; creating jobs and developing skills; attracting and retaining businesses revitalising places; and developing talent [...] There is strong evidence that participation in the arts can contribute to community cohesion, reduce social exclusion and isolation, and/or make communities feel safer and stronger. (pp. 7–8)

That said, just as the arguments made around the value of culture seem to have an impressive stab-ility, so now do the critiques made of these arguments. Arts Council England's review of evidence gathering since 2010 finds that 'most of the studies reviewed cannot establish causality between arts and culture and the wider societal impacts' (p. 8), again highlighting the need for longitudinal study. Nevertheless, such a document continues some of the circular reasoning which partially accounts for the lack of progress highlighted above. After stating that no causal relationship has been established between cultural activity and broader social impact, we find this statement:

> We know that arts and culture play an important role in promoting social and economic goals through local regeneration, attracting tourists, the development of talent and innovation, improving health and wellbeing, and delivering essential services. (p. 11)

Thus the social life of these methods continues even as it is being critiqued: we cannot establish the broader causalities suggested by policy rhetoric, but we (the Royal policy 'we') know that culture plays a role, or at least believe this.

Despite the limitations outlined in this paper, the methods cur-rently in use serve sufficiently to support this belief, and to provide ways in which the belief can be articulated, framed and developed further in future policy interventions. It is, on the whole, unclear what the role of 'better', and particularly of more fine-grained and/or longitudinal data, might be in policy development. What research may usefully now ask, therefore, lest these issues persist, is not what can be achieved by cultural activity, but rather what forms of social science are needed to break the hold of the current social life of methods in culture-led urban regeneration?

NOTE

1. A full list of sources consulted can be found in Campbell et al. (2015).

DISCLOSURE STATEMENT

No potential conflict of interest was reported by the authors.

FUNDING

This work was supported by the Arts and Humanities Research Council [grant number AH/L014505/1].

NOTES ON CONTRIBUTORS

Peter Campbell is a lecturer in Sociology and Social Policy at the University of Liverpool. His research to date has focussed upon cultural policy, and on attempts to align culture and creativity with processes of socio-economic urban regeneration. In addition to doctoral research studying political discourse and activity regarding the 'creative industries', and their broader social role, he has worked on evaluation of the European Capital of Culture research programme, and the London 2012 Cultural Olympiad.

Tamsin Cox is Head of Policy and Research at DHA, and an Honorary Research Fellow in the School of Sociology, Social Policy and Criminology at the University of Liverpool. She has undertaken a range of work with funding bodies, local authorities, organisations, networks, and events.

Dave O'Brien is a Chancellor's Fellow in Cultural and Creative Industries at Edinburgh College of Art, University of Edinburgh. He has published extensively on cultural policy, cultural and creative work, cultural value, and culture-led urban regeneration. His most recent books are the edited collections Routledge Companion to Global Cultural Policy, After Urban Regeneration, and the monograph Cultural Policy.

REFERENCES

1. ACAVA (ASSOCIATION FOR CULTURAL ADVANCEMENT THROUGH VISUAL ART) (2014) 'Regeneration Archive', [Online] Available at: http://www.acava.org/regeneration/regeneration-archive (accessed June 2014).
2. ARTS COUNCIL ENGLAND (2009) 'The North West Housing Market Renewal Arts Partnership', [Online] Available at: http://www.artscouncil.org.uk/media/uploads/publications/NW-Housing-Market-Renewal.pdf (accessed June 2014).
3. ARTS COUNCIL ENGLAND (2014) The Value of Arts and Culture to People and Society, Arts Council England, Manchester.
4. AUDIT COMMISSION (2011) 'Housing Market Renewal: Housing, Programme Review', [Online] Available at: http:// archive.audit-commission.gov.uk/auditcommission/SiteCollectionDocuments/Downloads/201103HMRprogramm ereview.pdf (accessed June 2014).
5. BARNARDO'S (2005) 'Art of Regeneration: Evaluating the Impact of the Arts in a Disadvantaged Community', [Online] Available at: http://www.dmss.co.uk/wp-content/uploads/2013/06/art_of_regeneration_report.pdf (accessed June 2014).
6. BELFIORE, E. (2002) 'Art as a means of alleviating social exclusion: does it really work? A critique of instrumental cultural policies and social impact studies in the UK', International Journal of Cultural Policy, vol. 8, no. 1, pp. 91–106.

7. BELFIORE, E. (2006) 'The social impact of the arts – myth or reality?', in Culture Vultures: Is UK Arts Policy Damaging the Arts?, ed M. Mirza, Policy Exchange, London, pp. 20–37.

8. BELFIORE, E. (2015) ''Impact', 'value' and 'bad economics': making sense of the problem of value in the arts and huma-nities', Arts and Humanities in Higher Education, vol. 14, no. 1, pp. 95–110.

9. BLANK, L., ELLIS, L., GOYDER, E. & PETERS, J. (2004) 'Tackling Inequalities in Mental Health – The Experience of New Deal for Communities', [Online] Available at: http://extra.shu.ac.uk/ndc /downloads/reports/RR34.pdf (accessed June 2014).

10. BUTLER, J. (2010) 'Performative agency', Journal of Cultural Economy, vol. 3, no. 2, pp. 147–161.

11. CABE (COMMISSION FOR ARCHITECTURE AND THE BUILT ENVIRONMENT) (2008) 'Artists & Places: Engaging Creative Minds in

12. Regeneration', [Online] Available at: http://www.liminal.org.uk /uploads/9/warwick_bar_masterplan_Artist_and_ Places_2008-pdf (accessed June 2014).

13. CALLON, M. (2010) 'Performativity, misfires and politics', Journal of Cultural Economy, vol. 3, no. 2, 163–169. CAMPBELL, P. (2014) 'Imaginary success? – The contentious ascendance of creativity' European Planning Studies, vol. 22,

14. no. 5, 995–1009.

15. CAMPBELL, P., COX, T., CRONE, S. & WILKS-HEEG, S. (2015) "Evidence of Things That Appear Not'? – A Critical Review of the Role of Arts and Culture in the Regeneration of Urban Places and Urban Communities', [Online] Available at: http://repository.liv.ac.uk/2035440/ (accessed November 2015).

16. CASE (CULTURE AND SPORT EVIDENCE PROGRAMME) (2011) 'The Art of the Possible – Using Secondary Data to Detect Social and Economic Impacts From Investments in Culture and Sport: A Feasibility Study', [Online] Available at: https:// www.gov.uk/government/uploads /system/uploads/attachment_data/file/77608/CASE_The_Art_of_the_ possible_ 2.pdf (accessed June 2014).

17. CEBR (CENTRE FOR ECONOMICS AND BUSINESS RESEARCH) (2013) 'The Contribution of the Arts and Culture to the National Economy', [Online] Available at: http://www.artscouncil.org.uk /media/ uploads/pdf/CEBR_economic_report_web_ version_0513.pdf (accessed June 2014).

18. COLOMB, C. (2011). 'Culture in the city, culture for the city? The political construction of the trickle-down in cultural regeneration strategies in Roubaix, France', Town Planning Review, vol. 81, no. 1, pp. 77–98.

19. COX, T. & O'BRIEN, D. (2012) 'The "scouse wedding" and other myths and legends: reflections on the evolution of a "Liverpool model" for culture-led regeneration', Cultural Trends, vol. 21, no. 2, pp. 93–101.

20. CROMPTON, J. L. (2006) 'Economic impact studies: instruments for political Shenanigans?', Journal of Travel Research, vol. 45, pp. 67–82.

21. DC RESEARCH (2011) 'Economic Value and Impact of Yorkshire Sculpture Park', [Online] Available at: http://www.ysp.co.uk/media/editor/file/YSP%20Economic%20Impact%20Final%20Report%20Web%2025101 1%20CF.pdf (accessed June 2014).

22. DCLG (DEPARTMENT FOR COMMUNITIES AND LOCAL GOVERNMENT) (2007) 'The Single Regeneration Budget: Final Evaluation', [Online] Available at: http://www.landecon.cam.ac.uk/pdf-files/cv-etc/pete-tyler/SRB_RESEARCHSUMMARY_2007. pdf (accessed June 2014).

23. DCLG (DEPARTMENT FOR COMMUNITIES AND LOCAL GOVERNMENT) (2009) 'National Evaluation of Housing Market Renewal Pathfinders 2005–2007', [Online] Available at: http://webarchive.nationalarchives.gov.uk/20120919132719/http:/ www.communities.gov.uk/documents /housing/pdf/1362833.pdf (accessed June 2014).

24. DCLG (DEPARTMENT FOR COMMUNITIES AND LOCAL GOVERNMENT) (2010) 'The New Deal for Communities Experience: A Final Assessment – The New Deal for Communities Evaluation: Final Report – Volume 7', [Online] Available at: http://extra.shu.ac.uk/ndc/downloads/general/A%20final%20assessment.pdf (accessed June 2014).

25. DCLG (DEPARTMENT FOR COMMUNITIES AND LOCAL GOVERNMENT) (2013) 'Investing in Your Future: Case Study Booklet – East Midlands European Regional Development Fund Programme, 2007–2013', [Online] Available at: https://www.gov. uk/government/uploads/system/uploads/attachment_data/file/147821/East_Midlands_ERDF_Case_Study_Bo oklet_Edition_1.pdf (accessed June 2014).

26. DHAMAK BEATS (2012) 'About Dhamak', [Online] Available at: http://dhamak.barefoot-hosting.com/wordpress/?page_ id=11 (accessed June 2014).

27. ELA PALMER HERITAGE (2008) The Social Impacts of Heritage-Led Regeneration, Ela Palmer Heritage, London.

28. ENGLISH PARTNERSHIPS (2008) 'Additionality Guide: A Standard Approach to Assessing the Additional Impact of Interventions', [Online] Available at: https://www.gov.uk/government/ uploads/system/uploads/attachment_data/ file/191511/ Additionality_ Guide_0.pdf (accessed June 2014).

29. ENNIS, N. & DOUGLASS, G. (2011) Culture and Regeneration – What Evidence Is There of a Link and How Can It Be Measured? GLA, London.

30. EUROPEAN COMMISSION (2013) 'Housing Investments supported by the European Regional Development Fund 2007– 2013: Housing in Sustainable Urban Regeneration', [Online] Available at: http://ec.europa.eu/regional_policy/ sources/docgener/studies/pdf/ housing/2013_housing_study.pdf (accessed June 2014).

31. EVANS, G. (2011) 'Cities of culture and the regeneration game', London Journal of Tourism, Sport and Creative Industries, vol. 5, no. 6, pp. 5–18.

32. EVANS, G. & SHAW, P. (2004). The Contribution of Culture to Regeneration in the UK: A Review of Evidence, DCMS, London.

33. GARCÍA, B. (2004) 'Cultural policy and urban regeneration in Western European cities: lessons from experience, pro-spects for the future' Local Economy, vol. 19, no. 4, pp. 312–326.

34. GARCÍA, B. (2005) 'Deconstructing the city of culture: the long-term cultural legacies of Glasgow 1990', Urban Studies, vol. 42, no. 5–6, pp. 841–868.

35. GARCÍA, B. & COX, T. (2013) 'European Capitals of Culture: Success Strategies and Long-term Effects', [Online] Available at: http://www.europarl.europa.eu/RegData/etudes/etudes/join/2013/5 13985/IPOL-CULT_ET%282013%29513985_EN. pdf (accessed June 2014).

36. GATESHEAD COUNCIL (2006) 'The Angel of the North', [Online] Available at: http://www.gateshead.gov.uk/ DocumentLibrary/Leisure /Angel/Angel%20Pack%20large.doc (accessed June 2014).

37. GENERAL PUBLIC AGENCY (2008) Art at the Centre Phase II – Final Evaluation Report 2005–2008, General Public Agency, London.

38. GHK (2009) Economic Impact of HLF Projects, Volume 1 – Main Report, GHK, London.

39. GOLDTHORPE, J. & MCKNIGHT, A. (2004) The Economic Basis of Social Class. CASE paper, CASE/80, Centre for Analysis of Social Exclusion, London School of Economics and Political Science, London.

40. GORARD, S. (2006) Using Everyday Numbers Effectively in Research, Continuum, London.

41. GRAY, C. (2006) 'Managing the unmanageable: the politics of cultural planning', Public Policy and Administration, vol. 21, no. 2, pp. 101–113.

42. GRAY, C. (2007) 'Commodification and instrumentality in cultural policy', International Journal of Cultural Policy, vol. 13, no. 2, pp. 203–215.

43. GRAY, C. (2008) 'Arts council England and public value: a critical review', International Journal of Cultural Policy, vol. 14, no. 2, pp. 209–214.

44. HELGESSON, C-F. & KJELLBERG, H. (2013) 'Introduction: values and valuations in market practice', Journal of Cultural Economy, vol. 6, no. 4, pp. 361–369.

45. HEPWORTH WAKEFIELD (2012) 'Annual Review 2011–12', [Online] Available at: https://ripassetseu.s3.amazonaws.com/ www.hepworth wakefield.org/_files/documents/dec_12/FENT__1355235958_THW_A nnual_Review_2011–12_LR. pdf (accessed June 2014).

46. HESMONDHALGH, D., NISBETT, M., OAKLEY, K. & LEE, D. (2015) 'Were new labour's cultural policies neo-liberal?',International Journal of Cultural Policy, vol. 21, no. 1, pp. 97–114.

47. HM TREASURY (2003) 'The Green Book: Appraisal and Evaluation in Central Government', [Online] Available at: https:// www.gov.uk/government/uploads/system/uploads/attachment_data/ file/220541/green_book_complete.pdf (accessed June 2014).

48. HOLDEN, J. (2007) Publicly-funded Culture and the Creative Industries, Demos, London.

49. HUGHES, G. (1989) 'Measuring the economic value of the arts', Policy Studies, vol. 9, no. 3, pp. 33–45.

50. HYSLOP, D. (2012) 'Culture, regeneration and community: reinventing the city', Gateways: International Journal of Community Research and Engagement, vol. 5, pp. 152–165.

51. JONES, P. & EVANS, J. (2008) Urban Regeneration in the UK, Sage, London.

52. KNELL, J. & OAKLEY, K. (2007) London's Creative Economy: An Accidental Success?, The Work Foundation, London.

53. LABADI, S. (2008) 'Evaluating the Socio-Economic Impacts of Selected Regeneration Heritage Sites in Europe', [Online] Available at: http://www.encatc.org/pages/fileadmin/user_upload/Forum/Sophia_Labadi_2008CPRA_Publication. pdf (accessed June 2014).

54. LARC (LIVERPOOL ARTS REGENERATION CONSORTIUM) (2011) 'Liverpool Thrive Programme Final Report', [Online] Available at: http://www.larc.uk.com/wp-content/uploads/2013/06/Thrive-Final-Report.pdf (accessed June 2014).

55. LAW, J. & RUPPERT, E. (2013) 'The social life of methods: devices', Journal of Cultural Economy, vol. 6, no. 3, pp. 229–240. LAW, J., RUPPERT, E. & SAVAGE, M. (2011) The Double Social Life of Methods, CRESC, Milton Keynes.

56. LEATHER, P., NEVIN, B., COLE, I. & EADSON, W. (2012) 'The Housing Market Renewal Programme in England: Development, Impact and Legacy', [Online] Available at: http://www.inta-aivn.org/images/cc/Habitat/background%20documents/HMR%20legacy%20paper%201%2012.pdf (accessed June 2014).

57. LEES, L. & MELHUISH, C. (2015) 'Arts-led regeneration in the UK: the rhetoric and the evidence on urban social inclusion',

58. European Urban and Regional Studies, vol. 22, no. 3, pp. 242–260.

59. LEES, L., SLATER, T. & WYLY, E. (2007) Gentrification, Routledge, London.

60. LGA (LOCAL GOVERNMENT ASSOCIATION) (2013) Driving Growth Through Local Government Investment in the Arts, LGA, London.

61. MADDEN, C. (2001) 'Using 'economic' impact studies in arts and cultural advocacy: a cautionary note', Media International Australia incorporating Culture and Policy, vol. 98, pp. 161–178.

62. MARKUSEN, A. & GADWA, A. (2010) 'Arts and culture in urban or regional planning: a review and research agenda', Journal of Planning Education and Research, vol. 29, no. 3, pp. 379–391.

63. MARRES, N. & WELTEVREDE, E. (2013) 'Scraping the social', Journal of Cultural Economy, vol. 6, no. 3, pp. 313–335. MEDIA AND ARTS PARTNERSHIP. (2008) 'Housing Market Renewal', [Online] Available at: http://www.maap.org.uk/sholver/(accessed June 2014).

64. MILES, A. & SULLIVAN, A. (2012) 'Understanding participation in culture and sport: mixing methods, reordering knowl-edges', Cultural Trends, vol. 21, no. 4, pp. 311–324.

65. MILLER, P. (2008) 'Calculating economic life', Journal of Cultural Economy, vol. 1, no. 1, pp. 51–64. MYERSCOUGH, J. (1988) The Economic Importance of the Arts in Britain, Policy Studies Institute, London.

66. NEW ECONOMY (2013) 'Beyond the Arts: Economic and Wider Impacts of the Lowry and Its Programmes', [Online] Available at: http://www.thelowry.com/Downloads/reports/The_Lowry_Beyond_the_Arts.pdf (accessed June 2014).

67. NFASP (NATIONAL FEDERATION OF ARTISTS' STUDIO PROVIDERS) (2010) 'Developing Affordable Artists' Studios in a Housing market Renewal Area', [Online] Available at: http://artspace.org.uk/download-file/downloads/Manor-Oaks-CS.pdf (accessed June 2014).

68. OAKLEY, K. (2004) 'Not so cool Britannia: the role of the creative industries in economic development', International Journal of Cultural Studies, vol. 7, no. 1, pp. 67–77.

69. OAKLEY, K. (2008) 'Any answer as long as it's right: evidence-based cultural policymaking', in Making Meaning, Making Money, eds L. Andersen, & K. Oakley, Cambridge Scholars, Newcastle Upon Tyne, pp. 18–41.

70. OAKLEY, K. & O'BRIEN, D. (2016) 'Learning to labour unequally: understanding the relationship between cultural pro-duction, cultural consumption and inequality', Social Identities: Journal for the Study of Race, Nation and Culture, vol. 22, no. 5, pp. 471–486.

71. O'BRIEN, D. (2013). Cultural Policy: Management, Value and Modernity in the Creative Industries, Routledge, New York.

72. O'BRIEN, D. (2016) 'What price evidence? The ethics of office and the ethics of social science in British cultural policy',Journal of Cultural Economy, vol. 9, no. 2, pp. 127–140.

73. O'BRIEN, D. & MATTHEWS, P. (2015) After Urban Regeneration, Policy Press, Bristol.

74. PENDLE BOROUGH COUNCIL (2014) 'Housing Market Renewal', [Online] Available at: http://www.pendle.gov.uk/galleries/ gallery/5/ housing_market_renewal_hmr (accessed June 2014).

75. PUBLIC ART LEICESTER (2005) 'Cultural Mapping Public Art Programme Leicester', [Online] Available at: http://www. leicester.gov.uk/culturalmapping/index.html (accessed June 2014).

76. REEVES, M. (2002) Measuring the Economic and Social Impact of the Arts: A Review, Arts Council England, London.

77. REKDAL, O. B. (2014) 'Academic urban legends', Social Studies of Science, vol. 44, no. 4, pp. 638–654.

78. ROGER TYM & PARTNERS (2011) 'Economic Impact of the Liverpool Arts Regeneration Consortium', [Online] Available at: http://www.larc.uk.com/wp-content/uploads/2011/10/LARC-Economic-Impact-Final-Report.pdf (accessed June 2014).

79. RUSHTON, M. (2015) 'On the Return to Public Investments in Museums', [Online] Available at: http://www.artsjournal.com/worth/2015/03/on-the-return-to-public-investments-in-museums/ (accessed June 2014).

80. SAVAGE, M. (2000) Class Analysis and Social Transformation, Routledge, London.

81. SAVAGE, M., DEVINE, F., CUNNINGHAM, N., TAYLOR, M., LI, Y., HJELLBREKKE, J., LE ROUX, B., FRIEDMAN, S. & MILES, A. (2015) 'A new model of social class? Findings from the BBC's great British class survey experiment', Sociology, vol. 47, no. 2, pp. 219–250.

82. SCHUTZ, A. (1960) 'The social world and the theory of social action', Social Research, vol. 27, pp. 203–221.

83. SELWOOD, S. (2006) 'A part to play? The academic contribution to the development of cultural policy in England',International Journal of Cultural Policy, vol. 12, no. 1, pp. 35–53.

84. SHARP, J. (2007) 'The life and death of five spaces: public art and community regeneration in Glasgow', Cultural Geographies, vol. 14, no. 2, pp. 274–292.

85. SHIN, H. & STEVENS, Q. (2013) 'How culture and economy meet in South Korea: the politics of cultural economy in cul-ture-led urban regeneration', International Journal of Urban and Regional Research, vol. 37, no. 5, pp. 1707–1723.

86. THRU (TOWNSCAPE HERITAGE RESEARCH UNIT) (2013) Townscape Heritage Initiative Schemes Evaluation – Ten Year Review Report, Townscape Heritage Research Unit, Oxford Brookes University, Oxford.

87. TYLER, I. (2015) 'Classificatory struggles: class, culture and inequality in neoliberal times', The Sociological Review, vol. 63, pp. 493–511.

88. UKCCA (UK CENTRE FOR CARNIVAL ARTS) (2010) 'Volunteer Pack', [Online] Available at: http://www.carnivalarts.org.uk/ Portals/0/ UKCCA%20Volunteer%20pack.pdf (accessed June 2014).

89. VAN HEUR, B. (2010) 'Small cities and the geographical bias of creative industries research and policy', Journal of Policy Research in Tourism, Leisure and Events, vol. 2, no. 2, pp. 189–192.

90. VICKERY, J. (2007) The Emergence of Culture-led Regeneration: A Policy Concept and its Discontents, Centre for Cultural Policy Studies, Warwick.

91. WHAT WORKS CENTRE (2014) 'Evidence Review 3 – Sports and Culture', [Online] Available at: http://whatworksgrowth. org/wp-content/uploads/2014/07/14-07-07-Culture-and-Sport.pdf (accessed June 2014).

92. YARROW, D. & KRANKE, M. (2016) 'The performativity of sports statistics: towards a research agenda', Journal of Cultural Economy,

13

ROUSSEAU'S CRUSOE MYTH: THE UNLIKELY PROVENANCE OF THE NEOCLASSICAL HOMO ECONOMICUS

Matthew Watson

Department of Politics and International Studies, University of Warwick, Coventry, UK

ABSTRACT

The neoclassical homo economicus has escaped the narrow confines of economic theory and is today embodied countless times over in the everyday behaviour that so much of the modern economy is set up precisely to serve. Not all of the authors of leading books on economic principles have named the neoclassical homo economicus, but when they have done so it is overwhelmingly in the same way. They have given him the human form of a Robinson Crusoe figure, despite the fact that his behavioural motivations and his practical conduct owe next-to-nothing to Daniel Defoe's original characterisation. I suggest that the route to today's cultural familiarity with the neoclassical homo economicus instead passes through the entirely unwitting hands of Jean-Jacques Rousseau. He substituted Defoe's account of the castaway's continuing deference to prevailing social norms with his own idealised vision of how the individual might use solitude to escape the corrupting influences of modern society. It is altogether another desocialised individual also bearing the Crusoe name who has latterly shaped many of the economics textbooks' renderings of the neoclassical homo economicus. However, we can get to him only by first understanding the essential features of Rousseau's Crusoe myth.

Keywords: Rousseau; Robinson Crusoe; homo economicus; natural self; virtue in solitude

INTRODUCTION

Homo economicus has become something of a cultural icon.[1] It is hardly an exaggeration to say that for some time now he has walked amongst us, stalking our everyday decisions. This is because behav-ioural interventions enacted through a variety of government policies today serve as encouragement for more and more people to think and act like him. However, to suppress the alternative forms of economic conduct that are always present as at least untapped potentials first requires learning what it means to occupy the archetypal neoclassical agent's economic mindset. In particular, it requires the ability to call into the imagination the successes of somebody who already inhabits that way of being. Given the widespread imprint that homo economicus has left behind, it is surely a great irony that almost his only appearance as a named person in economics textbooks is not a real person at all. The behavioural attributes of homo economicus are often taught through reference to Daniel Defoe's fic-tional character, Robinson Crusoe.

When homo economicus walks amongst us, then, he follows in the footsteps of a figure who has been lifted out of an early eighteenth-century novel and placed within much later economic theories. Yet this has only been possible because he was transformed out of all recognition in his move between these two contexts. In itself, this move was patently not a single moment of transposition as much as something significantly more complex. It appears to have entailed a series of appeals to previously partially transformed Crusoe figures, each of which differs substantively from its immedi-ate predecessor, and each of which was created for a different reason specific to a particular author working at a particular time and against the backdrop of a particular set of arguments. The relevant historiographical back-story is certainly somewhat messy, then, but it is no less important for that.

If it is noteworthy enough that nobody other than a fictional character can be found to put some 'real-life' flesh on the bones of homo economicus, it is surely more noteworthy still that the original fictional characterisation was itself deemed unfit for purpose. Appeals to some sort of Crusoe figure spread far and wide amongst the first two generations of self-identifying marginalists who were active from the 1870s onwards: Jevons, Menger, Edgeworth, Wicksteed, Böhm-Bawerk, von Wieser, Marshall, Clark and Wicksell all identified in him the 'someone' they needed to illustrate neoclassical behavioural principles (White 1998, p. 217). Yet not one of them had a Crusoe whose conduct resembled Defoe's character in anything but its desert island location. When Carl Menger ([1871] 1950, p. 135) repeatedly called the hypothetical agent of his neoclassical theory 'our Crusoe', the 'our' in the description was unintentionally more revealing than the 'Crusoe'. This character belongs indisputably to the early neoclassical economists. It is their creation not Defoe's, and the cultural imprints left today by homo economicus owe much to them and not to him.

Defoe's novel tells of how the castaway's life provides the perfect context for Crusoe to learn the early eighteenth-century bourgeois manners that he conspicuously failed to exhibit back at home as a young man. In the hands of the early marginalists, however, that same context is the means of illus-trating how the rational everyman who so entranced late nineteenth-century economic theorists might be expected to act. This is quite some jump between two characters who consequently appear to share little other than their name. In the final twist in the historiographical tale that underpins this article I suggest that Crusoe's transformation from reluctant early eighteenth-century English gentle-man to the archetype for the late nineteenth-century homo economicus was facilitated, however inadvertently, by Jean-Jacques Rousseau's writings in Émile. I say 'however inadvertently' because the whole of the rest of Rousseau's intellectual oeuvre features conscious refusal of the sort of economic socialisation that homo economicus represents. Rousseau, I argue, had his own personal Cru-soe myth, one which differs from that of neoclassical economics but nonetheless paved the way for it. There remains an important disjuncture here, then, but the essential difference between the various Crusoes should nonetheless prompt enquiries about how they are related. There is nothing in any of Rousseau's work that acts as a direct template for the neoclassical homo economicus. Yet my argu-ment is in any case much less bold than that. It is merely that it is impossible to understand how the neoclassical homo economicus might have been given the Crusoe name unless there is some appreci-ation to start with of the role played by Rousseau in changing the way that Defoe's novel was read from the middle of the eighteenth century.

Rousseau embraced Defoe's story because he thought he saw in Crusoe an Enlightenment anti-hero, someone who rejected the excesses brought about by attending to social opinion so that he might restrict his labour to catering only for natural needs (Rousseau [1762] 2003, p. 165). From this perspective Crusoe displayed a dignity in labour that Rousseau believed could break the bonds of having to work for a living and could therefore serve as the fulcrum of an alternative natural education. There is indeed a narrative of conversion that runs through the novel, but it is not this one (Hunter 1966, pp. 168–169). Rousseau's reading of Defoe's text emphasised the way in which salva-tion might occur in his own social system rather than Defoe's, and it does so only through selectively reading into the story a series of implications that are absent from the original (Fishelov 2010, p. 178). Despite Rousseau's determination to present Crusoe as a role model for his young charge Émile, Defoe's hero is a most unlikely instantiation of Rousseauian aspirations. His change of priori-ties results from increasingly explicit acknowledgment that he wishes to exhibit the characteristics of bourgeois respectability in order to ease his return to the society from which his shipwreck tempor-arily excludes him (Rogers 1979, p. 27). The fact that he adopts many attributes of Rousseauian asce-ticism in the interim is purely down to force of circumstance rather than being affirmation of a new lifestyle choice. He does not reject the social construction of early eighteenth-century economic man so much as try to become that man.

Rousseau disqualified this possibility by taking the return home out of the story. Moreover, he had to, because Crusoe's constant longing for a means of escaping the island and his delight in the thought of his physical and emotional restoration to a society in which his claims on property have meaning evidently contradict Rousseau's preference for a natural education that permanent abode on a desert island facilitates. The island setting for the original novel becomes meaningful only insofar as it becomes a means of excluding competing claims on ownership (Schonhorn 1991, p. 149). For Rousseau, solitude enabled a conscious retreat from society, but the Defoe scholar Ian Watt (1951, p. 110) says that we should instead see Crusoe as having been 'stranded in the utopia of the Protestant Ethic' that Defoe treated as the purification of his own society. Solitude, in this regard, is not the reward for rejecting society so much as the punishment Crusoe receives for prior-itising the intemperate pursuit of speculative riches over the bourgeois stability that Defoe treasured so highly (p. 121).[2] His restoration to society is conditional upon him learning how to become the type of man his father had always wanted him to be and that he latterly sees he should always have settled for being (p. 125).

In this form, though, the Crusoe figure would have been of no interest to the early marginalists. They thought that the most important task of economic theory was to strip away all social influences on behaviour so that the realm of the purely economic might be revealed. Rousseau's depiction of Crusoe as the manifestation of sustenance through hard work was easily turned into a morality play about a desocialised back-to-nature survivalism (Green 1991, p. 150). It was this re-character-isation that opened the door for the subsequent neoclassical depiction of Crusoe as the modern-day homo economicus. Yet his final fleshing out nonetheless involved a circuitous route that took a whole century and a half, by which time the connection back to Rousseau's Crusoe myth went unre-ferenced. My hope in the pages that follow is merely to draw attention to the need to think through the separate steps that allow that connection to be made anew.

The analysis will now proceed in three stages in advance of such a claim. The first section reveals the way in which Rousseau's Crusoe myth results from a selective reading of the text governed by his own prior analysis of fallen humanity that preceded the publication of Émile. It sidesteps almost entirely Defoe's description of the innermost thoughts that propel Crusoe's activities when living alone. Leopold Damrosch (1985, p. 197) accounts for the novel's ability to fire the imagination of the reader in terms of the tension it invokes between the island as a place of punishment and the island as a paradise on earth. However, Defoe's text concentrates solely on the former, and it is only post-Rousseau and following his reflections on the delights of a purely natural education that the idea of such a tension can be sustained. The second section contrasts Rousseau's depiction of the solitary state as a normative ideal with the psychological acts that Crusoe performs on himself to escape the full implications of being deserted on the island. Solitary existence for Rousseau is a mechanism for retreating from the social pressure to continually live in the opinion of others, but Crusoe spends much time imagining himself living up to the economic expectations of his social peers. The Crusoe figure that appears in Émile is therefore not Defoe's in any simple sense, but Defoe's rewritten via the philosophical model of human existence Rousseau had already outlined in his previous work. The third section focuses on the specific content of the individuals that Defoe's Crusoe summons in his imagination. He uses his time alone to experiment with imaginative devices that allow him to visualise himself assuming positions of economic power within social hierarchies. He continually calls to mind the image of subjects, and through this technique he becomes both fam-iliar and comfortable with the idea of subjecting others economically in the search for social advance-ment. In this way, Defoe's Crusoe ultimately affirms Rousseau's suspicions of status-driven economic behaviour as already laid out in his Discourse on Inequality. The neoclassical homo economicus there-fore has very curious historiographical foundations in Rousseau's appropriation of a literary figure that in its original formulation acts antithetically to his own philosophical wishes. Judged by the stan-dards of Defoe's novel, then, Rousseau must have invented a Crusoe myth if Émile was to learn from his actions. It is this, I argue, that subsequently propelled further Crusoe myths that eventually resulted in him being named as the archetypal neoclassical homo economicus. Rousseau's writings in Émile remain only a starting point for this process, but they are important for precisely that reason.

Rousseau's account of fallen humanity and the instruction of Émile

The usual way for specialist Defoe scholars to read Robinson Crusoe today is as an exercise in Pur-itan spiritual autobiography (Starr 1976, p. 83). Crusoe himself opines that the reason for his ship-wrecked state was his youthful decision to 'tempt Providence to my ruine' (p. 38) by the act through which 'I forsook my father's house and broke thro' all his good advice' (pp. 55–56). Despite his father's passionate plea for him to defer to the prevailing structure of society he ignored the move into a respectable bourgeois profession in preference for the much less assured rewards of prospecting (p. 28). The novel's narrative comes together only as Crusoe realises that physical deliverance from the island first requires spiritual deliverance via atonement for his previous trans-gressions of established social and economic norms (Hunter 1966, p. 188). Defoe must therefore be understood to have infused his text with cautionary tales about the dangers of rebelling against the social order of early eighteenth-century England: theological moralism was harnessed to political conservatism (Idelson-Shein 2014, p. 160). His readers were encouraged to act passively in regard to that order through the narrative trick of treating bourgeois respectability as the antidote to Cru-soe's 'original sin'. Today's dominant spiritual autobiography interpretation therefore organises Defoe's text around a clear cycle of fall and redemption. It associates Crusoe's fall with the purpo-seful denial of filial duty and his consequent punishment takes the form of exclusion from society. True redemption is reserved solely for when providential judgement affirms the success of Cru-soe's self-tutored adoption of bourgeois norms and arranges the opportunity for him to secure safe passage home.

Rousseau's rather different presentation of Defoe's story for his idealised pupil Émile's instruction involves a complete inversion of this particular cycle of fall and redemption. He treated the individ-ual's fall not as the moment at which exclusion from society takes place but as a necessary feature of the equally necessary requirement of taking the first step within society and being exposed to its deceptions. Redemption for Crusoe therefore cannot occur upon leaving the island for the return home but must be restricted to the time on the island when he lacks human company. This changes the content of the underlying idea of Robinson Crusoe as a success story. Defoe's narrative only works in its own terms because it draws the reader into assuming that Crusoe will have his one true desire satisfied by eventually being delivered home. In this regard the shipwreck is a deus ex machina that allows him to do his penance through solitary labour and thus earn his delivery (Billig 2014, p. 25). Rousseau ([1762] 2003, p. 166), by contrast, instructed Émile to treat solitary labour, not as a means to an ulterior end, but as an end in itself, especially insofar as it enabled him to feel closer to nature through the work that he does on it.

'Now, of all the occupations which can furnish subsistence to man', wrote Rousseau ([1762] 2003, p. 177), 'that which approaches nearest to the state of Nature is manual labor'. He asked his young charge to consider how Crusoe might free himself from the destabilising impact of social opinion and experiment with approximations of his hypothetical 'natural self' through the labouring tasks that Defoe's Crusoe called the 'strange multitude of little things' that make life liveable (p. 130). Émile is then encouraged to go one stage further and to think of himself as Crusoe, thus imagining the dis-missive responses he would give to some of modern life's peculiarities were he able to create in his mind a perfect replica of Crusoe's pre-social position, in which anything other than performing sub-sistence tasks through manual labour becomes meaningless (Rousseau [1762] 2003, p. 168). Rous-seau knew that Émile would ultimately have to reconcile himself to living within society, but he wanted to give him as many vicarious experiences as possible first of living as a Crusoe-type figure who could therefore take nature with him as he was eventually forced to enter society (McGrath 2010, p. 124).

It is notable in this regard that Rousseau would not allow Émile to read any other than the parts of Defoe's text when Crusoe is alone on the island (Rousseau [1762] 2003, p. 165). This amounts to only around 30% of the original novel's overall contents. In Rousseau's rather unflattering depiction it is the story 'divested of all its rubbish' (Rousseau [1762] 2003, p. 163). The providential intimations that frequently reappear to bind together Defoe's narrative have almost no role in what is left for Émile to study (Green 1991, p. 154). Defoe's theological moralism, which is so prominent especially in the early part of the story, thus gets replaced by Rousseau's pedagogical moralism (Fuchs 2004, p. 158). Rousseau would not sanction anything of a theological orientation that might help Émile to identify with Crusoe's efforts to reinvent himself as worthy of return to an explicitly bourgeois society. Indeed, he warned against giving children any uncensored view of modern literature. It bore the cultural imprints of a corrupted society, he said, by falsely attributing virtuous status to the bourgeois politeness of early eighteenth-century economic man. 'I hate books', was his typically forthright choice of words to illustrate the distance between the values he believed were depicted in modern literature and the values enshrined in his own principles of natural education (Rousseau [1762] 2003, p. 161).

The partial exception he was willing to make for Robinson Crusoe arose from reading into Defoe's novel the moral propriety he associated with solitude. To him, Crusoe was unique amongst literary heroes in being located 'in the place of an isolated man', from where he could live a life 'above preju-dices' (Rousseau [1762] 2003, p. 163). The main lesson for Émile to take from the story was the capacity to use the solitary state to transcend the pressures of other people's opinions: 'This is how we realize the desert island which first served me as a means of comparison', he wrote (Rousseau [1762] 2003, p. 163). In particular in Rousseau's eyes, an isolated existence eliminated the individ-ual's dependence on the opinion of others when attempting to derive forms of social consciousness that could carry information about perceived self-worth (Charvet 1974, p. 32). Put simply, the indi-vidual could not be an economic status-seeker when living alone. The Crusoe of Defoe's construction is a seed merchant who goes to extraordinary lengths to improve the property he claims as the ship-wreck's sole survivor. The Crusoe of Rousseau's construction is instead a botanist who revels in the natural landscape into which fortune places him (Engélibert 1996, p. 274).

Throughout his early work, but never more so than in his Discourse on Inequality, Rousseau endeavoured to explain his preference for solitude by historicising the impact of social forms of exist-ence on what he called the natural self. This distinctive concept is clearly nothing more than an abstraction, an idealisation of how human life might have been lived before the first impulses forced individuals for their own ease into communal habitation (Scott 1992, pp. 697–698). The concept of the natural self was designed to fill in the blanks of historical knowledge as plausibly as possible, sub-stituting for missing ethnographies of the past so as to rationally reconstruct the trajectory of human evolution whose end-point is confirmed by ethnographies of the present (Rousseau [1754] 1993, pp. 44–46). Rousseau's use of this method enabled him to situate the natural self at the very inception of consciousness, at the point at which self-awareness was first mutually constituted with the aware-ness of differences exhibited by others (Kuhn 2006, p. 17). After that point, consciousness of the self co-evolved with society's prevailing structure of manners, becoming as it did so increasingly insepar-able from the imagined expectations of one's most immediate peer groups (Banerjee 1977, p. 172). Crusoe cannot, of course, act as a guide for what human existence was like before consciousness, because he must be a product of the society from which the shipwreck excludes him and into which Émile must eventually pass. His interest to Rousseau lies in the temporary respite his island setting makes possible from social opinion and the clues that this provides for how Émile might be sheltered from the full corrupting effects of modern society by first having received an education conducted according to the principles of nature (Harari 1987, p. 119).

The natural self encountered in the Discourse on Inequality is afforded normative status that is elevated there way beyond anything that can be found in Émile. This is because it is in this condition only that individuals can take on an unqualified 'wholeness' and are thus capable of surrendering solely to themselves. Yet because it relates to a past to which there can be no return, the notion of an individual who is entirely self-contained and self-sustaining must remain an unrealisable ideal-isation within the context of a natural education. Rousseau's strictures on the latter are not an instruction manual for creating a natural self, only a second-best that recognises how far out of reach the natural self will always be. The contrast in both instances is to socialised forms of existence, where 'society offers to us only an assembly of artificial men and factitious passions' (Rousseau [1754] 1993, p. 115). It is unclear whether Émile will ever be able to avoid a future surrounded by such corruptions, but learning to be himself through a natural education provides the most assured means of mitigating their worst excesses (Vanpée 1990, p. 46). The natural self is able to live as a perfectly self-oriented individual because the opinion of others has no bearing on decisions about how to act. Such decisions are propelled by the survival functions that the actions satisfy rather than by the social effects of having the actions acknowledged (Rousseau [1754] 1993, p. 71). Rous-seau drew the distinction to socialised existence in the following way: 'social man lives constantly outside himself, and only knows how to live in the opinion of others' (Rousseau [1754] 1993, p. 116). With each person continually updating what they believe they know about themselves on account of other people's understanding of where the boundaries of social acceptability are posi-tioned, everyone becomes an imperfect mirror for everyone else to make assessments about their own subjectivity. Consciousness of the self consequently becomes a constant struggle for self-location with respect to a moving target that is the very opposite of personal self-containment (Rous-seau [1754] 1993, p. 102). Rousseau's account of fallen humanity centred decisively on this distinc-tion between what people have become within society and what they might otherwise have remained in an ideal realm where the natural self flourished beyond society. The principles of natural edu-cation accept that human history cannot simply be reversed to a time before consciousness prevailed, but they do commit to making the most of what results.

Nowhere were Rousseau's principles of natural education put into practice more extensively in the late eighteenth century than in Germany. The most prominent pioneer was Johann Bernhard Basedow, whose progressive school in Dessau, the Philanthropinum, was opened in 1774. This was six years after publishing his educational tract, Vorstellung an Menschenfreunde und vermögende Männer über Schulen und Studien,[3] which itself was published six years after Rousseau wrote Émile as his own manifesto for a natural education (Baggerman & Dekker 2009, p. 56). The objective of the Philanthropinum was to nurture self-activity on the part of the child by departing from the existing tradition of rote learning within a religious framework. Up until then, this had figured almost exclu-sively as the educational backdrop through which European societies had tried to instantiate the next generation of bourgeois subjects (Louden 2011, p. 143). Instead, and in line with Rousseau's con-struction of Crusoe – but, importantly, not Defoe's – Basedow emphasised the love of manual work as a means of dignifying labour and the love of tending the land as a means of respecting nature for itself (Sharma 2007, p. 76). This led to an ordered curriculum that has to be contrasted to the complete laisse-moi faire approach that Rousseau envisioned for Émile. Yet it still amounted to a revolutionary embrace, for its time, of the concept of learning readiness, through which the teacher was to use play as a mechanism for detecting the point at which each pupil was deemed able to move to the next stage of their learning (Bowen 1981, p. 200). Crusoe's desert island location, which Rous-seau had advocated as the primary setting for the games through which Émile would voluntarily begin to appreciate nature, was never far away in this regard.

One of Basedow's successors at the Philanthropinum, Joachim Heinrich Campe, took this reifica-tion of the lone desert island inhabitant to further extremes. He systematically reframed the political centrepoint of Defoe's original novel in his imitation, Robinson der Jüngere.[4] He used his Preface to say that his Crusoe would be an even better role model for his Emilius than Rousseau's Crusoe was for his Émile (Campe 1788, pp. 13–14). 'Mr. Rousseau is mistaken', wrote Campe (1788, p. 12).

> The Old Robinson Crusoe [that Rousseau had allowed Defoe to set the terms for] has plenty of tools and instru-ments, which he saves from the wreck of a ship; whereas the New Robinson Crusoe [that Campe created specifi-cally for an audience of children] has nothing but his head and his hands to depend on for his preservation. (emphasis in the original)

Campe overplayed his hand in this regard, because Rousseau's very first mention of Crusoe in Émile shows that what he had in mind is less Campe's 'old' Crusoe than his 'new'. The image to be pre-sented to his young charge, he wrote, was of 'Robinson Crusoe on his island, alone, deprived of the assistance of his fellows and of the instruments of all the arts' (Rousseau [1762] 2003, p. 163). Rousseau's Crusoe is a direct forerunner of Campe's in starting his solitary existence without the benefits of first salvaging a stock of tools from the shipwreck. Émile is to imagine himself as a Crusoe without the tools of the society from which he has been excluded, because this will help Rousseau to prepare him for his preferred entry into society: 'if he himself is at work, at each tool that he is using he will not fail to say to himself: "If I did not have this tool, how should I go to work to make one like it or to do without it?"' (Rousseau [1762] 2003, p. 169). Campe's Crusoe is therefore no more of a Rousseauian idealisation than Rousseau's own. This is probably only as is to be expected, because the world that Campe created for his real-life Emiliuses at the Philanthropinum was evidently much less rough-and-tumble than the purely natural surroundings in which Rousseau would happily have had Émile immerse himself. It was a sanitised point somewhere between nature and society (Baggerman and Dekker 2009, p. 134).

All of this might still seem to be something of a leap to the neoclassical homo economicus. As Michael White (1982, p. 34) demonstrated in an authoritative early account of how the neoclassical Crusoe came to economics, even though it was unbeknownst to what are usually still seen as the first-generation marginalists of the 1870s, they had been beaten to the punch by Hermann Heinrich Gos-sen when it came both to redefining the economic concept of value in marginalist terms and to using a Crusoe figure to exemplify that conception. When Gossen ([1854] 1983, p. 54) insisted that 'the results presented [for his theory of value] conform exactly to the experiences provided by actuality', he gave the following justification:

> In order to become fully convinced of this, one needs only to read Campe's tale for the young, Robinson Crusoe, up to the point when Crusoe finds Friday. One will then approve of Robinson's actions exactly insofar as they are in accord with our earlier pronouncements.

The important fact here is that the historiographical route from Defoe's original novel to the neo-classical Crusoe passes directly through Campe's reworking and, to his mind at least, perfecting of Rousseau's Crusoe figure. Gossen really could not have been any more explicit that this was the source for how homo economicus might latterly have been ascribed the state-of-mind of a pure maximiser. Rousseau's Crusoe escaped its author's censure because his retreat into solitude left him no-one else to please other than himself, Campe attempted to construct a Crusoe that was a flawless personification of such an escape, and it was this that caught Gossen's eye when he began his search for a suitable figure to act as his homo economicus.

The question that must be asked for my analysis, then, is which of these two forms of virtue Defoe's version of Crusoe more obviously manifests on his island. Is it the virtue born of a well-mannered engagement with bourgeois politeness or the virtue to be found in the embrace of a purely solitary state? Does it therefore involve the cycle of fall and redemption as described by literary scholars of Defoe's work or as described by Rousseau? The prospect of identifying a dis-tinctively Rousseauian Crusoe myth that populates Émile depends on whether Defoe's Crusoe ever genuinely comes to terms with pre-social forms of self-realisation that being cast away makes possible.

Crusoe's problematic relationship with solitude

Defoe required Crusoe to pay seemingly obsessive attention to domesticating his island. This was evidently something very different to Émile's lessons in botany or the real-life Emiliuses' in tending their garden plots. It is noticeable just how hard he works himself during his time alone, far too hard to invoke the idea of the desert island as an idyllic natural setting (Rogers 1979, p. 54).

His domes-tication strategy is explicitly one of domination, enshrining a procedural ethic through which anything or anyone coming into contact with the island immediately becomes his property. He has a freedom to own on the island which appears markedly more important to him than the freedom he also has to enjoy the island as an unspoilt natural landscape.

As Defoe allowed but Rousseau and Campe did not, Crusoe is cast away complete with the embo-died labour of capital goods that he and his dead shipmates were carrying on their doomed voyage. He therefore does not start his island sojourn with nothing, as would be the implication of taking Rousseau's principles of natural education as the point of entry, but is accompanied by useful rem-nants of his prior society. These goods are put to use specifically in acquisitive projects designed to enhance the value of his property. As Watt (1974, pp. 87, 88) suggests, 'Defoe's hero is not really a primitive nor a proletarian but a capitalist ... [H]is solitude is the measure, and the price of his luck' for having no competitors when asserting his property rights. Crusoe makes concerted attempts to exemplify his ability to own exclusively by fencing off his land, even though this stands in marked contrast to the contemporary accounts of the actions of marooned men on which Defoe could have drawn (White 1982, p. 37). Not one of them recounts expending labour on creating enclosures as a permanent reminder of property entitlement that might be issued to presumably only ever imagined others. Manuel Schonhorn (1991, pp. 144, 155–156) consequently associates Crusoe's efforts to enclose as much of the island as possible with Defoe's endorsement of an absolutist conception of property, whereby the first person in a state of nature to make a claim on a particular piece of land subsequently owns it fully and unconditionally.

Much can be said in this regard about how unlike the Rousseauian ideal the resulting situation is and how far Rousseau had to go in rewriting Defoe's original story to appropriate the Crusoe name for his own purposes. Perhaps most obviously, in the Discourse on Inequality Rousseau identified the first seizure of previously commonly-held land as the originating moment of humankind's descent into socialised forms of existence (Charvet 1974, pp. 24–25). It is, in effect, the moment at which the natural self is forever lost to a past to which Émile cannot return. 'The first man', he wrote, 'who, having enclosed a piece of ground, bethought himself of saying "This is mine", and found people simple enough to believe him, was the real founder of civil society' (Rousseau [1754] 1993, p. 84). In his historicisation of human nature it is the property-owning individual who was the first to become mindful of displaying the fruits of industriousness as a means of social comparison: '[T]here arose rivalry and competition [... as ...] the first effects of property' (Rousseau [1754] 1993, p. 96). Crusoe breathes life into such effects by turning what had once been a pristine landscape into land that serves the accumulation function (Curkpatrick

2002, pp. 258–259). This good husban-dry is celebrated by the Defoe scholar Maximillian Novak (1962, pp. 57–58) as evidence of the repli-cation under trying circumstances of the 'civilised society', but this is a condition that Rousseau repeatedly denounced so that the individual might instead live a self-contained and self-sustaining life. It is clear that Campe's Crusoe also went in for husbandry in a way that was mirrored in his pupils being given their own personal garden. Even an avowedly Rousseauian educational exper-iment therefore let the accompanying Crusoe figure keep some of the behavioural characteristics that Defoe gave him but that Rousseau wanted to take away. Finding the right balance between nature and society, either for the abstract Émile or the real-life Emiliuses, was therefore far from an assured affair.

Furthermore, the labour that Defoe's Crusoe undertakes during his period as a castaway appears to provide him with a mechanism for whiling away his time in preference to having to reflect on the implications of solitude (Richetti 2001, p. xxiii). Admittedly, he does utter a few brave but isolated words about the restorative capacity of the time he spends alone when trying to come to terms with the error of his previous ways: 'It was now that I began sensibly to feel how much more happy this life I now led was, with all its miserable circumstances, than the wicked, cursed, abominable life I led all the past part of my days' (p. 125); 'in my silent state of life in the island … I wanted nothing but what I had, and had nothing but what I wanted' (p. 281). Scratching the surface of these thoughts, how-ever, makes it clear that the relevant passages are only incidentally about solitude itself. Their driving force is his gratitude for not having gone the same way as his shipmates: 'I believe it is impossible to express to the life what the extasies and transports of the soul are, when it is so saved, as I may say, out of the very grave' (p. 65);

> With these reflections I worked my mind up, not only to resignation to the will of God in the present disposition of my circumstances, but even to a sincere thankfulness for my condition, and that I, who was yet a living man, ought not to complain, seeing I had not the due punishment of my sins. (pp. 142–143)

The defining theme of Defoe's Crusoe's thoughts about being on his own therefore has little – and perhaps even nothing – to do with the condition of solitude per se. Instead it is intimately bound to his attempts both to construct a providential account of how he came to be cast away and to convince himself that Providence was justified in dispatching the fateful storm. The premise of just punish-ment coheres in his mind as the thought that he has been placed on the island to repent for his prior lifestyle and to reconstitute his economic subjectivity accordingly (p. 107). The new forms of self-discipline that Crusoe learns when alone are almost all directed at accommodating himself to the prospect of leading a solid if unspectacular life of middle-class sobriety when he returns home. He understands his success in domesticating the island to be a reflection of how far he has come in domesticating himself to that end.

The domination he exercises over the natural landscape consequently has a direct analogue in the domination he exercises over his own outlook on life. Both would appear to be open contradictions of Rousseau's own stated ideals. Defoe's Crusoe performs psychological restrictions on himself to ensure that he emerges from the island more in tune with the social norms of early eighteenth-cen-tury England than he was when he arrived. This is an entirely alien state-of-being for what eventually emerged in Gossen's work as the neoclassical homo economicus, who serves his purpose for econ-omic theory precisely to the extent to which he is unaffected by any social norm whatsoever. This particular Crusoe figure, the isolated economising individual, can have no thought for how well he conforms to prevailing social norms, otherwise he would be forced to give up both his isolation and his status as an economiser. The psychological restrictions that Defoe's Crusoe enacts upon him-self are facilitated by his solitary confinement. That, after all, is the whole point of giving the story a desert island setting. At no stage in his personal renewal, though, does he find the process of embodying his new character traits either easy or pleasurable. It is specifically bourgeois virtue he tries to instil in himself, not Rousseau's virtue in solitude that subsequently facilitates, via a circuitous route involving Basedow, Campe and Gossen, the wholly desocialised depiction of the neoclassical homo economicus. Indeed, Defoe's Crusoe must find a way of ending his solitude if he is to demon-strate to his own satisfaction the success of his conversion to the distinctive pattern of social manners in operation in early eighteenth-century England.

Completely consistently with Rousseau's critique of socialised forms of existence, the more that Crusoe manages to turn the island from something inhospitably alien to something familiar from his previous life the more he wishes to see others marvel at his material accomplishments. He had always craved company, but the content of his craving changes markedly as he learns over time to become a 'compleat natural mechanick' (p. 89) who increasingly excels at making goods that he can imagine having a defined monetary worth. Where once he wished for companions to help him conduct his labour more effectively, increasingly he hopes for the presence of others to pass positive judgement on how well he has done for himself to be surrounded by so much property and so many possessions (pp. 192–193). For economists today, whether textbook writers or the theorists who provide the text-book writers with their base material, the most essential feature of the Crusoe construction continues to be that he is always 'doing the best he can' (Nechyba 2011, p. 546). However, there is a subtle development of meaning in operation here. Defoe's Crusoe does not attempt to transcend the social construction of eighteenth-century economic man so much as make great efforts to embody its most essential characteristics. He wants people to see how well he has done for himself, but only within that specific frame of reference. The marginalist originators of the neoclassical homo economicus, by contrast, believed that they had deprived him of all historically bound social constructions of economic man by mimicking the wholeness that Rousseau had first attributed to the natural self and later set as a goal for Émile. This enables him to do the best he can in a much more fundamen-tally self-enclosed sense.

Defoe's Crusoe, however, becomes the epitome of Rousseau's fallen humanity, attempting to live in the opinion of others even when there are no others physically present to hold a favourable opinion of him. Even his providentialist account of the fateful storm through which he was cast away serves two purposes. It means most obviously that he can rationalise the need to become the man of good bourgeois character as an act of atonement for past economic indiscretions (Rogers 1979, p. 52). More subtly, it also creates an authority figure in his mind from whom he can seek endorsement of the ongoing reconstruction of his economic subjectivity. By secularising his vision of an unseen deity, Crusoe is able to prepare himself for an untroubled return home (p. 146). What he needs to do to impress God with his attempts at spiritual redemption through hard work simul-taneously corresponds to what he will need to do to fit inconspicuously into the prevailing bourgeois order back in England. Rousseau's Crusoe, which eventually evolved into Gossen's, exhibits none of these thoughts, because he bears the influence of neither a theological moral nor the celebration of middle-class civility. Despite both Campe's and Gossen's personal deference to the religious norms of their day, the Crusoe figure that Gossen created for economic theory from Campe's is sufficiently abstract to deny the influence of all cultural promptings.

Interestingly, even Defoe's Crusoe ends all pretence to a truly providential reading of his circum-stances at the first moment company arrives (p. 269). This is also exactly the same moment as the prosperity that he works so hard to build through cultivating his land suddenly becomes socially sig-nificant. And it is also when Rousseau ([1762] 2003, p. 163) insisted that he ceased to be of interest to Émile and when Gossen ([1854] 1983, p. 54) insisted that he ceased to be of interest to economic theory. For Defoe's Crusoe, learning to be conditioned by the economic norms of early eight-eenth-century English society means learning to commit himself to accepting other people's assess-ments of the mark he has left upon the world. In the absence of company during his time alone on the island there are no human others in whose opinions he could attempt to live. Instead he creates for himself a God to whom he talks in human form (p. 146). He tries temporarily to live within the opinions of this God, albeit only to generate vicariously what in reality is secularly derived approval for having aligned his labour to the demands of middle-class domesticity. Insofar as he flirts with a real spiritual conversion at all this appears only ever to be a front for his economic conversion to a lifestyle that Rousseau ([1754] 1993, p. 109, [1762] 2003, p. 186) dismissed on purely philosophical grounds and tried his best in practical terms to shelter Émile from.

Defoe's Crusoe's instrumental appropriation of religion should therefore be understood as evi-dence of his failure to come to terms with the possibility, to use Rousseauian language, of 'living within himself' (Shinagel 1968, pp. 128–129). Albeit in different ways, for different reasons and guided by different motivations, the neoclassical homo economicus operates on this Rousseauian plane, but Defoe's Crusoe does not. Not once does he prepare himself for exiting the mindset appro-priate to socialised forms of existence, even when he is physically deprived of society. Every aspect of Crusoe's time alone on the island is haunted by a deep ambivalence about the possibility of being forced psychologically into himself (Sill 1983, p. 161). He makes no attempt to render himself whole again in the manner of Rousseau's depiction of a life lived solely in accordance with the pre-cepts of a purely natural education.

Crusoe's imaginative reconstruction of subjects

Defoe's Crusoe's solitary state during his time alone means that he experiences company at that time only ever vicariously. People's opinions come to him via mental practices of imaginative reconstruc-tion. Rousseau's perspective on the imagination in general was critical – 'abstractions [of the mind] are painful and unnatural operations' (Rousseau [1754] 1993, p. 67) – and he became increasingly entrenched in his criticism the more that the imagination was occupied solely with normalising socialised forms of existence. He first announced his suspicion that humankind's fall from the natural state was linked to imaginative acts in the opening passages of the Discourse on the Moral Effects of the Arts and Sciences. There, he described the needs of the mind as the 'ornaments' of society (Rousseau [1750] 1993, p. 4), the accomplishment of mental tasks serving initially to establish and then to reproduce the norms that elicit socialised behaviour. Governed by the realm of the imagination, 'We no longer dare seem what we really are but lie under a perpetual restraint' (Rous-seau [1750] 1993, p. 6). In his Letter to d'Alembert he described that restraint specifically as 'the empire of opinion' (Rousseau [1758] 1968, p. 22). Rousseau reduced the actions of modern economic man to the promptings of an imagination that is limited in its scope of possibility by the prevailing system of manners (Ryn 1997, p. 43). The desire to attain objectives that first enter the consciousness as aspirational devices arises only through the way in which contact with others establishes hierar-chies of possessive individualism in the mind (Scott 1992, p. 702). In Benjamin Barber's (1978, p. 82) words, 'Rousseau seems to reconstruct a classic ascetic case against [the imagination]'.

The one imagination that appears to be exempt from such pressures is Rousseau's own. According to his autobiographical work, this is because he successfully tutored himself to isolation and conse-quently deprived his imagination of the corrupting influences of socialised forms of existence (Yousef 2001, p. 262). Interestingly, though, the practices he described in The Dialogues situate him physically but not psychologically in isolation. The solitude that he willingly enforced upon himself was designed specifically to allow him 'to bring together the sweetness of study and the charms of intimacy' (Rousseau [1782] 1990, p. 14). That is, he used his time alone in an attempt to understand more about himself through the hypothetical reconstruction of his relationships with his closest friends. As he himself put it, 'I fostered [such thoughts] in an ideal world which my creative imagin-ation soon peopled with beings after my own heart' (Rousseau [1782] 1953, p. 398). The choice of imaginative companions is significant, because in Rousseau's schema a thoroughgoing egalitarianism structures the relationship between close friends. Social conventions do not interpose into the way in which such people relate to one another, restoring to them a wholeness that does not have to be sacri-ficed to the simulation and pretence of society (Barber 1978, p. 85).

However, the original Crusoe's imaginative reconstruction of company could hardly have been more different. Defoe failed to place in Crusoe's imagination friends to whom he can issue love, so much as temporary acquaintances whom he has no desire at all to know well (Grapard 1995, p. 33). It is arguably the defining feature of the neoclassical homo economicus that he has nobody other than himself to call to mind, imaginatively reconstruct and vicariously relate to. Insofar as Rousseau's Crusoe might be expected to follow Rousseau himself if he is to be the perfect role model for Émile, then he must use the imagination to engage at least his close friends. There are cer-tainly plenty of hints that Campe's Crusoe does so. Neither, therefore, is the neoclassical homo eco-nomicus in his own right. Defoe's Crusoe, perhaps unsurprisingly given what has already been said, also remains a resolutely imperfect template for the neoclassical homo economicus, because he is sure that temporary acquaintances are socially meaningful to him at the moments at which they impinge upon his stock of property in some way. However, the extra characters that Defoe intro-duced to his text so that he could write parables of property ownership only enter Crusoe's con-sciousness as either the purveyor of things or the judge of their social value once these things are physically in his possession.

Defoe's Crusoe takes such a perspective to its logical extreme in treating anyone he encounters in the same way as material goods by objectifying them and rendering them suitable for subordination. He does not relate to people through the pure human wholeness that Rousseau ([1782] 1953, pp. 212, 395) wrote about approvingly when describing the egalitarian relationship he enjoyed with his friends. This is the same human wholeness that he believed Émile could learn from his version of Crusoe. Instead, Defoe's Crusoe uses contractual obligations where the main aim is to enable him to dominate. This might explain why his mind appears to attach itself much more expediently to the idea of saving Europeans than non-Europeans (pp. 177–179, 212–213, 233). He recognises specifically in Europeans the likelihood that they will abide by the same standards of contractual obligation as he does (Hymer 1971, pp. 31–32). These are people who away from the island would be his equals in the face of the law, but who on the island will be culturally disposed to treat his antecedent claims to property ownership as the law (Grapard 1995, pp. 42–43). Even the captain of the ship that eventually restores Crusoe to his own society is required to submit himself to the pol-itical structure of legitimacy transposed from that society in order to respect the procedural ethics of Crusoe's right to property on the island (pp. 253–254). The use of contractual obligation to deter-mine the content of personal relations thereby becomes a means through which he establishes his dominion over the entire lifeworld associated with the island, whether inanimate or animate, non-human or human.

In all of this Crusoe's imagination departs from Rousseau's by calling up representations of sub-jects rather than of friends. Crusoe's instinct is always to narrate his relationship to others in terms of hierarchies that he stands atop, enacting quasi-regal prerogatives to be followed by subordinates: 'my people were perfectly subjected: I was absolute lord and lawgiver' (p. 241). As Schonhorn (1991,

\endash 152) notes, his 'rhetoric of absolutism and submission, of kingly authority and subject obedience, places the right and might of sovereignty in the office of the monarch'. The irony is completely lost on Crusoe that in expecting such a high level of compliance to a social order that he has established by convention he requires much more of other people than he was willing to countenance of himself as a younger man.

His political conversion to the idea of an established order begins when fantasising that his meal times in the company of his parrot, dog and two cats represent a social hierarchy with him at its apex: 'see how like a king I dined ... all alone, attended by my servants' (p. 157). This follows his decision, in his sixth year cast away, to set off in his hand-made canoe to sail around the island as a means of familiarising himself with the thought of property ownership. The decision is justified by his 'being eager to view the circumference of my little kingdom' (p. 147). Tellingly, this is when he initially begins to describe his time on the island as 'my reign' (p. 147): 'if I pleased, I might call my self king ... over the whole country which I had possession of. There were no rivals; I had no competitor, none to dispute sovereignty or command with me' (p. 139). The Defoe scholar J.R. Hammond (2001, p. 74) has gone as far as to suggest that Robinson Crusoe can consequently 'be regarded as a "god game" romance, a genre in which a masterful figure on an island assumes the attributes of a divinity'.

It is clear from this that the conception of sovereignty underpinning the novel's narrative struc-ture operates simultaneously at two distinct levels. Defoe's Crusoe's articulation of Puritan piety – however instrumental it might be deemed – places him under the control of providential sovereignty (Starr 1976, p. 91). Yet the manner in which he claims property rights over the land on which he is set down to ostensibly do God's will allows him to act upon an exclusive sovereignty with respect to the island's lifeworld (Novak 1962, pp. 62–63). Providential and imperialistic sovereignty thereby co-exist, with Crusoe seeking the approbation of God for involving himself throughout the text in the expropriation of the island's natural landscape for imperialistic purposes (Engélibert 1996, p. 269). The presumed legitimacy of such power is thus the ideological superstructure which main-tains the unequal relationships that he constructs to his own advantage.

For Rousseau ([1754] 1993, p. 85), the identification of power as a resource to be used self-inter-estedly represents a significant moment in his historicisation of the distance that humankind has tra-velled from the natural self. He argued that there are specific living conditions unique to socialised forms of existence that have to be in place for the concept of power to become meaningful as an aspect of individual consciousness. For anyone to exhibit patterns of behaviour consistent with the desire to incorporate anyone else into an effective dominion,

> he would have to know that there are men who set a value on the opinion of the rest of the world; who can be made happy and satisfied with themselves rather on the testimony of other people than on their own. (Rousseau [1754] 1993, p. 116)

He associated the quest for power unequivocally with 'this unremitting rage of distinguishing our-selves' (Rousseau [1754] 1993, p. 112). Everything once again relates back to the imaginative leaps that the natural self cannot make because of the absence of the comparative reference point arising from self-awareness. Only individuals experiencing the fall into socialised forms of existence know what it is to think of themselves in situations in which they might be advantaged by subordinating other people's interests.

Individuals seek superiority in a Rousseauian world because they compete for the esteem that constitutes external ratification of their social standing (McLendon 2003, pp. 121–122). Defoe's Cru-soe proves that he is not Rousseau's Crusoe by doing this in the imagination in the first place so that he can construct for himself a regal personality that he increasingly comes to internalise. Once man-ifested in this way it can subsequently be used in earnest to determine the content of his relationships when he is no longer alone on the island. The feeling of additional self-worth he derives from ima-ginatively depicting himself in positions of power translates latterly into attempts to acquire subjects as a means of enhancing his perceived self-worth still further (pp. 157, 207–209, 218–221). Crusoe's constant attention to domesticating his land is inexplicable in its own terms, as its intrinsic economic worth to him is exhausted the moment it meets his subsistence needs. Rousseau's Crusoe, the bota-nist who acts as Émile's guide to nature, will not work beyond the point of making the land sustain him. The actions of Defoe's Crusoe only become easier to understand when considering how, from the perspective of early eighteenth-century economic man, the implicit value of property serves as a direct proxy for the esteem that can be generated from owning it. He is therefore definitively both a socially constructed economic man, the like of which the early marginalists tried to write out of econ-omic theory, and the specific socially constructed economic man against whom Rousseau offered his principles of natural education as an alternative normative ideal-type.

It is therefore necessary to think more deeply about how the Crusoe figure that Rousseau refash-ioned to his own ends in Émile latterly re-emerged as another rather different Crusoe figure that the neoclassical economists made serve as their homo economicus. Ridding Crusoe of the specific social artefacts of Defoe's time and place was the first step in turning him into the blank canvas of a thoroughly desocialised individual. It was by no means preordained, though, that this would lead to Crusoe having the features of the neoclassical homo economicus latterly painted onto him. How-ever, every journey must start somewhere, and Crusoe's journey out of the pages of literature and into those of theoretical books on economic principles begins here, with Rousseau. The next steps involved Basedow's founding of a progressive school in Eastern Germany on Rousseauian principles, and his successor Campe's systematic rewriting of Robinson Crusoe in an attempt to provide his pupils with what he thought was an even better role model for a natural education than Rousseau had managed. The final steps were taken when Gossen seized upon Campe's Crusoe figure to illus-trate his very early marginalist theory of value and when what conventionally are still seen as the first-generation marginalists subsequently reconciled their abstract economising agent to Gossen's trailblazing theory of value. The marginalists of the early 1870s were unaware of Gossen's prior work when setting out their own analytical frameworks, but they soon accepted Gossen's right to precedence upon the publication of the first history of marginalism, which appeared in 1879 in the second edition of Stanley Jevons's Theory of Political Economy (see Jevons [1871/1911] 2013, pp. liii–lx). Each of these moves towards the neoclassical homo economicus required, in its own terms, something of a leap in the dark. None was necessarily suggested by what had gone before. Yet each would have been highly unlikely to have taken the form by which we now know it had the preceding stages not occurred as they did. There is thus still much to gain from examining closely Rousseau's Crusoe myth because of what came after it.

CONCLUSION

Rousseau remarked in his autobiographical writings that he stood outside of society most obviously in his rejection of contrived appearance and his commitment to providing a truthful representation of himself (Rousseau [1782] 1953, p. 17). The propensity for inauthenticity, he argued, is indicative of the extent of humankind's fall from the natural state (Rousseau [1750] 1993, p. 5, [1754] 1993, pp. 81–82, 88). In this respect it is something of a puzzle that he was prepared to present Émile, a boy whose natural education was to be conducted in line with his principles of life, with an egregious Crusoe myth (Rousseau [1762] 2003, pp. 163–165). The romanticised story of a socially-abstracted Crusoe acting in accordance with what nature allows is impossible to reconstruct from Defoe's text. But it is this that Rousseau fully committed himself to.

Rousseau is clearly culpable for this mischaracterisation of Crusoe as an effective approximation of how far his theory of a natural education could take an individual along the path to the natural self. Yet he is entirely blameless for the way in which his mischaracterisation has passed through several subsequent hands to re-emerge as the basis for the neoclassical homo economicus. It too trades on the instinctive association that the Crusoe name triggers to a back-to-nature survivalism. Most of us will recall from our childhoods retellings of the Crusoe story that take this form, and it is all-too-easy to substitute these re-workings for what is actually to be found in Defoe's original text. They become what the memory says is 'known', and it is not far from this understanding of Crusoe's efforts to do his best in the struggle against nature to the basic outline of the neoclassical homo economicus. There is a cultural suggestibility in operation here – Crusoe becomes the neoclassical homo econom-icus because that is what we want to believe he is – but it has only inadvertent roots in Rousseau's work. He was merely the first to impose upon Crusoe the attributes of a desocialised agent, an ideal-ised and potentially transcontextual 'economic man', that the early marginalists found so convenient for their theory.

Reading backwards from the 1870s, the marginalist pioneers Jevons and Menger were surprised to discover that their Crusoe figure was not, strictly-speaking, their own, because Gossen had pre-empted them by almost twenty years in illustrating marginalist principles via a Crusoe figure. Even then, though, Gossen's Crusoe figure was not, strictly-speaking, Defoe's, because he referenced Campe's imitation and not Defoe's original. Campe's Robinson der Jüngere was part of his broader pedagogical writings that, following Basedow, experimented with putting into practice the principles of a natural education that Rousseau outlined in Émile. But even then there were definite departures from what Rousseau had presented as the ideal. Nothing is as it seems at first glance, then, in the historiographical back-story to how the Crusoe figure has come to stand in for the neoclassical homo economicus. That back-story in itself plays no part in the economics textbooks' presentation of the neoclassical homo economicus, notwithstanding the times at which this presentation directly references the so-called Robinson Crusoe Economy (Hewitson 1999, p. 111). A Crusoe figure none-theless remains intensely important to the cultural precepts on which the modern economy is founded. Economic theory is a crucial source of authority for the inculcation of behaviour consistent with the neoclassical homo economicus, and it is still a Crusoe figure that is most readily brought to mind whenever attention turns to naming someone who might pass muster as the neoclassical homo economicus.

It is genuinely perplexing just how many jumps are necessary to get from Defoe's original novel to the cultural significance of today's economics textbooks. The neoclassical homo economicus is now pushed often really rather aggressively as a cultural project, but it is difficult to conclude anything other than he was created by accident. At the very least, he relies for his believability on a particular variant of the Crusoe figure who has a most unlikely provenance. Rousseau ([1754] 1993, p. 73), arch-critic of the modern economy's encouragement of 'purely relative and factitious feeling', appropriated Defoe's Crusoe figure and turned him from everything that he found so contemptible about socialised forms of existence into a role model for a 'natural' lifestyle that celebrated the radical autonomy that the individual gains when opting out of society. The early marginalists subsequently appropriated Rousseau's Crusoe figure, albeit only after it had passed through the hands of Basedow, Campe and Gossen, so that a named desocialised economic agent could be used to exemplify the maximisation properties of pure economic theory. This is a haphazard and entirely unplanned route to homo economicus's current status as a cultural icon. The flimsiness of the links through which he has been brought to life is well worth bearing in mind next time one feels the social pressure to be like homo economicus.

NOTES

1. I am extremely grateful to the journal's two anonymous referees, who have helped me enormously to clarify my argument and to make sure that it is as robust and as error-free as possible. They have alerted me to the need to remove a number of weaknesses from it, and if they are convinced that some weaknesses remain then that is, of course, solely my fault and not theirs.
2. All of the references to the text of Robinson Crusoe take this form and they relate to Defoe ([1719] 1985) listed in the bibliography.

3. This is typically translated into English as Proposal to Philanthropists and Men of Means Regarding Schools and Studies.

4. Robinson der Jüngere translates directly from the German as Robinson the Younger. However, Campe's book entered the English language from his French translation that he published as Le Nouveau Robinson, and for this reason it is usually translated into English as The New Robinson.

Disclosure statement

No potential conflict of interest was reported by the author.

FUNDING

This article was written with financial assistance from an Economic and Social Research Council Professorial Fellow-ship. The Fellowship [grant number ES/K010697/1] supports the project, 'Rethinking the Market' (http://www.warwick.ac.uk/rethinkingthemarket). I gratefully acknowledge the ESRC's ongoing support of my research.

NOTES ON CONTRIBUTOR

Matthew Watson is Professor of Political Economy in the Department of Politics and International Studies at the Uni-versity of Warwick. He is also currently a UK Economic and Social Research Council Professorial Fellow.

REFERENCES

1. BAGGERMAN, A. & DEKKER, R. (2009) Child of the Enlightenment: Revolutionary Europe Reflected in a Boyhood Diary, translated by D. Webb, Brill, Leiden.

2. BANERJEE, A. (1977) 'Rousseau's concept of theatre', British Journal of Aesthetics, vol. 17, no. 2, pp. 171–177. BARBER, B. (1978) 'Rousseau and the paradoxes of the dramatic imagination', Daedalus, vol. 107, no. 3, pp. 79–92. BILLIG, V. (2014) '"I"-lands: the construction and shipwreck of an insular figure in modern discourse', in Shipwreck and

3. Island Motifs in Literature and the Arts, eds B. Le Juez & O. Springer, Brill, Leiden, pp. 17–32.
4. BOWEN, J. (1981) A History of Western Education, Volume III: The Modern West Europe and the New World, Routledge, London.
5. CAMPE, J. H. (1788) The New Robinson Crusoe, Stockdale, London.
6. CHARVET, J. (1974) The Social Problem in the Philosophy of Rousseau, Cambridge University Press, Cambridge. CURKPATRICK, S. (2002) 'The Footprint in the Sand: providence, invention, and alterity in Robinson Crusoe', Pacifica, vol. 15, no. 3, pp. 247–265.
7. DAMROSCH, L. (1985) God's Plot and Man's Stories: Studies in the Fictional Imagination from Milton to Fielding, University of Chicago Press, Chicago, IL.
8. DEFOE, D. ([1719] 1985) Robinson Crusoe, edited by A. Ross, Penguin, London.
9. ENGÉLIBERT, J.-P. (1996) 'Daniel Defoe as character: subversion of the myths of Robinson Crusoe and of the author', in Robinson Crusoe: Myths and Metamorphoses, ed. L. Spaas and B. Stimpson, Macmillan, Basingstoke, pp. 267–281.
10. FISHELOV, D. (2010) Dialogues with/and Great Books: The Dynamics of Canon Formation, Sussex Academic Press, Brighton.
11. FUCHS, E. (2004) 'Nature and Bildung: pedagogical naturalism in nineteenth-century Germany', in The Moral Authority of Nature, eds L. Daston and F. Vidal, University of Chicago Press, Chicago, IL, pp. 155–181.
12. GOSSEN, H. H. ([1854] 1983) The Laws of Human Relations and the Rules of Human Action Derived Therefrom, translated by R. Blitz, MIT Press, Cambridge, MA.
13. GRAPARD, U. (1995) 'Robinson Crusoe: the quintessential economic man?', Feminist Economics, vol. 1, no. 1, pp. 33–52.
14. GREEN, M. (1991) Seven Types of Adventure Tale: An Etiology of a Major Genre, Penn State Press, University Park, PA.
15. HAMMOND, J. R. (2001) A Defoe Companion, Palgrave Macmillan, Basingstoke.
16. HARARI, J. (1987) Scenarios of the Imaginary: Theorizing the French Enlightenment, Cornell University Press, Ithaca, NY.

17. HEWITSON, G. (1999) 'Robinson Crusoe: the paradigmatic "rational economic man"', in Robinson Crusoe's Economic Man: A Construction and Deconstruction, eds U. Grapard and G. Hewitson, Routledge, London, pp. 111–132.

18. HUNTER, J. P. (1966) The Reluctant Pilgrim: Defoe's Emblematic Method and Quest for Form in Robinson Crusoe, Johns Hopkins University Press, Baltimore, MA.

19. HYMER, S. (1971) 'Robinson Crusoe and the secret of primitive accumulation', Monthly Review, vol. 23, no. 4, pp. 11–36.

20. IDELSON-SHEIN, I. (2014) Difference of a Different Kind: Jewish Constructions of Race during the Long Eighteenth Century, University of Philadelphia Press, Philadelphia, PA.

21. JEVONS, W. S. ([1871/1911] 2013) The Theory of Political Economy, Palgrave Macmillan, Basingstoke.

22. KUHN, B. (2006) '"A chain of marvels": botany and autobiography in Rousseau', European Romantic Review, vol. 17, no. 1, pp. 1–20.

23. LOUDEN, R. (2011) Kant's Human Being: Essays on his Theory of Human Nature, Oxford University Press, Oxford.

24. MCGRATH, B. (2010) 'Rousseau's Crusoe: or, on learning to read as not myself', Eighteenth-Century Fiction, vol. 23, no. 1, pp. 119–139.

25. MCLENDON, M. L. (2003) 'The overvaluation of talent: an interpretation and application of Rousseau's amour-propre', Polity, vol. 36, no. 1, pp. 115–138.

26. MENGER, C. ([1871] 1950) Principles of Economics, translated by J. Dingwall and B. Hoselitz, Ludwig von Mises Institute, Auburn, AL.

27. NECHYBA, T. (2011) Microeconomics: An Intuitive Approach with Calculus, international edition, Cengage, Boston, MA. NOVAK, M. (1962) Economics and the Fiction of Daniel Defoe, University of California Press, Berkeley, CA.

28. RICHETTI, J. (2001) 'Introduction', in Robinson Crusoe, by D. Defoe, Penguin, London, pp. ix–xxviii. ROGERS, P. (1979) Robinson Crusoe, George Allen and Unwin, London.

29. ROUSSEAU, J.-J. ([1782] 1953) The Confessions of Jean-Jacques Rousseau, translated by J.M. Cohen, Penguin, London.

30. ROUSSEAU, J.-J. ([1758] 1968) Politics and the Arts: Letter to M. d'Alembert on the Theater, translated by A. Bloom, Cornell University Press, Ithaca, NY.

31. ROUSSEAU, J.-J. ([1782] 1990) Rousseau, Judge of Jean-Jacques, Dialogues, translated by R. Masters, C. Kelly and J. Bush, University Press of New England, Dartmouth, MA.

32. ROUSSEAU, J.-J. ([1750] 1993) 'A discourse on the moral effects of the arts and sciences', in The Social Contract and Discourses, ed. J.-J. Rousseau, translated by G.D.H. Cole, Everyman, London, pp. 1–29.

33. ROUSSEAU, J.-J. ([1754] 1993) 'A discourse on the origin of inequality', in The Social Contract and Discourses, ed. J.-J. Rousseau, translated by G.D.H. Cole, Everyman, London, pp. 31–126.

34. ROUSSEAU, J.-J. ([1762] 2003) Émile, or Treatise on Education, translated by W. H. Payne, Prometheus Books, Amherst, NY.

35. RYN, C. (1997) 'Imaginative origins of modernity: life as daydream and nightmare', Humanitas, vol. 10, no. 2, pp. 41–60.

36. SCHONHORN, M. (1991) Defoe's Politics: Parliament, Power, Kingship, and Robinson Crusoe, Cambridge University Press, Cambridge.

37. SCOTT, J. (1992) 'The theodicy of the Second Discourse: the "pure state of nature" and Rousseau's political thought',

38. American Political Science Review, vol. 86, no. 3, pp. 696–711.

39. SHARMA, P. (2007) Education Administration, A.P.H. Publishing, New Delhi.

40. SHINAGEL, M. (1968) Daniel Defoe and Middle-Class Gentility, Harvard University Press, Cambridge, MA. SILL, G. (1983) Defoe and the Idea of Fiction, 1713–1719, Associated University Presses, London.

41. STARR, G. (1976) 'Robinson Crusoe's conversion', in Daniel Defoe: A Collection of Critical Essays, ed. M. Byrd, Prentice-Hall, Englewood Cliffs, NJ, pp. 78–91.

42. VANPÉE, J. (1990) 'Lessons in Rousseau's Emile ou de l'education', Modern Language Studies, vol. 20, no. 3, pp. 40–49. WATT, I. (1951) 'Robinson Crusoe as a myth', Essays in Criticism, vol. 1, no. 2, pp. 95–119.

43. WATT, I. (1974) The Rise of the Novel: Studies in Defoe, Richardson and Fielding, Chatto and Windus, London.

44. WHITE, M. (1982) 'Reading and rewriting: the production of an economic Robinson Crusoe', in Robinson Crusoe's Economic Man: A Construction and Deconstruction, eds U. Grapard and G. Hewitson, Routledge, London, pp. 15–41.

45. WHITE, M. (1998) 'Robinson Crusoe', in The New Palgrave: A Dictionary of Economics, Volume 4, eds J. Eatwell, M. Milgate and P. Newman, Macmillan, Basingstoke, pp. 217–218.

46. YOUSEF, N. (2001) 'Savage or solitary? The wild child and Rousseau's man of nature', Journal of the History of Ideas, vol. 62, no. 2, pp. 245–263.

14

VALUATIONS OF EXPERIMENTAL DESIGNS IN PROTEOMIC BIOMARKER EXPERIMENTS AND TRADITIONAL RANDOMISED CONTROLLED TRIALS

Claes-Fredrik Helgesson, Francis Lee and Lisa Lindén

Department of Thematic Studies – Technology and Social Change, Linköping University, Linköping, Sweden

ABSTRACT

This article examines the shifting conditions for biomedical knowledge production by studying trends in the design of biomedical experiments. The basic premise of the study is that the very act of establishing a research design entails a process involving a series of valuations where different values are evoked, ordered, and displaced. In focus is the articulation and ordering of what counts as central values in research design for two kinds of biomedical treatment trials, namely the traditional randomised controlled trial (RCT) and the emerging new form of biomarker trials used to assess biomarker/treatment combinations (BTTs). The empirical material consists of textbooks (RCTs) and journal articles (BTTs). We ask how these materials articulate the various scientific, medical, and economic values at play. Among the differences uncovered are a difference in relation to what counts as ethical in relation to prior knowledge, differences in the flexibility in design as well as the valuation of the risk for false positives and false negatives. More broadly, the study shows how textual accounts of different ways of producing knowledge are linked to partly different valuations of ethics, flexibility, and risk as part of establishing the research design of biomedical experiments.

Keywords: Valuation; knowledge production; knowledge as a public good; biomedical research; clinical trials; valuography

INTRODUCTION

The conditions for biomedical knowledge production are constantly being negotiated and renego-tiated in contemporary society. Political, ethical, medical, scientific, and economic constraints and possibilities are constantly shifting. The questions 'What is worth knowing?' and 'What should we do to get there?' are continually handled using a variety of yardsticks for biomedical knowledge production. What is effective and efficient research? What are marketable research outcomes? What is ethically justifiable research? Viewed in this way, answers to the question 'What is valuable research?' become potentially multiple and divergent. Any answer to this question is contingent on a complex set of valuations. This article approaches the shifting conditions for biomedical knowl-edge by examining trends in the design of biomedical experiments and the intertwining, balancing, and hierarchisation of different values and measures of value for biomedical research. As such it attempts to shine light on shifting yardsticks, values, and pressures in the contemporary research landscape.

The premise of this study is that the very act of establishing a research design entails a process involving a series of valuations that are linked to the question posed above. We treat this process as an activity involving many different yardsticks of value. These can include such things as cost of materials, speed of discovery, scientific interest, clinical relevance, and market prospects. These yard-sticks of value are intimately intertwined with ideas about research seen in terms of public goods, scientific goods, and/or commercial goods. Hence, we take an established design as the result of sev-eral valuations that deal with what is worth knowing, and what the appropriate means to generate this knowledge are. In short, we understand research design as a process that involves assessing different design parameters in light of, among other things, the expected knowledge outcomes.[1]

In this article we explore these issues by examining similarities and contrasts in design discourse between two different modes of experimentally assessing medical treatments: the traditional ran-domised controlled trial (RCT) and the emerging new form of biomarker trial used to assess bio-marker/treatment combinations (BTT). We are interested in exploring how the design discourse related to these two different modes of knowledge production about medical treatments could shine light on some of the complex valuations that are part of biomedical knowledge production. The empirical material consists of textbooks on the design of traditional RCTs and journal articles on BTTs. In this investigation we ask how these materials articulate the various valuations and scien-tific, medical, and economic values that are at play in contemporary knowledge production.

This article centres on examining the articulation and ordering of what counts as central values in the process of research design for two kinds of biomedical treatment trials, namely the traditional RCT and the emerging BTT. Our focus on valuations in research design is a way to examine articu-lations about what knowledge is worth pursuing and what counts as the appropriate means for these endeavours. More broadly, our choice to focus on the design phase as well as on two different kinds of trials is done to facilitate an exploration of the various yardsticks mobilised in biomedical research. We thus see design as a site where we glimpse the making of different stakes in biomedical knowl-edge production.

The medical RCT has a history from at least the 1950s as the prime method for testing drugs (Marks 1997; Fisher 1999). The primary design feature of traditional RCTs is some form of ran-domisation where two or more treatments (or placebo) are distributed among a group of selected trial subjects. The randomised allocation of treatment to individual trial subjects is generally double blind. This means that neither the trial subjects (single blind) nor the staff seeing them (double blind) knows who gets what treatment when. Trial subjects are regularly patients, but they are selected with reference to criteria set in the trial protocol that, for instance, could exclude patients suffering from other complicating diseases. The randomisation in effect creates different subgroups, or trial arms to use the vernacular of trials, where each subgroup principally ought to be similar in all aspects but for the treatment they receive. On average, the populations of trial subjects in each arm would be similar due to the randomisation (one should expect same average age, same gender distribution, and so on).

Biomarker-based experiments on patients is part of what has been suggested as a trend towards '"biomarkerization" of health and disease' (Metzler 2010, p. 407), where biomarkers are seen as a route to provide better and more efficient diagnosis, prognosis, and treatment. At the most basic level a biomarker is something that points to a biological condition. A biomarker can be a bodily mark, such as the redness of eyelids to hint at anaemia (cf. Mol 1999). More commonly today bio-markers are seen as genetic or proteomic 'profiles' that can be used to classify patients and their dis-ease using some sort of diagnostic or prognostic test. The iconic examples are the BRCA genes for predicting breast-cancer risk, and the screening for elevated levels of prostate-specific antigen for diagnosing prostate cancer. One often-expressed hope is that biomarkers can be used to stratify patients into subgroups where patients in each subgroup suffer from molecularly different types of cancer, or each subgroup has a different predicted response to a certain medication. In sum, the idea is that biomarkers can be used to identify therapeutically relevant differences among patients suffering from the same diseases such as, for instance, differences that express themselves in different responses to drugs. In keeping with these expectations of biomarker-based personalised medicine, a primary idea of BTTs is that there is some sort of biomarker that can be used to stratify trial subjects into subgroups as part of the experimental arrangement.

Values and valuations as topics in the study of knowledge production

In science and technology studies (STS) there has been a long-standing interest in how social and cultural values are intertwined with research and development. Different studies have dealt with things such as racism (Winner 1980; Bowker & Star 1999; Fujimura 2013), accuracy and precision (Wise 1995; Mackenzie 1999), gender (Haraway 1988; Harding 1991), and calculation (Porter 1995), while other studies have focussed on the political economy of biomedical science through predefined notions such as capitalism and commodification (Shiva 1997; Waldby 2002; Sunder Rajan 2006; Rose 2007; Mitchell & Waldby 2010).

Our approach to examine research design as a process of valuation is inspired by the meeting of the fields of STS and studies of economic practice (Callon 1998; Callon et al. 2007). Here we are inspired by studies that have used concepts and sensibilities from STS for studying the intertwine-ment of technologies and economical practices such as in social studies of finance (MacKenzie & Millo 2003; MacKenzie 2009) as well as more broadly in research on calculative practices and per-formativity of economics, on how calculative devices and economic theories shape markets and agencies (Callon & Muniesa 2005; Callon et al. 2007; MacKenzie et al. 2007; Sjögren & Helgesson 2007; Cochoy 2008; Skærbæk & Tryggestad 2010).

In this article we build on the above research while simultaneously furthering a more inclusive approach to the study of values. We here take a pragmatic approach that sees all values, regardless if they are social, economic, or scientific, as enacted in the process of designing trials. One conse-quence of this approach is that it does not take values as static norms of various equally stable cat-egories (economic, social, cultural, medical, scientific, and ethical) that influence action. This pragmatic approach to understanding values allow us to treat them as practical achievements where practices of valuation establish what values count and how various values are separated, ordered, or intertwined. We have elsewhere called this a valuographic approach (Dussauge et al. 2015). Such an approach works, for instance, well for the following scholars: Zelizer (1985, 2005), Appadurai (1986), and Stark (2000, 2009) who all have argued for analytically abandoning any sense of a priori and clear-cut distinction between (social and cultural) values and (economic) value. This is also similar to Bruno Latour's argument against social categories as points of analytical departure (Latour 2005).

One central advantage of this approach is that it takes seriously the complex and multifa-ceted practices that perform valuations. This opens up for understanding values as contingent as well as for examining how specific choices, devices, and orderings go into enacting certain values. The promise of this approach is to show how certain values (such as calculative or econ-omic) become shaped and formatted through specific practices as part of the valuation. This enables us to study what values are articulated as desirable and what values are ignored or made absent. We understand this approach as a 'flank movement' to the study of values where they are seen as enacted and ordered in practices of valuation (Dewey 1939; Muniesa 2012).[2]

This study's focus on research design as a site where valuations are performed is thus closely tied to a pragmatic approach to values where values are seen as articulated, enacted ordered, and dis-placed in practices. In this, valuations are understood as enacting values rather than being deter-mined by and therefore merely reflecting pre-stabilised values. This approach enables us to examine how different yardsticks are articulated, mobilised, and ordered in various aspects of research design. Moreover, it gives access to articulations as to what knowledge is seen valuable and on what grounds. Our choice to examine two different kinds of trials – traditional RCTs and emerging BTTs – further strengthens the valuographic approach in that it allows us to be sensitive to differences in the particular yardsticks articulated. In short, it allows us to examine differences in what values counts, what knowledge is worth pursuing and what is seen as the appropriate means for these endeavours.

Examining textual accounts of valuation in design

We will in the following present an examination of design as it is expressed in textbooks (on tra-ditional RCTs) and articles (on biomarker trials). Our focus has been to explore what they articulate in relation to trial design and the values and valuations at play in these articulations.

Regarding traditional RCTs, we have examined three textbooks. These were chosen on the basis of how well-used they seemed to be, something that was decided on the basis of how often they were borrowed at our local University library and how many University libraries in Sweden had used the books. Moreover, we did choose newer books in favour of older ones, as we wanted to know how design matters are articulated in a contemporary setting. All in all, this method gave us an indication concerning the books' relevance.

As BTTs are a less entrenched and emerging phenomenon in the biomedical research landscape, established textbooks in biomarker experiments were unavailable. Instead journal articles focussed on the design of biomarker experiments were used. To create a material on biomarker designs we searched for articles in the ISI web of science with 'biomarker* design' in the title that were published in the last five years (2008–2012). The focus was on biomarkers concerning humans. All articles that were published between 2011 and 2012 were included; articles published before 2011 that were cited more than once were included. From the remaining articles those concerning validation of BTTs were chosen in order to focus on experiments aimed to assess medical treatments, this as such focus is regularly the case in traditional RCTs.

The examination was conducted by thematically coding the relevant sections in three selected text-books and a few articles were coded thematically using a software for coding, search, and retrieval. In a Fleckian (Fleck 1979) sense this means that we are investigating articulations of value in different parts of the knowledge collective concerning medical trials: sedimented textbook knowledge versus emer-ging scholarly discussions. As such this article does not deal in a proper comparison, but rather in exploring emerging articulations of value in biomedicine and contrasting those with more established ditto. Thus, our focus is on emerging trends in biomedical knowledge production.

Our examination of certain textual accounts provides one, albeit narrow, glimpse into the valua-tions that participate in shaping medical research. First, it should be readily acknowledged that the processes of trial design practice are far more convoluted and complex than any textual rendition of them. Second, the actual implementation and logistics of trials contain more contingencies than can be captured in a stabilised trial protocol (see, for instance, Jonvallen 2005; Helgesson 2010). Third, the trajectory of medical knowledge production is also contingent upon the practices of interpreting and (selective) publication of results, which may involve so-called publication bias (see, for instance, Dickersin et al. 1987). Yet, the narrow focus of the present study on textual accounts about trial design provides one step in the study of valuations in design practices. In this way, it turns attention to a part of medical experimentation that has been given little attention in social science research on clinical trials and the shaping of biomedical knowledge.

Valuations in design: from traditional RCTs to BTTs

Our investigation of the valuations in the design of medical experiments is done along four themes:

(1) the broad-stroked characteristics of research design for RCTs and BTTs, respectively; (2) on the roles of uncertainty, ignorance, and absence of knowledge when designing trials; (3) design issues pertaining to scale, cost, and epistemic gain; and, finally (4) clinical relevance as a theme in trial design. For each of them we look both at how these valuations are discussed as regards design of traditional RCTs as well as for the emerging new form of BTTs.

The big picture

The pivotal design feature of an RCT is the randomisation of trial subjects to one out of two or more possible treatments (trial arms). The choice of treatments, influences – along with other design decisions – what kind of questions the trial can address. These questions could, for instance, be whether treatment A is superior to treatment B, or whether treatment A at least not is inferior to treatment B. Figure 1 is adapted from a textbook and shows three kinds of design for RCTs where the solid lines indicate the randomisation performed for allocating treatments to the trial sub-jects in a way that in effect creates two groups of patients.

On a highly general level a biomarker trial can test (1) the prognostic or diagnostic value of a bio-marker or (2) a biomarker and treatment combination. In the following we focus on (2), the BTTs, as these have goals similar to traditional RCTs for testing treatments. In general, rather than asking, 'What treatment is best for these kinds of patients', which is a frequent question in RCTs, the ques-tion in a biomarker trial becomes 'What treatment and patient combination is best?' Thus, the bio-marker trials we have chosen to discuss aim to test the efficacy of a BTT.

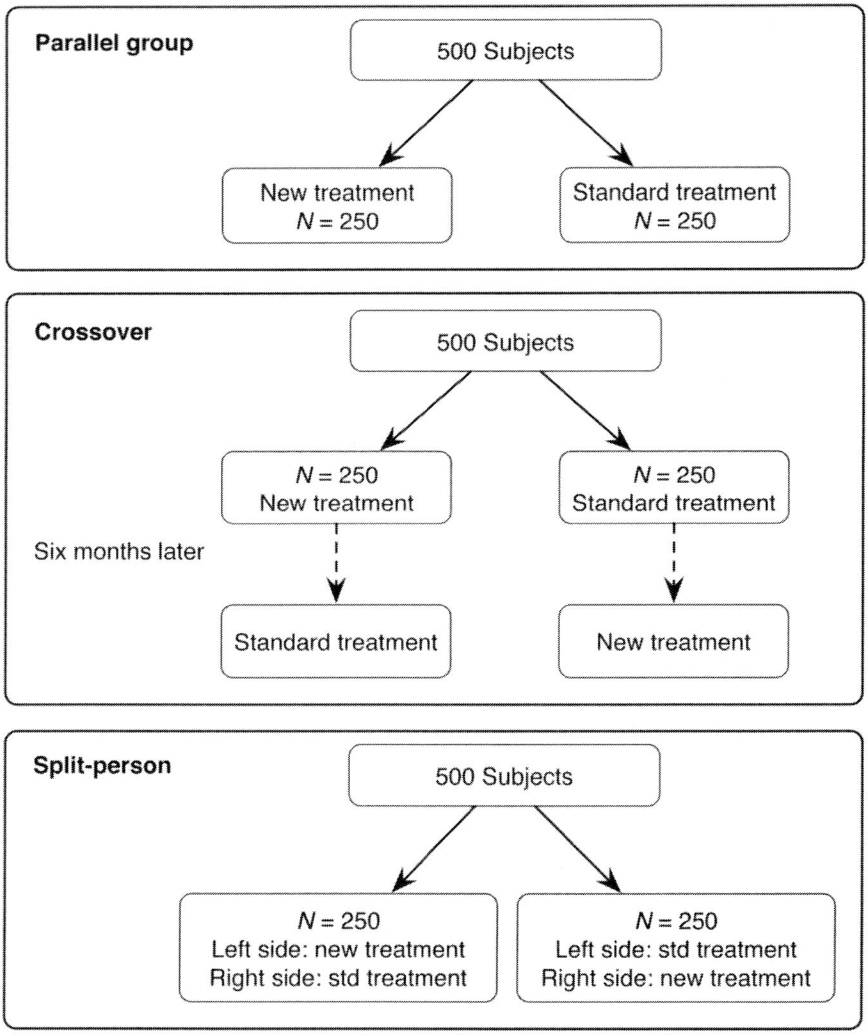

FIGURE 1. Three versions of trial design within the overall RCT design framework for testing different treatments. The split-person design could, for instance concern treatments distributed as an ointment where each trial subject gets two interventions one on different sides of their bodies (adapted from Hackshaw 2009, p. 59).

In a similar way to traditional RCTs, there is some sort of randomisation of the patient in BTTs. However, the random component of the trial is commonly performed after a patient stratification, and not, as in traditional RCTs, where it is often done at the very beginning of the trial. This later stratification is done in order to be able to test the efficacy of the BTT. The idea is that medical treatment could be tailored using patient classification on different genomic or protein expression pro-files. Thus, a major difference in the design of traditional RCTs and the BTT is that the randomisation in the former aims to create similar groups in the different arms whereas stratifica-tions in the latter are used to create subgroups of trial subjects that are dissimilar from one another. This means that in one case there is treatment stratification, while in the other there is patient as well as treatment stratification. As we will see, this difference has effects for what, and how, values are articulated in the design process. The pivotal design feature of biomarker trial is different from traditional RCTs, as the questions these trials ask are different than in regular trials.

Figure 2 shows a schematic image of the organisation of a biomarker-based trial designed to com-pare 'the MammaPrint 70-gene expression signature with a common clinical-pathological prognos-tic tool (Adjuvant! Online) in selecting patients with negative or 1–3 positive nodes for adjuvant chemotherapy in breast cancer'.[3] We can note that the randomisation occurs on the left-hand seg-ment in the fourth row. It has been demoted from the start of the trial, where it would reside in a traditional RCT, and is now one step of many in clinical/medical knowledge production. Further-more, it is only one out of the three initially identified patient strata that is made subject to randomis-ation, which randomises the trial subjects to one out of two decision rules for choosing the treatment.

The envisioned outcome of the design effort of a traditional RCTs is a protocol where the allo-cation of treatments to different subjects is to be done early in the trial using randomisation. In con-trast, the BTT design depicted in Figure 2 works with stratifying trial subjects into more internally homogenous subgroups before a randomisation is performed as regards one such subgroup. As Mandrekar and Sargent (2009) argue in an article assessing multiple trial designs for biomarker validation:

> While there is no one-size-fits-all solution, it is clear that the choice of a clinical trial design is driven by a com-bination of scientific, clinical, statistical and ethical considerations. The current era of novel agents and targeted therapies such as small molecules, antibodies, and vaccines are mandating intelligent clinical trial designs. Well-designed retrospective analyses of RCTs, supplemented by prospective trials whenever possible, will hasten this important progress. (Our emphasis; Mandrekar & Sargent 2009, p. 4033)

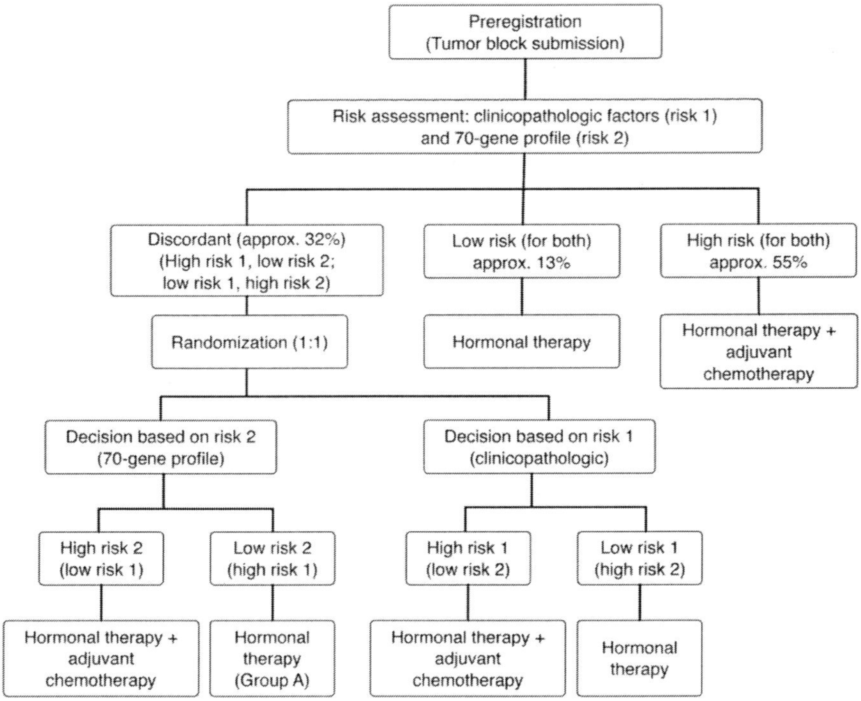

FIGURE 2. A schematic figure of the Microarray in Node-Negative Disease May Avoid Chemotherapy (MINDACT) trial design (adapted from Mandrekar & Sargent 2009, p. 4031).

In the case of biomarkers the design is envisioned to result in a protocol where the allocation of treat-ments to different subjects is to be informed by biomarkers during the trial. The advent of the dis-cussions about biomarkers and personalised medicine ('targeted therapies') is thus argued to be 'mandating intelligent trial designs' that, as we show below, reshape knowledge-making practices in contemporary biomedicine. The articulations of principles for allocating treatments in the RCT textbooks are therefore different from those in the articles discussing the 'intelligent trial designs' in BTTs. This articulates a need to not only understand the drug in question but also a need to under-stand how it interacts with different kinds of bodies (as identified by biomarkers). One effect of the drive towards personalised medicine is, in this way, that the trial imagined in the regime of person-alised medicine no longer solely tests the efficacy of a drug, but also attempts to test the interaction of the drug with specific bodily configurations. The resulting design, testing combinations of specified bodies and drugs, assumes a shape where different modes of stratification and sorting precede randomisation.

The differences in articulation of trial designs for RCT and BTT point to important tensions in the value practices of contemporary medicine. Below we examine further the articulation of values in relation to design discussions and these depict what could be recognised as specific versions of 'epis-temic', 'ethical', and 'economic' values. The use of the single quotation marks further stand to remind us that what would count as say 'ethical' values indeed might differ between different trial design contexts.

On the roles of uncertainty, ignorance, and absence of knowledge when designing trials

> When an established treatment exists, it is unethical to give a placebo instead because this deprives some sub-jects of a known health benefit. (Hackshaw 2009, p. 12)

A central discussion in textbooks about RCT design concerns which treatments can be given to trial subjects in the two parts of the trial (the different arms). This relates to the objective of the trial. However, it is also, as illustrated in the quote above, intimately related to what can be considered to be known prior to the trial since this determines what can be considered an ethically viable trial. This, in turn, relates to the uncertainty as to what treatment is best for the patient that is con-sidered to make it ethically possible to randomise different treatments among the trial subjects. In this way uncertainty is articulated as valuable to make a trial ethical. In these moments the epistemic values of uncertainty and ethical values are articulated in conjunction with one another:

> In addition there must be genuine uncertainty as to which of the options is best for the patient. It is this uncer-tainty which provides the necessary equipoise to justify random allocation to treatment after due consent is given. When a trial is planned, it is therefore clear that there must be considerable 'uncertainty' with respect to the relative efficacy of the 'therapeutic' options. Without this uncertainty, the trial should not commence. (Emphasis added; Machin & Campbell 2005, p. 149)

Trials are in this way understood as ethical if there is uncertainty about what treatment is best for patients. In the traditional RCT textbooks this is related to the notion of clinical equipoise. The notion of clinical equipoise is articulated as a strong formulation of how prior knowledge affects what can be considered possible ethical options when selecting the treatments in the different arms.[4] Genuine uncertainty is expressed as a necessity for the trial to be considered ethical and is connected to the principle of clinical equipoise. Hence, an absence of knowledge about differences in treatment effects is articulated as vital for it being considered ethical to randomise between differ-ent treatments (or placebo).

Another epistemic valuation hinging on absences is the notion of bias. The absence of bias is con-sidered highly valuable. Bias is understood as made possible by making sure that humans are not interfering in the conduct of the trial process: 'By removing all human influence from the random allocation process, possible biases are minimised' (Hackshaw 2009, p. 77). In RCT textbooks, the exclusion of human influence (and hence, what is understood as an ethical trial) is enabled through randomisation devices – in contrast with human interference. For instance, in one textbook it is said that:

> By the very term 'randomised', this design implies that the particular treatment given is chosen neither by the patient nor by the doctor, but by a randomisation device. (Machin & Campbell 2005, p. 149)

The use of a randomisation device is understood as making it possible to avoid biases related to undue human influence. Removing direct human involvement in treatment allocation makes the design more readily considered as able to produce unbiased results – and by extension outcomes that are objective and neutral. This focus on removing humans to enable objectivity can conceptually be understood as an expression of mechanical objectivity (Daston & Galison 1992). The concept mechanical objectivity expresses a non-intervening objectivity accomplished with the help of machines, technology, or other devices. The concept thus highlights the idea of machines as reliable in that they do not have any intentions nor do they intervene. Hence, they do not affect and disturb scientific practice. Mechanical objectivity stands in stark contrast to subjective judgements and decisions brought into scientific research by the researcher (Daston & Galison 1992).

In sum, the desirable epistemic starting point of RCTs hinge on uncertainty and ignorance among trial designers and clinical staff as tools for ethics and objectivity. Uncertainty about treatment effects is said to produce an ethical trial and ignorance about the allocation of treatments to trial subjects is argued to create unbiased objectivity. The ethical and epistemic cornerstones of biomedical knowl-edge production are therefore both related to absence of knowledge: absence of knowledge about differences in treatment effects, and absence of knowledge about which treatment patients receive.

The epistemic starting point and what counts as ethical is different in the case of BTTs. Prior knowledge about the biomarker and its possible relation to treatment effects is utilised in trials test-ing BTTs to stratify patients into different treatments (arms). The use of biomarkers for patient stra-tification thus shakes the above-delineated cornerstones of RCTs to their core. In a trial where a BTT is tested, there has already accumulated a large amount of biological knowledge about the predictive abilities of biomarkers prior to the trial, which makes the 'genuine uncertainty' of the RCT less strong. Thus, both the uncertainty about treatment effects and the ignorance of patient distribution are jettisoned in BTTs. In this vein, biomarker trials muddle the ethics anchored to the notion of equipoise and mechanical objectivity of RCTs.

In both traditional RCT design and BTT design, previous knowledge is viewed as raising ethical concerns. One discussion of the ethics of biomarker-based trial designs is how to handle the treat-ment of the patients about whom there is prior knowledge. Here the purported knowledge of the effectiveness of different treatments is seen as leading to two 'clinical dilemmas'. First, the notion of not knowing, of genuine uncertainty are in these discussions shifted to statistical and organis-ational handling of patients that are 'pan resistant' to the trial drugs. Second, the notion of knowledge informing the trials, rather than uncertainty and absence of knowledge, is articulated as being a pro-blem in that biomarker-based knowledge about the patients is seen as rapidly changing, making both knowledge and uncertainty moving targets that need to be handled by 'novel statistical methods'. In biomarker-based trials there are, thus, new ethical dilemmas that need to be handled:

> One of the clinical dilemmas that arises in studies of therapeutic biomarkers is the problem of what to do for patients in whom the biomarkers predict resistance to all of the drugs tested. We suppose that in preparation for a prospective randomized trial, such as we propose, investigators have some confidence in the stratification, based on a mix of biological knowledge and some data indicating the way the biomarkers predict response in observational studies of the outcomes of treatment given by physician's choice. The question of whether to include the 'pan-resistant' patients in the main trial, contributing to the hypothesis testing, depends on the trade-off of increased degrees of freedom for the tests versus capitalizing on an unexpected result (e.g., via a contribution to rejecting the intersection null). When theory and prior data suggest that there are no differences in treatment outcomes in a sub-group, there is little justification in spending degrees of freedom on the small chance of a surprise. So we would exclude them from the main trial. Since their biomarker measurements are already taken, they can be enrolled in an auxiliary trial in which we randomize them among the K treatments. (Lai et al. 2012, p. 153)

Thus, in biomarker-based trials the notions of equipoise and genuine uncertainty become replaced by different ethical framings that are tied to the biomarker-based prior knowledge. Rather than focussing on the importance of genuine uncertainty and absence of knowledge as the ethical bases of a trial, the discussion of the ethics of biomarker trial designs emphasises how prior knowl-edge based on biomarkers needs to be actively brought in as a ground for action. In this way, pre-vious knowledge, as in traditional RCTs, is articulated as a problem. In the case of BTTs it is not absence of knowledge that is the cornerstone of ethics, but a knowledge-based and ethical patient sorting. Thus, there is a shift from randomisation as tied to the ethics of equipoise to an ethical framing that encourage knowledge-based sorting. Going from an ethics of uncertainty to an ethics of knowing shifts the registers of vigilance needed: vigilance of the purported uncertainty versus vigilance of the state of knowledge. A negative epistemics of ignorance is replaced by a positive epistemics of knowing.

Let us now take stock of what emerges when setting the textual accounts regarding the design of RCTs and BTTs side by side. There is a clear difference in the articulation of what counts as ethi-cal. Our textbook sources on RCTs emphasise how the design must be such that there is a genuine uncertainty about the relative efficacy of the alternative treatments. The notion of clinical equipoise is to this effect put forward to specify what should characterise the design of the trial so as to make it ethical on behalf of the trial subjects. In the articles about BTTs we can discern a shift where prior knowledge reframes what is seen as ethically salient. Here genuine uncertainty is replaced by biomarker-based knowledge that should lead to a choice between different treatments, and what to do for patients for whom no treatment works. Another striking aspect of the difference discerned relates to mechanical objectivity and randomisation. Whereas randomisation is an espoused aspect for producing ignorance in the textbooks on RCTs, the texts on BTTs instead highlights biologically and statistically informed choices and stratifications as part of the design of an experiment.

Design issues pertaining to scale, cost, and epistemic gain

Deciding on the number of trial subjects involved, i.e. the sample size, is a crucial trade-off in trial design that interweaves several different registers of value. Three different reasons for why the size of the trial is an important concern are invoked: the possible research results, economic resources spent, and fairness. In other words, in articulations about sample size the epistemic, ethical, and financial sides of a trial appear as closely connected.

One trade-off central in our material is the one between research results and the use of time, as well as economic and human resources. This trade-off, then, brings forward one way in which scien-tific and economic registers of value are intertwined:

> A common situation is one where the number of subjects (often patients) that can be included in a trial is gov-erned by non-scientific forces such as time, money or human resources. With a predetermined (maximal) sample size, the researcher may then wish to know what probability he

> or she has of detecting a certain effect size with a trial confined to the size. (Machin & Fayers 2010, p. 193)

Another facet of the scale trade-off is how clinically important differences might be missed with a too small trial, and that an unnecessary large trial might delay the market introduction of a superior treatment:

> If there are too few subjects, a clinically important difference may be missed. If there are too many subjects, resources could be wasted and a delay may occur in offering a superior treatment to future patients. (Hackshaw 2009, pp. 65–66)

As indicated in the quote above, a central reoccurring trade-off in the textbooks on traditional RCTs is the one related to sample size: having too few subjects might mean that the trial produces no results whereas having too many subjects implies unnecessarily high expenses. Research results are hence repeatedly articulated as being balanced against resources. These quotes illustrate how many different considerations are made part of determining a trial size. Too many subjects would mean that recourses are wasted unnecessarily, but having too few subjects is articulated as not spend-ing enough resources to generate statistically significant (and conclusive) research results.

Another scale trade-off intertwines financial aspects with what is considered to be fair for patients and participants. Here, not only research results (a clinically meaningful difference) are staged as important, but also the ethical treatment of the patients. Fairness is articulated as being related to both the possible discomfort of those participating in the clinical trial and to the number of patients getting a more effective treatment. This can be illustrated with the following quote:

> A small trial with no chance of detecting a clinically meaningful difference between treatments is unfair to all the trial participants who are subjected to the risk and discomfort of the clinical trial. On the other hand, recruiting too many participants is a waste of resources and may be unfair if, for example, a larger than necess-ary number of patients receive the inferior treatment when one treatment could have been shown to be more effective with fewer patients. (Emphases added; Machin & Campbell 2005, p. 179)

In this context, what is ethical is not linked to the notion of equipoise discussed above, but to the knowledge about differences in treatment effects that the trial might or might not uncover. If the trial is too small, it will not be fair for trial subjects as they are exposed to unnecessary risks and dis-comforts during the trial without it producing any subsequent epistemic gain. In this way unnecess-ary denotes that the trial should be of value for the trial patients – and in extension for patients 'out there'. A too big trial might be unfair, on the other hand, since more than the necessary number of trial subjects might receive a treatment that we subsequently would identify as the inferior treatment. Deciding on scale (sample size) is hence an instance where the issue of the possibility to get unequi-vocal results is not only linked to the resources spent. It is also articulating a link between the welfare of the trial subjects and the possible epistemic gains of the trial. It is further here the notion of (statistical) power is central in RCT design since it denotes the probability that an effect is detected, pro-vided that this effect truly exist: (We could think of power as the probability of an epistemic gain under the assumption about reality to the effect that such an epistemic gain is there to be made.)

> This is why it is important to try to detect the smallest clinically worthwhile effect, with 80 or 90% power, in order to have an appropriately sized study. (Hackshaw 2009, p. 74)

BTTs and scale, on the other hand, implicates both the idea of personalised medicine, but also the idea about so-called flexible trial designs. One of the promises of biomarker-based trials is to combat the high failure rate of trials, by targeting subsets of the population identified by biomarkers. The quotes below illustrate how innovation in biomarker-based trials are articulated as a panacea for the high failure rates of trials, but that the large sample sizes needed for trials of personalised thera-pies also need adaptive designs to shave off costs and adapt to evolving biomarker knowledge. In our material, innovation in trial design is articulated as a trade-off between process-efficiency/economic costs and the epistemic risk of false positives:

Traditional clinical trial designs for development and validation of biomarker-guided therapies, as described for example in [2], often require large sample sizes; moreover, they cannot adapt to evolving knowledge about bio-markers. AR [a type of adaptive design] designs … 'which allows researchers to avoid being locked into a single static protocol of the trial', can 'yield breakthroughs, but must be handled with care' to ensure that they do not 'inflate the risk of reaching a false positive conclusion', … 'The [adaptive] approach has been controversial, but is catching on with both researchers and regulators as companies struggle to combat the nearly 50% failure rate of (cancer) drugs in large, late-stage trials'. It is hoped that innovative designs can 'drive down the cost of clini-cal trials 50-fold' in comparison with traditional designs for the development of personalized medicine, other-wise 'drug companies (won't) be interested in taking the risk of developing a drug for these small number of patients' [34]. (Lai et al. 2012, p. 149)

Here biomarker-based adaptive designs are described as yielding epistemic breakthroughs and cost savings. An interesting register of value in the material on biomarker trials focusses on the flexibility and rigidity of trial designs. Where the biomarker-based designs are heralded as a more modern and flexible way to organise trials, the traditional RCTs are described as fixed and rigid (Lai et al. 2012, p. 149).

This links epistemic and organisational registers of value. Where organisational flexibility of the trial is made possible by an epistemic change, where questions, randomisations, and trial designs can shift. However, there is also an epistemic anxiety linked to the aforementioned jettisoning of the rigid RCT protocols, that are still described as the gold standard: 'the gold standard ... continues (appropriately) to be a prospective RCT ... ' (Mandrekar & Sargent 2009, p. 4028). BTTs is tied to a similar trade-offs as regular RCTs, i.e. attempting to minimise the sample size and number of events with the risk of increasing false certainty:

> Preliminary work suggested that the [x] design may be superior to [y] design in terms of the number of events (and hence the total sample size) required (while keeping all the parameters the same for both designs) ... (Mandrekar & Sargent 2009, p. 4032)

Thus, the major trade-off between biomarker-based designs – i.e. 'targeted/enriched', 'unselected/all-comers design', and 'hybrid designs' (Mandrekar & Sargent 2009, p. 4028) is articulated as being one of costs versus epistemic risk. However, the trade-off is not solely tied to the scale of the trial, but also introduces innovation in trial design as a possible route to cost savings.

Summing up, there are major differences in how issues pertaining to scale, cost, and epistemic gains are articulated in the design of RCTs and BTTs, respectively. Cost is a highly present register of value in both cases, but it is differently linked to other facets. The possibility of a true epistemic gain, to take one example, is in RCT design strongly linked to trial size and the notion of power to safeguard against the risk of false negatives (i.e. the risk of not finding a treatment difference whereas there is one to be found). In BTTs, on the other hand the possibility of an epistemic gain is linked to flexible designs while safeguarding against the higher risk of false positives (i.e. the risk of falsely identifying a treatment difference whereas there in fact is none). Furthermore, issues of scale are further linked to ethical registers of value in expressions of the desirability to not involve an unnecessary large number of patients trial subjects in light of the possible epistemic gain (see also previous section).

Clinical relevance as a theme in trial design

The notion of clinical relevance is recurrently evoked as an important value in the traditional RCT textbooks. This notion denotes how the trial might produce knowledge of importance to the every-day practice of medicine. It is brought to the fore in discussions on what to measure as treatment outcomes as well as when the epistemic quality of the trial results is brought up:

> For many trials, the choice of endpoint will be easy, for example death, the occurrence or recurrence of a specific disease, or a change in habits. The main endpoint should be clinically relevant to both the trial subject and the researcher. (Hackshaw 2009, p. 61)

> There are circumstances where small therapeutic advantages may be worthwhile demonstrating, particularly in the fields of cardiovascular disease and cancer. In terms of trial size, the smaller the potential benefit, essentially the effect size, then the larger the trial must be in order to be reasonably confident that the small benefit envi-saged really exists at all. (Machin & Campbell 2005, p. 150)

Financial or commercial aspects of the trial results are not part of the textbook discussions related to clinical relevance. Instead epistemic gains from a trial are articulated as if it was a public good: the outcome of the research is measured against its relevance for practitioners and patients (and not say, a pharmaceutical company). In this sense, it is not merely a research design that should be of value for the research community that is desired, but research that is of relevance, too, for society. Hence, clinical relevance is articulated as a public good. The question(s) posed must have important conse-quences in that the answer should inform research and/or influence clinical practice in a meaningful way (Machin & Fayers 2010, p. 25). However, in discussing clinical relevance, the financial aspect of trial cost do implicitly appear since clinical relevance is related to trial size (see the latter of the two quotes above and the previous discussion on power). In this way, financial aspects are not explicitly discussed but are still brought to bear on the register of value pertaining to clinical relevance.

The notion of clinical relevance is somewhat differently configured in the realm of BTTs. The core idea of BTTs is that it is worthwhile to assess the efficacy of BTTs. The premise for this is that the efficacy of treatments may vary for different patients and that patients can be identified through the use of biomarkers. Hence, BTTs are aimed to produce knowledge about the efficacy of treatments in relation to patient stratifications that possibly could be replicated in clinical practice:

> Advancing new discoveries from the bench to the bedside is the ultimate goal of clinical and translational research. The concept of predictive biomarkers moves the field a step closer toward individualized medicine, whereby individuals who are likely to have a favorable clinical outcome such as improved survival and/or decreased toxicity from a treatment can be prospectively identified. (Mandrekar & Sargent 2009, p. 4033)

BTTs thus not only reconfigure how clinical relevance is understood in the realm of trials, but ties this to a reconfiguration of how clinics are to make use of the knowledge thus produced. In short, clinics are to use biomarkers to match patients to treatments on the basis of knowledge produced in BTTs.

The clinic can hence both appear as a stand-in for the epistemic gain that the trial is designed to produce, as in the articulations about favouring clinically relevant endpoints. Yet, it can also become a matter of ethics in trial design where the treatment of patients in the trial becomes the focus. By evoking yardsticks relating trials to the clinic, certain valuations and certain epistemic interests are presupposed and favoured in the trial design.

In traditional RCTs, then, clinical relevance is evoked as a way to discuss the epistemic gain from a trial as a public good. This is not that different from one of the ways the clinic is made relevant in BTTs. Yet, in the latter case it appears also in other guises.

CONCLUDING DISCUSSION

We have examined articulations about valuations entailed in the design of two kinds of biomedical experiments for testing treatments, namely the traditional RCT and the emerging kind of trials that assess BTT. Examining textbooks on the design of traditional RCTs and journal articles on BTTs, we have asked how these articulate various valuations and scientific, medical and economic values in contemporary knowledge production. Three different themes have been discussed: first, we discussed the roles of uncertainty, ignorance, and absence of knowledge when designing trials. Here, we dis-cussed what is articulated as an ethical basis for the different trial design. We also noted how the newer BTTs appear to represent a shift from emphasising a stable protocol and something akin to mechanical objectivity to flexibility and adaptability. Second, we discussed trial design issues per-taining to scale, cost, and epistemic gain. In this section we considered how trial cost, epistemic gain, and trial subject ethics appear as different yet linked registers of value that are to be balanced when deciding the scale of the trial. We further noted that there is a different emphasis between traditional RCTs and new BTTs as regards the risks of false negatives and false positives. Third, we examined to the notion of clinical relevance and the desired epistemic output of the different trials. In this discussion, we discussed how valuations of clinical relevance are articulated as having to do with the epistemic gain as a public good (rather than, say, a commercial value).

The basic premise of the study was that the very act of establishing a research design entails a process involving a series of valuations where different values are evoked, ordered, and displaced. The values related to research design has been examined with a valuographic approach; by seeing values as ongoing achievements established through articulations, negotiations, and orderings. In doing so, we have discussed what knowledge is articulated as worth pursuing as well as what means are deemed appropriate. Moreover, we have been able to see what registers of value are central in such valuations. Our reading of textbook accounts about the design of RCTs and articles about the design of BTTs indicate consequential differences as to how certain valuations are made in the design work – something that has consequences for what knowledge is seen as valuable.

The valuations described in our textual sources have, as depicted above, been related to assessing the possibility to produce results with some certainty and clinical relevance, and to relate the results to the costs of producing them. We have, moreover, discussed how the trend of personalised medi-cine includes a significant shift. In the design of the traditional RCT a stable protocol and genuine uncertainty are measures related to the value of something akin to a mechanical objectivity and a trial subject ethics of not knowing. In the design of the new emerging BTT, the adaptable protocol evokes values of flexibility and where the changing knowledge about trial patients is seen as an ethical dilemma vis-à-vis the trial subjects. In short, the valuations that are part of trial design differ in non-trivial ways between the two kinds of ways to perform bioedical experiments examined.

Our results suggest that the valuations in design entail important links between different versions of certain values. Several differences in what counts in the design of the traditional RCTs and emer-ging BTTs indicate that the valuations in design are interlinked in intricate ways. Consider, for instance, the specific and more complex allocation of trial subjects to treatments in the BTT trial involving booth stratifications and randomisation discussed previously (see Figure 2). The discussion of such a design tied both to a new assessment of what counts as clinically relevant results and a new understanding of the ethics related to trial subject enrolment. In short, the valuations in such a design interlink specific versions of 'epistemic' and 'ethical' values. Similarly, the discussions of the cost of an experiment often hinges on trial size and is entangled with both issues of trial subject ethics as well as with the quality of the knowledge thus produced. Hence, specific versions of 'econ-omic', 'ethical', and 'epistemic' values are interlinked in such valuations. Different kinds of exper-iment designs not only entail a certain configuration of how the experiment is going to be performed, they also entail certain configurations of the valuations. As a consequence, different kinds of trial designs appear to enact a different composite of what counts as 'ethical', 'economic', 'epistemic', 'clinically relevant', and so on.

This study has entirely relied upon textual sources regarding research design. This limited focus has nevertheless allowed us to depict the above summarised pertinent differences between traditional RCTs and BTTs in how different registers of values are evoked. It is certainly reasonable to deduce that the practices of research design are more convoluted and furthermore involve commercial assessments not so readily discussed in the textual accounts we have examined. It is further true that medical research is shaped by practices, including valuation practices, in other sites of biome-dical experimentation, such as when deciding if the results of a completed study should be published or not. Thus, we have in this study been able to map a few of the valuations that participate in shap-ing the biomedical knowledge production. Yet, the focussed study of textual accounts has neverthe-less clearly exposed how certain valuations related to the design of biomedical experiments differ somewhat between different kinds of design.

Different ways for conducting research involve not only differences in how things are done, but also differences in the valuations that are part of shaping this research. This is an important general lesson that goes far beyond the specific valuations of research design examined here. To us, this opens up for empirically examining a number of research fields. What valuations are part of determining what knowledge is worth pursuing? Given the power of knowledge, this is indeed a line of inquiry worth pursuing.

NOTES

[1]Within STS there is a long-standing tradition of doing empirical studies on the practices of medical research (Fujimura 1987; Epstein 1996; Löwy 1996; Keating & Cambrosio 2006). However, the practices of experimental research design has not been the object of extensive empirical study, which also holds for the recent and growing social sciences studies about RCTs in medicine (Fisher 2009; Petryna 2009; Sismondo 2009; Helgesson 2010; Will & Moreira 2010).

[2]The growing interest in valuation can be seen in different topics, from markets, to tomato tasting (Helgesson & Kjellberg 2013; Helgesson & Muniesa 2013; Heuts & Mol 2013; Kjellberg et al. 2013).

[3]http://www.agendia.com/clinical-trials-mindact/

[4]The notion of clinical equipoise was introduced in the 1980s and has also been subject to some criticism in that it puts too strict restrictions on what should be considered ethically viable options.

ACKNOWLEDGEMENTS

This paper reports a sub-study within the larger project 'Trials of Value' where Helgesson and Lee investigate the valuations performed in the designing of different kinds of experiments in medicine and biomedicine. The project has been made possible with a grant from Riksbankens Jubileumsfond. The authors want to thank Barbara Townley and Philip Roscoe as well as two anonymous reviewers for helpful and encouraging comments on earlier versions of this article. The article has furthermore benefited from comments on various occasions: the session 'Clinical research in post-genomic medicine' at 4S/EASST Copenhagen, October 2012; the workshop 'What price creativity? A workshop on the valuing of social/public goods' at University of St Andrews, December 2012; and the ValueS seminar within Technology and Social Change, Linköping University. In particular, we want to acknowledge comments and encouragement by Alberto Cambrosio, Andrew Hoffman, Nicole Nelson, and Teun Zuiderent-Jerak.

DISCLOSURE STATEMENT

No potential conflict of interest was reported by the authors.

NOTES ON CONTRIBUTORS

Claes-Fredrik Helgesson is professor in Technology and Social Change at Linköping University, Sweden. He works in the fields of economic sociology and science and technology studies (STS), currently in the emerging field of valuation studies which takes an interest in valuation as a social practice. He has published in Industrial Marketing Management,

Marketing Theory, and Journal of Marketing Management. Helgesson is co-founder and co-Editor-in-Chief of Valua-tion Studies. He is co-editor with Isabelle Dussauge and Francis Lee of Value Practices in the Life Sciences and Medicine (Oxford University Press, 2015).

Francis Lee is an assistant professor in Technology and Social Change at Linköping University, Sweden. His primary research interests lie in the politics, practices, and technologies of knowledge. He has published in Science, Technology & Human Values, Science as Culture, and History and Technology. He is a member of the Editorial Board of Valuation Studies and is co-founder of the academic network Algorithms as Devices of Power and Valuation. He has co-edited

Value Practices in the Life Sciences (Oxford University Press, 2015).

Lisa Lindén is a PhD candidate in Technology and Social Change at Linköping University, Sweden. Her main research interests concern politics of care, pharmaceuticals, and subjectivities. In her PhD dissertation project she studies HPV vaccination campaigns, with a focus on how digital media mediate care in this setting. She has published work on HPV vaccine advertisements in Girlhood Studies, a co-authored discussion note in Valuation Studies and a review and dis-cussion article in Catalyst: Feminism, Theory, Technoscience.

REFERENCES

1. APPADURAI, A. (1986) 'Introduction: commodities and the politics of value', in The Social Life of Things: Commodities in Cultural Perspective, ed A. Appadurai, Cambridge University Press, Cambridge, pp. 3–63.
2. BOWKER, G. C. & STAR, S. L. (1999) Sorting Things Out: Classification and Its Consequences, MIT Press, Cambridge, MA.
3. CALLON, M. (Ed.) (1998) The Laws of the Markets, Blackwell, Oxford.
4. CALLON, M., MILLO, Y. & MUNIESA, F. (Eds) (2007) Market Devices, Blackwell, Oxford.
5. CALLON, M. & MUNIESA, F. (2005) 'Economic markets as calculative collective devices', Organization Studies, vol. 26, pp. 1229–1250.
6. COCHOY, F. (2008) 'Calculation, qualculation, calqulation: shopping cart arithmetic, equipped cognition and the clus-tered consumer', Marketing Theory, vol. 8, no. 1, pp. 15–44.
7. DASTON, L. & GALISON, P. (1992) 'The image of objectivity', Representations, vol. 40, Autumn, pp. 81–128. DEWEY, J. (1939) Theory of Valuation, The University of Chicago Press, Chicago, IL.
8. DICKERSIN, K., CHAN, S., CHALMERSX, T. C., SACKS, H. S. & SMITH JR, H. (1987) 'Publication bias and clinical trials', Controlled Clinical Trials, vol. 8, no. 4, pp. 343–353.
9. DUSSAUGE, I., HELGESSON, C.-F. & LEE, F. (2015) 'Valuography: studying the making of values', in Value Practices in the Life Sciences and Medicine, eds I. Dussauge, C.-F. Helgesson & F. Lee, Oxford University Press, Oxford, pp. 267–285.
10. EPSTEIN, S. (1996) Impure Science: AIDS, Activism, and the Politics of Knowledge, University of California Press, Berkeley.

11. FISHER, L. D. (1999) 'Advances in clinical trials in the twentieth century', Annual Review of Public Health, vol. 20, pp. 109–124.

12. FISHER, J. A. (2009) Medical Research for Hire: The Political Economy of Pharmaceutical Clinical Trials, Rutgers University Press, New Brunswick, NJ.

13. FLECK, L. (1979) Genesis and Development of a Scientific Fact, University of Chicago Press, Chicago, IL.

14. FUJIMURA, J. H. (1987) 'Constructing 'do-able' problems in cancer research: articulating alignment', Social Studies of Science, vol. 17, no. 2, pp. 257–293.

15. FUJIMURA, J. H. (2013) Confounded Categories: Is the HapMap a Race-based Project? 4S/EASST Design and Displacement Social Studies of Science and Technology, Copenhagen.

16. HACKSHAW, A. (2009) A Concise Guide to Clinical Trials, Wiley-Blackwell, Chichester.

17. HARAWAY, D. J. (1988) 'Situated knowledges: the science question in feminism and the privilege of partial perspective', Feminist Studies, vol. 14, no. 3, pp. 575–599.

18. HARDING, S. (1991) 'Feminist standpoint epistemology', in The Gender and Science Reader, eds I. Bartsch & M. Lederman, Routledge, London, pp. 145–168.

19. HELGESSON, C.-F. (2010) 'From dirty data to credible scientific evidence: some practices used to clean data in large ran-domised clinical trials', in Medical Proofs, Social Experiments: Clinical Trials in Context, eds C. Will & T. Moreira, Ashgate, Aldershot, pp. 49–66.

20. HELGESSON, C.-F. & KJELLBERG, H. (2013) 'Values and valuations in market practice', Journal of Cultural Economy, vol. 6, no. 4, pp. 361–369.

21. HELGESSON, C.-F. & MUNIESA, F. (2013) 'For what it's worth: an introduction to valuation studies', Valuation Studies, vol. 1, no. 1, pp. 1–10.

22. HEUTS, F. & MOL, A. (2013) 'What is a good tomato? A case of valuing in practice', Valuation Studies, vol. 1, no. 2, pp. 125–146.

23. JONVALLEN, P. (2005) Testing Pills, Enacting Obesity: The Work of Localizing Tools in a Clinical Trial, Published PhD Diss., Department of Thematic Studies – Technology and Social Change, Linköping University.

24. KEATING, P. & CAMBROSIO, A. (2006) Biomedical Platforms: Realigning the Normal and the Pathological in Late-Twentieth-Century Medicine, MIT Press, Cambridge.

25. KJELLBERG, H., MALLARD, A., ARJALIÈS, D.-L., ASPERS, P., BELJEAN, S., BIDET, A., CORSIN, A., DIDIER, E., FOURCADE, M., GEIGER, S., HOEYER, K., LAMONT, M., MACKENZIE, D., MAURER, B., MOURITSEN, J., SJÖGREN, E., TRYGGESTAD, K., VATIN, F. & WOOLGAR, S. (2013)

26. 'Valuation studies? Our collective two cents', Valuation Studies, vol. 1, no. 1, pp. 11–30.

27. LAI, T. L., LAVORI, P. W., SHIH, M. C. I. & SIKIC, B. I. (2012) 'Clinical trial designs for testing biomarker-based personalized therapies', Clinical Trials, vol. 9, no. 2, pp. 141–154.

28. LATOUR, B. (2005) Reassembling the Social: An Introduction to Actor-Network-Theory, Oxford University Press, Oxford. LÖWY, I. (1996) Between Bench and Bedside: Science, Healing, and Interleukin-2 in a Cancer Ward, Harvard University Press, Cambridge.

29. MACHIN, D. & CAMPBELL, M. J. (2005) Design of Studies for Medical Research, Wiley, Hoboken, NJ.

30. MACHIN, D. & FAYERS, P. M. (2010) Randomized Clinical Trials: Design, Practice, and Reporting, John Wiley & Sons, Chichester.

31. MACKENZIE, D. (1999) 'Nuclear missile testing and the social construction of accuracy', in The Science Studies Reader, ed Mario Biagioli, Routledge, New York and London, pp. 342–357.

32. MACKENZIE, D. (2009) Material Markets: How Economic Agents Are Constructed, Oxford University Press, Oxford.

33. MACKENZIE, D. & MILLO, Y. (2003) 'Constructing a market, performing theory: the historical sociology of a financial derivatives exchange', American Journal of Sociology, vol. 109, no. 1, pp. 107–145.

34. MACKENZIE, D., MUNIESA, F. & SIU, L. (Eds) (2007) Do Economists Make Markets? On the Performativity of Economics, Princeton University Press, Princeton, NJ.

35. MANDREKAR, S. J. & SARGENT, D. J. (2009) 'Clinical trial designs for predictive biomarker validation: theoretical consider-ations and practical challenges', Journal of Clinical Oncology, vol. 27, no. 24, pp. 4027–4034.

36. MARKS, H. M. (1997) The Progress of Experiment: Science and Therapeutic Reform in the United States, 1900–1990, Cambridge University Press, Cambridge.

37. METZLER, I. (2010) 'Biomarkers and their consequences for the biomedical profession: a social science perspective', Personalized Medicine, vol. 7, no. 4, pp. 407–420.

38. MITCHELL, R. & WALDBY, C. (2010) 'National biobanks: clinical labor, risk production, and the creation of biovalue', Science, Technology & Human Values, vol. 35, no. 3, pp. 330–355.

39. MOL, A. (1999) 'Ontological politics: a word and some questions', in Actor-Network Theory and After, eds J. Law & J. Hassard. Blackwell, Oxford, pp. 74–89.

40. MUNIESA, F. (2012) 'A flank movement in the understanding of valuation', in Measure and Value, eds L. Adkins & C. Lury. Wiley-Blackwell, Oxford, pp. 24–38.

41. PETRYNA, A. (2009) When Experiments Travel: Clinical Trials and the Global Search for Human Subjects, Princeton University Press, Princeton, NJ.

42. PORTER, T. M. (1995) Trust in Numbers: The Pursuit of Objectivity in Science and Public Life, Princeton University Press, Princeton, NJ.

43. ROSE, N. (2007) The Politics of Life Itself: Biomedicine, Power, and Subjectivity in the Twenty-first Century, Princeton UP, Princeton, NJ.

44. SHIVA, V. (1997) Biopiracy: The Plunder of Nature and Knowledge, South End Press, Boston, MA.

45. SISMONDO, S. (2009) 'Ghosts in the machine: publication planning in the medical sciences', Social Studies of Science, vol. 39, no. 2, pp. 171–198.

46. SJÖGREN, E. & HELGESSON, C.-F. (2007) 'The Q(u)ALYfying hand: health economics and medicine in the shaping of Swedish markets for subsidised pharmaceuticals', in Market Devices, eds M. Callon, Y. Millo & F. Muniesa. Blackwell, Oxford, pp. 215–240.

47. SKÆRBÆK, P. & TRYGGESTAD, K. (2010) 'The role of accounting devices in performing corporate strategy', Accounting, Organizations and Society, vol. 35, no. 1, pp. 108–124.

48. STARK, D. (2000) For a Sociology of Worth. Working Paper Series, Center on Organizational Innovation, Columbia University.

49. STARK, D. (2009) The Sense of Dissonance: Accounts of Worth in Economic Life, Princeton University Press, Princeton, NJ.

50. SUNDER RAJAN, K. (2006) Biocapital: The Constitution of Postgenomic Life, Duke University Press, Durham, NC.

51. WALDBY, C. (2002) 'Stem cells, tissue cultures and the production of biovalue', Health, vol. 6, no. 3, pp. 305–323.

52. WILL, C. & MOREIRA, T. (Eds) (2010) Medical Proofs, Social Experiments: Clinical Trials in Context, Ashgate, Aldershot.

53. WINNER, L. (1980) 'Do artifacts have politics?' Daedaleus, vol. 109, no. 1, pp. 121–136.

54. WISE, M. N. (1995) 'Introduction', in The Values of Precision, ed M. N. Wise, Princeton University Press, Princeton, NJ, pp. 3–13.

55. ZELIZER, V. A. (1985) Pricing the Priceless Child: The Changing Social Value of Children, Basic Books, New York.

56. ZELIZER, V. A. (2005) The Purchase of Intimacy, Princeton University Press, Princeton, NJ.

INDEX